"GOD HAS MADE
US A KINGDOM"

James Jesse Strang, 1813-1856
Courtesy Clarke Historical Library, Central Michigan
University, Mount Pleasant, Michigan

"GOD HAS MADE US A KINGDOM"

VICKIE CLEVERLEY SPEEK

Signature Books • Salt Lake City • 2006

Jacket design by Ron Stucki

Cover images: James Jesse Strang, ca. 1855, probably photo-
graphed by Dr. Thomas Aiken; Sarah Wright and son James
Phineas Strang, ca. 1858; Elvira Field posing as Charles Douglass,
ca. 1849, courtesy Clarke Historical Library, Central Michigan
University; sketch of a merchant ship on the back of a letter from
Peter Hess to James Strang, Feb. 13, 1850, courtesy Beinecke
Library, Yale University.

www.signaturebooks.com

for Stupe

Contents

Preface

I wasn't looking for Mormons during the summer of 1991. I was simply looking for some basket-making materials and the nearest shop was about thirty miles away in Burlington, Wisconsin. I found the shop at the corner of Highway 36 and Mormon Road. "Mormon Road?" I thought to myself. "There weren't any Mormons in Wisconsin."

I figured I should know. After all, I was a sixth-generation Mormon from Idaho, active in my church, and a Mormon history buff. In all of my religious education, I had never heard of Mormons in Wisconsin. So I took the unfamiliar road that sunny day and what I found astonished me. It started me on the highway of an adventure, the like of which I never would have anticipated.

From a series of plaques and monuments installed near the edge of Mormon Road, I became acquainted with a group of Latter Day Saints from the 1840s and 1850s who called their community Voree, which they said meant "Garden of Peace." I saw their houses, the remains of their cemetery, their Hill of Promise, and groves along the river where they held their services. I learned about their leader, James Jesse Strang.

When the Mormon prophet, Joseph Smith, was killed in 1844, Strang claimed to be Smith's successor even though Strang had been baptized only four months earlier. He based his claim on a letter of appointment from Smith and the anointing of an angel. Over the next few years, Strang's leadership attracted hundreds, perhaps thousands of people to Voree and to the Beaver Islands, a remote area in the northern part of Lake Michigan.

The Strangites built temples and tabernacles, served proselytizing missions, practiced baptisms and sealing ordinances for the dead. They established a communal order of living which they called the Associated Order of Enoch. Strang found and translated ancient historical records. He experienced revelations and visions to guide his people. Twelve years to the very day of receiving his religious calling, he died of a gunshot wound administered by former friends and members of his church.

Curious about this religious group, I started researching their story in various historical repositories. I found that a great deal had been published about Strang and his life but that very little had been written about his five wives. I wondered what had happened to these women and their children. Their lives did not end when his did. In fact, four of Strang's five wives were pregnant at the time he died. The youngest children did not begin life until after their father's was over.

As I studied these women and children, I suddenly realized I was working on something of much broader scope. I began to comprehend that the story of the wives and children was, in a sense, the actual history of the Strangite people. All four of Strang's plural wives had family members who were similarly Strangite adherents. His first wife, Mary, continued to interact with her husband's followers. The trials and hardships of these women were echoed in the experiences of those related to them.

For most of the Strangites, the journey of faith began in Nauvoo, Illinois, with the death of Joseph Smith. Eyewitnesses to singular religious events and participants in the social upheaval that occurred when the Mormon people were left leaderless, they chose Wisconsin and Strang rather than Utah and Brigham Young. While building their own communities, they were witness to some important events in the broader history of America such as the emergence of Wisconsin as a state, the steamboat trade on the Great Lakes, and the demise of the great fur and fishing empire centered on Mackinac Island. They made their homes on the frontier in both Wisconsin and Michigan, lost their homes on Beaver Island, and made new homes and communities. For the most part, they were hardworking ordinary folk looking for simple religious truth.

I am not the first to write about the Strangites, and I am sure I won't be the last. At least two experts in Mormon history told me I should not waste my time studying the Strangites because everything about them had already been written. They were wrong. I learned that new facts and new resources are still being discovered. Old records are ready for re-examination and re-interpretation.

This book is not a biography of James J. Strang. Information about him can be found in other volumes. Nor is the intent to discuss whether Strang was a prophet or charlatan. This, too, has been debated again and again. It really doesn't matter to me whether Strang was a "genuine prophet" or not because the people who followed him obviously believed he was. This book is simply an attempt to tell the fuller story of the Strangites—their trials and tribulations and efforts to maintain the Strangite Church during their founder's ministry and after his death. I have drawn extensively on primary sources—letters, diaries, memoirs, public records, and Strang's newspapers and religious materials. Whenever possible, I have allowed the eyewitnesses to speak for themselves.

To avoid confusion in terminology, I have used the same names that were common in Strang's day for the different segments of the Mormon Church. Those who followed Strang will be called Mormons, Saints, or Strangites interchangeably, while those who followed Brigham Young will generally be called Brighamites. Members of the Reorganized Church of Jesus Christ of Latter Day Saints, now the Community of Christ, will be referred to as Josephites. Those who did not belong to any of these churches were known as "gentiles." I have referred to Strang's wives and most of the women in this narrative by their maiden names.

The story of this movement is a compelling and intriguing one. Many writers, including Strang's own descendants, have struggled with the logistics of how to relate the tale without sensationalizing it, and so have I. Strang's grandson, Mark A. Strang, wrote the following words to a cousin in 1956:

> Over the past hundred years, hundreds of thousands of words have been written about Strang. Much of it has been based on downright lies and vindictive gossip of his enemies.... My correspondence with writers of sensational articles on the subject indicates a general complaint of a dearth of search materials from which to paint the brighter picture. I am at work now on a project assembling the *historical facts* about him and his followers; many of his remarkable concepts; and anecdotes illustrative of the fine qualities of his character. My thought is that if I make this material easily available, some of the future writers (and there will be many of them, the subject is so intriguing) will use some of it and thereby truth and justice will to some extent be served.

Mark Strang was later successful in obtaining and deciphering his grandfather's diary and getting it published. Mark left behind a number of letters written to and from Strangite leaders in the 1950s and 1960s. James Strang's sons, Charles and Clement, similarly struggled to tell a more sympathetic story of their father. They obtained the original letter of appointment and their father's autobiography and collected a huge number of letters written to and from the church founder during the 1830s-50s.

Other writers have also added to the collection of knowledge over the years, the most notable being Milo M. Quaife, author of *The Kingdom of Saint James: A Narrative of the Mormons,* and Roger Van Noord, author of *King of Beaver Island: The Life and Assassination of James Jesse Strang.* In the 1920s, Quaife interviewed the last of the original Strangites, including Sarah Wright, one of Strang's widows, Wingfield W. Watson, and James Oscar McNutt. Van Noord discovered a number of sources that had never before been used and produced a more modern interpretation of Strang and his followers.

I have made a number of friends during the writing of this book and am grateful for the kind assistance of William Shepard, a member of the Strangite Church and trustee for the Wingfield Watson Land Trust. Bill introduced me to the Strangites in Burlington—a small but gracious and very patient group. I admire their faith and devotion more than I can say. I am also grateful to Norma Jean Drebin Herzman and Jerry Gorden, descendants of people who lived on Beaver Island; Bill Cashman, director of the Beaver Island Historical Society; and the members of the Society for Strang Studies. All have helped me immeasurably. Others have assisted me, including the librarians at the Clarke Historical Library at Central Michigan University, the Wisconsin Historical Library in Madison, and the State Library of Michigan in Lansing. Ron Romig of the Community of Christ spent an entire day running files to and from the archives for me in Independence, Missouri. All of these people went out of their way to help me find the documents I needed. The librarians at the Morris Area Library in Morris, Illinois, allowed me to make hundreds of prints from their microfilm readers.

I would not have been able to write this book if it were not for the help of my dear husband and best friend, Bob. He read every word of this book time after time. His faith in me kept me going long after I was ready to give up. I also owe a debt of gratitude to my four children, Mike, Kaatje, Keri, and Rob, and to my parents, Joyce and Dick Cleverley. I sorely neglected them during the research and writing, yet they never complained. I want my mother-in-law, Truis Speek, to know that she does not have to worry about my health anymore because I am finally taking it easy. Thanks for caring about me.

I.
THE RISE AND FALL OF ST. JAMES

THE PROPHET AND HIS WIFE

1813-1843

Thus we were left in destitution and ... [were] left on the dock at Chicago to go where we pleased and find a home ... where we could. Here we were left without shelter, the sun beaming down at fever heat. Here we were made a gazing stock for all kinds of people to stare at. One man began to swear at the [onlookers] ... and with some manly feelings he shoved the large warehouse doors apart and said, 'Here, ladies and gentlemen, come in here out of the sun and stay until you can find places.' This was the first kind word that we had heard from any one during the whole proceedings. —Wingfield W. Watson to Milo M. Quaife.[1]

It was indeed a hot day in early July 1856 when a large group of Mormons stood in the sweltering sun on a dock in Chicago, uncertain what to do. Only two days before, they had been forced from their homes on Big Beaver Island in the middle of Lake Michigan, herded onto departing ships like cattle, and stripped of their possessions. Their religious leader, James Jesse Strang, lay on his death bed in Wisconsin, dying of wounds administered by former friends and followers. Homeless and leaderless, the destitute Mormons prayed for divine guidance....

. . .

Jesse James Strang was born in the town of Scipio, Cayuga County, New York, on March 21, 1813, the son of Clement Strang and Abigail James. There was no indication the child would grow up to be a leader, let alone a prophet. Both of his parents were small in stature. Clement stood only about five foot three, while Abigail measured even less. However, James wrote that his were "comely in appearance, amiable, affectionate, charitable,

---

1. Wingfield W. Watson, interviewed by Milo M. Quaife; see Quaife's notes for Dec. 10-11, 1918, Clarke Historical Library, Central Michigan University, Mount Pleasant, Michigan; John Cumming, "Wingfield Watson: The Loyal Disciple of James J. Strang," *Michigan History*, Dec. 1963, 316.

remarkably industrious, skillful in labor, and judicious in business." They were also "unsullied in moral and religious character."[2]

Their oldest child, David, was two years older than James, and their only daughter, Myraette, was five years younger. The family was close and there was never "so much as a momentary coldness between any two members of the family."[3]

James's childhood and school days were quiet and uneventful, although he was precocious and addicted to reading. He exhibited a rare ability in debate at an early age. Before he had even turned nineteen, he had attained the reputation of a debater among his schoolmates. At the age of twenty-one, he began to study law. At first he borrowed law books, then hired out as a farmer to earn the money to buy his own books.[4] Sometime during his teenage years, he reversed his first and middle names and thereafter became known as James Jesse Strang.[5]

In June 1836, James began practicing law in a small village near Cherry Creek, New York, called Clear Creek at the time.[6] Twenty-three years old, the future prophet was, like his parents, slight of frame and stood about five foot seven. His hair was a light "sandy red" and "seemed to send out rays of light," while his beard was a "lambent reddish-brown."[7] He had large, dark

---

2. "Ancestry and Childhood of James J. Strang, written by himself in 1855," Strang Letter Book 1, James Jesse Strang Papers, Yale Collection of Western Americana, Beinecke Rare Book and Manuscript Library, Yale University, New Haven, Connecticut. Items in the Strang Letter Book are numbered, the autobiography being item 1. Most other correspondence, in the Strang Collection rather than the Strang Papers, is indexed according to folder number.

3. Ibid.

4. Elvira Field Strang and Charles J. Strang, "Biographical Sketch of James J. Strang," unpublished manuscript, n.p., Strang Manuscript Collection, Library and Historical Center, State Library of Michigan, Lansing, Michigan.

5. Ibid.; *Gospel Herald*, Oct. 28, 1847. At a Voree debate with William E. McLellin over the proper name of the Mormon Church, Strang remarked, "I prefixed the name Jesse to my original name of James Strang, and many years after I changed it about so as to make Jesse the middle instead of the first name; yet I never heard till today that I was not the same identical individual that was formerly James Strang." The *Gospel Herald* was the official voice of the Church of Jesus Christ of Latter Day Saints in Voree, Wisconsin, from September 1847 through June 1850. It continued the *Voree Herald,* Jan.-Oct. 1846, and *Zion's Reveille,* Nov. 1846-Sept. 1847.

6. Strang and Strang, "Biographical Sketch."

7. Mark Strang to Russell B. Nye, May 25,1960, Clarke Historical Library. Sarah

brown eyes that some said were "dreamy and meditative." He was nearly blind in his left eye, although it was not a noticeable defect.[8] At age twenty-one, he remarked in his diary that for the first time in many years he was able to read a word with his right eye covered.[9]

His manner was "ingratiating and attractive," "sensitive and tender in his emotions"—artistic, in other words. He sometimes drew original embroidery patterns for ladies. Both he and his brother, David, were "inclined to invention" but were discouraged from that occupation by their father.[10] A newspaper reporter once made the following observation: "In person, Strang is rather below the ordinary size, very plainly dressed, red face, bold, prominent forehead, large eyes and mouth and cheekbones; possesses considerable talent, great shrewdness, and an earnest, energetic manner, is very loquacious, and speaks very fast and loud when preaching." In fact, while preaching, the reporter noted:

> he appears like a man trying with all his might to convince others that he had something very important to tell them, and that it was absolutely necessary they should believe it. He is perfectly familiar with the Bible, and very persevering in his efforts to convince others of the truths of particular passages.... On the whole, I should think him well calculated to make converts and get together a large body of people and control them, as he possesses the talent, energy and shrewdness. He is very pernicious in argument, and has ready wit.[11]

In the early part of 1836, James, now twenty-three, began courting Mary Abigail Perce, a young woman of eighteen. James was familiar with her

---

Wright said Strang's eyes were blue, but all other accounts report that they were brown or black.

8. Eugenia Phillips to Stanley Johnston, June 15, 1937, Clarke Historical Library.

9. James Jesse Strang, diary, Feb. 25, 1835, microfilm, James Jesse Strang Papers, Beinecke Library; also folder 3, Strang Collection, Beinecke Library. The diary was obtained by Milo Quaife from Henry Denio of Lamoni, Iowa, in the 1920s. Strang's grandson Denio apparently inherited this heirloom from his grandmother Betsy McNutt. To avoid confusion with the published diary, I cite Strang's entry dates rather than page numbers. A portion of the diary was written in code, which was not fully deciphered until the 1950s by Strang's grandson Mark Strang, *The Diary of James J. Strang: Deciphered, Transcribed, Introduced and Anotated* (Michigan: Michigan State University Press, 1961).

10. Eugenia Phillips to Stanley Johnston, Oct. 31, 1936, Clarke Historical Library. Eugenia said her father was a light eater and fond of milk but abstained from pork later in his adult life.

11. "The Mormons," *Rochester Daily Democrat*, rpt. in *Gospel Herald*, Sept. 23, 1847.

family, having been a member of the wedding party when her paternal aunt, Freelove Perce, married Jarvis Bennett.[12] James was also a friend of Ellen Waitee (Weata) Perce, another paternal aunt. In fact, it was Ellen who introduced James to Mary.[13] His best friend was Benjamin Carpenter Perce, another member of the extended family.[14] Only nine years older, Benjamin may have seemed more of an older brother to Mary than an uncle.[15]

The previous year, 1835, Benjamin had joined a group of people who were moving to Wisconsin Territory, which was newly opened for settlement. The party included Benjamin's sister Lydia; her husband, Moses Smith; and Aaron Smith, Moses's brother. The Smiths settled in an area along the White River near what is now Burlington, Wisconsin, and Benjamin moved about a mile and a half farther west to found the community later called Spring Prairie.[16]

Mary was the second oldest child of William Livingston and Lydia Brown Perce. Born on April 10, 1818, in Madison County, New York, she had an older sister, Harriet, and two younger brothers, William Jr. and Samuel Y.[17] Her father was a contractor in the canal business; by 1836 he was digging a water channel in Virginia.[18] At least two of Mary's siblings lived with

---

12. Strang, diary, coded entry, Aug. 21, 1834. Strang and the young woman he was courting at the time, Wealthy Smith, "stood up" as a witness for Freelove Perce and Jarvis Bennett. Wealthy was probably related to Aaron and Moses Smith.

13. Ibid., coded entry, May 29, 1836; James Strang to Mary Perce Strang, Feb. 20, 1837, Strang Letter Book 127. Myraette Mabel Strang verifies that Ellen Waitee Perce is the "Weata" listed in Strang's diary. Perce Family History, unpublished manuscript, n.p., State Library of Michigan.

14. Perce Family History. For almost 100 years, researchers have incorrectly reported that Benjamin was Mary's brother and Lydia was Mary's sister.

15. Ibid. Ellen Perce was only eleven years older than her niece, Mary.

16. Ibid. Benjamin and Sarah Perce, parents of Benjamin C. and William L. Perce, made the 700-mile trek from New York to Wisconsin by wagon when they were sixty-seven and sixty-eight years old. They moved in with Benjamin, where their daughter Ellen did the housekeeping chores. According to the obituary of Moses Smith in the *Gospel Herald*, June 14, 1849, a large number of relatives and friends accompanied Moses and Aaron Smith to Burlington, Wisconsin.

17. Ibid.

18. Researchers have claimed William Perce was in the "candling" business, but a close examination of letters shows the word to be "canaling." See James Strang to Benjamin C. Perce, Feb. 28, 1837, Strang Letter Book 24; Strang to Perce, Aug. 20, 1838, Beinecke Library; Moses Smith obituary, *Gospel Herald*, June 14, 1849.

their father while he was away in Virginia, while Mary and her mother lived in Elliottville, New York, where Mary attended school.

James proposed marriage to Mary within a few months of meeting her. She apparently had apprehensions and soon called off the engagement. James was upset and embarrassed over this turn of events. He wrote in a coded portion of his diary on May 7, 1836, that his engagement had been "a total, radical and unmitigated failure, without one redeeming circumstance. She could have gone but one act more," he wrote, which would have been to say that when "we meet again it must be as total strangers." But undaunted, James persisted. "By heavens, she is mine," he acclaimed. "I will steal her heart in an hour she thinks not. I know she can and must and will love me."[19]

Three weeks later, on May 29, he was no longer as eager to be married as Mary's Aunt Waitee was that the two should be reconciled. "Weata has done me a twofold kindness," James wrote in code. "It was on her introduction that I formed the engagement with Mary. Now she has procured its renewal. I did not [seek] or wish for this, preferring an entirely different course. Yet it may answer well," he conceded. If not, Aunt Waitee "shall fail for once. One interview will decide. I know I shall finally conquer," he added confidently.[20]

James decided to write to Mary's father in Virginia to ask for her hand in marriage. "It is with feelings of more than ordinary diffidence that I now address you," he wrote. "I have been introduced to your daughter Mary Abigail. I have corresponded with her since last winter—have avowed my affection for her, and after her assurance that my high regard was kindly and fully reciprocated, I have said to her that with the permission of her parents I was ready to offer her (what I believe I have to bestow) an honour unsullied, a heart uncorrupted." James then got to the point:

> I now write by her permission to desire your approbation of an alliance between us.... I will not insult your understanding by pretending myself a subject of those violent passions which so often 'die in their sweetness.' On the contrary, my partiality to Miss Perce is the result of a perfect conviction of her moral and intellectual worth, and I think I may say is of a kind and degree which may endure ... as long as life lasts. If you resolve to grant my request, you will have

---

19. Strang, diary, coded entry, May 7, 1836.
20. Ibid., coded entry, May 29, 1836.

done what was in your power to consummate the happiness of two persons pecu-
liarly adapted to each other's society.[21]

Within three weeks, William Perce replied to Strang's letter with one of
his own, agreeing to the marriage. "Mary is very dear to me & I am very so-
licitous for her comfort and happiness," he answered. "But I am certainly as
well pleased to trust her to you as any gentleman in the circle of my acquain-
tance. You have therefore my entire approbation & I fervently hope you may
neither of you have cause for sorrow & that you may not be disappointed. You
must not expect too much." William then wrote to his daughter:

Now Dear Mary, I have at once & frankly complied with what is doubtless your
wish although young. You have a right to judge for yourself in this all important
matter, but it gives me great pleasure to say that your choice accords well with
my own.... I am now about to surrender my authority but you must not forget
that your part is still obedience—you have been a dutiful daughter. Do not let
me hear that you are a stubborn wife, but remember to make home pleasant to
your husband.[22]

The wedding took place on November 20, 1836, in a Presbyterian
church in Silver Creek. James was twenty-three and Mary eighteen. It was a
cold day, "ushered in by rain, and sleet and snow, and November wind and
gloom—a fit precursor for the tragic life of Mary Abigail Content Perce,"
wrote their daughter, Myraette, many years later.[23] On that day, Mary became the first of James's five wives—the only one to whom he would be legally married. "Who could have imagined, as they walked up the aisle to the
altar that Sunday morning, the sorrow and trouble, the heartache, and woe
and pain the years were holding for her?" Myraette mused.[24]

As a wedding present, James gave his new wife a copy of the *Complete
Works of Shakespeare,* a handsome brown-leather volume that can still be seen
in the archives at the State Library of Michigan. Mary's name is carefully
written in script on the inside cover.[25] James wrote to his friend Benjamin,
Mary's uncle, telling him of the marriage:

---

21. James Strang to William Perce, Sept. 22, 1836, Strang Letter Book 62.
22. William Perce to James Strang, Oct. 10, 1836, Strang Letter Book 63.
23. Perce Family History.
24. Ibid.
25. Strang Manuscript Collection, State Library of Michigan.

I ever regretted that fate had not made us members of the same family, and had I wanted other sufficient inducement [to be married into the Perce family,] that should have been one [toward] forming of the alliance I have lately entered into.... Whether I have done wisely or unwisely, it would not be well to ask you now—but I have chosen the companion of my life for those qualities that are enduring and agreeable in every stage of life and every possible circumstance of fortune. If it is not well done, I have only to say that I have acted with the utmost care and deliberation—and that every appearance is yet more than satisfactory."[26]

For a few months after their marriage, the young couple lived apart. Mary studied Latin and French in Elliottville, New York, while James studied law in Randolph about twenty miles away. Three weeks into their marriage, Strang wrote to his wife:

Tis midnight, I sit here in my room, tired and jaded and alone with half a day in papers on my table unopened and a dozen on the floor just read. My clothes are on every chair in the room ... not three sticks of wood in the world and too much business to get any.... I need not tax your credibility when I ask you to believe that I, who have concentrated upon you the affections of a feeling and changeless heart, feel your absence even now.... Before this very short absence I did not know that I loved you so much as I really do, though I thought I loved you as much as possible.[27]

He continued to tell his wife the next day he had

since slept and dreamed of you. This is the first time I ever dreamed of you at least since we were married.... Now it is very pleasant to dream of agreeable objects as it is the most exquisite torture to dream of things that are not so.... [D]o be very careful with your health and follow the physicians directions in everything. I fear you will not be careful enough. Forever that spirit and animation which renders you so lovely must be sometimes curbed or your loveliness will cease and your health and happiness, too.[28]

He included a love poem he had composed for her:

---

26. James Strang to Benjamin C. Perce, Feb. 23, 1837, Strang Letter Book 24.
27. James Strang to Mary Perce Strang, [Dec.] 5, 1836, Strang Letter Book 99.
28. Ibid.

There be more of Beauty's daughter
With a magick like thee;
And like musick on the water
Is thy sweet voice to me.
When, as if its sounds were causing
The charmed oceans pausing,
The waves lie still and glistening
And the [chilled] winds seem gleaming[,]
And the midnight moon is weaving
Her bright [hair] o'er the deep;
Whose breast is gently heaving
As an infant's asleep;
So my spirit bows before thee,
To listen and adore thee;
With a full but soft emotion,
Like the swell of summer's ocean.[29]

Mary, too, was lonely. "I received the books you sent me, James, but [I] was not here when they arrived, & had I been, I would have written you by the bearer." She continued:

> James, why did you not write, did you suppose a letter from you would not be welcome to me[?] If you did, you have not known the heart of her for whom you resigned all you had hitherto held most dear.... I am some melancholy this evening[.] Why should I be[?] I am surrounded with friends, and dear ones, too—because one dearer than these ones for whom I have left Father and Mother, Sister and Brothers is away. Are you sick? I know it not. Are you well[?] I am not assured of it. Had you written were it only enough to say you were well perhaps I should not feel thus.

Mary added that she had heard something that hurt her feelings: "They say I ought not to go to school that I am going to be more expense to you than I shall be profit. James is this truth? If it is I had rather not attend school. Perhaps I have done wrong in wishing to attend."[30] David Strang was one of those who thought Mary was unnecessarily depleting his brother's finances.

---

29. Ibid. Some of the writing in this letter is difficult to read.
30. Mary Perce Strang to James Strang, [winter] 1836-37, Strang Letter Book 92.

"I should think you had better stop sending your wife to school," he advised a few months later.[31]

Mary was frequently ill, which may have contributed to her worry about James's health. Her mother and sister believed she could regain her health if she would drop her studies. But James continued to encourage her, frequently buying her quills and school supplies and such books as Thomas Nugent's French-English dictionary, a French grammar, an edition of Fénelon's *Les Aventures de Télémaque,* and Samuel Putnam's *Sequel to the Analytical Reader.*[32]

Besides being physically ill, Mary was also often depressed. Her mother, Lydia, now living away from her daughter, wrote the following: "Do not, my Dear Mary, harbor melancholy. [I]t is hurtful to your health and without doubt, likewise to your husband's feelings. I judge him by myself when I used to see you dejected. It always grieved me." Perhaps instinctively knowing that Mary needed some cheering, Lydia added that she had "written till I am almost beside myself. I would say to you how much I want to see you but it is useless. I could not give you an idea of my feelings on the subject[;] I am not eloquent enough to describe them but I must close by wishing the best of heaven's blessings may attend you here and hereafter."[33]

In early 1838, James and Mary traveled to the eastern United States and visited her father in Virginia.[34] When they returned a few months later, they moved in with James's parents. But the young couple was living on their own by the time Mary gave birth to their first child on July 5, 1838. The baby girl was named Mary Elizabeth and nicknamed "Little Mary." Exactly what disease ailed Strang's wife and caused frequent illness throughout her life cannot be determined, but there is some evidence she may have suffered from chronic depression. After giving birth to her second daughter, Myraette (Nettie) Mabel, on May 23, 1840, Mary was very ill, presumably with postpartum depression. Her mother-in-law took the older child into her home for a time.

"Little Mary is well and contented & happy," James's sister, Myraette, wrote from her mother's home in a note addressed to Mary. "She is so good that mother don't mind her noise. Mother says she brought her home because

---

31. David Strang to James Strang, Jan. 31, 1837, Strang Letter Book 140.

32. Mary Perce Strang to James Strang, Jan. 14, 1837, Strang Letter Book 113.

33. Lydia Perce to "My Dear Children [James and Mary Strang]," Feb. 23, 1838, Strang Letter Book 121.

34. Strang and Strang, "Biographical Sketch."

she was afraid she would not be taken care of when you were sick & now she thinks you had better let her stay till you can take care of her yourself." Myraette continued by describing how "Mary stands by this stand while I write[,] jabbering[,] & is as happy as a little queen, she says she is happier than Victoria. We do not wonder that you want to see her; we love her so well that it's no trouble to wait on her, but we are willing that you should send for her when you think best."[35]

Myraette had written to her brother a few days previously:

I suppose by this time you are anxious to hear from Mary. She is well & contented and has been so. She says she is perfectly happy. She has not had a crying spell since she has been here. She sleeps in the settee sitting by mother's bed. Mother says she is the most playful child she ever saw & Maryann V. Tassel says she is the prettiest thing in the entire world ... she gives away so many kisses that there will be none left for you. She behaves as well as when she was at home, has room enough to play in[,] & minds as well as before she came. [S]he sits up at the table & eats like a woman.[36]

Out in Wisconsin, Mary's relatives had heard of the new baby and of Mary's illness. Benjamin and Ellen Perce wrote to say they were "well-situated," selling land at speculation prices. They encouraged the Strangs to join them in Burlington. "I am truly sorry to hear of your ill state of health and I know ill health brings misery and no enjoyment of life," Ellen wrote Mary. She enclosed some prairie flower seeds in her letter, telling Mary how beautiful Wisconsin Territory was.[37]

By this time, James had become postmaster of Ellington, New York, and was practicing law. In 1843 he purchased a weekly newspaper, the *Randolph Herald,* and served as publisher and editor. Mary frequently helped him, at least once taking over her husband's duties while he was away. "I think [Mary] must be a capable woman to take care of the post office[,] law office[,] & other offices without your assistance," James's cousin wrote.[38] Although James was periodically away, he appeared to be a good husband and father. On one occasion he wrote his wife to tell her he would not be home for

---

35. Myraette Strang to Mary Strang, May 24, 1840, Strang Letter Book 141.

36. Myraette Strang to James Strang, May 16, 1840, Strang Letter Book 135.

37. Ellen Perce to Mary Perce Strang, June 28 [1840], Strang Letter Book 55.

38. Manly James to James Strang, July 6, 1839, Strang Letter Book 142.

a few days. "Kiss the children for me and pat the dog on his head," he wrote warmly.[39]

By 1840, Mary's father had moved his family to Illinois, where he worked as a contractor on the I&M (Illinois and Michigan) Canal.[40] He purchased land both in northwestern Illinois and Burlington, Wisconsin, and urged James and Mary to join them.[41] After considering the idea for three years, James sold the *Randolph Herald* and placed an advertisement in his paper offering to act as land agent for anyone interested in Wisconsin property. On August 18, 1843, the Strangs loaded their belongings into a carriage and left their home in Clear Creek, New York, for Burlington, Wisconsin.[42]

---

39. James Strang to Mary Perce Strang, Oct. 15, 1841, Strang Letter Book 167.

40. William L. Perce, Land Records, Will County Courthouse, Joliet, Illinois.

41. William Perce to James Strang, June 27, 1840, Strang Letter Book 31.

42. "Refuge of Lies," *Voree Herald,* May 1846.

2.

GOD'S OWN GOOD TIME

1844-1845

I seal upon thy head against God's own good time, the keys of the Melchisedec Priesthood ... Thou shalt hold the keys of the Melchisedec Priesthood; shalt walk with Enoch, Moses, and Elijah and shalt talk with God face to face. —Joseph Smith, as recalled in the Chronicles of Voree.

I perceive by the spirit which is in me that thou shalt carry the gospel with the spirit like flowing fire to many nations, and by thee shalt God save the pure of his people. —Hyrum Smith, as recalled in the Chronicles of Voree.[1]

After reaching Wisconsin, the Strang family settled in Spring Prairie with Mary's aunt and uncle, Ellen and Benjamin Perce. Mary's paternal grandparents may have also been living in the same house. The Perces seem to have had a close familial relationship, so the arrangement may be assumed to have worked out well. The nearby town of Burlington was home to a number of Latter Day Saints (LDS), also known simply as Saints or Mormons. Mary's Aunt Lydia, who married Moses Smith, was an early convert to the Mormon Church. As early as 1837, Moses and his brother Aaron had set up a branch of the church with six members in Burlington.[2]

Within a couple of years, the little branch had grown to about 100 adherents. Moses and Aaron shared joint stewardship over the flock. However, by 1839, Moses had left Burlington to settle closer to the main body of the

---

1. "Chronicles of Voree, A record of the establishment and doings of the Stake of Zion called Voree in Wisconsin made by the Scribes appointed to that office," 6-7, microfilm copy, Library-Archives, Wisconsin Historical Library, Madison, Wisconsin; cf. John J. Hajicek, comp., *The Chronicles of Voree, 1844-1849* (Burlington, WI: JJRR Publishing, 1991).

2. *Latter Day Saints Messenger and Advocate,* June 1837. Moses Smith reported to the newspaper that there were six members of the church, including himself, in Foxville (now Burlington), Racine County, Wisconsin. Moses and Aaron Smith are not believed to be related to the originator of the Mormon Church.

church in Knox County, Illinois. The following year, Moses sold his property and gave the proceeds to Joseph Smith to help in purchasing land for a new gathering place and homeland for the Saints in western Illinois.[3] The swamp lands Smith bought on the shores of the Mississippi River at what was then known as Commerce, Illinois, were drained to become the town of Nauvoo.

James Strang had undoubtedly heard of the Mormon Church before moving to Wisconsin. Besides the fact that his wife's relatives were members, the religious sect had certainly been a theme of village gossip in Chautauqua County, New York, where Strang grew up. Hanover Township was located only about 140 miles southwest of Palmyra, where the Mormon prophet, Joseph Smith, was raised to manhood.[4] The stories coming out of Palmyra were hard to ignore. For instance, Smith said he was visited on the night of September 21, 1823, by an angel who led him in vision to a nearby hillside. There, Smith said, the angel showed him the location of a buried chest containing a book written on plates of gold. A few years later, Smith went to the location and acquired the chest. With the help of a seer stone called the urim and thummim, after the biblical adornment, Smith translated the golden plates into the Book of Mormon. It was a chronicle of people who had allegedly come to North America hundreds of years before the birth of Jesus Christ. Soon, Smith organized a church in Palmyra and Fayette, Seneca County, New York, based in part on the Book of Mormon. Strang turned seventeen in 1830, the year Smith founded the church. In addition, Kirtland, Ohio, the first gathering place for church members, was less than 100 miles southeast of Strang's New York home.

James opened his law practice in Burlington about a mile and a half away from Spring Prairie. His law partner, Caleb P. Barnes, was well known in the community. Strang had apparently considered becoming a contractor or engineer on the Illinois Canal with his father-in-law, but work on the canal had

---

3. Moses Smith obituary, *Gospel Herald*, June 14, 1849. Born in March 1800, Moses was a quiet, reserved man who was nevertheless known for his generosity and kindness. His obituary gives an interesting account of his life and an early history of lumber production at the so-called "pineries" in Wisconsin. His brother, Aaron, was uneducated but widely respected as a man of faith and wisdom.

4. "An American King," *Harpers Monthly Magazine*, Mar. 1882, 554, copy in the Legler Collection, Wisconsin Historical Library. Strang's son, Charles J. Strang, acknowledged that he contributed much of the information for this article.

been temporarily suspended.[5] It is possible that Strang would have also joined with his law partner in support of the Burlington Library Association, a semi-secret abolitionist organization which aimed to assist escaped slaves.[6] Barnes is known to have sheltered slaves in Spring Prairie, as did Lemuel Smith, brother of Moses and Aaron, who lived nearby.[7]

In October 1843, the Strang family became seriously ill and five-year-old "Little Mary" Strang died, a tragedy that would have weighed heavily on her parents' minds.[8] Some speculate the child's death may have been the catalyst that moved her parents to investigate the Mormon Church.[9] A few months later, during early January or February 1844, James was involved in trying a lawsuit in Ottawa, Illinois.[10] Aaron Smith, who was also in the city, convinced him to travel to Nauvoo and hear Joseph Smith preach. Nearly 11,000 people lived in Nauvoo at this time, making it a rival to the city of Chicago in population. Hancock County, where Nauvoo was located, boasted a population of nearly 23,000—most of them Mormons—and was the most populous in the state.[11] At first skeptical of the doctrine he heard from Joseph Smith, Joseph's brother Hyrum, and converted Campbellite preacher Sidney Rigdon,[12] Strang became convinced of their message and consented to be baptized before he left the city. Joseph Smith performed the baptism on February 25, 1844, in the basement of the unfinished Mormon temple in

---

5. "The Mormons," *Rochester Daily Democrat,* rpt. in *Gospel Herald,* Sept. 23, 1847.

6. Manual Hahn, "Freedom of the Press," unpublished manuscript ca. 1940, 72, Wisconsin Historical Library. Hahn was a member of the Burlington Historical Society and may have written the manuscript for that organization.

7. *Burlington, Wisconsin: The First Hundred and Fifty-Plus Years* (Burlington, WI: Burlington Historical Society, 1991), 18.

8. Perce Family History, unpublished manuscript, n.p., Library and Historical Center, State Library of Michigan, Lansing, Michigan. Mary Elizabeth Strang died on October 19, 1843.

9. Myraette Strang Losee to "Friend" Dennison, 1878, James Strang Collection, Clarke Historical Library, Central Michigan University, Mount Pleasant, Michigan.

10. Elvira Field Strang and Charles J. Strang, "Biographical Sketch of James J. Strang," unpublished manuscript, n.p., State Library of Michigan. This lawsuit may have had something to do with the Illinois & Michigan Canal.

11. Robert Bruce Flanders, *Nauvoo: Kingdom on the Mississippi* (Urbana and Chicago: University of Illinois Press, 1975), 322. Flanders took these data from the Illinois State Census of 1845.

12. "Chronicles of Voree," 6.

Nauvoo.[13] Witnesses to the ordinance were Moses and Aaron Smith, by now both high priests of the Melchizedek Priesthood order, and Thomas S. Edwards, Moses Smith's son-in-law.[14]

On March 3, Strang was ordained an elder in the church by Hyrum Smith. "I perceive by the spirit which is within me that thou shalt carry the gospel with the spirit like flowing fire to many nations, and by thee shalt God save the pure of his people," Hyrum prophesied, his hands on Strang's head.[15] Once again, Moses and Aaron Smith witnessed the ceremony.[16] As Strang was being initiated into the Mormon Church over the space of several weeks, he would have become aware of signs of discord in the city. Due to persecution both within and without, it was becoming increasingly obvious to Joseph Smith and his counselors that they would soon have to leave Nauvoo. Threats had been made on their lives, as well as against other Mormon leaders. There were a number of reasons why the Saints were not liked in Illinois. They were viewed by their non-Mormon neighbors as a fanatical sect bent on aggressively converting anyone with whom they had contact. In addition, the church members considered themselves to be God's chosen people, with a right to land and governance.

In addition, the city of Nauvoo, by virtue of its 1840 charter, had enjoyed enormous political power and independence beyond anything seen in any other city in Illinois. The city council was allowed to pass any law "not repugnant to, or inconsistent with, the constitution of the United States or of this State." In Nauvoo, this was interpreted to mean that the city was exempt from any state or federal law.[17] There was also a growing fear of the concentration of political power, as church members tended to vote in a unified block according to how their prophet directed them. Faithful to their church, the city

---

13. Ibid.

14. James J. Strang, minister's license, Clarke Historical Library. The document was issued by Walworth County, Wisconsin Territory, and filed on December 25, 1845, "for Record and Recorded on page 38 001 of Ministerial Records." It was signed by Leland Rockwell, clerk.

15. "Chronicles of Voree," 6-7. Hyrum also revealed through revelation that Strang was descended from the same ancient biblical tribe of Judah as King David and Jesus Christ himself.

16. Strang, minister's license.

17. Andrew F. Smith, *The Saintly Scoundrel: The Life and Times of Dr. John Cook Bennett* (Urbana and Chicago: University of Illinois Press, 1997), 94-95.

leaders answered only to Smith, who was simultaneously city mayor, the ranking officer of the Nauvoo Legion—the largest militia in the United States—and the presiding official of the Mormon Church. The officers of the militia were also devout Mormons, as were the leaders of the city's social organizations, including the Masonic Lodge. Non-Mormons viewed this concentration of religious, military, and political power as extremely dangerous and a threat to their own existence.

There was also a growing faction within the church that was opposed to Joseph Smith, especially after he declared to a few trusted associates his revelation from God regarding polygamy. Although this would be denied in public, many high-ranking church leaders became involved in the practice, including most of the twelve apostles. Other church leaders who were opposed to polygamy began to form a powerful opposition, which James Strang would undoubtedly have noticed. It also makes sense that Strang would have known about polygamy since Moses Smith's daughter Sarah became a plural wife of Thomas S. Edwards on February 1, 1844, in a ceremony performed in Nauvoo by James Braton.[18] Considering Strang's close association with Moses and Aaron Smith, it can be assumed he would have known something about this marriage and its implications.

Because Strang was well versed in geography, he attracted the attention of Joseph Smith in at least one discussion about the possibility of moving the church from Illinois to Wisconsin. This occurred about the same time Smith set up the Council of Fifty, a clandestine organization made up of the twelve apostles and others of the most devout men in the church. The council was charged with "consulting on the best manner of obtaining redress for grievances from our enemies and to devise means to find and locate in some place where we could live in peace."[19] It was this council, under the direction of Brigham Young, which later directed the movement of the Saints to Utah.

Throughout the history of the Mormon Church, members had spoken of establishing the kingdom of God on earth to usher in the second coming of Jesus Christ. It was believed that when the Second Coming occurred, all gen-

---

18. Lyndon W. Cook, comp., *Nauvoo Deaths and Marriages, 1839-1845* (Orem, Utah: Grandin Book, 1994), 109. The fact that Sarah was a plural wife is confirmed in family records currently in the possession of a living descendant of Thomas Edwards.

19. Joseph Smith, *History of the Church of Jesus Christ of Latter-day Saints* (Salt Lake City: Deseret Book, 1980), 7:213.

tiles—a term meaning anyone who was not Mormon—would be destroyed. The Council of Fifty was literally charged with setting up God's kingdom, including a ruler who would be revealed to them by God. In this manner, they believed they could promote the anticipated parousia.[20] On March 11, 1844, in a secret meeting of the Council of Fifty, Joseph Smith was ordained "King on earth" while surrounded by fifty-three "princes of the kingdom," or members of his secret council.[21]

No doubt, James Strang, who was still lingering in Nauvoo at this time, would have been more or less aware of this secret council. It was meeting at a time when, almost overnight, Smith's friends had become his enemies and no secret could remain so for long. Strang had at least one very close friend who was a member of the Council of Fifty, Moses Smith. A well-known frontiersman, Moses was given the responsibility of scouting out possible areas in the Rocky Mountains where the Saints could go to live.[22] Another piece of evidence showing that Strang would have known about the Council of Fifty appears in the Strangite record, *Chronicles of Voree*, in which Strang records Council of Fifty assignments immediately after mentioning his own baptism into the church.[23] In fact, Strang would institute a similarly structured council and kingdom when he established his own religious organization in 1850.

James arrived back home in Spring Prairie at the end of March or first of April 1844 and immediately began investigating the logistics of receiving emigrants from Nauvoo. In May he wrote a report to Joseph Smith apprising him that Burlington and Spring Prairie would be particularly favorable areas for such immigration. Aaron Smith added a few notes to Strang's letter and

---

20. Klaus Hansen, "The Making of King Strang: A Re-examination," *Michigan History*, Sept. 1962, 208. This information was taken from the diaries of John B. Lee. Because of the secrecy surrounding the Council of Fifty, it is difficult to reconstruct what the entire purpose of the organization was. Information exists only in a few fragmentary letters and journals.

21. Ibid., 208-209. This information comes from an unpublished manuscript by George Miller, now located in the Mormon Miscellaneous Collection, Humanities Manuscripts and Archives, New York Public Library, New York City.

22. Moses Smith obituary. Other Council of Fifty members included George J. Adams, William E. Marks, George Miller, William Smith, and John E. Page, all of whom became influential in Strang's church.

23. "Chronicles of Voree," 7-8.

mailed it to Nauvoo toward the end of the month.[24] But just as everything seemed to be proceeding well for Mormons in Wisconsin, they were becoming worse in Illinois. On June 27, Joseph and Hyrum Smith were murdered in their Carthage, Illinois, prison cell, creating a grief-filled panic in Nauvoo. In addition, the deaths set up a succession crisis due to the fact that Joseph had not publicly designated an heir.[25]

Although reports of the Smith brothers' assassinations spread rapidly through the Mississippi River towns, it was some time before the rest of the country heard the news. A week after the murder, word reached Milwaukee, which was located about thirty miles northeast of Burlington. The *Milwaukee Commercial Herald* printed the story on July 5.[26] It normally took four to eight days for the mail to travel between Nauvoo and Burlington, routed first through a distribution center in Chicago, and from there by daily dispatch to Southport (Kenosha). Southport, in turn, relayed the mail at least twice a week to Burlington.[27] Under normal conditions, the information of Smith's death could also have reached Burlington by July 5.

However, Strang claimed the news did not arrive until July 9, the day he received an unexpected letter from Joseph Smith. The letter was postmarked Nauvoo, June 19, and arrived at the post office in Burlington after being routed through Chicago. Strang's law partner, Caleb Barnes, picked the letter up from Box 71 at the post office[28] and hand-delivered it to Strang the same day. Aaron Smith was with Strang when Barnes delivered the letter. James immediately opened it and sat down with Aaron to read it.[29] The two-page letter, dated June 18, nine days prior to Joseph Smith's death, was purportedly written by Smith in answer to the May letter from Strang and Aaron Smith. It was written on three successive pages, while the fourth page con-

---

24. Ibid., 7-8. Strang returned to Ottawa, where he spoke about the church with William L. Perce Jr., Mary's brother, then returned to Spring Prairie by way of the Fox River Valley. According to Manuel Hahn in "Freedom of the Press," William Perce Jr. was one of the trustees of the early Strangite Church.

25. For an excellent explanation of the Mormon leadership issues, see D. Michael Quinn, "The Mormon Succession Crisis of 1844," *BYU Studies* 16 (1976): 187-233.

26. Roger Van Noord, *King of Beaver Island: The Life and Assassination of James Jesse Strang* (Urbana and Chicago: University of Illinois Press, 1988), 7.

27. Hahn, "Freedom of Press," 48.

28. Ibid.

29. "Chronicles of Voree," 8-9.

tained Strang's name and address, the postage rate, and a red postmark, hand-stamped in Nauvoo.[30]

Smith began by acknowledging Strang's proposal to move the church to Wisconsin. Smith wrote that he had originally thought to respond unfavorably but changed his mind after speaking with his brother Hyrum. "I have long felt that my present work was almost done, and that I should soon be called to rule a mighty host, but something whispers me it will be in the land of spirits," the letter read.[31] Prophesying his own death, Smith added this revelatory word: "And now behold my servant James J. Strang hath come to thee from far ... [and] had faith in thee ... and to him shall the gathering of the people be, for he shall plant a stake of Zion in Wisconsin and I will establish it, and there shall my people have peace and rest, and shall not be mooved."[32]

Smith's letter included additional instructions, saying that God had chosen Aaron Smith to be Strang's counselor, that Strang should proceed to set up the holy city of the kingdom of God: "The name of the city shall be called Voree, which is being interpreted, garden of peace, for there shall my people have peace and rest and wax fat and pleasant in the presence of their enemies.... The city of Voree shall be a strong hold of safety to my people, and they that are faithful and obey me[,] I will there give them great prosperity ... and unto Voree shall be the gathering of my people, and there shall the oppressed flee for safety and none shall hurt or molest them...."[33] The letter was ostensibly signed by Joseph Smith.

This letter could have hardly come as a surprise to James Strang. It was not the first indication of an assumption that he would lead the Mormon Church. As he later explained, he was visited by an angel at 5:30 p.m. on June 27, 1844—the exact moment of Joseph Smith's death—and anointed to be Smith's successor.[34] The angel, Strang said, stretched forth his hand and touched his head, anointing it with oil.[35] Almost immediately, James set out to claim the leadership of the church. However, instead of going to Nauvoo,

---

30. Charles Eberstadt, "A Letter that Founded a Kingdom," *Autograph Collector's Journal*, Oct. 1950, 7.

31. "Chronicles of Voree," 1-6. For the complete letter of appointment, see appendix A.

32. Ibid.

33. Ibid.

34. Ibid., 10-12.

35. Ibid.

22

where other would-be successors had already begun to gather, Strang set out on foot for a conference of church leaders that was scheduled to get underway in Florence, Michigan. A member of the church for only four months, Strang presented his letter of appointment to the conference and was immediately excommunicated by the presiding high priest. Moses Smith, who was in Florence for the meeting, volunteered to take a copy of Strang's letter to Nauvoo. Strang became ill and returned to Wisconsin by boat across the Great Lakes.[36]

In Nauvoo, Strang's letter came under immediate suspicion. Critics claimed the two sheets of the letter were of different types of paper. They wondered if Strang had received a genuine letter from Nauvoo, which he had discarded, retaining only the page containing his name, address, and postmark. They thought it was obvious that someone had substituted a new page of paper, written a new message on the front and back of the page, and continued writing on the back of the original address sheet.[37] They also criticized the postmark, which they said should have been black rather than red and that it was too large, also that there was no record of the mailing in the mail ledger at Nauvoo.

The register was in fact missing for that particular day, but there was a record of the letter having been received at the Chicago Distribution Office, and the postmark was obviously red and the correct size. Critics still weren't satisfied and discovered what they believed was proof the postmark was false. There was a small dot at the left of the "J" in June, which should not have been there. Strang located a number of letters known to have been mailed from Nauvoo on June 19, and they all had the small dot in the same place on the postmark. A speck of dust or a splinter had gotten into the stamp that day and was marked on all the letters, something Strang could not have known.[38]

Joseph Smith's signature on the letter was also closely examined, quibblers claiming it bore no resemblance whatever to Smith's known signatures.[39] Other skeptics maintained Smith sent the letter but intended only

---

36. Ibid., 13-14.

37. Eberstadt, "Letter that Founded a Kingdom," 7.

38. James J. Strang, *Prophetic Controversy* (St. James, MI.: by the author, 1855), 39, copy at the Clarke Historical Library.

39. Eberstadt, "Letter that Founded a Kingdom," 7. The letter of appointment was printed in block script. Along with other matters of style, this was unlike anything Joseph

that Strang set up, and become the head of, the church in Voree. Brigham Young, who had been president of Smith's twelve apostles and temporarily placed in charge at Nauvoo, hotly disputed Strang's leadership claims and promptly excommunicated him a second time. However, there were others in Nauvoo who remained undecided about who should succeed Smith as head of the church and wanted to hear Strang's claims. A number of Mormons, including Smith's own family, maintained that Joseph's oldest son, Joseph III, was the intended successor. Several other church members claimed leadership rights. Brigham Young was finally selected by the main body of the church until a successor could be chosen, and he was later appointed second president of the Church of Jesus Christ of Latter-day Saints.[40]

Unimpressed by Young's leadership, Strang and his followers retreated to Wisconsin, where they quietly began preparing the community of Spring Prairie to become the new Mormon community of Voree. Although he claimed close friends and relatives were well aware of his divine call, Strang decided not to say much about it to his neighbors for fear they might ask unreasonable prices for their land.[41] In January 1845, he changed tactics and sent supporters, including Aaron Smith, to congregations in Wisconsin and Illinois, informing them of his letter of appointment and angelic ordination. Little by little, the small community of Voree began to grow.

On September 1, 1845, Strang told followers he had learned by revelation about some ancient plates of brass buried in a nearby hillside. He claimed an angel appeared before him and showed him the plates in vision and gave him his own urim and thummim to translate the records. The plates were said to be the history of another ancient people who had lived in the Americas and had died in battle at that location many years before.[42] This was, of course, reminiscent of Joseph Smith's discovery and translation of the Book of Mormon plates.

Two weeks later, Strang called together four of the most honest and re-

---

Smith had ever written. Eberstadt notes that some passages were very close to phrases Strang had used in his own diary.

40. Hansen, "Making of King Strang," 210nn. Even though the church has been known as the Latter-day Saints since 1838, it is spelled differently by the various churches. Brigham Young retained the hyphen between the words *Latter* and *day* and Strang took out the hyphen but capitalized *Day*.

41. "Chronicles of Voree," 14.

42. Ibid., 20-23.

spected men of the community: Aaron Smith, Jirah B. Wheelan, James M. Van Nostrand, and Edward Whitcomb. He disclosed his vision and led them to an oak tree on a nearby hillside. Strang noted the men would find a case of rude earthenware buried under the tree at a depth of about three feet. He instructed them to dig up the case and, while they were doing so, examine the ground closely so they would know the case had been buried there before the tree grew up. Strang kept entirely away while the men were digging.[43]

The tree, which had a trunk about one foot in diameter, was surrounded by a patch of deeply rooted grass, and the men could not see any indication the sod had been cut through or disturbed. The roots from the tree stuck down on every side and were closely interspersed with the roots from other trees. None of them had been broken or cut away. The men carefully dug up the tree and continued to dig to a depth of three feet, where they found a case of slightly baked clay. Over the case was a flat stone about one foot wide and three inches thick, which appeared to have been subjected to a fire. The case was imbedded in clay that was so hard packed, it broke when removed. The earth below it was so hard, it had to be dug with a pickaxe.[44]

The case contained three small plates of brass, scratched on all six sides with queer writings and drawings. The plates measured about 2½ inches long by 1¼ inches wide; they were about the thickness of tin. One of the sides contained what appeared to be a landscape drawing of the prairie and hills where the plates had been dug up. Another plate held drawings of a man with a crown and scepter, the moon and stars, and a strange looking eye. The plates seem to have been fastened together with a ring.[45] The other four sides of the brass plates were closely covered with what appeared to be alphabetic characters, but in an unknown language. Strang took the three small plates home and translated the markings and drawings with the aid of his urim and thummim.[46]

A week later, Strang invited his supporters to a meeting where he read his translation of the plates.[47] Quite a crowd had gathered to see and handle the brass objects. Strang told the crowd the plates were the ancient record of a

43. *Voree Herald,* Jan. 1846.

44. Ibid., Jan. 1846.

45. "The Mormons," Sept. 23, 1847.

46. "Chronicles of Voree," 25-27.

47. Ibid., 29.

man called the Rajah Manchou of Vorito, who had fallen in battle at that site. Before the raja died, he had managed, under the command and direction of God, to bury a short history of his people. Strang read the words transcribed on the plates:

> My people are no more. The mighty are fallen and the young slain in bat-
> tle. Their bones bleached on the plain by the noonday shadow. The houses are
> leveled to the dust and in the moat are the walls.... They sleep with the mighty
> dead, and they rest with their fathers. They have fallen in transgression and are
> not, but the elect and faithful there shall dwell.
>
> Other strangers shall inhabit thy land [where] I an ensign there will set
> up.... The forerunner men shall kill, but a mighty Prophet there shall dwell. I
> will be his strength and he shall bring forth thy record. Record my words and
> bury it in the hill of Promise.[48]

The forerunner referred to in the transcript was obviously the Mormon prophet Joseph Smith, and the mighty prophet who would succeed him was clearly James Strang.

The translation produced general astonishment and generated tremendous support for Strang among those who had come to see him as a true prophet. His supporters published his claims and distributed them in an effort to convert the scattered Mormons. Strang himself wrote an epistle to the elders of the diaspora. One thousand copies of the epistle were printed for distribution by missionaries in Nauvoo and the Fox River Valley of Illinois where many Mormons lived.[49] Strang did not mince words. "Follow not after any who usurp the authority of God in the holy city" of Nauvoo, he wrote. "Be not unmindful of the flock who know not the true Shepherd, but are following hirelings among whom are grievous wolves."[50] He cautioned against such pretenders as Brigham Young, who Strang said was usurping the true line of authority in the church.

The epistle came at an opportune time in Nauvoo. The so-called Mormon War between the Saints and their neighbors was escalating and Young was preparing to vacate Nauvoo for the Rocky Mountains. "Let not my call to you be in vain," Strang warned, continuing:

---

48. "Chronicles of Voree," 30-31.
49. Ibid., 33-34.
50. Ibid., 35-36.

26

You are preparing to resign country and houses and lands ... Many of you are about to leave the h[a]unts of civilization and of men to go into an unexplored wilderness among savages, and in trackless deserts to seek a home in the wilds where the foot print of the white man is not found. The voice of God has not called you to this. His promise has not gone before to prepare a habitation for you.... Let the oppressed flee for safety unto Voree and let the gathering of the people be there.[51]

The choice between what seemed to be a pleasant hamlet in Wisconsin Territory or the wilds of some unknown remote location was enough for some of the residents of Nauvoo to give Strang a second look.

---

51. Ibid., 45-46.

3

GATHERING TO VOREE

1846-1847

*I have all confidence that Joseph was
a prophet and that your appointment was legal as successor in office or else I
am worse deceived than ever and [surely] their cannot be but one in truth
in office as Prophet, Seer and Revelator. Now such a time of lo hears and lo
theres I have never seen and all making their claims[.] Come follow me
Brigham Young proclaims follow me McLellin says follow me William
Smith says follow me Lyman Wight proclaims follow me James J Strang
proclaims follow me and all their various places of gathering and commanding to build temples and come and bring all you have and rear up the
Lord's house or they can't have no inheritance in the kingdom of God[.]
Now so much of this makes confusion and delusion and who knows what is
right for there cannot be but one right.* —R. Stephens to James J. Strang.[1]

B y the beginning of January 1846, Strang had thrown his heart and
soul into the Mormon Church and to proving the authenticity of
his claim as Joseph Smith's successor. It was a time-consuming job and at a
time when he had a pregnant wife and a small child to feed. In addition to his
religious duties, he also retained his law profession for a time.[2] Soon he obtained a printing press and began production of the *Voree Herald,* a monthly
newspaper designed to present his religious views. The first edition reprinted
the letter of appointment from Joseph Smith and an accounting of Strang's
anointing at the hands of an angel, as well as the testimonies of the men who
had dug up the Plates of Voree. A number of papers were sent with missionaries to Nauvoo and to the Fox River settlements where about 300 members

---

1. R. Stephens to James Strang, Jan. 6, 1849, Burton Historical Collection, Detroit
Public Library.

2. Elvira Field Strang and Charles J. Strang, "Biographical Sketch of James J.
Strang," unpublished manuscript, n.p., Library and Historical Center, State Library of
Michigan, Lansing, Michigan. This article said Strang litigated at least nine cases in 1846.

of the Mormon Church resided.[3] Other copies were sent through the mail to prospective converts.

Gilbert Watson, who would later play a supporting role in both the Strangite and Reorganized LDS Churches, heard Strang's claims and was "partially convinced" of their truth. He traveled to Voree, hoping to meet Strang personally before committing to the sect. When he arrived, Strang had gone to Ottawa, Illinois, on church business. The young man decided to wait for him. "I visited Aaron Smith who was appointed his Counselor," Watson wrote in his journal. "Though he [Aaron] was what the world calls a very illiterate man, yet by the wisdom which God had given him [,] he understood the doctrines of the gospel of the Son of God. I found his conversation on this and on various other subjects both interesting and instructive. I also visited all the witnesses of the plates and found them men of truth and veracity." When Strang returned home, Watson questioned him closely. "I was fully satisfied that he was the lawful successor to the prophet Joseph," the young man wrote.[4]

Strang's claims attracted a number of prominent people who had served in leadership positions in the Mormon Church, including Martin Harris, who had been one of the three witnesses to the Book of Mormon translation; William Marks, former Nauvoo stake president; and Reuben Miller, one of Brigham Young's most trusted leaders. Joseph Smith's younger brother, William, made plans to move to Voree and bring his mother with him. He said his brother's widow, Emma, was also willing to move to Voree along with her children.[5] William wrote to Strang, representing the entire Smith family except Hyrum's widow, to uphold Strang as Joseph Smith's successor. The letter included the family members' signatures affirming that they concurred

---

3. "Chronicles of Voree, A record of the establishment and doings of the Stake of Zion called Voree in Wisconsin made by the scribes appointed to that office," 48, microfilm copy, Library-archives, Wisconsin Historical Library, Madison, Wisconsin; cf. John J. Hajicek, comp., *The Chronicles of Voree, 1844-1849* (Burlington, WI: JJRR Publishing, 1991).

4. "Journal of Gilbert Watson Comprising Also a Short Account of His Life and Travels Written by Himself," unpublished manuscript, Library-Archives, Community of Christ (formerly Reorganized Church of Jesus Christ of Latter-Day Saints), Independence, Missouri. Watson was born in 1822 in Scotland, where he was a weaver. He came to America in 1841 and was baptized into the Mormon Church in 1844. He learned the masonry trade, and at the time Joseph and Hyrum Smith were murdered, he was cutting stone for the Nauvoo temple. Watson later became a prominent member of the RLDS Church.

5. "Opinions of the Smith Family," *Voree Herald,* June 1846.

with the sentiments expressed. However, Joseph's sister, Catherine Salisbury, later denied having ever signed such a letter. Emma's name was not included on the manuscript, and there is no indication she ever intended to move to Voree, despite what William wrote.

Strang corresponded with a number of other Mormons, including Louisa Sanger, a disabled woman known for her quick wit and great intelligence.[6] Sanger had been part of the inner circle of Nauvoo as a secret plural wife of Hyrum Smith.[7] She wrote to Strang demanding evidence of his calling as a prophet.[8] At the time, she was living in Ottawa with her father, David Sanger, and brothers Lorenzo, William, James, and Lucien. Her father "opposed" Strang's message, but William was "much moved" by it.[9] Louisa never committed her religious favor to either Strang or Young.

Early in January 1846, Strang sent a message to Nauvoo ordering Young and the twelve apostles to appear in Voree to be tried for usurping authority.[10] Young scoffed at Strang's presumption. However, Strang's missionaries created a tremendous amount of excitement among Nauvoo's residents. In order to stop the Strangites from wooing away the populace, Young threatened to excommunicate any Mormon caught listening to the missionaries.[11] The people at that time were in a state of agitation in Nauvoo after the Illinois legislature revoked the city charter and disbanded the Nauvoo Legion, leaving

---

6. Louisa Sanger, obituary, *Ottawa* [Illinois] *Free Trader*, Aug.18, 1877.

7. D. Michael Quinn, *The Mormon Hierarchy: Origins of Power* (Salt Lake City: Signature Books and Smith Research Associates, 1994), 584; also on the *New Mormon Studies CD-ROM: A Comprehensive Resource Library* (Salt Lake City: Smith Research Associates, 1998). Louisa may also have been a plural wife of Reuben Miller. According to Devery S. Anderson and Gary James Bergera, eds., *The Nauvoo Endowment Companies, 1845-1846: A Documentary History* (Salt Lake City: Signature Books, 2005), 505n38, Louisa was sealed by proxy "for time" to Reuben Miller on January 27, 1847, in the Nauvoo temple.

8. "Correspondence," *Northern Islander*, Nov. 2, 1854. It is not entirely certain the woman Strang corresponded with was Louisa Sanger because her letters are signed simply "Louisa" or "L. S." However, historian Dale L. Morgan, who inventoried the Strang manuscripts in the Coe Collection at the Beinecke Library, was convinced it was Sanger, corroborated by references to "Louisa" in several letters from Reuben Miller; remarks made about "Dr. Sanger," Louisa's brother, in the "Chronicles of Voree"; and a mention of Louisa Sanger in the Nov. 2, 1854, *Northern Islander*. The *Northern Islander* was edited by Strang at Beaver Island from December 1850 through June 1856.

9. "Chronicles of Voree," 56.

10. Ibid.

11. Ibid., 57-59.

the Saints without a government and no legal way to defend themselves. Church members living in the outlying areas were frequently victims of mob attacks and were beaten and robbed of their possessions, their houses burned down around them. State authorities appeared either unable or unwilling to protect the city from the rising tide of deprivations. Some of the Saints engaged in retaliatory raids.

People had hoped the deaths of Joseph and Hyrum Smith would end the conflict between Mormons and gentiles in Illinois. This was not to be. If anything, the hostility intensified. It was soon obvious to everyone that, in order to bring an end to the warfare, the Mormons would have to leave the state. In the summer of 1845, a group of citizens from Warsaw, the gentile town a few miles south of Nauvoo, appealed to Illinois Governor Thomas Ford to expel the Mormons for the sake of "public safety." When this proved unsuccessful, they planned to incite an uprising against the Mormons. In September, notices appeared in several gentile newspapers announcing an upcoming "wolf hunt," a well-known code word for night riding against the Mormons.[12] By mid-month, a mob of about 300 had destroyed at least fifty-four Mormon buildings by fire, and there was every indication the arson would continue.[13]

Brigham Young felt he could do nothing more than publicly announce his intention to abandon the city of Nauvoo to the church's enemies. Leaders began making preparations to move the entire church—not just the Saints in Illinois but from communities throughout the Midwest and Northeast—to the far-off Rocky Mountains. The plan was to leave before the summer of 1846.[14] Members struggled to make preparations at the same time as they tried to sell their homes and farms with little success. Gentiles assumed they would be able to appropriate Mormon property for free once the inhabitants were driven out, and this assumption was later shown to be right. Valuable homes, farms, and businesses in Nauvoo ended up being sold for pennies on the dollar, if they sold at all.

By early February 1846, persecution had become so intense in Hancock County that Young and the twelve apostles decided to vacate Nauvoo immediately. On February 4, a large contingent crossed the frozen Mississippi

---

12. Robert Bruce Flanders, *Nauvoo: Kingdom on the Mississippi* (Urbana and Chicago: University of Illinois Press, 1975), 323.

13. Ibid, 327.

14. Ibid, 306.

River in covered wagons for their journey west when the temperature outside hovered below zero. Over the next eighteen months, nearly 20,000 Mormons would be banished from Nauvoo and the surrounding countryside, leaving behind an estimated $4-5 million in personal property. This included the un-completed Mormon temple.

For obvious reasons, Voree, 270 miles northeast of Nauvoo, may have been more attractive to many of the Saints who were sick, elderly, poor, or had family members who were incapable of traveling to the Mexican frontier. Strang claimed it had not been Joseph's design for the Saints to go to west into an uninhabited country, only that twenty-five men "without families" had been intended to "take a mission among the Indians and take measures for establishing a stake of Zion." This, Strang reported in the *Voree Herald,* was "quite another thing from taking out thousands of women and children to perish by famine, flood and Indian war."[15]

Reuben Miller wrote to Strang from Nauvoo on February 15, giving an assessment of the Mormon exodus from the city:

> The work of God is progressing with unexpected rapidity—The church is crossing the river as fast as they can and it is expected they will take up the line of March in a few days—The mob papers have lately come out and say that they cannot stay in the county longer than the tenth of May.... Now we have many poor with us—and many who cannot raise money to go out of the county. Many that have land that they cannot sell.... There are many that will be at Voree in the course of six weeks—Many that would go if they could—But cannot for want of means.[16]

On April 6-8, the Strangites held a conference in Voree to sustain James as their prophet, seer, revelator, and translator. Aaron Smith was upheld as Strang's first counselor, William Marks as bishop of the Voree congregation, and Reuben Miller as president of the Voree stake. Brigham Young and all but two of Joseph Smith's apostles were excommunicated for "usurping the authority belonging to the first presidency, taking to themselves the powers

---

15. "Going into the Wilderness," *Voree Herald,* Mar. 1846.

16. Reuben Miller to James Strang, Feb. 15, 1845 [1846], folder 14, James Jesse Strang Collection, Yale Collection of Western Americana, Beinecke Rare Book and Manu-script Library, Yale University, New Haven, Connecticut. Although the letter is dated 1845, references to events taking place in Nauvoo indicate that it was 1846.

and duties of the high quorums, and commanding the church to go into the wilderness."[17]

Through the pages of the *Voree Herald,* Strang sent an open letter to the Nauvoo refugees encouraging them to sell or rent their homes and farms and come to Wisconsin Territory. "If you have not the means of coming to Voree, but can move part way, take the Mississippi route and seek employ in the mineral country; or the Illinois route and seek employ on the Illinois and Michigan Canal, and among the farmers, till you can gather with your brethren," he wrote.[18] He urged "non-resistance" to the mobs threatening Nauvoo. He said this would be "a stronger defense than the strongest artillery on earth. If your enemies smite you on one cheek, turn them the other."[19] It was advice Strang would later issue to his own people.

By late April, teams were crowding into Strang's City of Peace from every direction and the community soon looked like "an encampment rather than a town."[20] "A very few families came in last fall," Strang wrote to a friend. "But the gathering may be said to have commenced the first day of this month, since when it has not been below four families any day, beside about the same number settling in the country around."[21]

A Pittsburgh Mormon wrote to Strang about a dream he had previously had, months before he heard of Strang, in which he saw himself settling down in Voree. He said he had not understood the dream until Moses Smith arrived with a copy of the *Voree Herald.* Another adherent, Benjamin Chapman, wrote that his "heart was so rejoiced that the Great God had fulfilled his word in appointing a man through our beloved Joseph ... that I go for the man that has the Tools," which he explained were the "Urum & Thumum." "For," he wrote, "I know that the first President of the Church of Jesus Christ of Latter

---

17. "Chronicles of Voree," 73. Apostle Wilford Woodruff was not among those charged because he was away on a mission when Young "seized" the power of the church. Another apostle, John E. Page, renounced Young's leadership and within months was sustained as one of Strang's own apostles. Strang looked on Page's conversion as a *coup d'état* over Young because Page had been a devout follower and apostle of Joseph Smith. However, Page left Strang's church in 1849.

18. "To the Saints in Hancock County," *Voree Herald,* Apr. 1846.

19. Ibid.

20. James Strang to John C. Bennett, Apr. 16, 1846, Library-Archives, Community of Christ.

21. Ibid.

Day Saints must have those things or he cannot be a Seer and Translator."[22] Chapman said he had "advocated [Strang's] claims with a number of individuals here. And the greatest objections are, why did you not come out sooner with your claims. And another is they have understood that you have two or three sections of land in Voree, and they fere [fear] that it is a speculation in you, in order to get your land sold and make yourself rich thereby."[23]

Another prospective convert wrote asking for information about Voree. "I would make further inquiry of you relative to the town of Voree. Whether it is laid out yet," James W. Pugh wrote. "And if it is, you will do me a kindness by giving me a description of the lots, their size, and present value. As the members here feel desirous of obtaining an inheritance before it falls into speculators hands. And we are desirous of knowing the numbers of latter day saints in the vicinity and wheather the immigration has begun there yet."[24]

Strang answered both men through the pages of his newspaper, replying that he had claimed his place as successor to Joseph Smith at the very time of Smith's death. "It is others who have kept the church in ignorance on the subject," he explained.[25] There were several hundred lots for sale in the best part of the town, he continued, which "are very large, varying from one-fourth of an acre to an acre. They all sell for the same price, $50 per lot. Parts of lots in proportion so that a quarter lot four rods by ten very prettily located can be had for $12.50."[26] Strang had added an interesting clause to the property deeds for the town, stipulating that at no time could spirituous liquor be sold on the property, in which case the property would revert back to the original owner, who was usually Strang.[27]

In September 1846, Strang had written in his newspaper that "as the place [Voree] began to be built last April, principally, by a plundered and exiled people,"

22. Benjamin Chapman to James Strang, Mar. 24, 1846, folder 16, Strang Collection, Beinecke Library.

23. Ibid.

24. "Correspondence," *Voree Herald*, April 1846.

25. Ibid.

26. James W. Pugh to James Strang, Mar. 23, 1846, folder 20, Strang Collection, Beinecke Library; "Correspondence," *Voree Herald*, Apr. 1846.

27. "Opinions of the Smith Family," June 1846; [Mr. and Mrs. Theron Drew] to Mark Strang, June 20, 1956, James Strang Collection, Clarke Historical Library, Central Michigan University, Mount Pleasant, Michigan.

it certainly is not a very rich city. Its population dwell in plain houses; in board shanties, in tents, and sometimes many of them in the open air, and if any of those good truth telling christians who say Voree is NON EST will call here of a sunday we will show them a congregation of from one to two thousand people besides those who stay at home. The place is more prosperous than could have been expected in the present impoverished state of the church.

All who come here find plenty of employment at good wages and a bountiful supply of all the necessaries of life at low prices.... The expense of a removal from any place east of the mountains to Voree is less than half the cost of going to Nauvoo. There is none of the exposure to river fevers, and when you get here industry is rewarded and rights respected by a peaceable law abiding people.[28]

William Hickenlooper later wrote to his son and daughter, both Strangites, explaining in 1855 his decision to follow Brigham Young and trying to convince them to leave Strang. "The first evidence I received that Brigham was the true successor of Joseph, was on the day when Sidney [Rigdon] set up his claim for the presidency," he wrote. "Brigham's countenance his voice, gestures and everything truly represented the martyred prophet in such a striking manner I shall never forget—I was convinced by the spirit of the Lord that the mantle of Joseph had fallen on Brigham."[29]

S. S. Thornton responded to his father-in-law, explaining his conversion to Strang:

I shall show by successful contradiction by your own arguments that he (Brigham Young) is an usurper, and has acted as such ever since Joseph's death. Because Mr. Young had tried to mimic Joseph for several years before his death, and on his return from Boston after his (Joseph's) martyrdom even went out and got a dentist to take out a tooth on the same side that Joseph lost one, to make himself appear as much like him as possible, that even his voice, gestures and likeness would seem like Joseph, and did, at the August conference, as you related, which was evidence to you that he was the man Joseph appointed, yet it is no evidence without he had come in at the gate, and been ordained, as the Lord had told Joseph before, which was by an angel.[30]

Thornton said his wife, Jane, also wished her parents to know the evi-

---

28. "Voree," *Voree Herald,* Sept. 1846.

29. "Correspondence from GSLC," *Northern Islander,* Aug. 16, 1855. The Hickenloopers were probably Jane Thornton's parents.

30. Ibid.

dence she had to prove the truth of Strangism. "She says the testimony she received under their preaching and the strong evidence they brought from the scriptures and revelations is one reason. Another was, she prayed that if it was right the Lord would send a man to buy our place and property, and in a few days a man came and would not give it up until he bought it, and first we knew we were ready to start."[31] Thornton added that his wife had "another evidence":

> It was impressed in her mind if we did not go to Beaver Island that she would die in a short time.... Brother Hickey came to our house, he being the Apostle that was sent to preach with us that winter. He was impressed by the spirit and spoke out and said that if we did not go she would die, and he should never see her again. She then said this had been the impression in her mind for some months, but she had told no one of it, not even me; but that she then was confident it would be so if we did not obey the voice of the good shepherd, which was to go. We accordingly hitched up and started.[32]

Through such personal witnesses that Strang was to be their prophet, converts continued to file into Voree during the summer of 1846. Strang was often seen in Burlington wearing a blue shirt, black-and-white checked trousers, and a straw hat as he conducted business for the church. A newspaper reporter from Ottawa described him.

> The Prophet is thirty three years old, rather below the middle size, slender constitution, of nervous temperament, enjoys but very indifferent health, of mild temper and retiring habits, and is apparently honest and earnest in all he says. Phrenologically the moral and intellectual faculties predominate most decidedly, in a large head; among other organs, self-esteem is rather large and the organs of the animal passions are quite deficient. Mr. Strang was bred to the law, is entirely self-educated and a man of extensive and general reading. He is now engaged in connection with several leading citizens, in devising an enlarged and liberal system of com[mercial] Schools for Wisconsin; is a warm advocate of temperance, and more or less connected with most of the benevolent enterprises of the age. In public speaking, his enunciation is tolerably distinct, very rapid and somewhat too loud. He is a close debater, generally mild in criticism, but in invective comes down like an avalanche. — Both his views and his

---

31. Ibid.
32. Ibid.

plans are very comprehensive and look forward to future generations as much as the present.

He depreciates both the military and the mob spirit; looks upon the organization of military bands in the church as uncalled for, and … goes very near as far as the Quakers for non-resistance; looking to peaceful avocations as a better security against molestation, than any armed defense whatever.…

The prophet lives in a most unostentatious style, in a room eight feet by twelve, furnished with a stove, table, and two chairs. This with a small sleeping apartment, makes the accommodation for him, his amiable wife and two children. Well will it be for his people if they do not make him proud by flattery and adulation.[33]

While most of those attracted to Voree were honest, upstanding citizens looking for a religious journey, there were a few who may have sought profit from their friendship with the Saints. Included in the latter may have been three who were widely considered to be among the most notorious rogues in Mormon history: George J. Adams, John C. Bennett, and William Smith.

Of these three, Adams was a preacher and a sometimes actor who sought out Strang in July 1846. He had an exceedingly "glib tongue" and was a "perfect terror with Bible verses." With a Bible and a volume of Shakespeare constantly at his fingertips, Adams was noted for his burning eloquence and withering sarcasm. Strang wrote of him: "His oratory is like the mountain torrent quenching the flames of iniquity—his faith is Abrahamic, and takes hold on heaven—his heart is filled with the milk of human kindness, flowing like the rivers of waters. God speaks, and he obeys—let the earth keep silence."[34]

In 1846, George J. Adams was thirty-five years old, "of medium size, black curly hair, sharp dark eyes, intelligent forehead, Roman nose, lips that shut up like a clamshell, showing great firmness if not absolute obstinacy." His countenance was "Jewish," and he claimed to have "Israeliteish blood flowing in his veins."[35] He had moved quickly through the ranks of Mormon

---

33. "The Mormon Prophet," *Ottawa Constitutionalist*, rpt. in *Voree Herald*, Apr. 1846.

34. "The Star in the East," *Zion's Reveille*, Dec.1846.

35. Clarence Day, *The Journey to Jaffa* (no publication data), 30, copy in the Doyle C. Fitzpatrick Collection of Strang Papers, State Library of Michigan. The "J" in George Adams's name may have stood for Jefferson, Joshua, or Jones and has been reported all three ways. Adams was born about 1811 in Oxford Furnace, New Jersey, not far from the Delaware River. He supposedly inherited a dark complexion from his mother, who is said to have

leadership following his conversion in 1840. At one time he was considered "the thirteenth apostle," but was never an official member of the quorum. In 1843, however, he was charged with adultery after he returned to Nauvoo from a two-year mission to England accompanied by a wife and child. The complication was that he already had a wife and a child waiting for him at home in Nauvoo. The following year, he was excommunicated, both for teaching and practicing polygamy and for embezzling church funds.[36]

A member of the Mormon Church from Massachusetts wrote to Strang to caution him against Adams. "The brethren with one accord denounce George J. Adams as being decidedly a bad man," Alden Hale wrote.[37] Adams was said to be involved with "a drunken set of rowdies, fighting and rolling in the gutters," and to "play on the stage, where he would get drunk, preach, and fight," all at the same time. He was also known to consort with prostitutes, according to Hale. "Adams says he does not care about Mormonism at all, all he wants to do is make a living. I have to add," the writer alerted Strang, "if G. J. Adams has set in flame all places where he has been as he has Boston[,] that it would take but few such fires to nearly obliterate Mormonism from the world."[38]

Adams wrote Strang from Ohio in July 1846, claiming he had received a testimony of his prophetic nature in the same way he had previously come to be convinced of Joseph Smith's authority.[39] He asked Strang for his "old position" in the church and told Strang not to listen to the "lies" that were being told about him. "People will tell you I am a drinker—it is a lie[,] … a base phalsehood," he wrote.[40] The prophet freely forgave Adams for his faults. "As for these complaints that you say are made against you," Strang wrote, "I

---

had Jewish blood. *The Journey to Jaffa* is the true account of Adams's attempt to found a colony in Palestine in 1866.

36. Flanders, *Nauvoo: Kingdom on the Mississippi*, 276. Even though many of the Mormon Church leaders, including Joseph Smith, had multiple wives, the practice of polygamy was denounced publicly from the pulpit.

37. Alden Hale to James Strang, Jan. 1, 1849, folder 359, Strang Collection, Beinecke Library. Hale explained that Adams had borrowed money from several of the Saints in Massachusetts. By stratagem, all except a Brother Skimming recovered their money. Skimming went to Adams's room to collect $40 the actor had borrowed from him and found two of Adams's associates drunk in bed and Adams himself so drunk he was barely able to stand.

38. Ibid.

39. George J. Adams, "Correspondence," *Voree Herald*, July 1846.

40. George Adams to James Strang, Mar. 27, 1846, Detroit Public Library.

have only to say <u>now</u> that if you are guilty, <u>you</u> <u>must</u> <u>do</u> <u>so</u> <u>no</u> <u>more</u>."[41]

Adams's friend John C. Bennett was another notorious individual in Mormon history. At one time, Bennett had been one of Joseph Smith's closest advisors and had even lived with Joseph's family for a time. Suave, sophisticated, and intelligent—his black hair sprinkled with gray—Bennett was nine years older than Strang. He stood about five-foot-six, was broad shouldered and weighed about 142 pounds. His eyes were dark, face thin; he had a dark complexion, "roman" nose, and was missing his upper front teeth. He was said to be "sharp-eyed" and to speak with a Yankee accent. There was no question that Bennett was knowledgeable in several subjects and was an able administrator in many respects. He had been Nauvoo's first mayor and wrote the Nauvoo charter. His high energy and flowery public speech were complemented by his fondness for pomp and ceremony. He was extremely deft at the art of flattery.[42]

His falling-out with Joseph Smith came in early 1841 when Smith received an anonymous letter telling him Bennett had abandoned his wife and children in Ohio. Smith sent a trusted friend, George Miller, to investigate. Miller interviewed a number of people in Ohio before concluding that Bennett was "an imposter, and unworthy of the confidence of all good men."[43] The most unsavory part of Bennett's reputation was that he was a womanizer. In Nauvoo several women confessed to "unchaste and unvirtuous conduct" with him, and he supposedly told at least one woman "that it was right to have free intercourse with women and that the heads of the church also taught and practiced it."[44] Church leaders charged Bennett with seduction and promising women medicine for abortions should they become pregnant.[45]

Bennett was excommunicated in 1842, although he claimed he resigned

---

41. James Strang to George Adams, May 5, 1846, folder 60, Strang Collection, Beinecke Library.

42. Andrew F. Smith, *The Saintly Scoundrel: The Life and Times of Dr. John Cook Bennett* (Urbana and Chicago: University of Illinois Press, 1997), 56. Bennett was born in Fairhaven, Massachusetts, in 1804.

43. Ibid, 56.

44. Ibid, 78-79.

45. Ibid, 88-89, 113. Bennett supposedly told one woman "he could cause abortion with perfect safety to the mother at any stage of pregnancy and that he had frequently destroyed and removed infants before their time to prevent exposure to the parties. In addition, Bennett was said to have built a brothel in Nauvoo. Whether or not it was true, the city council declared it a public nuisance and tore it down.

beforehand and left Nauvoo with the "best of feelings." Whatever good feeling may have existed at his departure evaporated when, within months, he produced a "tell-all book" that was extremely damaging to his friends. In his *History of the Saints; Or an Exposé of Joe Smith and the Mormons,* Bennett claimed Joseph Smith had planned to overthrow the western states of Illinois, Indiana, and Iowa and that the Mormon founder was setting up an empire in which Smith himself would be the king. Bennett disclosed that members of the Nauvoo Legion were members of the secret Danite organization, whose members swore loyalty to the prophet, right or wrong, and who took vengeance on gentiles for their supposed crimes against the Mormons.[46]

The most damaging information in Bennett's book was about polygamy. He claimed the Nauvoo hierarchy had set up an elaborate system of "prostitution" for the special benefit of church leaders. Joseph Smith had participated in a marriage ritual whereby Smith obtained at least seven "secret" or "spiritual wives," Bennett disclosed. These claims of kingship, corruption, polygamy, and other supposed Mormon offenses—most of them somewhat exaggerated—became sources of persecution directed against the Saints and likely contributed to the deaths of Joseph Smith and his brother Hyrum two years later.

In 1846, Bennett approached Strang by letter about getting his "old" church position back and gave Strang instructions on how to successfully win over a congregation. "Do you intend to have me in my original place in the First Presidency as one of your councilors?" Bennett asked in March. "I am willing to acknowledge you and sustain you as President, Chief, first in all things, with Elder George J. Adams as an equal councilor; but I am not willing now, nor will I ever be, to yield supremacy to ignorant men, simply because they are reported pious."[47] "I shall unite with _you, or with none_," he reiterated two days later. "There is nothing attractive to me under any other leader than yourself. I take _you_ to be the '_man with a crown upon his head and a scepter in his hand_,' the _Imperial Primate_ over all Israel; and that I am the '_upright line_,' or your _General-In-Chief_, 'standing before,' as seer upon one of your plates. I hope to be restored to my place by you. No other man in this

---

46. Fawn M. Brodie, *No Man Knows My History: The Life of Joseph Smith* (New York: Vintage Books, 1995), 314-15.

47. John C. Bennett to James J. Strang, Mar. 24, 1846, Library archives, Community of Christ.

church ever filled exactly the same place; so I should not interfere with the claims of any other man."[48]

Strang answered Bennett cautiously. "Taking your place in the church, confiding in your wisdom," he ventured, "I should not hesitate one moment to appoint you a councellor." But "you are doubtfully aware that my associates in the Presidency are appointed by revelation & consequently it is impossible for me to write anything on the subject."[49] In fact, Strang did not think it wise for the two men to be seen working together in public for the time being. "You are doubtless aware of the strength of prejudices against you in many quarters, growing out of the controversy between you & Joseph," Strang told Bennett. "As a counsellor and confidential assistant you are a host. You have proved that already. But if publickly known I doubt not old scandall would be raked up and given to the winds again."[50] Convinced that Bennett had repented of his wrongs against the Mormons, Strang gave George Adams instructions to rebaptize him. "Let him [Adams] send to me a certificate of that fact & in return I shall send you an appointment as counsellor to be followed by ordination the first time we meet," Strang wrote. "These things we may as well keep quiet about," he added.[51]

The third man of dubious character to join with Strang in 1846 was William Smith, the younger brother of the prophet, Joseph Smith. William was five years younger than his martyred brother but three years older than James Strang. William presented an imposing physical presence. He was tall and had a gaunt, raw-boned look to his face but was strong and muscular. Those who knew him said he possessed nothing of the kindness and gentleness that had characterized his brothers Joseph and Hyrum.[52] In fact, he was "lusty, hot-tempered and always in debt."[53] There was no doubt he was energetic as an apostle after his ordination at twenty-three years old and after his election to the Illinois House of Representatives in 1842 at the age of thirty-two. He

---

48. John C. Bennett to Dear Friend [James Strang], Mar. 28, 1846, Library-Archives, Community of Christ.

49. James Strang to John C. Bennett, Apr. 16, 1846, Library-Archives, Community of Christ.

50. Ibid.

51. Ibid.

52. Preston Nibley, *Joseph Smith, the Prophet* (Salt Lake City: Deseret News Press, 1946), 234. William Smith was born in Windsor County, Vermont, in 1811.

53. Brodie, *No Man Knows,* 163; Nibley, *Joseph Smith,* 234.

was successful in the legislature, particularly in defending Nauvoo's charter.[54] He was also editor of a secular newspaper published in Nauvoo.[55] Even the publication's name, *The Wasp*, told something of the editor's disposition.

Although he was a firm believer in the doctrines his brother had brought forth, William was handicapped by his fierce, uncontrollable temper that often caused him to regret his impulsive actions.[56] For instance, when Joseph was jailed in Missouri in 1838 and many were calling him a "false prophet," William was among those who turned against him. He hotly declared he hoped Joseph would never escape the hands of his enemies alive. "If I had the disposing of my brother," he shouted to some of the apostles, "I would have hung him years ago."[57] In response, the Quorum of the Twelve Apostles suspended him from office until Joseph later indulgently reinstated him.[58]

On another occasion, William had organized a debating society that became notorious for its "malicious and carping criticism." Joseph walked in one night and reproached his brother for the tenor of their discussion. William answered with a stream of abuse. Joseph got up to leave, but William attacked him, causing Joseph to fall to the floor, upon which William pummeled him until their older brother, Hyrum, dragged William off.[59] As a result of this beating, Joseph was unable to either sit or rise without assistance for some time thereafter and occasionally felt the effects of his injuries through the rest of his life.[60]

Grieved by William's actions toward him, Joseph wrote of the "wickedness of his brother, who Cain-like had tried to kill him." William later expressed remorse, and Joseph again freely forgave him; but the last time the brothers saw each other, William had once again physically threatened his older brother.[61] This disagreement took place in May 1844, a month before Joseph's death. William had asked for a city lot in Nauvoo near the temple. Joseph told him he would do so "with great pleasure" if William would build

54. Preston Nibley, ed., *History of Joseph Smith by His Mother, Lucy Mack Smith* (Salt Lake City: Bookcraft, 1945), 342-44.

55. Brodie *No Man Knows,* 288.

56. Nibley, *Joseph Smith,* 234.

57. Brodie, *No Man Knows,* 245-46.

58. Ibid., 163-64.

59. Ibid., 344-45.

60. Ibid.

61. Nibley, ed., *History of Joseph Smith,* 343-44.

a house on the lot and live in it, but not if William wanted the property for speculative purposes. William assured his brother he wanted to live near the temple. The lot was worth over $1,000. However, within a few hours of obtaining title to the land, William tried to sell it for $500. Hearing this, Joseph told the Nauvoo city clerk not to transfer the property deed and to nullify the transaction. William became so angry, he once again threatened Joseph's life. Aware of his brother's tendency toward violence, Joseph stayed out of his way until William left on a steamboat for the East.[62]

On October 1, 1845, Brigham Young ordained William to be patriarch of the Mormon Church even though personally Young did not trust him. Within five days, William was claiming that his position as patriarch entitled him to preside over the church as president, for which Young revoked the calling. Seven days later, on October 12, Young excommunicated the patriarch for "appropriating public funds of the church for his own private use—for publishing false and slanderous statements concerning the church and for a general looseness and recklessness of character which ill comported with the dignity of his high calling."[63] Like John Bennett, William Smith was also suspected of having taught the principle of "spiritual wifery" to various women in Nauvoo; several women claimed to have had illicit sexual intercourse with him.[64] He is known to have had at least four plural wives before his first wife died in 1845.[65]

Strang's lack of judgment in choosing church officers was one of several issues that created dissension in the summer of 1846, but it would be the most enduring threat. To the outsider, Voree appeared to be a peaceful, growing community. However, internal tension threatened to split the community apart. Beginning already in April, the question was raised about whether those who came to Voree from the Brigham Young faction needed to be rebaptized. Strang claimed that since he was Joseph Smith's true successor, his church was the continuation of the original movement and his followers did not need to be rebaptized. Others in the community, including Aaron Smith, felt it would be advisable for anyone of standing in Voree to demon-

---

62. Susan Easton Black, *Who's Who in the Doctrine and Covenants* (Salt Lake City: Bookcraft, 1997), 300-301.

63. Nibley, ed., *History of Joseph Smith*, 344.

64. Smith, *Saintly Scoundrel*, 88-89.

65. Brodie, *No Man Knows*, 303-304.

strate their commitment to Strang by submitting to a second baptism.[66]

Bennett and William Smith arrived in the midst of this controversy and immediately created suspicion among some members that Strang had invited "scoundrels" and "traitors" into his inner circle. Strang was also making moves at this time to extend a leadership role to George Adams. The fact that all three men had been associated in some way with polygamy in Nauvoo added to the dissatisfaction. Most of the Voree community were intently opposed to plural marriage and had only joined Strang's church after being assured that it would oppose the practice.

Most of those who had lived in Nauvoo had heard whispers that their leaders were secretly practicing polygamy or "spiritual wifery." In actuality, Smith had produced a revelation on the "new and everlasting covenant of marriage" on July 12, 1843, and shared it with some of his closest associates.[67] The revelation laid out the principle of "celestial marriage," whereby a husband and wife were given the opportunity to be "sealed " together in a ritual which promised them "eternal increase" in life and in the afterlife. A couple could have posterity as numerous as that of the prophet Abraham, as plentiful as "the dust of the earth, the stars of the sky and the sands of the seashore."[68] Celestial marriage was "essential" for an individual's complete "eternal salvation," according to the revelation.

However, the polygamy doctrine actually predated the revelation and had roots that reached as far back as February 1831. As Smith was studying the Old Testament and wondered how biblical prophets justified the practice of polygamy, he prayed for guidance in the matter. The Lord replied with an early version of the celestial marriage revelation and warned that "all who have this law revealed unto them must obey the same." In other words, Joseph was required to obey the law of plural marriage, just the same as the prophets of old, or be damned.[69]

Over the succeeding years, Smith secretly married a number of wives and taught the principle to a few family members and trusted friends. Grad-

---

66. "Story of the Late Apostacy at Voree," *Zion's Reveille*, Feb. 25, 1847.

67. Doctrine and Covenants, Section 132. The Community of Christ and the Strangite LDS Church recognize portions of the Doctrine and Covenants as scripture.

68. Todd Compton, *In Sacred Loneliness: The Plural Wives of Joseph Smith* (Salt Lake City: Signature Books, 2001), 10. Compton documents thirty-three plural marriages for Joseph Smith, while other historians have identified as many as forty-eight.

69. Ibid, 27; Doctrine and Covenants, Section 132.

ually most of the apostles took additional wives. Smith taught that "all real marriages were made in heaven before the birth of the parties." In its simplified form, this concept of kindred spirits, who had known each other in a life before this one, who were destined to be together on the earth as husband and wife, was called the "spiritual wife" doctrine.[70] Smith had intended for it to be kept secret until some future time when the main body of the church would be ready for it, but John Bennett's book, with its charge of prostitution, colored the practice so that it looked profane. It excited the revulsion of Mormons and gentiles alike.

In 1846, Strang was firmly opposed to polygamy. In September, at a conference in Kirtland, Ohio, under Strang's direction, his high council resolved unanimously to disclaim the whole spiritual wife system and vowed not to practice or to hold fellowship with anyone who believed in or practiced such things.[71] "The man or woman does not exist on the earth, or under the earth who ever heard me say one word, or saw me do one act, savoring in the least of spiritual wifery, or any of the attending abominations," Strang wrote in *Zion's Reveille* (the *Voree Herald* under a new name). "My opinions on the subject are unchanged, and I regard them as unchangeable. They are established on a full consideration of ALL the scriptures, both ancient and modern, and the discipline of the church shall conform thereto," he wrote.[72]

John Bennett became situated in nearby Burlington, which was less than two miles from Voree, and announced himself in flyers as a "professor of the principles and Practice of Midwifery and the Diseases of Women."[73] He also

---

70. Compton, *Sacred Loneliness,* 19-20.

71. "Kirtland," *Voree Herald,* Sept. 1846.

72. "Official," *Zion's Reveille,* Aug. 12, 1847. This article was written in response to another by John E. Page, who said he represented Strang's sentiments toward polygamy.

73. Flyer by John C. Bennett, July 4, 1846, Library-Archives, Community of Christ. The flyer reads: "Doctor Bennett has had the most ample experience in the treatment of western diseases, in an extensive and successful practice of more than 20 years, and having imported the most safe and efficacious French remedies, is now fully prepared to effect radical cures in the shortest time possible. Such remedies as De la Roche's Extract of Dogwood (one dose of which will cure the ague and fever in six hours ... together with Otto's Female Restorative and J. Xavier Chabert's French Female Monthly mixture for the diseases of females, which will be treated with the above famous remedies, prescribed by the female hospitals of Paris and Vienna, which are so especially adapted to the female frame and which now stand unrivaled and have obtained such universal celebrity both in Europe and America.)." The flyer listed testimonials from hospitals and doctors across the United States.

wasted no time in huddling up with Strang to help him organize his church. Within days, the two men had set up a secret organization called the Halcyon Order of the Illuminati. The structure of this secret society included an imperial primate, a grand council, viceroys, and noblemen, and it was designed to be the "governing council of the Strangite Kingdom of God on earth."[74] Bennett claimed the revelation for the Illuminati had been received by Joseph Smith in 1841 and that Smith had left instructions for Bennett to establish the order after Smith's death in order to "perpetuate the Kingdom of God."[75] According to Bennett, the oath for the Order of the Illuminati was the same one given to Constantine the Great in defense of Christianity. It was supposedly delivered to Constantine by an angel who appeared holding "a cross of gold" in her hand.[76]

The first meeting of the secret order was held on July 6, 1846. At this meeting, Strang was confirmed Imperial Primate and Bennett was appointed General-in-Chief of the new kingdom. In a series of meetings that month, at least twenty-four men were made chevaliers, marshals, earls, and cardinals. Several women were ordained to the entry-level office of *Illuminatus*. A list was kept containing the members' names and biblical lineages.[77] The initiates were introduced into the order by placing their right hand on a cross, which was positioned on a Bible, as Bennett recited the following: "Receive thou the accolade by which I now create thee an Illuminatus, in the name of the Father, and of the Son, and of the Holy Ghost, and by the authority of the Holy Priesthood, and the special edict of the Imperial primate our absolute monarch."[78]

New members were then anointed with oil while Bennett continued: "In behalf of the true, holy, catholic and apostolistic Church of Jesus Christ of Latter Day Saints; by an edict of the Imperial Primate, I now extend to thee the right hand of fellowship on the fine [five] points." This was followed by

---

74. Order of the Illuminati Papers, folder 188; also folder 4, Strang Collection, Beinecke Library.

75. Klaus Hansen, "The Making of King Strang: A Re-examination," *Michigan History*, Sept. 1962, 211. According to Hansen, the Order of the Illuminati borrowed its structure and ritual from the Council of Fifty, whether or not Strang was aware of this.

76. Order of the Illuminati Papers, folder 4, Strang Collection; also Strang Letter Book 188, Strang Papers, Beinecke Library.

77. Ibid.

78. Ibid.

the revealing of secret handshakes, signs, and code words by which members could identify each other and be warned if an intruder came into their midst.[79] Swearing an oath not to "ever conceal and never reveal" any of the secrets of the order and to faithfully warn others of the group of any approaching danger, the initiates swore to obey all the edicts, decrees, and commands of the general-in-chief (Bennett), sanctioned by the "Imperial Primate and Absolute Sovereign" (Strang). Their pledge of total obedience to Strang was said to supercede any law, obligation, or mandate of any other person or power. The final act was for members to sign their names in a record book, some later claiming they were required to sign in their own blood.[80]

Bennett became so obsessed with the formalities surrounding the Illuminati that he proposed membership diplomas or certificates that would contain the member's age, height, hair, eyes, forehead, nose, chin, face, tribe, particular marks, and signature. He asked Strang to have at least 500 of them printed on good quality parchment and suggested charging members at least one dollar each for the diplomas, but there is no indication that this was ever done.[81]

On the first Monday in August, Strang left for a two-month mission to the eastern states. Aware of the growing undercurrent of rebellion in his community, he spoke for three hours on the Sunday before he left, warning his followers about disagreement and controversy.[82] However, by the time he returned in October, the dissidents, whom Strang labeled "pseudo-Saints," or simply "pseudos," had drawn away a number of members.[83] Gilbert Watson wrote in his journal that "in the summer and fall of 1846, many apostatized from the church because they would not abide the Covenant spoken of in a revelation given to the church through the prophet James on the first day of July that same year." Watson noted that "Aaron Smith was among the number that apostatized, and I also was nearly carried away, but the Lord delivered me."[84]

---

79. Ibid.

80. *New Era and Herald of Zion's Watchman,* a semi-monthly publication by dissenters from Strang, Jan. 1847; see also the Order of the Illuminati Papers, Aug. 15, 1846, Beinecke Library.

81. John C. Bennett to James Strang, Aug.18, 1846, Strang Letter Book 165.

82. "Story of Late Apostacy."

83. *Zion's Reveille,* Dec. 1846. In the note at the bottom of page 3, Strang explained that "pseudo" was "of Greek derivation, and signifies false, counterfeit, spurious."

84. "Journal of Gilbert Watson."

One of the dissidents was Reuben Miller, formerly one of the staunchest supporters of Strang, and Aaron Smith apparently refused to take the oath of the Illuminati. The pseudos blamed most of the problems on John Bennett and were determined to rid the church of him. They said he was carrying on the same type of treasonable activities he had been excommunicated for in Nauvoo, namely seducing women, saying there was nothing wrong with extra-marital intercourse, and performing abortions for those who became pregnant.

While Strang was in the east, Aaron Smith held a church court and excommunicated Bennett.[85] However, on his return to Voree in mid-October, Strang reversed the excommunication, claiming it had been performed illegally.[86] Mormons in other communities heard of these developments and made their feelings known to Strang. "We have been Confidentially informed that Since Br. Strang left Voree that the Devils of the lowest grade have busily <been> at work and organized a secret Society among the Saints," four men wrote from Kirtland, Ohio. "We shall not at this time undertake to innumerate the many damnable heresys and doctrines that the devil J. C. Bennett W. M. Smith and others have introduced or tried to, but thanks be to God there is Eyes Eares [ears] and Some understanding in and among the Saints." The writers said they were concerned for the safety and reputation of the women of Voree and that they could not, in good conscience, refer potential immigrants to Voree while the "devil" Bennett was there.[87]

Strang decided it was time to set his church in order. Between the end of October and the end of December 1846, a substantial number of members were brought to trial for misdeeds against the church. In November the Lord revealed that Aaron Smith, Strang's counselor in the First Presidency, "hath yielded himself unto evil doers to contend against thee [Strang] and to bind thee with bands that thou shalt not speak my words, and hath weakened thy hands and tore them down; therefore shall he not be anymore thy Counsellor." Aaron was excommunicated for covenant breaking, lying, schism, and heresy. In his place, William Smith was made a counselor.[88] Two months pre-

---

85. "Chronicles of Voree," 124.

86. "Story of Late Apostacy."

87. Jacob Bump, Leonard Rich, Amos Babcock, and S. B. Stoddard to James Strang, Oct. 16, [1846], Library-Archives, Community of Christ.

88. "Chronicles of Voree," 119.

viously, Strang had also appointed George Adams to the first presidency.

These were not good moves for a man who wanted to instill harmony in the church. As the new year opened, the inner circle consisted of three men whose reputations were the worst of any in Mormon history. William Smith and George Adams were Strang's first and second counselors and John Bennett was Strang's general-in-chief.

4.

ORGANIZING THE KINGDOM
1846-1848

I have just received a letter from my mother, in the Western Mormon Camp, dated Feb. 6th, 1847, detailing unparalleled sufferings. My father (Freeman Nickerson) died of exposure and suffering. Three others of our family, making four out of six, have fallen victims to this rash undertaking. And my mother, now 66 years of age, has been compelled to sleep on the open prairie, in the snow, without tent or bed. This is but the common tale of woe in all the camp. Dear brother, is not this sufficient, with the many evidences we have of the sufferings of those who have gone west, to prove that God has rejected them?
—Uriah C. H. Nickerson to Brother John Greenhow.[1]

While Strang's claims of succession appeared to have attracted the wrong type of leaders in 1846, it also attracted men of high moral standing and good reputation such as William Marks, John E. Page and his brother Ebenezer Page, Zenas H. Gurley, Jason W. Briggs, Samuel Shaw, and Samuel Graham. Among those who investigated Strang's claims were also Benjamin, Phineas, and Samuel Wright—three brothers who were married to three sisters. Two of these three men would later have a patrimonial relationship with Strang as over the next ten years Benjamin and Phineas became the prophet's fathers-in-law.[2]

The Wright brothers were early members of the Mormon Church in Leeds, Ontario, Canada, who were probably converted through the efforts of the Mormon Apostle John E. Page, who baptized over 600 people in the area in 1836-37. Benjamin Wright was ordained an elder at a conference in Canada on November 18, 1836, where Page presided. Phineas is also known to

---

1. "Important from the Camp of Israel," *Zion's Reveille*, Feb. 25, 1847.

2. The Wright brothers were descendants of American loyalists who had fled to Leeds, Ontario, Canada, during the Revolutionary War. All were born in Leeds—Benjamin on Mar. 6, 1809, Phineas on Oct. 25, 1811, and Samuel on Feb. 20, 1814.

have later served a mission in Canada with Page.[3] Sometime between 1836 and 1838, the Wright families moved as a group from Leeds to Fort Defiance, Ohio, and continued on to Nauvoo in 1840. Dissatisfied with the organization of the church in Nauvoo, the families moved two years later to Potosi, Wisconsin, a small town about twenty-five miles from Galena, Illinois, where they worked in the lead mines.[4] The brothers may also have worked in the Wisconsin pineries, cutting lumber for the Nauvoo temple and other structures in Nauvoo.

Phineas was living and working in Potosi when he learned of Joseph Smith's death and Strang's claim to leadership of the Mormon Church. "He went to Voree [and] talked with Strang, who told him he had been called of God to lead the people in the ways of riteousness," Phineas's daughter later reported. "I think my father and his brothers thought he was the true prophet of God. They bought the land to put church buildings on. He [Strang] ordained my two uncles his counselors, my father one of his twelve apostles, but his word was law."[5]

Benjamin was ordained a high priest on July 3, 1846, the same day Phineas was made an elder.[6] He later wrote from Potosi: "The church in this region are mostly from Nauvoo; all acknowledge Strang as first president and are anxious to get to Voree. I am making every effort to dispose of my property so as to move to Voree in the spring, for I am tired of living among gentiles; I thank my Heavenly Father that I have not had a doubt in my mind [about Strang]."[7] The Wrights were not the only Mormons temporarily working in the lead mines. George Brownson and Zenas H. Gurley eventually built up at least two branches of the Strangite movement in the same area. There was a branch with at least thirty-two members near the Yellowstone Mines and the Pine Bluff diggings branch had eleven members.[8]

---

3. *Messenger and Advocate,* Jan. 1837.

4. Sarah Wing to Milo Quaife, June 28, 1920, Clarke Historical Library, Central Michigan University, Mount Pleasant, Michigan.

5. Ibid.

6. "Chronicles of Voree, A record of the establishment and doings of the Stake of Zion called Voree in Wisconsin made by the Scribes appointed to that office," 84, microfilm copy, Library-archives, Wisconsin Historical Library, Madison, Wisconsin; cf. John J. Hajicek, comp., *The Chronicles of Voree, 1844-1849* (Burlington, WI: JJRR Publishing, 1991).

7. "Extract of a Letter from Elder Wright," *Gospel Herald,* Feb. 11, 1847.

8. Hiram P. Brown to Sister Strang, Aug. 6, [1851], Strang Letter Book 265, James

Following the excommunication of a large number of pseudos in December, Strang turned his attention to the faithful membership. On New Year's Day, 1847, members prepared "a most sumptuous feast, of which 130 partook, notwithstanding the weather was extremely inclement." An article in *Zion's Reveille* reported that this was "one of the most pleasant festivals the church has ever witnessed. It was truly a feast of love (as well as a corporeal feast), an outpouring of the most noble feelings of the human heart—a flow of souls co-mingling with this spirit of God."[9]

Strang's new house and that of another member were dedicated that day, and a special meeting of the Order of the Illuminati was held in the evening. Members were taken to a dark room where their heads were anointed with a special oil that mysteriously glowed in the dark, giving a halo appearance to the initiates. Strang said the ordination was "an extraordinary and visible manifestation of the spirit, which rendered the members at once and thereafter impregnable to all the shafts of Satan."[10] William Smith, who later grew dissatisfied with Strang, claimed the oil had a queer smell so he secretly took a small sample of it to examine. He found the oil was a mixture of oil and phosphorous. When rubbed too roughly, it could have set a man's hair on fire. When Strang was confronted about the oil, he apparently acknowledged the ingredients. But he preached a sermon maintaining that the miracles of Christ, Moses, and other prophets were wrought the same way, by natural means.[11]

There is little doubt the Strangite Mormons considered themselves fortunate to be in Voree. The Saints who had left Nauvoo with Brigham Young and traveled to a camp called Winter Quarters on the Missouri River in present-day Nebraska experienced widespread illness and starvation. One of the Strangites in Voree, Uriah Nickerson, received a letter from his family members gathered with Young at the "Camp of Israel." The news was not good. Nickerson's father, Freeman Nickerson, had died of exposure, and his mother, age sixty-six, had been compelled to sleep on the open prairie in the

---

Jesse Strang Papers, Yale Collection of Western Americana, Beinecke Rare Book and Manuscript Library, Yale University, New Haven, Connecticut. After Strang started practicing polygamy, Gurley left and became one of the originators of the RLDS Church.

9. "The First of January, 1847," *Zion's Reveille,* Jan. 14, 1847.

10. *New Era and Herald of Zion's Watchman,* Feb. 1847. See also "A Late Mormon Miracle," *Ottawa Free Trader,* rpt. in *Gospel Herald,* Dec. 23, 1847.

11. *New Era and Herald of Zion's Watchman,* Feb. 1847.

snow.[12] Others at Voree had friends and relatives on their way west who wrote of similar situations.

The community of Voree was "so successful, and prospered so finely," Strang decided to start another Mormon colony on the same basic principles. He chose the main island in the Beaver archipelago in Lake Michigan. The previous summer he had experienced a vision, in which he was shown a land mass "amidst great waters," where the land covered with heavy timber and a deep bay lay to one side of the land. In the vision, Strang wandered across the land finding the air pure and a serene setting among the little hills and rich valleys. He was told he would see the land with his own eyes before he returned to Voree.[13] On returning home from the eastern states, the boat Strang was traveling on took refuge during a storm inside the harbor of one of the islands in Lake Michigan. For the first time, Strang saw the promised land with his own eyes—Beaver Island. He was so impressed, he made immediate plans to return as soon as possible.

In the spring of 1847, Strang and four companions—Gurdon Brown, Nathan Wagner, R. F. Mills, and William Savage—arrived at the island to explore and prepare for settling it. The group was so destitute of means, they sold their blankets for passage to the island and arrived with no money and only enough provisions for two days. There were two gentile trading posts located on the island, although neither proprietor was pleased to see the five men. Strang and his companions went into the woods, where they made a camp and started a thorough exploration. By "perseverance and a willingness to work," they obtained supplies and the use of a boat from the traders. After exploring the entire group of islands, they built a small cabin. Brown and Mills remained on the island while Strang, Savage, and Wagner returned to Voree.[14]

In the summer and fall of 1847, several families moved to Beaver Island but became dissatisfied and eventually left. By winter, eighteen Strangites on the island seemed content to stay; within a year the population had grown to

---

12. "Important from Camp." Mrs. Nickerson later joined Strang at Voree.

13. This revelation was received on August 25, 1846, while Strang was visiting the community of Elizabeth, Pennsylvania, located about ten miles south of Pittsburgh on the Monongahela River. "Chronicles of Voree," 114-15; see also *Zion's Reveille*, Jan. 14, 1847.

14. Elvira Field Strang and Charles J. Strang, "Biographical Sketch of James J. Strang," unpublished manuscript, n.p., Strang Manuscript Collection, Library and Historical Center, State Library of Michigan, Lansing, Michigan.

sixty-two.[15] In early 1848, a number of families were considering moving to the island. They were advised to take a year's provisions, including two barrels of flour, one barrel of meat, and other articles in proportion to each adult. "No one should think of going with a less supply," Strang counseled.[16]

The prophet was encouraging emigration through his newspaper, now called the *Gospel Herald,* in which he published instructions on how to ship household items to the island:

> Persons coming from Lake Ontario and all places beyond will usually find it best to ship by propellers coming up the Welland Canal directly for Beaver. Those from Lake Erie and beyond should ship on propellers in the Buffalo and Chicago line and contract expressly to be landed at Beaver Island. Most boats in this trade stop there. But if you can't get to Beaver, stop at Mackinac, whence you can go to Beaver at $1.00 a passenger and 50 cents a barrel for freight. Persons from Lake Michigan and beyond ship from the most convenient port directly for Beaver.... Any honest, industrious man who is able to take himself and family to Beaver with one month's provisions has nothing to fear, and may be sure of as much labor as he ever needs, in an excellent country.[17]

Plans for colonization progressed through the remainder of 1847 as the Saints in Voree continued to build their city of peace. Numerous homes were under construction in Voree, as well as a temple and a "tower of strength," a building that would be used to store provisions. Converts continued to arrive, often met at the outskirts by pseudos who tried to convince them Strang was an imposter, a "false prophet" surrounded by unscrupulous schemers. In fact, Strang himself began to have doubts in the summer of 1847 about the leadership and morality of his two closest advisors, John C. Bennett and William Smith. They initially had Strang's support, but Bennett and Smith seemed to be flirting with the kinds of activities that had gotten them into trouble in Nauvoo, in particular spiritual wifery and adultery. The two men were often targets of the pseudos' condemnation of the whole church and drew unwanted attention to the imperfect nature of Strang himself and his organization.

John Bennett was quietly excommunicated on October 7, 1847, for "apostasy, conspiracy to establish a stake by falsehood, deception and various

---

15. Ibid.

16. "Indian Mission," *Zion's Reveille,* Jan. 14, 1847.

17. *Gospel Herald,* Nov. 25, 1847, [7].

immoralities."[18] The following day, William Smith was excommunicated for adultery and apostasy.[19] Both of them had apparently already moved from Voree by that time and neither appeared at his church trial. Their departure silenced the pseudos and stabilized the Voree colony for a time. This relative calm and peacefulness between the fall of 1847 and the summer of 1849 allowed members to establish a society that would try to equalize the wealth of the membership.

On January 12, 1848, twelve families under Strang's direction formed an "equality association" they called the Associated and United Order of Enoch. The purpose was for the Saints to "become as one in their temporal things and thus put an end to inequality among the people of God."[20] Besides Strang, the twelve original members included the families of the three Wright brothers, Finley Page, Francis Cooper, Luther and Anson Prindle, Samuel E. Hull, Seth C. Child, Lyman Reynolds, and William Savage.[21] A month later the association increased to include sixty members[22] and by the end of the year to about 150 people, approximately half the Strangite population of Voree.[23]

Members of the association pledged to organize their families into one large household with Strang as the presiding patriarch. They promised to "consecrate" their substance to the Lord so that rich and poor would share alike. However, for the most part, members who had wealth were reluctant to join. "The few brethren who engaged in this most laudable of all causes (with few exceptions) labored and struggled on in póverty," James Blakeslee wrote. "And, in some instances, in want of almost all things, incessantly through the remainder of the winter." However, by the time April conference was held, most of the crops were in the ground and several houses had been built, "so that Conference found us in a prosperous situation both at home and abroad."[24]

Members met together regularly to govern the association and distribute

---

18. "Chronicles of Voree," 151.

19. Ibid, 152.

20. "Chronicles of Voree," 178.

21. "Journal of Gilbert Watson Comprising Also a Short Account of His Life and Travels Written by Himself," unpublished manuscript, Library-Archives, Community of Christ, Independence, Missouri. Child, Reynolds, and Savage later withdrew from the organization.

22. "Pastoral Letter," *Gospel Herald*, Feb. 3, 1848.

23. *Gospel Herald*, Dec. 28,1848, [3].

24. "A Report for the Herald," *Gospel Herald*, Apr. 19, 1849.

food, clothing, and wood to participating families. Children who were sixteen years of age or older had the right to vote alongside the adult members.[25] In addition to holding all their goods in common, members of the order voted to live by certain rules, resolving not to incur debt, to be sure their children were trained properly in religious matters, and not to partake of such luxuries as sugar, spices, or dried fruit. They also abstained from the religiously forbidden coffee, tea, tobacco, and alcohol.

The voting members decided to conserve funds by dressing in "uniform style without needless material or ornamentation." Women agreed to make their dresses out of drillen, a durable cotton fabric commonly used for work clothes, and aprons out of a check-printed fabric. Women who did not already have a dress suitable for attending meetings were furnished with a calico dress for that purpose. The men agreed to wear clothing made of sheep jersey and homemade flannel in the winter and drillen and "factory" in the summer. Winter headgear consisted of homemade cloth caps in a predetermined design. "Good heavy leather boots of uniform style" were to be worn, but light shoes were acceptable for those who needed them for indoor work. Everything was to be of a uniform style and manufactured by members of the group as speedily as possible.[26]

When a church member decided to join the order, he dedicated his property to the Lord and renounced all claim to it. An appraiser would examine the property and give Strang, the association's administrator, an estimate of its worth. Once the property was consecrated, it could be used individually, communally if so directed, or it could be sold for funds. For most of the Strangites, the communal way of life was a foreign concept. No matter how much a member's spirit might be willing to give, his or her mind might rebel when it came to their more expensive possessions such as horse teams, wagons, and machinery. Several families withdrew after discovering they could not live the communal principles. At first, such members were allowed to reclaim their possessions when they withdrew, but this placed a burden on the others who needed to replace what was withdrawn and had freely contributed their own much needed food, clothing, wood, and other necessities. Before

---

25. Depositions from members of the Order of Enoch in a lawsuit by John W. Archer, Order of Enoch Papers, folder 177, James Jesse Strang Collection, Beinecke Library. In September 1849, Archer tried to withdraw from the order and retrieve his property.

26. Order of Enoch Papers, folders 171-79, Strang Collection, Beinecke Library.

long, it was decided that consecrated items, which had been deeded to the church, would stay in the church's possession and would not be returned.

In a revelation given to Strang on January 7, 1849, the Lord chastised his people for rebelling against the Order of Enoch. If the church repented and its members paid their tithes and offerings, the Lord proclaimed, he would reveal many "precious things" to them to give them strength over their enemies. In fact, God had prepared a land for them where they could live without disruption. The implication was that Beaver Island was to be this refuge: "Moreover, I have given you the Islands in the Great Lakes for a possession. There shall you dwell apart from the Gentiles, and none shall make you afraid." The members were told "their inheritances shall be appointed unto them and to their houses, and their posterity after them for a perpetual possession. Let many gather to the islands which I [God] have appointed for your gathering, that this Order [of Enoch] may be kept more perfectly; for there will I give you much possession for an inheritance, if ye will go up and possess it."[27]

On April 13, Strang accompanied three families to Beaver Island in advance of several others who planned to embark within a few weeks. Strang's group of about twenty-one individuals traveled to Racine, Wisconsin, to obtain passage across the lake. Racine was a rapidly growing city of about 3,000, about twenty-five miles directly east of Burlington. The docking facilities consisted of two precarious-looking piers that extended fifty feet on either side of the Root River where the river flowed into Lake Michigan. The water under the piers was only about five feet deep, but all of the community's shipping business was conducted on these two piers. Vessels came in and took freight until their keels were nearly to the bottom, then they would back into deeper water where they could receive the rest of their cargo, either from smaller boats called lighters or from a spring pier which was a temporary extension to the loading dock.[28]

At any hour of the night or day, a variety of ships could be located on the docks, including sailing ships—schooners, scows, barks, and brigs—and paddle-wheel steamships, which had been used on the Great Lakes since at least 1818. There was also a new kind of steamship called a "propeller," which was becoming more common for both freight and passengers. These new

---

27. "Revelation, Given Jan. 7th, 1849," *Gospel Herald*, July 26, 1849.
28. "Editorial Correspondence—No. 3," *Gospel Herald*, May 10, 1849.

ships were driven by a steam-powered propeller instead of a side wheel.[29] The Strangites waited for a ship that was delayed because of bad weather, and they found themselves with an indeterminate amount of time on their hands. Not used to whiling away his time, Strang quickly became bored. As the wait extended into Sunday, he complained of missing his routine and the religious services he was used to in Voree. He wrote a letter to Frank Cooper, editor of the *Gospel Herald*, giving an account of the company's travels.[30] "In the afternoon my heart ached to [be with] the class in the study of the prophets at their lessons. But it could not be. Even the short sleep which I habitually take during the evening service is denied me," he wrote tongue-in-cheek. "Here I stand mentally tired with one days rest, feeling about for the ideas which I usually have rolling up faster than I can put them on paper."[31]

Four days later, the group had increased to thirty-eight Strangites waiting to catch a ship to the islands. The propeller *Troy*, for which they had purchased passage, was still delayed in Milwaukee due to unfavorable winds. Strang was so stir-crazy, he had the ticket agent in Racine telegraph the *Troy* that its passengers would arrive in a small boat he had arranged for them, the *Lady of the Lake*, which would immediately sail for Milwaukee.[32] Strang wrote to Cooper about the short trip to Milwaukee, saying they were "now on our way over rough sea, in a small unsteady, rolling Propeller, neither a sea worthy craft, nor, as far as I can observe, a gentlemanly officer on board. Nearly all the company are seasick. The weather is cold and the wind high. The women and children sleep on the deck, pretty well closed in to be sure, but without fire." He was frustrated. "I have met more difficulties than I usually do thus far, and if I had known any such word as fail, should have given up the expedition before today."[33]

They arrived at Milwaukee Harbor just before midnight on April 20, cold, tired, and seasick. A northeastern wind was sweeping across the lake as the passengers rushed from the small boat to the wharf, another spring pier extending approximately sixty rods out into the lake. The pier was loosely

---

29. Haillan Hatcher and Erich A. Walter, *A Pictorial History of the Great Lakes* (New York: Crown Publishers, 1963).

30. By this time the church newspaper, *Zion's Reveille*, had been renamed the *Gospel Herald*.

31. "Editorial Correspondence—No. 2," *Gospel Herald*, May 3, 1849.

32. "Editorial Correspondence—No.4," *Gospel Herald*, May 17, 1849.

33. Ibid.

covered with plank boards through which the water occasionally dashed up. To their surprise, the *Troy* had already left. To add to their discomfort, the captain of the *Lady of the Lake*, who had been paid in advance, augmented their fares before they disembarked, a practice that was apparently not uncommon in frontier America, and seized some of the passengers' goods in payment. While the others huddled together waiting, Strang engaged passage for the group on the *Sciota*, another propeller that was soon due in port. The Strangites retrieved the rest of their possessions from the *Lady of the Lake* and by torchlight made beds on the wharf, a "privilege" for which the wharf master charged them $8.75. Strang haggled the wharf master down to $4.00 while the temperature fell to below freezing.[34]

Shortly before sunrise, the *Sciota* arrived. With some difficulty because of the wind and waves, the passengers stepped off the wharf onto the propeller at about noon on Saturday, April 21, seven days from the time the group had first arrived in Racine. Nevertheless, Strang would report to the *Gospel Herald* that the last leg of the trip was "a rapid and rather pleasant passage" although the weather was "quite foggy and it was not till past nine o'clock that we discovered the Big Beaver." Enraptured by the "first glance of it, but dimly seen in the misty distance," the island "gave the most sincere joy to more than a score of hearts. Indeed, though the weather was most uncomfortable, men, women and children kept the deck, gazing with satisfaction and cheerfulness at our future home. The desponding heart, worn with care, toil, suffering, disappointment and injuries, became exuberant in joy and happiness. A new face was on all of us. We felt at home again, because we could see the home God had given us. Every gift of God is good."[35]

Big Beaver Island, also referred to simply as Beaver Island, was the largest in a string of ten islands in the northern part of Lake Michigan. About thirteen miles long and seven miles wide, the main island contained about 50,000 acres of fertile, well-timbered land. A natural harbor located on the northeastern half of the island was almost entirely encircled with land and provided safe refuge for boats. The water around the island was rich in fish.

By July, 300 Mormons had made passage to the island. Houses were going up everywhere. There were two wood yards and three stores in operation, a steam mill was going up, and a newspaper was in the planning stages. The

34. Ibid.
35. "Editorial Correspondence—No.5," *Gospel Herald*, May 24, 1849.

settlers had brought cows and other stock with them and were devoting a good deal of attention to agriculture. A school was established for the children. Indian children in the area were invited to attend school free of charge.[36] The men started constructing a road through a swampy area into the island's interior where the land was more suitable to agriculture. A small schooner was under construction.[37]

A branch of the Order of Enoch was formed, but this was soon disbanded in favor of a system of tithing and "inheritance."[38] Each member was to tithe one-tenth of his time and increase to the church, which would be applied to common needs such as road improvements. In return, each family was to be granted an inheritance consisting of a plot of land large enough for the livelihood of the family. Just exactly where the money was to come from to buy the land is not clear. However, Strang assured his followers that the Lord intended Beaver Island to be just for them.

As the busy prophet struggled with the concerns of a growing church, he spent less time with his wife and children, often staying away for months on church business. This contributed to a deteriorating relationship with his wife, Mary, who accused him of being "neglectful." James responded that she was "jealous minded."[39] Admitting that he was not easy to live with, he once politely refused the advances of a married woman who propositioned him by mail. He wrote back, "I am not very selfish, but I bear no contradiction; my remarks on the most commonplace subjects, are sharp and cutting. I am cold, stern, uncommunicative, petulant, and exceedingly difficult to please."[40] He judged himself to be above meddling in most people's business, but for those he took an interest in, he "exact[ed] the most rigid and implicit obedience." "I never give a reason why I should be obeyed. I bear no importunity. No excuse can be satisfactory. I cannot be trifled with a single moment, and not infrequently am most seriously vexed because my unspoken wants are not anticipated."[41] Setting aside the disingenuous tone of his letter, there was more than a scintilla of truth in Strang's amusing self-evaluation.

---

36. "Beaver Islands," *Buffalo Express,* rpt. in *Gospel Herald,* July 26, 1849.

37. Strang and Strang, "Biographical Sketch."

38. Ibid.

39. James Strang to unknown woman, n.d., folder 75, Strang Collection, Beinecke Library.

40. Ibid.

41. Ibid.

There were also rumors of other women. Strang denied these, claiming his enemies were willing to believe the worst about him. But he must have given some encouragement to the women who wrote personal letters to him and gave him locks of their hair.[42] Interestingly, it seems that Mary initially hesitated to join her husband's church, but finally did sometime before May 1846 and conveyed that information to her parents. "I shall make no other mention of the information contained in your letter," her mother responded, "only [that] I hope the Lord will make you a sincere believer in the lord Jesus Christ, though it matters not what name you call yourself. Your father said he was sorry Mary had become a Mormon, but I am too tired to write more."[43]

One member thought it odd that Strang's own children, Nettie, William, and Hattie, were not baptized into his church.[44] It is equally telling that Mary's name is not listed as a member of the Order of Enoch or as a covenant taker for the Order of the Illuminati. Tea, sugar, and raisins—forbidden foods—were later listed in an inventory of Mary's home in Voree.[45] In fact, the years 1843 to 1848, the time James spent establishing his church, were difficult for Mary Perce. Her daughter died in October 1843, and her grandfather and patriarch of the family, Benjamin Perce Sr., became senile and died in 1844.[46] Benjamin's wife, Sarah—Mary's grandmother—followed him to the grave a few months later.[47] In 1844 a difficulty also arose with Mary's father when the land he had contracted to dig for the Illinois and Michigan Canal proved to be low-lying and required additional soil for embankments. William Perce and his partner were unable to construct their

---

42. Folder 95, Strang Collection, Beinecke Library. Lucy Waldo, Olive Scott, Lucretia Wait, Mary Anne Barker, and Jane Brown presented the hair locks in ornamental designs to Strang on June 23, 1847, at Rutland Hollow, New York. Some of these women later settled on Beaver Island.

43. [Lydia Perce] to Mary A. P. Strang, Sept. 20, 1846, folder 135, Strang Collection, Beinecke Library.

44. Elvira E. Baker to Dear Friend [Wingfield Watson], Mar. 22, 1883, Clarke Historical Library.

45. James Strang, Probate Records, Walworth County Court House, Elkhorn, Wisconsin.

46. Benjamin Perce Sr., Probate Records, Grundy County Court House, Morris, Illinois. Benjamin Perce Sr.'s personal property consisted of a gun worth $8.00 and a coat worth $1.00.

47. Perce Family History, unpublished manuscript, n.p., State Library of Michigan.

portion of the canal on schedule and sustained heavy financial losses. His partner committed suicide.[48]

Misfortunes continued to plague the Perce family. Before moving back to New York in October 1846, Benjamin Perce Jr., citing a "natural affection" for his niece Mary, sold to her his home and half an acre of land for the sum of one dollar.[49] On September 19 the following year, Benjamin was killed in a construction explosion at the age of thirty-seven.[50] In July 1848, Mary's beloved mother, Lydia, died at the age of fifty-five.[51] In the space of just five years, as many relatives in Mary's closely-knit family had died or been killed, and her father had suffered financial ruin. Her husband was busy with his newfound profession as a religious leader. Already given to melancholy, the circumstances must have affected Mary immensely. She gave birth twice during this five-year period and may have suffered once again from postpartum depression.

James told at least three followers that Mary refused to have "wifely relations" with him after the death of their daughter in October 1843.[52] This cannot be entirely true as Mary gave birth to a son, William J., on December 20, 1844, and a daughter, Harriet (Hattie) Anne, on October 17, 1848. However, it had clearly become an unhappy marriage. According to at least one member of the Strangite movement, Mary separated herself from her husband for a time, then returned to the marriage sometime before 1849.[53]

In the spring of 1848, Mary Perce Strang, now thirty years old, was pregnant with her fourth child and had been married to James for twelve

---

48. *I&M Canal Stories* (Chicago: Canal Corridor Association, 1999), 12; *Report of the Board of Trustees of the Illinois and Michigan Canal* (O. L. Baskin & Co., 1882), 197.

49. Benjamin Perce, Land Records, Walworth County Court House, Elkhorn, Wisconsin. Benjamin also sold 320 acres of Wisconsin farmland to his brother William L. Perce.

50. Edw. Learned to James Strang, Apr. 9, 1848, folder 136, Strang Collection, Beinecke Library. Benjamin C. Perce died on Sept. 19, 1847, in Albany County, New York.

51. Perce Family History. The details of Lydia Perce's death are not known.

52. Wingfield W. Watson, interviewed by Milo M. Quaife, Dec. 10-11, 1918, Clarke Historical Library. Watson said Strang made these comments when Watson was having his inheritance assigned at Beaver Island. Watson said Strang made the remark to him and to two or three others who were present.

53. Notes probably written by Charles Strang in the margin of a newspaper clipping from the *Detroit Evening News*, Sept. 19, 1892, Clarke Historical Library. Charles wrote that he learned this from his mother, Elvira Field.

years. She had seen many people come and go in the community since 1844, but there was something different about Elvira Field, a young woman who accompanied her parents to Voree for a church conference in April. Mary could not have known it, but this eighteen-year-old woman would change her life in a very unusual way.

Elvira Eliza Field was a healthy, attractive but not strikingly beautiful girl.[54] She was physically small and was described as delicate, but she was also extremely intelligent and articulate. Born July 8, 1830, in Streetsborough, Portage County, Ohio, near Akron, Elvira was the daughter of Reuben Field and Eliza Granger. She had an older brother, Albert, who was born in 1828, and a younger sister, Anna Miranda, who was born in 1832 but died when Elvira was eight.[55] Her father was a true frontiersman. He purchased "wild land," cleared and improved it for farming, and sold it, then moved on. Elvira's mother, Eliza, was trained in the use of medicinal herbs and plants and had developed a reputation for good medical skills.[56] The family lived in log cabins they built with their own hands.[57] As a child, Elvira enjoyed short hunting trips and was an expert in the use of a rifle. She could kill a hawk on the wing and on one occasion killed the finest buck in a herd of deer drinking at a stream.[58]

In 1831, Reuben and Eliza Field came into contact with a missionary from the newly organized Church of Jesus Christ of Latter-day Saints.[59] They were baptized and moved to the Mormon community of Kirtland, Ohio. As

---

54. Clement Strang interviewed by Milo M. Quaife, Feb. 12, 1921, Clarke Historical Library.

55. Elvira Field Strang Baker Memorial Book, State Library of Michigan. Reuben Field was born on April 22, 1801, and Eliza Granger Field on June 20, 1798, both in Massachusetts.

56. Clement J. Strang, "Why I Am Not a Strangite," *Michigan History*, fall 1942, 469.

57. *The Past and Present of Eaton County, Michigan* (Lansing: Michigan Historical Publishing Association, n.d.), 304-306.

58. Baker Memorial Book; Milo M. Quaife's notes, Clarke Historical Library. The incident involving a hawk occurred in Voree in 1856 or 1857, following Strang's death. Elvira would have been about twenty-six or twenty-seven years old. She shot the buck in 1897 near her home in Baldwin, Michigan, when she was about sixty-seven years old.

59. Jan Shipps and John W. Welch, eds., *The Journals of William E. McLellin, 1831-1836* (Provo and Chicago: Brigham Young University and University of Illinois Press, 1994), 434. Reuben and Eliza were baptized in November but had already begun to have doubts by February. McLellin wrote that he "restored their faith" in the church.

an elder in the church, Reuben was one of the signers of the Kirtland Safety Society,[60] which was an effort by Kirtland residents to establish a community bank, a common practice in early America. Most of the prominent men of the church, including the founder, Joseph Smith, were instrumental in the society's organization and involved in encouraging members to buy stock. Like many other fledgling banks in 1837, the Safety Society collapsed. The Depression of 1837 was as significant as the stock market crash of 1929, affecting banks and communities across the entire United States.

The failure of the bank was disastrous for Mormons in the area around Kirtland. Most lost everything they owned. One byproduct of the collapse was that it exposed the incompetence of the management, something that was laid at Joseph Smith's feet. In fact, Smith had become uncomfortable with the bank's involvement in land speculation preceding its failure and had withdrawn his support, warning others to do the same. But the church's membership became so embittered by the bank's failure, half the members either fell into inactivity or were excommunicated for speaking against church leaders.

Elvira grew up as other children of Mormon families did in Kirtland. She was probably baptized at age eight, according to the religious tenets of the church. Her family closely associated with many of the early prominent members, including the prophet, and such men as John E. Page, Martin Harris, and Moses and Aaron Smith, all of whom left the mainstream church, just as the Field family did, to join James Strang.

Many members in Kirtland had practiced a form of communal living called the United Order. The Field family may have belonged to this organization,[61] and this probably laid the foundation for them to join Strang's communal society in Voree. After the collapse of the Safety Society, Reuben Field and his family opted not to relocate with the main branch of Joseph Smith's people in Far West, Missouri, or later in Nauvoo, Illinois. They apparently continued to live in Ohio, possibly to recover from losses sustained in the Depression of 1837 and to live near other family members.

There was a great deal of persecution at the time against the Ohio Mor-

60. Lyndon W. Cook and Milton V. Backman Jr., eds., *Kirtland Elders' Quorum Record, 1836-1841* (Provo: Grandin Book, 1985), 101.

61. Under the United Order, families deeded all of their property to the bishop of the church. The bishop, in turn, acting as trustee for the entire community, conveyed back to each family the lands and possessions needed for their livelihood according to family size and circumstance. The rest of the property became community surplus, which the bishop

mons. The Field family may not have practiced their religion openly, if at all, for this reason. However, Reuben was said to be serving a mission in 1844 when Joseph Smith was killed.[62] That same year when Elvira was fourteen, her father bought eighty acres in Section 36 of Eaton township, Eaton County, Michigan, where other relatives were living. There, near the present town of Eaton Rapids, Reuben and Albert cleared about twenty-five acres of land and built another log cabin.[63] Elvira lived in Washtenaw County, Michigan, about seventy miles away, with her mother's relative Israel Smith. There she continued her schooling and learned the tailor's trade. She attended church in Milan, Michigan, with her uncle, who was a devout Presbyterian. During a series of revival meetings, Elvira became converted to the Presbyterians. However, she would not stay long with the Milan congregation. At age sixteen, she fulfilled a dream in the nearby town of Henrietta of becoming a teacher.[64] In 1847 she secured another teaching position in the town of Eaton Rapids in Eaton County, Michigan.

During the winters of 1846 through 1848, missionaries from the Strangite Church preached extensively throughout Michigan. Strang's apostle Samuel Graham, in Michigan on a mission during the winter of 1847-48, wrote to the prophet telling him of Elvira. "Sister EE Field of Eaton will come up to Voree for the April Conference and if you want a good schoolmistress, she has the name," Graham wrote. "She wants to join the Order of Enoch."[65]

There is no way of telling just how or when Elvira attracted more intense attention from James Strang. He told at least three or four of his followers that he was a man of "strong passions" and that this was especially true when he married his second wife. If Mary did indeed separate from James for a period, it probably would have been at about this time. Strang said he was "subject to much temptation—as many women would have been glad to live with him."[66] If true, a temporary separation from Mary may have been the catalyst

---

then distributed to the needy in the community, the poor, the sick, and the widowed who had no property.

62. Clement Strang interview.

63. Baker Memorial Book.

64. Ibid. The twelve-week contract in Henrietta paid one dollar per week, plus room and board.

65. Samuel Graham to James Strang, Jan. 15, 1848, folder 320, Strang Collection, Beinecke Library.

66. Wingfield W. Watson interview.

that drew Strang to the young attractive schoolteacher. Strang may also have believed that God had sent her to be his companion. By strange coincidence, Elvira's birthday was the same day Strang received the revelation to organize his church.

Elvira, her parents, and her brother, Albert, then nineteen, arrived in Voree in April 1848. Elvira and Albert would remain after the church conference to spend the summer in Voree and join the Order of Enoch. Their parents returned to Michigan to make preparations to sell their farm and move to Voree.[67] Elvira and Albert returned to Michigan in the fall of 1848 because Elvira had a contract to teach school near the town of Charlotte. In March 1849, school ended and the Fields completed their preparations to move. The night before they left, March 19, they were treated to an impromptu gathering at Samuel Graham's house in Parma, Michigan, where church members said their goodbyes. "This evening, members of the Springport branch convened at the house of S. Graham and although accidentally collected, the spirit seemed to suggest the propriety of having a conference meeting, as Br. R. Field and family and Elder Brownson were to leave on the morning for the Stake of Zion," Graham wrote. The Saints unanimously voted to "commend Reuben Field and his family to the confidence and fellowship of the church of the Saints at Voree." They offered sincere thanks to Elder George Brownson, a Strangite missionary from Chicago who was traveling with the Fields to Voree.[68]

The group most likely traveled to Chicago, where they planned to catch a steamer headed up the Great Lakes for Racine or Kenosha, Wisconsin, and from there by stage or wagon to Voree. But sixty miles into their journey, Brownson received a letter from Strang directing him to take the company to Beaver Island and settle there instead of in Voree.[69] The group probably continued on to Chicago and caught a steamer to Beaver Island. When they arrived in early April, Elvira would have had numerous occasions to meet Strang because he was on and off the island from the end of April through the

67. *Past and Present of Eaton County,* 305. This compilation erroneously states that Reuben Field sold his farm in Eaton Rapids and lived in Wisconsin for some time before moving to Beaver Island.

68. Samuel Graham to James Strang, Mar. 19, 1849, folder 323, Strang Collection, Beinecke Library.

69. George Brownson to James Strang, Mar. 27, 1849, folder 266, Strang Collection, Beinecke Library. Brownson sent his reply to Strang from Chicago.

first week of August. The smart, handsome young woman would have been a good intellectual match for the prophet at a time he was having marital problems. Sometime between the spring of 1848 and the summer of 1849, Strang sent his prime minister, George J. Adams, to "sound out" Elvira as to her attitude if the prophet made "certain proposals" to her. The most probable time of this visit would have been in July 1849, just before the onset of conference.

Elvira told Adams she had always been taught to regard Strang as a prophet and that anything he said to do, she would regard as a commandment of God.[70] She said she had been taught from early childhood that the teachings of Joseph Smith were inspired and that everything he commanded should be strictly obeyed because only through obedience could "this life be worth living" and "a happy hereafter be assured."[71] On behalf of Strang, Adams offered Elvira the unique opportunity of becoming a plural wife to the "prophet of God." Adams told her Strang's plans for the establishment of God's kingdom included her investiture as queen. However, the marriage could not be revealed to the world, and not even to her brother or parents, until such a time as God would reveal it to the people.[72]

Adams may also have told the young woman that Strang was making preparations for a church mission to the eastern United States and wished her to accompany him, but that it had to be done secretly. There is no way of knowing how long Elvira considered the marriage offer, but she accepted. The July 6-9 conference on the island was a huge success. Despite the fact another prominent member, John Page, has recently left the church, thirteen people came forward for baptism and seventeen children were blessed. The conference was held in a grove of trees because there was not yet a house large enough to hold all the people who wished to attend.[73]

On July 13, a few days after the conference, Elvira Field and James Strang were united in a secret marriage performed by George Adams. Two other apostles witnessed the ceremony. She was nineteen, he thirty-six and already married.[74] Although he had previously been a strong opponent of po-

---

70. Clement Strang, unpublished manuscript, n.p., State Library of Michigan.

71. Clement Strang to Dorothy Strang of the Strang Family Association, Aug. 3, 1939, Clarke Historical Library.

72. Ibid.

73. "Minutes of a Conference," *Gospel Herald,* Aug. 2, 1849.

74. Baker Memorial Book; Clement Strang to Milo Quaife, Aug. 13, 1920, Clarke Historical Library.

lygamy, Strang had now come to see the advantage of it. Five days later, Elvira and James left Beaver Island with fifteen other Mormons on the propeller *St. Joseph.* "I am just off after the most pleasant, interesting and spirited Conference that I ever had the happiness to attend," Strang wrote to Frank Cooper at the *Gospel Herald.*

> Tomorrow I shall be at Sault St Marie, in conference with the Indians. Bros. G. J. Adams and S. Graham go with me. There are 17 of us onboard the *St. Joseph,* this being the second division who have left since Conference to carry the gospel to the nations. A few Elders are yet behind, but our present party are not quite all elders. From the Sault I shall take a rapid journey to the Central College in Michigan and [be] home in a few days, say possibly two weeks from this day. Bro. Adams will accompany me.[75]

Even though Strang's marriage ceremony was discretely performed, it was not long before rumors were circulating about an illicit affair. Gilbert Watson wrote to Strang telling him of a report that Strang, Adams, and three others had gone up to the Sault with Mrs. Brownson and "somebody else" and participated in a regular drinking and "frigging" spree. "There are very few of the saints that are in any way troubled about it. As far as I am concerned I didn't believe a word of it," Watson added.[76] In fact, Strang was opposed to alcohol his entire life, so it is unlikely he was on a drinking spree. George Adams, on the other hand, was a known drinker and womanizer. Strang may have been seen with Elvira in a hotel or rooming house where they spent their honeymoon. In any case, Strang considered it prudent to leave Elvira situated at Albion, a small town in the south-central portion of Michigan, rather than bring her back to Beaver Island.[77]

Accompanying Strang on board the *St. Joseph,* Adams wrote to the *Gospel Herald* that he was enthralled with the Beaver Islands.

> I have no hesitation in saying that the Islands are by far the best places that God has ever given the saints for temporal or spiritual blessings and prosperity....

75. "Dear Frank," *Gospel Herald,* Aug. 2, 1849.

76. Gilbert Watson to James Strang, Oct. 7, 1849, folder 509, Strang Collection, Beinecke Library. In the nineteenth century, *frigging* was a slang term for sexual intercourse. See the *Shorter Oxford English Dictionary: On Historical Principles,* 5th ed., 2 vols. (Oxford and New York: Oxford University Press, 2002), s.v.

77. A. J. Graham to James Strang, Jan. 22, 1850, folder 317, Strang Collection, Beinecke Library.

The most common laborer can get a dollar per day, and if he wishes, can make more than that by management. And if one thousand should land there tomorrow they need not be out of employment two days. If a man is a farmer, and wishes to take up a farm of 40 or 80 or 160 acres of land, he can do so without money or price, and own it by gift and promise of God.... In fact no man can explore these Islands and find out their great resources without seeing the goodness of God in keeping them for the saints, where they may gather until the indignation of the Lord is overpast.[78]

Adams also made his first visit to Voree after leaving Strang in Michigan and wrote another glowing report for readers of the *Gospel Herald*. "The temple is going up steadily and constantly, and a most beautiful structure it will be when finished," he wrote. "It covers 2½ acres of ground, has twelve towers, and the great hall [is] two hundred feet square in the centre. The entire walls are eight feet through, the floors and roofs are to be marble, and when it is finished it will be the greatest building in the world." He said that the "strong Tower of Zion," the storage facility, was "being erected on the Hill of Promise, the walls of which are three or four feet thick, which when finished is for the carrying out of the Order of Enoch in all its beauty and fullness."[79]

Adams saw theological justification in this. "It may be truly said," he wrote, "that in fulfillment of revelation[,] God has given his people peace and rest at Voree, and they are waxing fat and pleasant in the presence of their enemies." He continued:

Every saint of God throughout the world can see that the word of the Lord given through his servant Joseph [Smith,] in the letter of appointment of James [Strang,] has been literally fulfilled, and God has now given them a better place to gather in, even the Islands in the great lakes, where they can have land without money and without price—have them because God has said go there and possess them, and there we can teach the Lamanites or the sons of Joseph the fullness of the everlasting gospel. There we can keep the law of Zion. There we can build up the kingdom of God, and get our first dominion. There we can hold land without the mark of the beast—hold it by virtue of the law of the God of heaven. We can take possession of it without fighting for it, as the children of Israel had to when they went to inherit the land of Canaan. Therefore I say unto

---

78. "To the Editor," *Gospel Herald*, Aug. 23, 1849.
79. "To the Saints Scattered Abroad, Greeting," *Gospel Herald*, Sept. 6, 1849.

the saints in all the world, be of good cheer, for God is with us to give us peace, dominion and power from this day forth.[80]

It was an upbeat assessment of the state of affairs and an endorsement of the prophetic vision of James Strang. One can see why the prophet placed such confidence in Adams, who was as loyal a booster for Strang's endeavors as there could be, whether in colonizing the frontier and islands of the Great Lakes or more personally in matters of the heart.

---

80. Ibid.

5

THE PROPHET AND HIS NEPHEW

1849-1850

I am informed that J[ohn]. E. [Page]
had a letter from Philadelphia stating that your clerk was in the habit of
wearing petticoats untill very recently, and also that he had another from
Baltimore confirming the same thing. Of course the Pseudos all believe it,
and some that don't call themselves so seem to credit it. If it should be so it
makes it all the better; for what is more endearing and consoling than the
kind care and attention of a bosom companion when one is afflicted with
sickness? —Gilbert Watson to James Strang[1]

I n August 1849, Strang returned to Voree from Michigan to preside
over a conference at which members of the Order of Enoch performed baptisms for their dead ancestors. "Not withstanding there was only
nine days notice given of this conference, large numbers were in attendance,
and there was more faith, more unity of heart, more oneness of spirit, more
confidence in the prosperity of the cause, and a better feeling than we have
ever before witnessed at any Conference in Voree," wrote Gilbert Watson, a
clerk for the conference.[2]

At this time it was Strang's intention to maintain colonies in both Voree
and the Beaver Islands. "It is a mistake that Voree is to be pulled up," Strang
reported in an effort to quell gossip originating with the pseudos. "It is making steady improvement, and a large company of masons and assistants are at

---

1. Gilbert Watson to James Strang, Feb. 11, 1850, folder 515, James Jesse Strang
Collection, Yale Collection of Western Americana, Beinecke Rare Book and Manuscript Library, Yale University, New Haven, Connecticut.

2. "Chronicles of Voree, A record of the establishment and doings of the Stake of
Zion called Voree in Wisconsin made by the Scribes appointed to that office," 206, microfilm
copy, Library-archives, Wisconsin Historical Library, Madison, Wisconsin; cf. John J.
Hajicek, comp., *The Chronicles of Voree, 1844-1849* (Burlington, WI: JJRR Publishing,
1991).

work on the temple. We do not begin a work to look back, and are in a country where mobs are not in vogue."[3]

While the church was progressing well in Voree and on Beaver Island, Strang's missionaries in other towns and cities were being rejected. Rumors about the secret Order of the Illuminati and Strang's association with John C. Bennett were rapidly and widely circulated among church members. Strang decided he had better go into the mission field to reclaim some of his lost flock and recruit settlers to go to Beaver Island.

He planned to take his wife Mary and their children with him when he left Voree, or at least take them as far as his parents' home in Cherry Creek, New York, and may have even intended to take Mary with him to the eastern cities of New York, Philadelphia, Baltimore, and Washington, D.C. "I shall be in Buffalo in about five weeks on my way to [New York] to hold a Conference," he wrote his brother David. "My family will accompany me.... I shall spend the winter in N.Y. Washington & other Eastern Cities. I don't know how much of the way Mrs. S. may take with me, but probably she will spend nearly all winter in the Atlantic Cities."[4] He may have wanted his wife to leave town to avoid hearing the rumors about his alliance with Elvira Field, or maybe he wanted time to prepare his wife for the change that was taking place in their marital relationship.

On August 28, Strang's family was one of five that departed for Racine to catch a steamer for Beaver Island. The weather was fair and clear. Three of the families planned to settle on the island while another headed for Canada.[5] With two children ages nine and four and an eleven-month-old baby to care for, Mary told her husband she would rather stay home in Voree, but James insisted she go, promising to help her with the children.[6] Upon arriving on Beaver Island, Strang met with George J. Adams, who had just returned from a short mission to Milwaukee. The two men conducted a conference in the new town of St. James, named after Strang, on September 8 and 9. Three

---

3. "The Strang Mormons," *Gospel Herald,* Aug. 23, 1849.

4. James J. Strang to David Strang, n.d., Clarke Historical Library, Central Michigan University, Mount Pleasant, Michigan.

5. "Journal of Gilbert Watson Comprising Also a Short Account of His Life and Travels Written by Himself," unpublished manuscript, Library-Archives, Community of Christ, Independence, Missouri.

6. Mary Strang to James Strang, Jan. 9, 1850, folder 115, Strang Collection, Beinecke Library.

days later, James, his family, and six elders boarded the propeller *Oneida* to attend a church conference in Franklin, Oakland County, Michigan, in the Detroit area. It was a somewhat rough passage and most of the passengers became seasick.[7]

Though not always comfortable or entirely safe, travel by ship was much quicker than overland travel. Steam ships no longer depended solely on wind power to propel them, but fierce storms often rose up rapidly and could sink a ship before it reached a safe harbor. Under ordinary conditions, the trip from Beaver Island to Detroit would have taken only a couple of days. Many passengers were required to provide their own food and sleeping blankets, and most chose easy-to-prepare foods such as bread, butter, cheese, dried beef, sausage, and crackers. They drank from the lake to quench their thirst.

In this case, all arrived safely for the conference in Franklin, after which Strang obtained a horse and buggy from a member and used it to take his family to his parents' home in Chautauqua County.[8] Strang had indicated that Mary might accompany him to the eastern cities, but now the plan was for her to remain behind with the children. James then left to take a steamer to Buffalo in order to meet up with his new wife, Elvira Field. The young woman looked much different than she had appeared on Beaver Island. Her long dark hair had been cut short and she was dressed in men's clothing. She had taken on the new identity of Strang's sixteen-year-old nephew, Charles Douglass. James and Elvira probably stayed at Huff's Hotel[9] and went to a daguerreotype shop in Buffalo where "Charley" posed for a picture.[10] From Buffalo, they traveled together to New York City for the October conference there.

Exactly how Elvira was able to leave her parents' home on Beaver Island and join Strang undetected cannot be determined, although some of it can be surmised. She probably told her family she was returning to Michigan to teach school for another year. She was already staying in the town of Albion in southwest Michigan in early September. Strang may have left her there when he traveled from Michigan to Wisconsin in early August. From Albion, she

---

7. "On Board Propeller Oneida, Lake St. Clair," *Gospel Herald,* Sept. 27, 1849.

8. "Eighteen Miles West of Cleveland, Ohio," *Gospel Herald,* Oct. 11, 1849.

9. James J. Strang to David Strang, n.d., Clarke Historical Library.

10. Clement Strang, interviewed by Milo M. Quaife, Feb. 12, 1921, Clarke Historical Library.

would have traveled to Detroit, where she could have boarded a steam ship to Buffalo—probably not the same steamer Strang traveled on, as that would have raised suspicions. It would have been necessary for her to have a male chaperone and a female companion since it was not customary in those days for a woman to travel by herself or even alone in the company of a man who was not a relative. Elvira's male companion was probably George Adams or one of the two other apostles who had witnessed her marriage. It may have even been Samuel Graham, one of Strang's most trusted advisors, because Strang mentioned that Graham was ahead of him on his way to the conference in New York City and that Adams was on his way to Baltimore.[11]

Elvira was trained as a tailor and could easily have made her own men's clothing.[12] Strang himself had explained the necessity of Elvira disguising herself as a man, telling her he was in the process of preparing the church for a revelation on plural marriage but it would not yet be good for church members to know their prophet was traveling with a woman, even if she was his wife.[13]

A woman by the name of Orria Brown may have been involved in Elvira's disappearance from Michigan. As previously mentioned, Gilbert Watson had reported a rumor that Strang, Adams, and three others had gone up to the Sault, accompanied by "Mrs. Brownson" and someone else, to participate in a regular drinking and frigging spree. Watson could have confused the names Brown and Brownson. Several letters mention a "Mrs. Brown" in association with Elvira's disappearance. "Albert Field is here after his sister," A. J. Graham wrote to Strang. A. J. was Samuel Graham's brother in Albion, Michigan.

> But she [Elvira] is not here. She left here last fall with Mrs. Brown to go, as I supposed, to the island. But it seems that she has not been there. He [Albert] is quite anxious to learn where she is. He was at my brother's yesterday and has gone to Samuel's wife about it. But she knows nothing about her. I cannot imagine where she has gone unless it is to Voree. You I presume can find out if she is there in a short time.
>
> If you know of her being at Voree, I trust you would let me know so I can

11. "Eighteen Miles West."

12. George Adams may have also provided the men's clothing. See Lois Austen to Samuel Graham, Nov. 20, 1848 [1849], folder 221, Strang Collection, Beinecke Library.

13. Clement Strang interview.

tell Mr. Fields as he is quite anxious to know something about her. Mrs. Brown's gearls [girls] are at the island and they do not know anything about their mother as they left her at Detroit, I suppose. Mr. Field says that Mrs. Brown told the [girls] that she was coming to the island in three weeks after she left them.[14]

A letter to Samuel Graham in October 1849 tells of a "faint whisper" circulating on Beaver Island since Strang's visit there in early September according to C. P. Moon. But "as there are no Ears to hear, it all fades away."[15] Yet when the propeller *Ohio* arrived on October 4 with "boxes of furniture for O. Brown" and two young ladies, presumably Orria Brown's adolescent daughters staying with the Hickeys until Orria's arrival, "Mrs. Hickey and Mrs. Aldrich are a trying to raise the wind."[16] Mrs. Hickey had apparently pieced together where the girls' mother was.[17] Within days of the girls' arrival, Mrs. Hickey sent a series of letters to her husband, Lorenzo Dow Hickey, in New York telling him the rumors about the Strang scandal.

Lois Austin, a Strangite woman on Beaver Island, wrote to Samuel Graham about the same time Moon wrote Graham, reporting there were "some operations going on here with Mrs. Hickey which I think you ought to be appraised of. She is going to leave the Island and I understand yesterday, that She said She would make herself good, with some of your things, for the trouble of those girls of Mrs. Brown's."[18] Austin considered Mrs. Hickey to be "a verry foolish woman, to give a loose to her tongue in the manner She does, for there is nothing she does not say of you and others, and as for Bro. Adams, She puts it on to him the worst way. She has spread the most Shameful reports of him, that could be, relating to some clothing, but she has not many friends, to take up for her, there is Mrs. Greig and one or two others, believes her stories."[19]

---

14. A. J. Graham to James Strang, Jan. 22, 1850, folder 317, Strang Collection, Beinecke Library.

15. C. P. Moon to Samuel Graham, Oct. 6, 1849, Clarke Historical Library.

16. Ibid.

17. James Greig to James Strang, Nov. 16, 1849, folder 354, Strang Collection, Beinecke Library.

18. Lois Austin to Samuel Graham, Nov. 20, [1849]. Lois Austin and her family joined the Strangite Church but later left it. Their daughter, Sophia, married Eri J. Moore, a trader on Beaver Island and one of Strang's archenemies.

19. Ibid.

Austin repeated again in the same letter that Mrs. Hickey:

> took the liberty to talk of you and Bro. Adams [and] Bro. Strang most Shamefully. She said she thanked God her tongue was not tied … and She would tell what She pleased…. Mrs. Aldrich feels sorry She has listened to Mrs. Hickey as much as She has in regard to yourself; She says She is convinced that Mrs. H. is a dangerous woman to associate with for She has quizzed [the young] Miss Brown too much, and got many things out of her. At least this is Mrs. H[ickey].'s story, but the girl says, She has never told her any such stuff, of her own Dear mother, as Mrs. Hickey said She did….
>
> I am verry, verry sorry the children Stopped with Mrs. H. At all, for She has misused them verry much with her tongue…. After She has left, times will be better[,] I hope[.] We shall rejoice to See her leave the Island and I pray the Lord to keep all such Saints as She is from coming here…. Mrs. Brown has not come to the Island yet, nor Does her children expect her now, for the last boat up was in last week.[20]

Another resident of Beaver Island wrote to Strang in November to give a general account of the settlers, including the interesting detail that he had visited with some of the pseudos and had become "about half a pseudo myself." Sister Hickey, she reported, had the support of her husband and was planning to "leave the island on the next boat. The daughters of Mrs. Brown are with her, but will be left for Brother Aldrich or myself to look after. Reuben Fields has sent Albert to Michigan to find Elvira."[21]

The mother of the two girls, Orria Brown, remained mysteriously absent from the island and out of contact with her daughters. Her name was mentioned in another context in the Strangite record in March 1850, when Samuel Graham wrote in cipher asking Strang if he had heard anything about "ORRA."[22] There is also a strange story told about a Mrs. Brown, possibly

---

20. Ibid.

21. James Greig to James Strang.

22. Samuel Graham to James Strang, March 13, 1850, folder 340, Strang Collection, Beinecke Library. The 1850 federal census for Beaver Island lists a thirty-year-old male from New York named Oren Brown living with the Thomas E. Dodge family. Also listed in the household are two female children, Harriet Brown, twelve, and Sarah K. Brown, nine. Harriet and Sarah were in attendance at the conference Strang conducted on Beaver Island in Sept. 1849, but Orria, or Oren, is not listed. However, all three took the Oath of the Covenant before Strang's coronation in July 1850. An Orria Brown subscribed to the *Gospel Herald* in April 1849.

Orria, who had run away from her husband. "Since the commencement of the Beaver Island settlement here in 1847," Strang wrote in 1855, "three run-away wives have reached here. Mrs. Brown and Mrs. Coltrin from Parma, and Mrs. Bebee from Thetford, Mich."[23]

Strang tells that Mrs. Bebee's husband came to retrieve her and that Mrs. Coltrin returned to her husband after only a few weeks and that nothing further had been heard from either of them. "But," he added, "Mrs. Brown, not having the good fortune to be followed, and finding no Mormon who would take her, connected herself in succession with ... several different Gentile traders, and has finally taken a mission [to] Kenosha, Wis[consin], 'as a lover of freedom and a friend of humanity,' to 'unburden the minds of those led astray by the cunning devices of Strang and his adherents.'"[24] Strang claimed Mrs. Brown mattered little to him, yet he wrote about her in detail and knew the latest facts of her whereabouts, quoting statements she had apparently made. It is highly unlikely he would have taken enough interest to attempt to defame her character if she had not been of some significance to him or to the community at one time.

Whatever connection Mrs. Brown and others had to the disappearance of Elvira Field from Michigan, Elvira's disappearance was total. Albert Field left Beaver Island and traveled by foot throughout Michigan for several months searching for his sister without finding a single clue as to her whereabouts. He became angry when he later learned the particulars of her marriage, but not incensed enough to leave Strang's church.[25]

Whether he knew about it or not, Strang was not the first Mormon to disguise a secret wife in men's clothing. In April 1841, Joseph Smith married his third plural wife, Louisa Beaman, in Nauvoo. The bride was disguised as a man during a ceremony which took place in a grove near Main Street in full view of the public.[26] It is entirely conceivable that John Bennett, William Smith, and other confidantes knew the lengths Joseph Smith had gone to in order to conceal his secret relationships and conveyed their information to Strang.

---

23. "Beaver Island—Mormon—Strang the 'Saint,'" *Northern Islander,* Oct. 11, 1855.

24. Ibid.

25. Clement Strang interview.

26. Todd Compton, *In Sacred Loneliness: The Plural Wives of Joseph Smith* (Salt Lake City: Signature Books, 2001), 59.

Contrary to his wife's expectations, Lorenzo Dow Hickey would eventually turn from his suspicions and doubts to become one of Strang's staunchest supporters, as well as himself a polygamist. He later wrote to Charles J. Strang, one of Elvira's sons, in defense of plural marriage. "You are like thousands who seem to think that prophets must conform to their views of propriety, while they are of all men the most independent and self-controlling." He asked the prophet's son what the biblical prophet Noah cared regarding what "the wise men of his age said of his ark philosophy.... You can talk of Strang's little trip with C—— D——. He did it because he chose to and it was his own business. And if the men that take so much pains to find fault with him would look to home they would find plenty of splinters in their own morals."[27]

In this remarkable letter to the prophet's son, Hickey concluded:

> But one thing I will state here. Any man that says that J. J. Strang ever abused his wife is a liar. I know all about the wife business. And if you understood matters you would say he done right. That Mary Strang (his first wife) was —— [left blank]. If your wife would do by you as she did by him (long before he thought of C. D. or any other wife) you would come [to] C. D. or some other fair deal. I don't want to say anything about Mary. But the less said the better for all parties. She was the perfidy you speak of, not him. I don't want to say anything against her, and don't, only when parties blame him. I told you years ago some things and if you had heeded them all would have been well. Yet I find no fault. God almighty called and ordained him by Angels. Who is the man to throw stones at a prophet because he tells, or asks, his wife to lay aside her long dress and petticoat and put on drawers and pants for convenience while traveling from place to place? You make a great sin of it. I fail to see it. I can tell of things old prophets done, better than all that and the world did not get mad about it. You are too impulsive, too quick to condemn, you should not forget that prophets of all ages do things often in opposition to the customs of the land and that is why they got killed.[28]

From September 1849 through March 1850, Elvira traveled with her husband disguised as his nephew Charles J. Douglass. As his personal secretary, she took notes and answered correspondence. In order to keep up the

---

27. Lorenzo Dow Hickey to Charles J. Strang, July [22,] 1882, Strang Manuscript Collection, Library and Historical Center, State Library of Michigan, Lansing, Michigan.
    28. Ibid.

charade of being a sixteen-year-old male, she may have assisted in Strangite priesthood responsibilities otherwise reserved for men, such as administering the sacrament, baptizing new converts, and healing the sick. In "his" spare time, Charley acquired an accordion and tried to learn to play but found it "proved not good" and returned it.[29] He/she was aware that a search was underway and felt uncomfortable about it. "As I read A. J. Graham's letter I saw some things which make me feel a little sad to heare of other people's sadness. You know what I mean," she wrote to Strang, who had left her in Baltimore for a few days while he traveled to Washington, D.C.[30]

As Charley Douglass, Elvira also wrote several articles for the *Gospel Herald.* One piece, "The Kingdom of God," which appeared in the November 15, 1849, issue, is signed by "C. J. D."[31] Elvira, posing as Charley, wrote another article about the benefit of secret societies such as the Masonic Order.[32] She was probably the author of an unpublished paper about the plight of working women.[33] It was also Douglass who reported the minutes of a church conference in New York City to readers of the *Gospel Herald,* notable for its mention of the priesthood ordination of a black man, Moore Walker. "The impression had gone forth in the conference that a colored man could not hold the priesthood, which was not true," the article reported. "Pres. Strang proposed by revelation that Bro. Walker (colored) be ordained an Elder, which was concurred in unanimously. Pres. Strang disclaimed any intention of courting the favor of emancipationists; holding that the revelations of God, and not the devices of men, are the foundation of all national freedom." And so, Brother Walker was ordained an elder under the hands of James Strang and George Adams.[34] The latter prophesied that Walker would "carry the gospel to the nations of the earth."[35] The ordination is significant because the Brighamites would not allow blacks to hold the priesthood until 1978, a full 129 years later.

---

29. Charles Douglass to James Strang, Feb. 7, 1850, folder 147, James Jesse Strang Papers, Beinecke Library.

30. C. J. Douglass to James Strang, Feb. 4, 1850, folder 146, Beinecke.

31. "The Kingdom of God," *Gospel Herald,* Nov. 15, 1849.

32. "Secret Societies," *Gospel Herald,* Dec. 13, 1849.

33. Unpublished manuscript, which appears to be in Elvira Field's handwriting, Clarke Historical Library.

34. "Minutes of A General Conference ... Oct 7. Evening Session," *Gospel Herald,* Nov. 15, 1849.

35. "Minutes of a conference held in New York City on Oct. 5-8, 1849," *Gospel Her-*

Charley kept the minutes for a subsequent conference held in New York City nine days later on October 17. "His" report appeared in the November 22, 1849, edition of the *Gospel Herald.* Charley began by stating he wished to give a history of "some strange proceedings" initiated by Increase Van Dusen and Lorenzo Dow Hickey. Van Dusen, a former Methodist preacher, had joined the Mormon Church in Oakland County, Michigan, but had moved to Nauvoo in 1843 to be with the bulk of the Saints. He and his wife had joined Strang by April 1846 and were among those who testified against Brigham Young and other apostles when Young and his colleagues were excommunicated by Strang *in absentia.* Van Dusen was frustrated by the choice of what he called "corrupt" men to lead the church and decided to leave Voree in 1847, although still considering Strang to be a prophet. For the next two years, he and his wife published and sold a small crude pamphlet that exposed the Nauvoo temple ceremonies, creating "an image of Mormonism as a licentious cult engulfed in a system of falsity and perversion."[36] In June 1849, Van Dusen repented of this course of action and reconciled with Strang.

Lorenzo Dow Hickey's father was a Methodist minister. Four years younger than Strang, he was born four miles away from Palmyra, New York, where Joseph Smith had begun his ministry. Hickey was named for the great revivalist preacher, Lorenzo Dow. Much like his namesake, he knew the scriptures so thoroughly that "Biblical phrases rolled from his tongue or pen with ease and fluency and his very manner of speaking was in the language of the Bible."[37] He had followed the same path as Van Dusen to Oakland County, Michigan, where he joined the Mormon Church in 1842, then relocated to Nauvoo with his wife in 1845 and converted to Strang in 1846. Al-

---

ald, Nov. 8, 1849. Walker planned to travel to Beaver Island in the spring of 1850 and settle here with his own family and several other "colored people," but there is no evidence he did. See also Moore Walker to James Strang, Feb. 2, 1850, folder 506, Beinecke Library.

36. Craig L. Foster, "From Temple Mormon to Anti-Mormon: The Ambivalent Odyssey of Increase Van Dusen," *Dialogue: A Journal of Mormon Thought* 27 (Fall 1994): 275-86, also available on the *New Mormon Studies CD-ROM: A Comprehensive Resource Library* (Salt Lake City: Smith Research Associates, 1998). Increase was born on May 25, 1809, in Hillsdale, New York. In 1833 at the age of twenty-four, he traveled to Lapeer, Michigan, where he met and married Maria Hoffman. Not much is known about Maria.

37. John Cumming, "Lorenzo Dow Hickey: The Last of the Twelve," *Michigan History,* Mar. 1966, 50-55.

though he had served a Strangite mission to Michigan, Hickey was not considered a member of Strang's inner circle.

During the conference on Beaver Island in early September, Hickey had been chosen to accompany Strang to New York and New Jersey, leaving his wife and three small children behind on the island. Both Hickey and Van Dusen were among the elders present in New York City earlier in the month at the October 5-8 conference.[38] Apparently, Van Dusen and Hickey had anticipated continuing on to Philadelphia to serve a mission together, but Strang surprised them by suggesting action on the proposal be postponed. At the next meeting in New York City, Van Dusen and Hickey, both known to be staunch opponents of polygamy, began spreading rumors about Strang, as well as about Samuel Graham, George Adams, and James Blakeslee. The following day just before another meeting, according to Charley Douglass, Hickey greeted Strang and his secretary very cordially. "The cloud which had rested on Hickey's brow for several days was gone, but a kind of nervous twitching, which sometimes marks incipient insanity, and not unfrequently follows great mental excitement, remained," the sensationalized report in the *Gospel Herald* read. Strang, by contrast, preached with "great spirit" and power from the text, "I will not know a wicked person."[39]

Initially, Hickey and Van Dusen seemed to be enthusiastic about the sermon, assuming the objects of the "scathing rebuke" and "deep toned admonition" were George Adams and Samuel Graham; but when they realized Strang was instead talking about them, the "smiling demon in Hickey and Van Dusen was roused to fury." "Sitting on their seats in the congregation," Charley reported, "they writhed, changed color, and gesticulated like the infuriated in the fierce encounter, when life is the stake and death the doom."[40] By the conclusion of the meeting, Hickey was trembling with rage and tried to speak to the congregation. Strang forbade him, insisting he would have no disorder in the meeting. Hickey retorted he had something to tell to the church. Strang responded he could wait until that evening when another meeting was held. Hickey sat down and said he was satisfied, but when the meeting was being dismissed, he called for the attention of the congregation and again said he had something important to communicate. He then launched

---

38. Foster, "Temple Mormon," 275-86.

39. "New York City, Oct. 22nd, 1849," *Gospel Herald*, Nov. 22, 1849.

40. Ibid.

into a tirade against Strang as "a liar, an imposter, a false prophet and danger-ously wicked man," and said he would prove it by letters he had in his pocket, which he had just received from his wife on Beaver Island. He pronounced Strang guilty of adultery, fornication, spiritual wifery, and "all the abomina-tions which ever existed in Nauvoo."[41]

Strang attempted to speak as soon as Hickey was done, but the confu-sion in the room was "too great." Van Dusen thrust his hands into Strang's face and chest and screamed "You are guilty! You are guilty! You are guilty!"[42] Both Van Dusen and Hickey kept up such intense shouting that Strang's voice was drowned out. Strang, along with Charley Douglass and the congre-gation, was forced to leave the building. However, they returned later that day for an afternoon session, at which Strang at first alluded to the distur-bance and then recapitulated the charges Hickey had made against him. He said the accusations had come from three letters Hickey's wife had sent him, which contained nothing of substance. They were simply the words of a "homesick woman, complaining of the hardships she suffered and feared during the absence of her husband."[43]

The following day, Monday, October 18, 1849, several officers and members of Strang's church met to investigate the conduct of Van Dusen and the charges Hickey had made against Strang. Two men testified that Van Dusen's conduct was the most abusive they had ever seen, saying Van Dusen had physically assaulted Strang. Moore Walker, the black man who had re-cently been ordained to the priesthood, remarked that persons of color were not usually expected to behave on the same level with white men but that he had never known a colored man to behave in such a shameful, abrasive, and insulting manner as Van Dusen.[44] Van Dusen was present and arose to ac-knowledge that he had not acted with the right spirit. He reminded the men that they themselves knew how excited he could become when under the in-fluence of passion and that the reason for his behavior was that Hickey had told him of "some very wicked things in respect to President Strang."

Hickey's case was presented to the general membership. Strang denied

41. Ibid.

42. "Proceedings of a Meeting in New York City on the Case of Hickey and Van Dusen," *Gospel Herald,* Nov. 22, 1849.

43. "New York City, Oct. 22nd."

44. "Proceedings of Meeting."

the charges Hickey had made against him, saying they were not true, in whole or in part. He called on Hickey to produce the letters from his wife, along with any other evidence he had of Strang's alleged misdoing, but Hickey said he no longer had the letters.[45] Thereupon, it was unanimously agreed that the church should withdraw all confidence and fellowship from Hickey. Van Dusen received the harsher punishment of excommunication. On November 1, 1849, the *Gospel Herald* published the following notice: "Lorenzo Dow Hickey, one of the Twelve, has been suspended of all jurisdiction and authority, for most gross lying and slander upon Bros. G. J. Adams and Samuel Graham and neglecting his mission to follow after the diabolical revelations of Increase McGee Van Dusen."[46]

The Saints back on Beaver Island were not surprised to hear of the action. "I learned by your letters that Hickey has pseudoed. I am not surprised. His wife has also pseudoed and she is constantly sending her pseudo letters to Dow ever since he left," Marvin M. Aldrich wrote to Samuel Graham. "She left this morning on the *Oneida*.... The girls are with me and verry likely to remain with me through the winter. Mrs. Brown has not arrived."[47]

Hickey took his suspension especially hard. Forced to reexamine his religious beliefs, he apparently suffered a "nervous breakdown" and ended up in jail and then a mental institution. George Adams said he found him in December and wrote to Strang asking for compassion. "Brother Hickey [was] like a lamb—the most humbel man that I ever See—he made the Strongest kind of Confession, and has given full evidince of a lasting repentance—he is like a child—he humbelly Desired that I would Cast the Devils out [of] him—which I did, and he is now clothed and in his right mind," Adams wrote.[48] In fact, Hickey had lost his clothes in a cemetery where he was found before he was sent to an asylum. "I found him at Bro. Leaches—he was afraid we would not forgive him," Adams explained; "he said he had wronged two of the Best men on earth, viz.—You and me. —he said [he did] it because the devil was in him.... James[,] let us have mercy on him—Suppose you recall

---

45. Ibid.

46. "Suspension," *Gospel Herald*, Nov. 1, 1849.

47. Marvin M. Aldrich to Samuel Graham, Nov. 23, 1849, folder 215, Beinecke Library.

48. George J. Adams to James Strang, Dec. 3, 1849, folder 201, Beinecke Library; "Forgiveness of L. D. Hickey," *Gospel Herald*, Dec. 27, 1849.

his Suspension—I think he will make one of the Best friends we ever had.... [T]he Hickey affair has done great good here, and it will do immence good in Philadelphia. —it is looked upon as the mighty power of God."[49]

A few nights later, the Saints in New York City held another meeting. "Van Devil Duzen, was there—but we Bound up the Devil so tight in him, that he could not open his mouth, and he trembled like a reed Shaken by the wind," Adams wrote to Strang. "After the meeting [Van Dusen] raged a little—Bro. Hickey told him to his face, that he was a liar, a knave, a puppy and a Scoundrel."[50]

Hickey himself wrote to Strang asking for forgiveness:

> I feel as Nebuchadnezzar did after he had [been] driven out [from among] men ... & all I have to say is I love you as I never loved before. I have confessed to God & man, & I ask your forgiveness & I ask your prayers that I may be just such a man as God shall own & bless in the future. I would like to see you, & tell you what I have passed through since I saw you. I feel like a child, I ask your counsel & advice that I may do the thing that would please God.... I ask your forgiveness for talking as I did in the Hall at New York & by the grace of God & the prayers of the saints I will try to do the thing that is right in the future.... [W]hip me when & where I deserve but remember mercy, for I am weak & not strong. I thought I was strong but alas I am as a little child.[51]

In a postscript, Hickey wrote to Strang that "Brother Greig wrote a good letter. [Y]es[,] one that was calculated to do good[,] one that will learn me as well as others to mind my own business."

Strang willingly forgave Hickey for his actions. "Again our brother is clothed in his right mind," he wrote, "because he has been forgiven and blessed by the priesthood, which holds the keys of the kingdom."[52] From this point on, Hickey would become a fierce apologist for Strang and remain loyal to him until his death, even taking three plural wives of his own. He

---

49. Ibid.

50. George J. Adams to James Strang, Dec. 5, 1849, folder 202, Beinecke Library. Increase Van Dusen never returned to Strang. In fact, he published a pamphlet alleging that Strang and Adams were inspired by the devil. The Van Dusens later moved to Kirtland, Ohio, where Increase died in 1882.

51. Lorenzo Dow Hickey to James Strang, Dec. 6, 1849, folder 384, Beinecke Library; "Forgiveness of L. D. Hickey."

52. "Forgiveness of L. D. Hickey"; *Gospel Herald*, Dec. 27, 1849.

named the first child born to his first plural wife Elvira after Elvira Field.

Even from the beginning, the intimate relationship between James Strang and his personal secretary raised suspicions among the members, especially in Philadelphia. George Adams considered Philadelphia to be a seat of apostasy. "Every foul and corrupt spirit seems to be located there," he wrote. "It is a perfect 'cage of unclean birds and filthy croakers,' and God has, or will, spew the most of them out of his mouth."[53] He found "few there that have not departed from the faith," with the exception of "Elder Thomas Braidwood [who] has faithfully discharged his duty as a man of God, and his skirts are clear."[54] Adams's words are ironic in that Braidwood would soon raise a ruckus about Charley Douglass's "skirts," which would result in nearly all the members in Philadelphia falling away.

Several members noticed the womanly curves of Douglass's body. One member, John Ursbruck, wrote to Strang citing the "physiological peculiarities" of the prophet's secretary. Ursbruck thought Charley Douglass resembled a young woman he had seen on Beaver Island. Strang tried to turn the subject by replying that Ursbruck must have seen Charley's sister. But Ursbruck told other members he knew it was the same woman he had seen on Beaver Island because of a certain mark on her face.[55]

Strang said the physiological peculiarities of his private secretary were none of Ursbruck's business and chastised him for spreading the story. "Don't you know that the mere suspicion; no matter how unfounded that I traveled with a female in disguise, would be taken up by a thousand tongues, each of whom would assist a story as holy writ? Are you so ignorant of human nature as not to know that the mere suggestion that a traveling friend of mine had one single genuine Physiological peculiarity must inevitably fall upon me as a distant charge of keeping a concubine?" he scolded. He went on to accuse Ursbruck of egotism and hypocrisy:

> Your good name is of so much consequence to you, that you have taken pains to write me a letter, "to prevent having statements inferred to you which you never made." You are so sensitive of your good fame that you can not endure that one person should think you guilty of falsehood, And therefore you write to

---

53. "Baltimore, Md., Oct. 2nd, 1849," *Gospel Herald*, Oct. 18, 1849.
54. Ibid.
55. Peter Hess to James Strang, Nov. 22, 1849, folder 70, Beinecke Library.

me to deny having made the statements attributed to you which I alone know to be false.... And yet you care so little for my good name that it is "a matter of no consequence to you" though your Physiological speculations, without the slightest pretense of knowledge, may damn me to infamy in the mind of three fourths of the land.[56]

Another member, Mrs. Long, dreamed Charley Douglass was a woman. Strang responded to this sardonically, saying: "A pretty way that is to pretend to have the gift of revelation. I wonder if she has a daughter that she would be willing to give to him for a bedfellow. Well, Mrs. Long is a kind-hearted woman and has nothing malicious about her. I shall be there some of these times to stay overnight and if she thinks I have a girl with me she will of course send him with the girls to bed. That will tell what she thinks."[57]

In November, Thomas Braidwood was informed anonymously that the young man with Strang was indeed a woman, and he wasted no time telling other members of the congregation.[58] He began to realize the obvious about Strang's companion, that he had the head, eyes, round breasts, and arms, hands, thighs, feet, and posterior of a woman. Charley was, "from the crown of his head to the soles of his feet ... every whit a woman."[59]

The gossip about Charley's identity had begun to fade by January but was suddenly brought up again. Strang heard from Amos Lowen that the story "had died away" except in the mind of "Tom Braidwood [who] believes that Charley is a woman[,] he laughs and winks when the name of Charley Douglass is mentioned. [T]he matter gives me no concern and I would not have alluded to it but for your inquiry."[60] Meanwhile, the rumors about Charley reached Voree. "There is considerable excitement about a letter that John E. Page has got from a man in Philadelphia saying that your scribe is some young lady who has been on Bever," Benjamin Wright wrote to Strang.[61]

---

56. James Strang to John Ursbruck, Nov. 20, 1849, folder 66a, Beinecke Library.

57. James Strang to Amos Lowen, Nov. 21, 1849, folder, 69, Beinecke Library.

58. Peter Hess to James Strang, Nov. 22, 1849, folder 70, Beinecke Library.

59. Ibid.

60. Amos Lowen to James Strang, Jan. 10, 1850, folder 417, Beinecke Library.

61. B. G. Wright to James Strang, Jan. 29, 1850, folder 535, Beinecke Library.

A few weeks later, James Canney reported to Strang that in New York City the members had held a private meeting to discuss Douglass's identity. He said the rumors were like "the Monsoons, whirlwinds," for their effect on the members' imaginations. They were "eruptions in the church," although he quickly assumed a dismissive tone, saying he would relate the content of the discussions in the form of "a historical romance," thereby covering all the "affairs which transpired here since Br. [Samuel] Bennett went away to Beaver."

With some hilarity, he explained how a former member of the church, Peter Hess, had appeared in Philadelphia with "tidings" of polygamy and how he had transformed the "wiseacre" elders into "old women," wondering "What shall we do?" The only way to convince members that Charley was a girl, they decided, was to organize a jury composed of old matrons, "without mercy or even benefit of the clergy." In Canney's telling, Hess becomes the judge presiding over a fictional courtroom. Warming to his story, Canney explains that the judge calls a "Sister L"[62] as his first witness. Sister L says when Charley returned from Haarlem High Bridge, he was lame, so she washed his feet for him. "And I told my husband soon's we got to bed, that Charley was a Gal and I node [knew] it, for I node that was a woman's foot and I could swear to it." The judge says, tongue-in-cheek, that the evidence "smells quite strong against Charley."

A second sister takes the stand to say she doesn't have a child, but ...

> when Strang brot Charley to our boat, he seemed very carefull about him (or her). [Be]fore he left him, he said, "Charley, take care of yourself till I come." And Strang said to me, "Sister—don't let Charley sleep with the boys!" I declare Judge, I begin to smell a Rat somehow or other—Well, I took good care of Charley & didn't let him sleep with the boys!... [But when we washed Charley's clothes, we found] a mess of bloody cloths, which women sometimes use, all rolled up.... O Gemini thought I! The Cat's out of the Bag, sure enough! O Dear! This Pseudo Charley turns out to be a filthy and abominable minsinians [minian's] Hussey! But when I examined the Bed, O Dear! It beat old Adam's Pantaloons! O Twang, Whang-Strambang, hocus pocus-pocus!!!

"The judge," writes Canney, thinks "this matron's evidence beats all ... for Charley's a Gal—sure a nuff!"

Next the judge calls a "Sister R.," an unassuming middle-aged women.

---

62. "Sister L." may have been Mrs. Long.

"Well, Judge, I don't know much—Strang had the one he called Charley with him at our house & was there himself off and on for 6 days. Charley appeared to be sick; ... but when Strang came to see him & doctor him, he seemed very private about it. I smelt something like a <u>Rat</u> and I mentioned it to my husband. But," she adds with a double entendre, "he said Strang was giving Charley <u>injections</u>. Well, I felt easy then, supposing it was only a conjunction between Strang & Charley. But since Hess came here[,] my husband owned that he smelt a rat ... and shore enuff Charley's a Gal!"

"The last witness on the stand" is a "widowy, middle-aged sort of matron, who said she knew nothing at all about the matter, but if such were true[,] it was very bad for it set a bad example, but she always liked Strang, Adams and Graham & if they never do anything worse, she should be glad.... She thought it was best to ... punish the Crime & let the criminals go—for accidents will happen in the <u>best of Families</u>, for she knew it by experience."

The judge gives his opinion that the evidence is "abominably strong against the accused," as against George Adams, who is all "menstrum and monstrous." The judge commits Strang, Douglass, and Adams to perpetual exile. Canney says he has "written the above Burlesque & have sent you the Copy of their Conferences here in the Church so you can form some idea of how matters stand here in New York. I was not in their secret Councils at all until Hess was gone home & everything fixed for a meeting of Condemnation of yourself, etc.... I kept them at Bay, all I could & then certified my Veto against them—I do not meet with them."[63]

Although Charley Douglass did not fool the members in Philadelphia, her disguise was apparently good enough to fool at least one family in New York. In her memoirs, Sarah Livingston, the daughter of one of the traders on Beaver Island who opposed Strang, related a story she heard as a child about Douglass. She recalled that Virginia Johnson, the fifteen-year-old daughter of a merchant in New York, said Douglass "made love to her" in 1850. Douglass promised marriage, if only the young woman's family would join Strang's church and move to Beaver Island.[64] The family was baptized

---

63. James and Clarissa Canney to James Strang, June 16, 1850, folder 277, Beinecke Library.

64. Sarah McKinley Livingston, unpublished manuscript, 27-28, Clarke Historical Library.

and relocated to the island, where they opened a store. They waited for Charley so the two young people could marry, but to their surprise Elvira suddenly came into the store one day wearing bloomers, sunbonnet, and boots, the style of dress among Mormon women. She was recognized as the "young man" who had been in New York. At first Elvira denied she was Charley, then admitted it. A few years later, Virginia married Alexander Wentworth, one of Strang's assassins.[65] Another version of the tale has Strang himself as the girl's seducer.

There is a partially true element to the story. According to census records, a family headed by Franklin Johnson, a merchant from New York, lived on Beaver Island in 1850. Johnson's fifteen-year-old daughter, whose name was actually Phoebe rather than Virginia, married Alexander Wentworth, one of the men who murdered Strang.

During the long fall and winter months of 1849 and 1850, Mary Perce Strang waited for her husband's return while she lived with his parents, Clement and Abigail Strang, in New York. Two of her children were so ill she thought they would die. "I wrote to you and directed [the letter] to Baltimore not having any idea that you would remain so long in New York," she wrote to her husband. "The baby had the whooping cough the Friday after you left here. Ellen was taken down with bilious fever. She had chills every day until lately."[66] In another letter she wrote that she had held herself "in constant reddiness for traveling the last three months and shall continue to do so until further direction."[67]

In early January, she wrote to James to tell him of the death of his brother David's wife. Downhearted, she wrote, "Now James, I tell you as I told you before that I would much rather go home than to go east. If I had money I would take the children and go home. You told me before I left home that you would help me take care of the children ... Do write something what you are intending to do."[68] She seems to have no reason yet to suspect her husband of infidelity. Neither Mary nor Strang's parents seemed to know anything about Charley Douglass. For some reason, they did not receive any letters from

---

65. Ibid.

66. Mary Strang to James Strang, Nov. 4, 1849, folder 113, Beinecke Library.

67. Mary Strang to James Strang, [Dec. 1849], folder 114, Beinecke Library.

68. Mary Strang to James Strang, Jan. 9, 1850, folder 115, Beinecke Library.

friends and relatives in Voree that season and did not receive any of Strang's newspapers.[69]

As with Elvira Field when George Adams acted as an intermediary between her and the prophet, it was Adams again who was apparently chosen to explain to Mary the principle of plural marriage and what God's wishes for James and his secretary were. Mary seems to have expected Adams to visit her at James's parents' home, asking in several letters to her husband where George was. "I have neither heard from or seen Brother Adams though I suppose it still continues to be some days past Christmas," she wrote.[70] Again, "I have had no letters since I left home from anyone. Where is Brother George?" She added that "Ellen and William need cloaks, a large warm shawl would not be out of place if you could conveniently get them. They both want shoes."[71]

To the prophet, Adams wrote assuringly "in regards to Sis. Strang," that he would "manage everything the Best I can."[72] But in this instance, George would not satisfy Strang's expectations and never make the trip to Mary's temporary residence in New York. In January, Adams suggested that Samuel Graham go to Cherry Creek to meet with her. "Bro. Graham is in Albany—or Utica," he wrote to Strang. "Perhaps I will arrainge for him to fill the mission and Bring your family to meet me in Albany. [H]ow would you like that?"[73] Graham became ill and was unable to make the trip.

The Saints in New York City had taken up a collection to bring Mary to the city. Moore Walker wrote to Strang in February 1850: "There is much dissatisfaction in consequence of the proceedings of Elder Adams. As we where told that he was on a mission of great importance & saith it was connected [to] the bringing of Sister Strang and children to New York. And as some of the saints gave money for that object, they feel aggrieved as they think that they have been imposed upon & that the mission was not for that purpose."[74]

---

69. Mary Strang to James Strang, Nov. 4, 1849.

70. Mary Strang to James Strang, [Dec. 1849].

71. Ibid.

72. George Adams to James Strang, Dec. 11, 1849, Clarke Historical Library.

73. George Adams to James Strang, Jan. 15, 1850, folder 205, Beinecke Library.

74. Moore Walker to James Strang, Feb. 2, 1850, folder 506, Beinecke Library.

Frantic to hear from her husband, Mary remained wholly ignorant of Strang's new marital status. James finally wrote to her in January apologizing for the delay in his letters. He had just received her news about the death of David's wife. He responded:

I should not have delayed my answer one moment but I was overwhelmed with grief and knew not what to say. To all my other sorrows was added that I have been subjected to so many disappointments, that I am not able to do what I know I ought to, and am at a loss which way to turn....

I have felt sorrow enough that you could not be with me here, but, Mary, I feel a little down now and am glad you are not here. Since the first of December I have seen but one tolerably fair day. It rains incessantly. There has been either rain or snow every day but one for 3 [?] weeks....

I have not been well one hour of that time and my spirits begin to lag. I have only kept up by the exercise of an iron will and if that gives way I shall sink.

Then Strang mentioned his secretary:

Charlie, is sinking rapidly and today can scarce help me at all. [On the] 28th [of] Nov[ember] I weighed 162 pounds, now I weigh about 145 pounds. It is a week since I have heard from Geo., and I don't know anything what prospects are. But I shall be on the move immediately.... Kiss the children for me. Tell them their father is coming to see them. I dream about them every night and you are scarcely absent from my thoughts waking or sleeping.[75]

In March 1850, James finally trekked to his parent's home to reclaim Mary and the children, then hurried them on to Buffalo, where he planned to meet a group of new converts going to Beaver Island. By the time they arrived in Buffalo, Mary and the children were ill, so he left them there and continued on. "We felt very bad to think that Mary and the children were left at Buffalo, unwell, and among strangers & very little money," James's mother wrote to him. With a hint of suppressed indignation and perhaps a mother's intuition, Abigail continued: "I would like to know what engaged your attention last winter to keep you so long absent from your family. I hope you will endeavor to be with them more, and try to make things comfortable around you.... Do not let [your] whole soul be taken up in trying to make yourself

---

75. James Strang to Mary Strang, Jan. 25, 1850, Strang Letter Book 73, Beinecke Library.

appear great in the eyes of man that must soon die and turn to dust."[76]

Like Mary, the Saints in Voree and on Beaver Island were anxious about their prophet. "We received your letters, one from Detroit and one from Bever," Phineas Wright wrote from Voree. "I am sorry to here that sister Strang is sick. I hope she will be up in a few days[;] we ware overjoyed to receive a letter from you so close to home[;] the constant query is when will Brother Strang be at home?"[77]

---

76. Abigail Strang to James Strang, spring 1850, folder 117, Beinecke Library.
77. Phineas Wright to James Strang, Apr. 17, 1850, folder 538, Beinecke Library.

6

MEANWHILE BACK WITH THE SAINTS
1849-1850

*I must say, then, with regard to Voree
that the saints are in the "unity of spirit, in the bond of peace" of one heart
and of one mind in the purposes of God, to work with all their might in the
great work of the last days.... The temple has progressed more this season
than it has before since Voree became a place of gathering; and although
there is but a little done compared with what there is to do, yet we think
our brethren abroad would not consider us slothful, if they knew the poverty and want that their brethren here had passed through. —Samuel P.
Bacon in the Gospel Herald.* [1]

W hile Strang was casting missionary nets in the eastern cities, the
Mormons left behind in Voree and on Beaver Island struggled
to make ends meet. During the fall and winter of 1849-50, the members of
the Order of Enoch in Voree pooled their financial resources, but they were
still very poor. Each time they seemed to get caught up financially, someone
left, taking their money and belongings with them, and the order had to re-
group all over again. If the members decided not to return the consecrated
possessions, they found themselves the object of a lawsuit.

The decision not to return consecrated property may have been based on a
section of the Book of Commandments, considered by members of the church
since Joseph Smith's day to be scripture. In it, members were commanded to
remember the poor and consecrate property for their support. Once properties
were consecrated, "they cannot be taken from the church," Section 42 read,
"and it shall come to pass that he that sinneth and repenteth not shall be cast
out of the church, and shall not receive again that which he has consecrated
unto the poor and the needy of my church, or in other words, unto me." [2]

---

1. "Voree," *Gospel Herald,* Nov. 29, 1849.

2. The Book of Commandments was later renamed the Doctrine and Covenants (see
D&C 42:30-37).

Wingfield W. Watson, one of Strang's followers, later explained: "Those who had means were required to buy out the lands of Voree so that the poor might have a home as well as the rich, and that a temple might be built and the work of the dispensation might go on. The lands in Voree at this time were nearly all in the hands of speculators and the poor could not reach [buy] them."[3] It was Watson's view that Strang never intended to abandon Voree for the Beaver Islands, but that there should be two colonies of the church. Strang, in fact, thought if a few leading men from Voree started businesses on the island, it would provide work and land for poorer members. The plan was to start fishing and wood-cutting industries, build houses and docks, obtain necessary merchandise and supplies, and then offer the poor a place there.

Once the immigrants arrived on the island, each family was given a parcel of land, or "inheritance," on which to live and produce goods. For instance, settlers could cut wood on their inheritances and sell it to Mormon businessmen, who in turn would sell it as fuel to the steamboats that called throughout the shipping season. "So the work went on, one business creating and calling for others, and blacksmiths, carpenters, boot and shoemakers, sawmill, and other mills and every one was busy winter and summer," Watson noted.[4]

While they supported such visionary concepts, the Saints in Voree struggled to get by. They set aside their resolution not to go into debt as they were forced to borrow heavily to purchase supplies and equipment. By mid-September 1849, the order was being sued by two former members. Strang's old law partner, Caleb P. Barnes, represented the church and its members in court.[5] Determined to see the settlement succeed, Benjamin Wright, who had been put in charge of the Voree stake, decided to take a group of men to work in the western Wisconsin lead mines to earn some much-needed capital.

"I have taken the diggins to work and we shall do well," Wright communicated to Strang in mid-September.[6] The participants in this project included Benjamin's brother Samuel, Zenas Gurley, David Powell, and a few

---

3. Wingfield Watson to Milo Quaife, Jan. 21, 1919, Clarke Historical Library, Central Michigan University, Mount Pleasant, Michigan.

4. Ibid.

5. B. G. Wright to James Strang, Sept. 13, 1849, folder 532, James Jesse Strang Collection, Yale Collection of Western Americana, Beinecke Rare Book and Manuscript Library, Yale University, New Haven, Connecticut.

6. Ibid.

others. They had heard about the success of the mining in Galena, Illinois, about 150 miles west of Voree, which was considered to be one of the richest lead-bearing regions in the world at the time. In addition to quantity, the lead was particularly pure. The deposits would later play a roll in assisting the Union in the Civil War. However, the Strangite group went to work in the Snake Diggings in nearby Potosi, Wisconsin, where Benjamin and his brothers had worked for several years before moving to Voree.

The richness of the lead mines appealed to people of all professions. Those who tried their hand at exploiting this natural resource included physicians, editors, lawyers, statesmen—all of whom saw an opportunity for great wealth. Investors tended to purchase or lease a plot of land and begin "sinking a shaft" into the ground about four to six feet wide and from ten to twenty feet deep. The ground was dug out with pick and shovel and shored up with timbers as the digging progressed. The miners worked by the light of tallow candles. After the initial hole was dug, they excavated additional shafts branching away from the opening. These were sometimes several hundred feet long. Ground water was the biggest obstacle the miners faced, as it had to be pumped out. When they hit lead ore, the miners would bring it to a central mine works where the smelters and furnaces melted away the impurities.[7]

The work was difficult. The men worked up to ten hours at a time underground in the wet and cold. Often they became sopping wet despite the short leather covering they wore on their backs. At times they could not find a dry spot on their clothes to lite a match.[8] Some of the Voree Mormons considered mining to be dangerously speculative and opposed Wright's plans, which proved to be a well-founded concern. After three months of hard digging, the first mineshaft failed to produce any ore.[9] Back in Voree, Gilbert Watson wrote to Strang in late November 1849: "The last news from Benjamin was very unfavorable. He had sunk a shaft smartly through rock sixty feet and realized very little. He has commenced on another."[10] Watson hoped Wright would be:

---

7. "Galena and Its Lead Mines," *Harpers New Monthly Magazine,* May 1866, 681-96.

8. Autobiography of Wingfield Watson, unpublished manuscript, 10, Clarke Historical Library. Watson worked in the lead mines before joining the Strangite Church.

9. Dennis Chidester to James Strang, Nov. 16, 1849, folder 282, Strang Collection, Beinecke Library.

10. Gilbert Watson to James Strang, [Nov. 30, 1849], folder 512, Strang Collection, Beinecke Library.

fortunate enough to realize something handsome for it has been attended to by a
good deal of expense and trouble & we need the means. Our taxes must be paid
and if possible, men, women & children shod for the winter. A considerable
many are somewhat dissatisfied about the speculation out in the mines, especially in having the steward of the Order out there all the time.... Not a few are
anxious to have our business carried on with more order and fear it cannot be
done under the stewardship of Bro. Wright.[11]

The Saints who remained in Voree prepared for winter by harvesting
their crops and finishing off the building of several houses. Some of them
were ill with typhoid fever. Still, even with Strang gone for an extended period of time, most remained strong in the faith. "Our meetings are very instructive and interesting, also attended by manifestations of the spirit of
God," Dennis Chidester wrote to Strang.[12] In spite of their relative poverty,
the Strangites were assisting those who were less fortunate. An example of
this was the care they offered to a young pregnant woman from Canada. "The
girl had the misfortune to get knocked up and left her home in Canada that
[her] family might not be disgraced," Gilbert Watson wrote to Strang. She
and her family had been baptized by Jehiel Savage when she was eight and
"she recognized him [and] clung to him as her protector. After counseling
the matter over ... [he] decided to bring her here and take care of her." The
girl was taken in and cared for by the family of Phineas Wright. She gave
birth at the Wright home a few months later.[13]

Samuel P. Bacon gave an update of the situation in Voree for the November 29, 1849, issue of the *Gospel Herald,* saying they were in "unity of spirit,"
that "the warm part of the season has passed away, and very little time has
been misspent or unimproved."

The fore part of the season was spent in repairing and making fences, assisting
brethren in emigrating to Beaver, at work on the [storage] Tower upon the Hill
of Promise, putting our seed in the ground, expecting by the blessing of God to
reap a rich harvest, when the harvest season should roll around. And so it has
been. Our crops are now secured, or nearly so. Quite a number of our houses

---

11. Ibid.

12. Dennis Chidester to James Strang.

13. Gilbert Watson to James Strang, Oct. 7, 1849, folder 509, Strang Collection,
Beinecke Library. Phineas Wright was away from Voree on a church mission during this
time.

have been finished inside, and more are in progression, and probably nearly all the rest will be completed soon. The Tower has been raised one and half stories high for about twenty-five feet in length, a roof put on, lathed, plastered and finished up for habitation the coming winter.

He noted that the temple was progressing reasonably well, although there was still much to be done, on the temple and otherwise, for Voree to meet people's expectations for "a place of gathering."[14]

As the Saints struggled to construct the temple out of stone, the quarry at Voree kept filling up with water. It was time consuming and expensive to pump it out. They wanted to buy more land adjoining the quarry to expand it but had no funds to do so.[15] Gilbert Watson wrote that the brethren were "generally firm in the faith" even though "it is pretty hard times, but nothing so bad as it was last year at this time. Our houses are mostly [ready for] occupancy for the winter. Yet cold weather is coming on and there is a great lack of clothing, especially for the children. There are a great many much in want of boots and shoes. And very little means of getting any."[16]

The members earned some money by fishing and hunting and selling the meat in Burlington.[17] Most families shared their homes with others. Like ordinary folk throughout the world, they also bickered and griped about their neighbors and fellow church members. Someone complained that John Comstock had left the Order of Enoch because "he thinks we are not religious enough," and a henpecked Brother Stiles left the order under the direction of his wife "who wears his underclothes." Mrs. Stiles threatened to do anything she could to prevent new members from joining the association.[18]

---

14. "Voree"; Manual Hahn, "Freedom of the Press," unpublished manuscript, ca. 1940, 90, Library-archives, Wisconsin Historical Library, Madison, Wisconsin. Hahn said the door for the Tower of Strength was made of stout oak, "bossed" and protected by heavy iron spikes. During the Civil War, the heavy doors were torn down and used for a nearby barn.

15. Wingfield W. Watson, interviewed by Milo M. Quaife, Dec. 10-11, 1918, Clarke Historical Library.

16. Gilbert Watson to James Strang, Nov. 30, 1849, folder 512, Strang Collection, Beinecke Library.

17. John Cole to James Strang, Dec. 3, 1849, folder 514, Strang Collection, Beinecke Library.

18. Alden Hale and Gilbert Watson to James Strang, Dec. 30, 1849, folder 513, Strang Collection, Beinecke Library.

Two Strangites, Alden Hale and Gilbert Watson, thought the problems in Voree were due to some people feeling they were superior to others. "Some people will apostatize," they said, "when they get their first suit of [communal] clothes and find out they are plain."[19]

As New Year's Eve approached, the youngsters in Voree wanted to stage a dance, but older members thought it was inappropriate for God's people to dance and that it would be an unnecessary extravagance in any case. They suggested a feast instead, followed by a religious fast, or abstaining from food, on New Year's Day itself. Hale and Watson wrote to Strang asking what to do. However, Strang was busy in the East and did not respond. The subject of the dance exposed the extent of dissatisfaction in Voree among the young people. One young man, who had married the previous fall, owned a new broadcloth suit and a pair of expensive boots to wear to the ball. Other young men complained about their rough, plain clothes and exclaimed they would "rather go to hell" than submit to the indignity of such attire "when others wore their broadcloth and fine boots."

Hale became so concerned about this attitude, he decided to let the people vote whether or not to have a dance. "I laid the matter before the brethren nearly on this wise," he explained to Strang. "The Lord one year gave us a severe rebuke by saying he had given us good gifts & we had consumed them on our own lusts ... & that it was the same to lust after fine clothes, or to satisfy ourselves in dancing." Hale explained that there were "good and honest men" among them who would "bolt" from the church if members held a dance, "having been trained in the gentile tradition that dancing is one of the most damnable sins that there is in the world." He was concerned about paying for items considered absolutely necessary for the occasion, estimating the order would have to pay ten to sixteen dollars for shoes suitable for dancing.[20]

Community members drew lots to decide whether or not to hold a dance or feast on New Year's Eve. Those who wanted the feast won the draw, "but the young people were determined to have their ball." Several of them, including F. Baxter, Andrew Hale, Andrew Porter, Ulysses Porter, and Anson W. Prindle went to Burlington and "paid 75 cents a couple" to attend a dance "and went in debt for slips for themselves and ladies," Watson wrote to

19. Ibid.
20. Ibid.

Strang. "This created no little feeling. And I am afraid it will be the cause of quite a fuss," he continued, "for besides injuring the feelings of many brethren and sisters, [some] difficulty with the gentiles has grown out of it. There being some misunderstanding between A. J. Porter and a fellow from Vienna." Gilbert added in code that a "collector" had arrived from the nearby town of Vienna claiming some clothing had been stolen and that he wanted to search the community. He was allowed to do so but nothing was found.[21]

Benjamin Wright returned to Voree in early December and again in January with money for property taxes[22] even though he had not made any progress with his search for lead. Corresponding with Strang from Potosi, he admitted that "after a great deal of hard work we find the water so strong that we are obliged to abandon the diggins." He tried to justify his venture by saying that what he had done was "with a hope to forward the cause." Recently he had taken $195 to Voree "that helped pay our taxes and some other things and am in debt as much here." He could not understand why he had not been successful in the mining venture. "Are we not the children of the Lord," he asked, "and as such called upon to build the temple and tower and to redeem our possessions at Voree?" In desperation, musing over the underlying problem, he suggested a radically different approach.

> Has not the Lord said that he would give his saints the riches of the earth? After a good deal of anxiety for the cause, Brother Cole and myself has agreed to ask [you] Brother Strang if it would be right for [you] to look in the Urim and Thumim and tell us where we should get a lead for the building of the temple and tower. If it is right tell us and if not tell us what to do and we will obey. The Lord [is] helping us for we have no other hope but in obedience to the commandments of the Lord. Now Brother you may smile at our folly, but in exposing our folly we often learn wisdom whether in adversity or prosperity.[23]

Strang did not reply, and Wright continued to fret about his failure to earn money for the gathering place in Voree. "Since my failure in the mines, I have not eat[en] nor slept with composure," such were his "anxieties" over "the building of the temple and tower." Comparing Strang to Moses in a let-

---

21. Gilbert Watson to James Strang, Jan. 4, 1850, folder 158, Strang Collection, Beinecke Library.

22. Ibid.

23. B. G. Wright to James Strang, Jan. 10, 1850, folder 287, Strang Collection, Beinecke Library.

ter at the end of January, Wright said he hoped "that when you come down you will not break the tables of stone nor withhold from us the celestial law."[24]

The lawsuits against the Order of Enoch were not going well either. In early February, Watson wrote that Strang was being sued for $42 for books and $150 for a threshing machine. A "dunning letter," or collection notice, had been received from the mines for $225. Another collection notice had been delivered to a particular member, and the order owed $200 to someone named Shelden.[25] "These all taken together make quite a sum, especially when we have nothing to pay it with," Gilbert conceded. "Our enemies think that we are down. And unless God delivers us we are. We are worse off now than we were a year ago.... But I have not lost hope yet, I believe God will open some way for our deliverance. I believe that thos[e] what remain in the Order now are all firm and unshaken in the faith."[26]

Hoping to redeem the mining fiasco, Benjamin Wright bought half interest in a cooper shop where he and another member worked making barrels and other items. "I have not ritten to you for some time and hardly [k]now what to rite, things are in such a state," he communicated to Strang in April. "The reason I have not ritten oftener is that I have nothing very comeferting and to disturb your mind with things that you could not remedy I did not wish to do[.] We expected you in March. Until of late we are like sheep without a shepherd."[27]

While most of the Strangites were struggling in Voree, the Beaver Island population had grown rapidly. In the first year of settlement, only four Mormon families wintered there. In 1848 that number had tripled to twelve, and by the winter of 1849 there were nearly fifty families permanently settled on the island.[28] The number of steam ships stopping for wood or supplies had increased from no more than four ships in 1847 to sixty-two ships which stopped to take on supplies and fuel the following year. One observer, Mr.

24. B. G. Wright to James Strang, Jan. 29, 1850, folder 535, Strang Collection, Beinecke Library.

25. Gilbert Watson to James Strang, Feb. 11, 1850, folder 515, Strang Collection, Beinecke Library.

26. Ibid.

27. Benjamin Wright to James Strang, Apr. 3, 1850, folder 537, Strang Collection, Beinecke Library.

28. "Progress of Beaver Island," *Gospel Herald,* Jan. 3, 1850.

Greeley, calculated at least 100 harbor visits during 1849 and estimated the amount of freight and passengers to and from the island during the upcoming season would reach at least $3,000, a substantial amount of money in 1850.[29] Fishing proved to be the most extensive industry, the fisheries extending north of Beaver Island for fifty miles, south for forty miles, and east and west the entire width of Lake Michigan.[30]

Several eastern newspapers noticed the sizeable migration to Beaver Island. The *Boston Globe* published the following:

> It is on these Islands that the Latter Day Saints, or the peace party of the Mormon people in pursuance of a professed revelation ... to Mr. James J. Strang, ... have commenced a settlement and invite all industrious Law abiding people of their faith to come and possess an inheritance forever, without money and without price, asserting that God has given them the right of soil, on which to establish the Kingdom of God, or the fifth universal Empire that is to subdue all nations and stand forever. This people claim no fellowship with the Salt Lake Mormons or any of their high handed wickedness, but expect to conquer all by love and rendering good for evil.[31]

Strang had left several trusted followers on the island in the fall of 1849 to maintain stability and apprise him of developments. One of those men, James Greig, wrote to the prophet in November 1849 to report that "as to our temporal matters, as a people, they are as good as any other people in a new country. Some of the brethren were a little fearful about provisions not being brought on to the Island," Greig wrote, "but we think there is enough and to spare; And those who deal in wood are bidding up to 62½ c[en]ts per cord for wood in the woods, and provisions will be much cheaper than they were last [year]. With the exception of a grumbler or two, we are sanguine of a pleasant and prosperous winter."[32] His account continues, full of details:

> We have four good substantial dwelling houses, which make eight in [the village of] Troy. We expect now to go on with the Mill until it is completed; we have been partly eaten up by lazy men, but think we shall outlive all these things. As

---

29. Ibid.

30. "Beaver Islands," *Gospel Herald,* Feb. 7, 1850.

31. Ibid.

32. James Greig to James Strang, Nov. 16, 1849, folder 354, Strang Collection, Beinecke Library.

for spiritual matters, we have but little to say as there is but little [or] has been no material change since you left us. There is no schism or rebellion. We meet four times each week, and generally have good meetings. Sometimes [we] rub each other up a little, just to keep from rusting; We all enjoy first rate health, and the spirit of the Kingdom, and a mind for the establishment thereof....

I wish you to bear in mind, that the gentiles are spreading themselves abroad on the Island; and cutting off all the valuable timber. [Peter] McKinley and [Alva] Cable have gone largely into the lumber business, and employ all the fishermen they can persuade to winter on the Island. Can no means be devised by which the timber can be spared to actual settlers[?][33]

On December 26, 1849, a group of Strangites, including Elvira's father, Reuben, and her brother Albert, gathered at the "new city" of Troy to form their own branch of the Order of Enoch on Beaver Island. Members resolved to be governed by the law of God, to conduct their business as if they were one family, and to pay a tithe on their increase beginning the first of January. They also resolved to keep their proceedings to themselves until Strang returned, then to ask him in person for his approval or disapproval.[34]

By the end of February 1850, a few "warm, strong" dwellings had been constructed. Locked in by ice on the Great Lakes, the Saints created their own fun on the island. "For amusement we have had dancing frolics until we have run that thing into the ground," Greig wrote to Strang. "We resolved in the stake not to associate with the gentiles in our amusement, but this raised such a fuss that the resolution was rescinded." He said the sailors on the island "abused our people and raised such a disturbance" that "it gave us a fine opportunity and a good excuse to let the gentiles alone," which pleased Greig.

"I do hope you will bring some good Mormons with you in the spring when you come on, and some of the best," Strang's informant implored. In the meantime, Greig thought they had gotten "the [gentile] sailors and fishermen by the ears." He continued:

I have been at Cable[']s [trading post] at the [head of] the Island and ... find they expect help from their friends east and intend to monopolize that end of the Island. McKinley, with Young and others, are stripping the Island of all the best <u>pine</u> and <u>ash</u> for staves, etc. I bethought me they could not do much without

---

33. Ibid.

34. "Resolutions of the Order of Enoch," Dec. 26, 1849, folder 76, Strang Collection, Beinecke Library.

saws, froes [cleavers], etc, so I have been up two or three times to look after some of our [missing] tools. I found some and some are lost altogether. The Cables have got some 200 stave bolts off the peninsula in Lake Gennesaret.... A stop must be put to this plundering or our home will soon be desolate.[35]

All the while in the eastern United States, James Strang was enjoying his mission with his personal secretary, Charles Douglass. When Charley became ill, James left her to recuperate in Baltimore while he traveled to Washington, D.C., in an attempt to meet with government leaders. He hoped to see the Beaver Islands granted exclusively to the Mormons for colonization but was unsuccessful. He wrote to Voree apprising the Saints of his plans to return home: "I am going hastily from here to New York and Boston, where large numbers are getting ready to go up with us," adding that "a company of 30" were "now on their way from the far-off State of Texas bound for Beaver. We shall go up and divide the land by lot, and a beautiful possession it will be." Realizing that he was luring people to the island with the promise of free land, he acknowledged that the Bible says "it is better to give than to receive. This is true; but its truth depends on circumstances. When one has given all he has, then it is better to receive. Many of the saints have been in that situation a long time. It is better for them to receive. They shall now inherit the earth."[36]

George J. Adams wrote an article for the same issue of the *Gospel Herald* encouraging the Saints to move to Beaver Island:

Let every saint who wants an inheritance without money and without price, as the gift of God, come to Beaver as early this season as possible. Let them that want sickness, accidents, vexatious law-suits, and other troubles and disappointments, stay among the Gentiles, that they may be robbed and plundered a little longer. Let them that want to be deceived, and deny the faith, put their money in a Gentile bank, and spend about $50.00 in going up to see if it is a good place, and find out whether the servants of God have lied to them or not. Let them that want to stand in the kingdom of God and prosper, and become mighty men of renown, take their means and go to Beaver, get their inheritance, go into busi-

---

35. James Greig to James Strang, Feb. 28, 1850, folder 355, Strang Collection, Beinecke Library.

36. "Philadelphia, Pa., March 8th, 1850," *Gospel Herald*, Mar. 28, 1850. Strang was in contact with the George Miller and Clarke Whitney companies, Miller's group being at the time in Zodiak, Texas, with another would-be successor to Joseph Smith, Lyman Wight.

ness as a steward over their own house, and God will prosper them on every side, just as surely as he will curse the others.[37]

Both Strang and Adams gave the impression they had obtained title to the islands from Congress and that the Mormons could settle there without paying for the land. Unfortunately, this was not true.

On April 10, 1850, Strang wrote to the *Gospel Herald* from on board the propeller *Illinois*. Accompanied by a small party of Saints, he had departed from Buffalo and was headed home. They arrived on Beaver Island two days later, on the evening of April 12, in the midst of a fierce storm.[38] Neither the prophet's nephew, Charley Douglass, nor his second wife, Elvira Field, were mentioned in the letter. Elvira's return to Beaver Island would be as mysterious as her leaving it.

---

37. "Baltimore, Md., March 6th, 1850," *Gospel Herald,* Mar. 28, 1850.

38. "Propeller Illinois, Detroit River, April 10th, 1850," *Gospel Herald,* Apr. 25, 1850; also a note in the paper that Strang and his family had landed on Beaver Island. The part about his family arriving with him may have been an incorrect assumption because Strang's mother said Mary and her children had been left behind in Buffalo. See note 76, chapter 5 of this volume.

7

THE IMPERIAL PRIMATE

1850

It pleased God to call together a general Assembly of the Saints, through his Apostle & Prophet James J. Strang, ... to assemble on Big Beaver Island in Lake Michigan, for the purpose of Establishing the Kingdom of God on the Earth according to the scriptures.... Our enemies were numerous & determined, by the spirit of wickedness which was in them, to prevent the Lord & his people from Establishing the Kingdom. On the other hand: the Saints were diligent, in doing the things which God required of them, & by their vigilance by day & by night, accomplished what the ancient Saints were not able to accomplish. —Warren Post, "Record of the Apostles"[1]

S trang traveled from New York to Beaver Island to evaluate the growing colony, then continued on to Voree, where the poverty of the Order of Enoch was painfully obvious. Members were anxious to be on their way to the island where they could get an "inheritance" for free. Land, when available for purchase in the Burlington area, was expensive. The association was still involved in several lawsuits with former members.

In mid-June 1850, Strang chartered a ship to transport settlers and his newspaper press to Beaver Island, arranging for a skeleton crew, including Benjamin, Phineas, and Samuel Wright and their families, to remain behind to manage the church's property. Strang then traveled to Racine to assist the members who were to board the schooner *J. C. Spencer.* He wrote to Benjamin Wright with last minute instructions: "[Samuel] Shaw arrived here yesterday morning early with the [indecipherable] J. C. Spencer in fine condi-

---

1. Warren Post, "The Record of the Apostles of James, Written During 1854-1863, Relating to the Events of 1844-1856, James J. Strang, the Mormons, and Beaver Island, Lake Michigan," unpublished manuscript, 1, Clarke Historical Library, Central Michigan University, Mount Pleasant, Michigan; cf. *Record of the Apostles of James, 1844-1856,* facsimile ed. (Burlington, WI: John J. Hajicek, 1992).

tion & we [will] go on her. It is a better charter than we could otherwise get and saves much expense—all can go who can get ready. No lack of room.... Do not fail to send the heavy box of type [for the press]," he reminded.[2]

The Mormons who arrived on Beaver Island about a week later found it to be a virtual paradise. James Blakeslee, writing earlier in the *Gospel Herald*, had expressed the same impression. In fact, he found the land to be as good or better than represented, with plenty of sugar maple, cedar for posts and rails for fences, fine stands of balsam fir, good quality white and Norway pine, and some oak and beech. The land was good for farming except immediately at or about the harbor and on the shores, which were sandy and rocky.[3] Wood sold quickly for $1.50 per cord, he reported, because it was needed by the steamboats which traveled up and down the lakes. Men who chopped wood earned as much as fifty cents per cord. "Any smart boy, of a dozen or thirteen years of age, can chop a cord of steamboat wood in a day, and do it easy," he observed. "All with whom I have conversed say that they have wanted for nothing since coming to the Island, and no industrious person need want for any of the comforts of life on this land." "Come, then," he urged his "brethren who are scattered abroad," and "gather up your families and property and come up to the places that God has appointed for the saints to gather to, and take an active part in preparing places of safety against the day when the wrath of God is poured out upon the wicked."[4]

Another Strangite, Nathan Foster, echoed Blakeslee's praise. "I am much pleased with this land, much better than I had anticipated," he wrote to readers of the *Gospel Herald*. "This is a good place for the rich and the poor, the widow and fatherless, freedom and equal rights to all the saints throughout the world, and no deaths from starvation. Thanks be to God. Now, brethren, you that can gather up with me when I return from the east for my family, which will be in the course of two months, I should be glad of your company."[5]

When Strang first set foot on the archipelago in 1847, the big island was

---

2. James Strang to Benjamin Wright, June 13, 1850, folder 62, James Jesse Strang Collection, Yale Collection of Western Americana, Beinecke Rare Book and Manuscript Library, Yale University, New Haven, Connecticut.

3. "For the Gospel Herald," *Gospel Herald*, May 17, 1849.

4. Ibid.

5. "To the Brethren in Kos Konong and Porter," *Gospel Herald*, May 17, 1849.

home to three white families, four or five white men with Indian wives, and a few individuals of French Indian extraction. About twenty or thirty single men came to the island each year to spend the winter.[6] About 2,000 Native Americans, members of the Ottawa and Chippewa tribes, lived nearby in five Indian villages. Some of the Indian men and women could read and write, although most, except for the children, could not speak English. The Indians were devout members of the Catholic Church and had a priest who made periodic visits.[7]

Over the course of three years, the handful of gentiles on the island grew increasingly antagonistic toward the new immigrants, who upset the established order of business in the small community. Until recently, the island had been under the influence of the powerful fur and fishing interests centered on Mackinac (also called Mackinaw) Island, about forty miles to the east where Lake Michigan, Lake Superior, and Lake Huron join together. In 1608, the French had built a fort on Mackinac, and over the years it had served as an important defensive position for the French, English, and Americans because of its sheer bluffs and cliffs.

At the end of the War of 1812, Mackinac had become one of the main headquarters of John Jacob Astor's American Fur Company. Between 1816 and 1834, Mackinac traded as much as $3 million worth of furs in exchange for merchandise, making American Fur Company the largest business concern in America. Its chief activity involved bartering furs, skins, and buffalo robes, which were in demand for hats and other apparel, in exchange for manufactured goods from the east coast and Europe.[8] Mackinac was ideally located for such trade. Furs, fish, and other products could be easily loaded onto ships and transported to the Atlantic Ocean. The cost of transportation was much less by water than attempting to send heavy pelts overland.

By 1850, Mackinac had a population of about 3,600. Most residents were employed in the fur trading and fishing industries.[9] However, Mackinac was a community under stress, the fur trading industry having nearly

---

6. "Emmet County," *Northern Islander,* Feb. 2, 1854.

7. Ibid.

8. Roger Pilon, "Introduction to the American Fur Company Records, 1832-1851," Joseph H. Steere Special Collections, Bayliss Public Library, Sault St. Marie, Michigan.

9. James Strang, *Ancient and Modern Michilimackinac, Including an Account of the Controversy between Mackinac and the Mormons* (1854; Ann Arbor: University of Michigan Library, 1987).

run its course; nor was there any longer the need for defense, and the rocky ground proved to be an impediment to crop production. The island had depleted its wood supply and had to import lumber to feed the steamships that stopped at the island for refueling. The profitable Great Lakes fishing industry, which had previously produced up to 250,000 barrels of fish a year, was in similar decline. Once, at least half the fish caught in the entire Great Lakes region had come to Mackinac to be salted, repacked, and sent to market, and merchants and traders on the island had provided fishermen with equipment, boats, and supplies—but no longer on the same massive scale.

When the main group of Strangites began settling the Beaver Islands in 1850, more than half of Mackinac's fishing trade had been relocated closer to the fishing areas, such as at Washington Island, St. Johns, St. Helena, Detour, and Duncan. These communities had wood for steamships and other support for the shipping trade. Mackinac was no longer the hub for Great Lakes-centered commerce and was rapidly losing its power as an administrative center for frontier government. For its survival, the island had come to rely on retail trade through its extensive sale of liquor, especially to fishermen and Indians.[10]

The Mormons represented competition for the gentiles not only on Beaver Island but also on Mackinac and the other surrounding islands. Located in the middle of the fishing industry, Beaver Island had an abundance of lumber, a hardworking labor force, and a natural harbor that could provide protection and shelter to many ships at a time. The Mormons could not have been more different than their gentile neighbors. Mormons tended to be educated farmers from the northern half of the United States, driven by religious commitment, willing to better the plight of the black man and "noble savage." They were idealists anxious to build a civilization filled with government, schools, and churches and had little tolerance for anyone who opposed them. They were clannish—suspicious of anyone who was not of their religious movement—and teetotalers dedicated to ridding the world of alcoholic beverages. They also voted en masse according to how their religious leader instructed them. As a whole, the Mormons believed they were God's chosen people, with a responsibility to convert others to their religion. They believed that the second coming of Jesus Christ was imminent and that

---

10. Ibid., 9-13.

this grand event would include the destruction of all who opposed the Mormon expansion.

By contrast, most gentiles were hardworking and honest, but they were not necessarily well educated. Many had come to the fisheries to get away from civilization rather than out of a desire to transform the wilderness. They saw larger government as an infringement on civil rights and liberties. Some of them were fugitives from the law and hid out in the fisheries because it was difficult for law enforcement to track them there. Whatever reason each man had for locating in the expansive Great Lakes area, none was eager to see more settlers, implying competition and decreased fish harvests. The gentiles were apprehensive of the political power implied by bloc voting, distrustful of people who blindly followed a religious leader, no matter what religion he represented. Some were willing to take advantage of outsiders. The traders sold adulterated whiskey and other inferior products to Indians in exchange for hard-earned fish and furs. An increasing number of Irish Catholic settlers escaping the famine and poverty of their homeland presented more easy targets and a ready clientele for alcoholic beverages.

During the fall of 1849, several of the gentile traders on Beaver Island announced they would not sell provisions to the Mormons and advised those who lacked their own supplies to get off the island before winter came. One of the Strangites, Samuel Shaw, went to Chicago and persuaded a lumber firm to ship provisions to the island in exchange for wood. When the ship arrived, the gentile traders dropped their prices so that Shaw had a hard time trying to make up the cost of the cargo.[11]

Before long, the conflicts between the two groups escalated. During the winter of 1849-50 as several Mormons were busy cutting down trees, they were attacked by large group of men from Whiskey Point, the trading post run by Peter McKinley on the eastern side of Beaver Harbor. A young Mormon, Spaulding Lewis, was severely beaten because he refused to quit harvesting wood. In another incident, a group of gentiles crashed a Strangite debating school, interrupting the proceedings with "rude and filthy conduct, sometimes accompanied by threats and violence." On New Year's Day 1850, a large number of men appeared uninvited at a Strangite party; before the evening was over, they had beaten two men for the "sole reason that they were Mormons."

---

11. Ibid., 24

The post office at Whiskey Point was an unavoidable destination for Strangites even though they were "subject to all manner of abuse" when they went there to collect their mail. Sometimes they were beaten. Others had their letters taken from them before they left the post office. Some gentiles, pretending to be drunk, went to Mormon homes while the men were absent and exposed themselves to the women and children in a "beastly manner, accompanied by vile language and threats of violence."[12]

Most of the ships visiting the island landed at Whiskey Point, including the ships carrying Mormon passengers. The immigrants were frequently threatened on the boats and wharves, typically a dozen or more surly men surrounding a family and ordering them back on the boat. The men would shout that they were going to drive off and kill all the Mormons on the island and prevent anyone else from landing. For this reason, more than a few immigrants lost heart and reconsidered their decision to settle on Beaver Island. One company of fifty-four Strangites from New York on the steamer *Empire State* expected to disembark at Beaver, but the boat passed by the island and refused to land, "undoubtedly" intimidated by "the traders and fishermen," Strang wrote in an account of the controversy between Mormons and gentiles.[13]

At first the Strangites "neither resisted nor retaliated" and adhered strictly to the principle of non-violence. This changed as more and more Mormons arrived and the power began to shift in their favor. By late spring 1850, between 600-700 Mormons had settled on the island. They publicly announced they would no longer submit to injury and aggression, that they would return "blow for blow" and "stroke for stroke" and would punish every man who "insulted or intruded' upon them.[14]

Gangs of gentile fishermen and sailors sometimes attended Mormon church services in order to interrupt them. The Strangites countered by assigning guards to patrol the meetings. Strangers coming to the services were escorted to seats dispersed throughout the congregation, then the guards would walk up and down the aisles with heavy canes. At the first show of dis-

---

12. Ibid.

13. Ibid.

14. Ibid., 25; also Elvira Field Strang and Charles J. Strang, "Biographical Sketch of James J. Strang," unpublished manuscript, n.p., Strang Manuscript Collection, Library and Historical Center, State Library of Michigan, Lansing, Michigan.

turbance, the stranger was pulled out of his seat and escorted from the building. If anyone spoke up for the offender, they too were shown the door. After two or three instances, the gentiles stopped disturbing the meetings, although they quickly found another way to annoy their pious neighbors. As Strangites kept their Sabbath on Saturdays, a typical workday for gentiles, the workers found one reason or another to drive their oxen past the Strangite meeting place, creating noise and confusion.

To many uneducated people living on the rough frontier, the men's antics were considered good fun, a little "horseplay" performed at the Mormons' expense. The Strangites took these "high jinks" more seriously than they might have had they not been driven from Ohio to Missouri to Illinois for the sole purpose that they were different than their neighbors. The bulk of the church membership had lost their homes and some had been tarred and feathered, raped, and robbed in three states before their arrival in Michigan. They were not inclined to put up with horseplay on Beaver Island.

One of Strang's followers was a fifty-five-year-old woman, Ruth Napier, whose husband, William, had been killed at Haun's Mill, Missouri, in 1838.[15] In that incident, more than 200 Missouri militiamen had surrounded the small community and fired on men, women, and children. When the shooting stopped, eighteen men and boys had been murdered and another twelve to fifteen seriously wounded. An unarmed ten-year-old boy who was found hiding under the bellows in a barn was shot in the head at point blank range while his father, lying mortally wounded nearby, pleaded for the boy's life.[16]

Some of Strang's followers had been exiled from Missouri in the dead of winter under an "extermination order" signed by the governor of Missouri, Lilburn W. Boggs. Many Mormons had left behind valuable homes and farms in Nauvoo and Hancock County, where members of the sect had once

---

15. Finley Page, deposition, *People of Michigan vs. Joseph W. Vincent,* Burton Historical Collection, Detroit Public Library; Parley P. Pratt Jr., ed., *Autobiography of Parley P. Pratt* (1874; Salt Lake City: Deseret Book Company, 1994), 174.

16. Stephen C. LeSueur, *The 1838 Mormon War in Missouri* (Columbia: University of Missouri Press, 1987), 167. To be fair, LeSueur also documents Mormon depredations in Daviess County, where armed Mormon militia rode out against the county seat of Gallatin, burned it to the ground, and sent gentile women and children packing in the snow. Mormon mobs also destroyed the town of Millport and plundered and burned outlying gentile farms (112-37, esp. 117-18). The war is traditionally dated to a Fourth of July speech delivered in 1838 in Far West, Missouri, by Mormon leader Sidney Rigdon, in which he threatened retaliation against the gentiles (49-53).

again been driven out. Persecution was constantly on the minds of the Strangites who made their homes on Beaver Island. To a person, they were not going to put up with any fun from Irish rowdies, fishermen, or anyone else.

Strang and his family set up housekeeping in the main settlement on the island, St. James, named after the prophet. Other small villages such as Troy, Enoch, and Galilee were soon to dot the island. According to the federal census of 1850, Elvira Field is listed in the census as a member of both Strang's household and that of her own parents.[17] Elvira's children later said their mother had not lived with Strang until after his coronation. If this was true, the duplicate listing may be because it was Strang who reported the names of the members of his household and had not wanted his second wife to be excluded.

Exactly when Mary first learned of her husband's relationship with Elvira is unknown. Church members in Potosi, Wisconsin, and the eastern cities had been gossiping about the union from as early as 1849. There is no official record of when the marriage was announced, but presumably it occurred about the same time the Strangite scripture, Book of the Law of the Lord, was published in 1851. If Elvira lived in the Strang household, she could have been introduced as a live-in schoolteacher, James's secretary, or as someone to help Mary with her children. It was not uncommon in early 1850 for families to live together on the island under the same roof until separate homes could be built. According to census records, the Strang household also included Catherine Hall, a thirty-six-year-old unmarried woman, and her daughter, Augusta, seven.[18]

It is also possible that James was already becoming involved with other women. Two of Elvira's sons, Charles and Clement Strang, later said their father had an unknown number of concubines on the island. "In addition to these [plural wives], there were 'concubines' who bore children for him, but who were not publicly classed or recognized as wives," Charles J. Strang wrote. "Of these I do not know how many, nor their names and addresses."

---

17. 1850 Federal Census, Mackinac County, Michigan, entries 517-33, 536, 554. The person who answered the census taker's questions did not know where Elvira was born and answered "unknown."

18. Ibid., entries 517, 533; *United States vs. James J. Strang*, Detroit Public Library. Hall was unmarried, as evidenced by her deposition in Strang's Detroit trial, wherein she is referred to as Katherine Hall or Miss Hall, while the other women are identified by their husbands' last names.

Charles said this was based on "statements made to me by mother, and partly on facts learned elsewhere."[19] Chauncey Loomis, a Strangite who later left the church, confirmed that Strang had concubines.[20] A letter from 1893 suggests that one of the women's surnames was Kinney.[21] There was, in fact, a woman by that name, Eunice Kinney, who was a strong supporter of Strang all her life. She was also married. If the information in the letter was true, Kinney's marriage would have been a good reason for Strang to claim her as a concubine instead of a plural wife. Historian Milo Quaife interviewed many Strangites in the 1920s for his book, *The Kingdom of Saint James*,[22] and happened on the following entry from Charles Strang's diary: "During conversation with Clement [Strang] in regard to [his] father, the subject of 'concubines' was touched. I asked him if he had ever heard of any. Said he had.... He mentioned 'the raising up of seed' by the childless widow, with the aid of the 'prophet[,]' to the glory of the departed husband. One of these [children] named Kinney is a young and prosperous lawyer in Wisconsin; another, [Clement] did not know the name, lived in Illinois or Indiana."[23]

Another possible concubine was a woman named Townsend. A newspaper article at the Clarke Historical Library includes the following notation in Charles Strang's handwriting: "Concerning concubines, Clement has told me there were two sons, one a lawyer named Kinney, believed somewhere in Illinois. Mother says there was one by the name of Townsend. She [Elvira] was always mad about this transaction as it seemed to her nothing but whoredom."[24] There was a family named Townsend among Strang's followers.[25]

By early summer 1850, the Mormons in St. James were preparing for a special conference to take place beginning the first of July. The concluding

---

19. "Some Corrections Made by One of the Family," *Detroit Evening News*, Feb. 26, [no year]. The article was pasted onto a sheet of paper, and Charles Strang, the correspondent for the article, wrote these words on the sheet next to the article. Strang Manuscript Collection, Clarke Historical Library.

20. Chauncey Loomis, "Experience on Beaver Island with James J. Strang," *Saints Herald* 35 (Nov. 1888): 718, copy in the Library-Archives of the Community of Christ, Independence, Missouri.

21. Charles E. Dyer to Wingfield Watson, Mar. 27, 1893, Clarke Historical Library.

22. Milo M. Quaife, *The Kingdom of Saint James: A Narrative of the Mormons* (New Haven: Yale University Press, 1930).

23. Quaife's notes, Charles Strang diary, Sept. 2, 1880, Clarke Historical Library.

24. Charles Strang, "Some corrections." See note 19 above.

25. William Townsend, deposition, *United States vs. James J. Strang*.

ceremony on the eighth day would commemorate the fourth anniversary of Strang's original revelation to organize the church. It would also be Elvira's twentieth birthday. Strang's Quorum of the Twelve Apostles were told to be at the conference without fail. It was apparent to everyone that something extraordinary was going to take place.

In the days leading up to the conference, almost everyone living on the island, including the women and children, were invited to take the oath of the Illuminati or oath of the covenant. Placing their hands on a cross, which was placed in a Bible, they swore allegiance to Strang as "the Imperial Primate and actual Sovereign Lord and King on Earth" and their "true and lawful Sovereign wheresoever and in whatever kingdom state or Domain" they lived, all in "preference to the laws, commandments and persons of any other Kings, Potentates or States." They pledged to "yield obedience to the revelations he shall give … and the decrees he shall make, as the supreme Law, above and superseding all laws, obligations and mandates of any other person, authority or power whatsoever."[26]

The gentiles on the island must have heard about the secret oath and felt threatened by it. Already suspicious, they would have seen these clandestine developments as a threat to open political discussion. In particular, the rumors circulating about an oath of loyalty sounded treasonous. Most Strangites had no problem swearing fidelity to Strang, and some later claimed they saw nothing disloyal to the United States in it. One member, Alonzo Cheeseman, testified there was "nothing in the covenant he could not live up to—nothing rendering a man liable to any law." Cheeseman said if there was anything in the covenant a man could not live up to, he should not take the oath. Another Strangite, Hiram Beckwith, stated that when he got to the part about acknowledging Strang as king and renouncing other laws, or words to that effect, he took his hand off the cross. He said he could not consent to it and would not sign the document.[27]

While the Mormons were making plans for their conference, the gentiles were initiating a Fourth of July celebration. According to an account

---

26. "Book of the Covenant," folder 188, Strang Collection, Beinecke Library, in which the complete oath appears in an appendix. This document includes the names of 234 people who took the Oath of the Covenant. The original document was obtained by Clement Strang, who said the book from which these pages were cut was given to him by Anson Prindle, a former Strangite residing at Black River Falls, Wisconsin, in 1890 [1880].

27. Depositions from Strangites, *United States vs. James J. Strang.*

published four years later in Strang's newspaper, the *Northern Islander*,[28] the neighboring fishermen and traders planned "a glorious and patriotic celebration of Independence—to be consummated by the expulsion of the Mormons."[29] The plan was to transport men and guns on board several small vessels from Mackinac Island to arrive at Whiskey Point on the night of July 3. The next morning, carrying concealed weapons, the men would go to the meeting the Strangites had scheduled. They would arrive either alone or in small groups and find seats as close as possible to each other near the speaker's stand and clerk's table.[30] The fishermen were to start "talking, drinking and swearing" during the service and initiate a fight with anyone who tried to stop them. Then they would surprise the congregation with their pistols and bowie knives, scatter the crowd, and kill the Mormon leaders before their people had time to organize a defense. This was to be followed by a general debauching of the women and burning of houses.[31]

The Strangites learned of the plans and called in church members from distant places to serve as reinforcements. With utmost secrecy, they obtained a cannon, guns, and a stock of ammunition, and began drilling in an area where they would not be seen. From Chicago they obtained a large schooner and anchored it in the harbor. During the night, the ship was filled with armed men who kept out of sight below the deck.[32] As the gentile fishermen began to gather at Whiskey Point on Tuesday, July 3, the Mormons assembled to hear instructions from Strang and other leaders. James W. Greig kept notes. "I have been much pleased by the remarks of my brethren in relation to mobs," Strang told the congregation. "Their words are my words and I reit-

---

28. The *Northern Islander* was the first newspaper published in northern Michigan. It appeared once a week on Thursdays during the shipping season and intermittently throughout the winter and spring. For a few weeks in early 1856 it was published daily.

29. "First Attempt to Drive the Mormons from Beaver," *Northern Islander*, Mar. 2, 1854. Strang wrote the only known account four years after the incident allegedly occurred; also in James Strang's *Ancient and Modern Michilimackinac, Including an Account of the Controversy between Mackinac and the Mormons* (1854; Ann Arbor: University of Michigan Library, 1987), 25-26. Historian Roger Van Noord in *King of Beaver Island: The Life and Assassination of James Jesse Strang* (Urbana and Chicago: University of Illinois Press, 1988), 103-104, gives his belief that the incident never happened, that Strang invented it to whip up hysteria against the gentiles and make himself appear the hero.

30. *Northern Islander*, Mar. 2, 1854.

31. Ibid.

32. Ibid.

erate them. I will execute with my own hands the sentence of death against the enemies relative to putting up a mob.... Give me 4 men who don't falter where I lead and I will make a full end of all our enemies." Greig remarked that Strang spoke so rapidly, he could not keep up and eventually had to abandon his note taking.[33]

George J. Adams told the assembled Saints he had been "informed that a mob is to be convened on the fourth for the purpose of breaking up our assemblies and also to drive us from the island. We wish all persons to understand us," he continued, "and remember this declaration: We will not be the aggressors[.] We will not go out of our way to avoid the threats of those who make them, and we give this warning that all men may know what to expect at our hands[.] Whoever comes against us as a mob shall have their names Hated and from under heaven! ... I give them notice that every person who [is] not of this church and are found in the ranks of our enemies or with mobs shall die!"[34]

For safety, the Strangite women and children stayed in the tabernacle that night rather than return to their homes. With a carefully selected group of men, Strang sneaked out to reconnoiter developments at the trading post where the fishermen were partying. The Strangites poured some of the fishermen's gunpowder into the lake and put tobacco in one of the barrels of whiskey, causing the revelers to become even more drunk.

At dawn the next morning, the Fourth of July, the Mormons used their cannon to fire a "national salute" in the direction of their gentile neighbors at Whiskey Point. It was apparently the first indication the fishermen had that the Strangites were in possession of a cannon. "The men were more than a little alarmed to discover that, at every boom of the cannon, the balls skipped along the water, past Whiskey Point, scarcely two rods from them, and were regularly getting the range for their buildings," Strang would report to the *Northern Islander.*[35]

The Strangites then assembled together within the unfinished walls of their tabernacle. Eight men with guns stood guard while twelve men kept the

---

33. Remarks of James Strang, Tuesday, July 3, 1850, noted by James W. Greig, folder 187, Strang Collection, Beinecke Library.

34. Remarks of George Adams, Tuesday, July 3, 1850, noted by James W. Greig, folder 187, Strang Collection, Beinecke Library.

35. *Northern Islander,* Mar. 2, 1854.

cannon ready for use and the cannon balls heated. Other patrols were constantly on the lookout for the enemy. Strang addressed his congregation and related the circumstances of the "scrape," as he called it. According to the notes Greig made of that speech, Strang remarked: "They think they can kill the church by killing me, but I tell you that tho they kill me ... they cannot kill the work or church. It depends on God only."[36]

Before evening, the Strangites learned that the plans to exterminate them had been postponed because several companies had not arrived on time. Some of the gentiles had grown afraid of possible retaliation, especially from the Mormon artillery. Eventually, all the rabble dispersed and the Mormons continued their conference without disturbance. Some of the gentiles who had been involved in the Fourth of July celebration later tried to make friends with their neighbors, pretending there had been no hostile intent, the *Northern Islander* reported. Others kept up a "continual clamor that the destruction of the Mormons had been only postponed, not abandoned.... From time to time a new day was fixed for the onslaught, and confidentially committed to some timid persons among the Mormons, in the hope of frightening them away," the article explained.[37]

Only a few select Mormons realized what grandiose ideas Strang had in store for the July 8 convocation. Elvira Field knew because she had helped Strang make a crown out of heavy paper, covered with gold tinsel.[38] George Adams knew because he was providing the stage props and scenery; but there is no indication Mary Perce knew anything about it. Strang's intention was to be crowned king and imperial primate of Beaver Island.

John C. Bennett was living and raising chickens in Plymouth, Massachusetts, but he had advance knowledge of the coronation. He wrote to Strang on May 29 to give his regrets for not being able to attend the "organization of the kingdom as they had discussed.... However, I wish you every success and you can rely upon me as I told you, in any regular position." Bennett offered to assist Strang by overseeing the imperial guards at the coronation, then sent some special cross-bred chickens as a coronation gift for use

36. Remarks of James Strang, Wednesday, July 4, 1850, noted by James W. Greig, folder 187, Strang Collection, Beinecke Library.

37. *Northern Islander,* Mar. 2, 1854.

38. Clement Strang, interviewed by Milo M. Quaife, Feb. 12, 1921, Clarke Historical Library.

on the island. Bennett clearly still considered himself part of Strang's organization. He concluded by writing, "I hope you will organize in a grand [fashion]—let the 'Imperial Guards' be <u>magnificent</u>—and as the 'General in Chief' I desire it well issued with able, energetic and efficient men."[39]

On the morning of July 8, the Strangites assembled in the unfinished Mormon tabernacle, which had been completed to a height of seven or eight feet. The building was made of hewn timbers and had a temporary cover so meetings could be held inside. That morning about fifty or sixty members simultaneously swore the oath of allegiance, the officiators holding several crosses and bibles at the same time. The initiates waited for the unique events of the day to begin. It was just about noon. "There was a curtain drawn in front of the stand so as to conceal from view anything that might occur behind. But as George Adams was a play actor, we expected to see some great performance," Chauncey Loomis recalled. "When ready to exhibit, the curtain was drawn aside and to our great astonishment we beheld Strang sitting in a large chair with a crown on his head and scepter in his hand.... Such a scene never presented itself before or since."[40]

A young woman, Cecilia (Seaman) Hill, later remembered that the coronation was preceded by a procession of about seventy "dignitaries of the church" dressed in scarlet robes, who walked to the altar of the church. The men walked with impressive dignity.

Like any young woman under similar circumstances, I was anxious to be present and managed to get into the tabernacle. At one end was a platform and towards it marched the procession of elders and other quorums, escorting the King. First came the King, dressed in a robe of bright red, and accompanied by his council. Then followed the twelve elders, the seventy and the minor orders of the ministry, or quorums, as they were called. The people were permitted to occupy what space remained in the tabernacle.

The chief ceremonials were performed by Geo. J. Adams, president of the council of elders. Adams was a man of imposing presence. He was over six feet tall and he towered over the short-statured King, who however, made up in intellect what he lacked in frame. Adams had been an actor, and he succeeded in making the crowning of the King a very imposing ceremony. It ended by placing

---

39. John C. Bennett to James Strang, May 29, 1850, folder 288, Strang Collection, Beinecke Library.

40. Loomis, "Experience on Beaver Island."

upon the auburn head of Strang a crown of metal. The crown was a thin circlet, with a cluster of stars projecting in front.[41]

Cecilia's husband, Ludlow Hill, a former resident of Beaver Island, said of the coronation that "the president of the council, George J. Adams, a man of the most striking personality, was master of ceremonies. He had been an actor and arranged the rites so as to appeal to the spectators."[42]

Strang was clad in a long gown that some said was part white and part red,[43] others remembering it as having been just red. Adams called for the president of the apostles, Samuel Graham, to bring forth the "royal diadem." With his own hands, Adams placed the crown "studded with stars" on Strang's head and proclaimed him "king of earth and heaven."[44] The ceremony continued with several men being ordained to various positions in the priesthood and a few being tried for transgressions.[45] John E. Page, Joseph Smith's former apostle who joined with Strang rather than Brigham Young, was among those who were excommunicated. As "James, the Anointed" sat upon his throne swaying his royal scepter, the congregation raised their hands and "covenanted with God to be His people and to keep His laws and statutes."

Warren Post wrote that God had chosen the Strangites to be "his people, and then gave us a portion of his footstool for an everlasting inheritance, as it

---

41. "Saw a King Crowned: Woman Living at Fish Creek Recalls a Most Curious Incident," *Green Bay Advocate*, Feb. 7, 1905; also in Henry E. Legler, *A Moses of the Mormons: Strang's City of Refuge and Island Kingdom* (Milwaukee: Parkman Club, ca. 1897), 163. Some details of the coronation, such as the use of the curtain, appear to be in contradiction, but it is also possible that, for instance, the procession may have proceeded to the front, at which time Strang may have separated himself to take a position behind the curtain. When the curtain opened, it may have shown him sitting on a throne, crowned or about to be crowned. That Cecilia Seaman thought the paper crown appeared to be metallic only confirms the artistry of those who prepared it.

42. Ibid. Ludlow Hill would later say his family was Mormon but that he was not. In any case, he would become one of Strang's opponents.

43. Mercy Ketchum, deposition, *United States vs. James J. Strang.*

44. "Saw King Crowned." In the eyes of Ludlow Hill, the coronation was "one of the most spectacular impositions ever practiced before deluded American citizens."

45. Post, "Record of the Apostles," 1-2. The apostles called during the meeting were Samuel Graham, as president of the quorum, and James Blakeslee, Ebeneezer Page, Jehiel Savage, and Phineas Wright. There were already seven apostles: Samuel P. Bacon, Samuel Bennett, Hiram P. Brown, Lorenzo Dow Hickey, Albert N. Hosmer (an assumption by Post), Edward Preston, and Warren Post.

is written in the Book of the Law of the Lord." Post said a passage was read from the Book of the Law of the Lord at the coronation, "namely the second chapter concerning the true God," after which, "with uplifted hands," the congregation "covenanted with God" and bore "record that the Kingdom of God is set up on the Earth no more to be thrown down."[46]

Warren's brother Stephan wrote in his journal that it had been a day "long to be [re]membered," among the "grand features of this day" being "the crowning of a king in Zion & the electing of a grand council of 8 for the setting up of the kingdom of God on the earth[.] The scene was solemn & impressive[.] King James was hailed as king in Zion by one unanimous voice of the whole congregation[.] The day[,] long looked for by prophet[s,] was [declared] at length [to have] arrived."[47]

There are a number of similarities between the coronation of James Strang and of Joseph Smith in March 1844 by the Council of Fifty. Strang was surrounded by men like George J. Adams and George Miller, former members of the Council of Fifty who had been present at Smith's crowning in Nauvoo, and it would have been a natural progression for Strang, as Smith's successor, to organize his own coronation. An important part of the Mormon belief structure was the future establishment of an actual kingdom of God on earth. Only then could the wicked—the gentiles who oppressed the Saints— be destroyed.

Some Strangites said their leader claimed only the Mormon people as his subjects, that he had asserted this office through revelation, just as Old Testament prophets had done.[48] Whether or not Strang actually committed treason against the United States may ultimately be less important than the fact that his enemies believed he had.[49] Reports of a coronation and rumors of Strang's polygamy were discussed in the public square. Not a few members and would-be followers became disenchanted. "A report carrying about here," James Blakeslee wrote Strang from Illinois, that "you have two wo-

46. Ibid., 5.

47. Stephen Post, journal, July 8,1850, Archives Division, Historical Department, Church of Jesus Christ of Latter-day Saints, Salt Lake City, Utah.

48. Wingfield Watson to the *Charlevoix Sentinel*, July 17, 1877, Clarke Historical Library.

49. Klaus Hansen, "The Making of King Strang: A Re-examination," *Michigan History*, Sept. 1962, 202-205. Hansen believes the coronation was consistent with Strang's character, considering the coded portions of his diary relating to ambition and power.

men, and the people seem to be more willing to Believe evil, than good."[50]

Charles Greenwood in Boston wrote in September about "certain evils that are practiced on the Island by some of the Saints and appear to be approved of." He chided Strang, writing:

> In the first years of your administration, the Saints truly had reason to rejoice for the noble stand you took in behalf of virtue, truth, and righteousness. It causes me much pain and sorrow to think that some of those that should be our teachers by example, as well as by theory, are the first to teach false doctrine.... And contra to the Doctrines taught in your own writings.
>
> I do hope that those that have been teaching those things that are contra to the laws of the church will see their folly and be brought to repentance. As to the Doctrines that are taught and practiced by certain individuals—I understood they [are] kn[o]w[n] also in Baltimore [and] N.Y.[51]

Amos Lowen said he stood almost alone in Philadelphia in defending Strang. "As to the cry of Polygamy against us[,] I will neither deny or affirm at present[,] but the time is at hand when I shall publicly avow the doctrine and I expect to make more converts to the faith than I ever have before," he boasted.[52]

Even Louisa Sanger, Strang's disabled friend in Ottawa, Illinois, rebuked him for his shocking behavior. She summed up the feelings of the disenfranchised Mormons searching for a leader:

> You will perceive that I have not yet departed this life, nor started for the Salt Lake, nor the Colorado, nor even for Beaver Island, and it seems quite uncertain when I shall do either. There is so much light in this 'enlightened age' that I am quite dazzled and bewildered; for before my eyes become accustomed to one good 'luminary' another starts up like a comet and scatters so many sparks that I am entirely blinded by its brilliance; and I am not always this sure, but it would be the wisest course to let the motions all pass and return to the sober 'lights of service.'[53]

---

50. James Blakeslee to James Strang, Oct. 4, 1850, folder 244, Strang Collection, Beinecke Library.

51. Charles Greenwood to James Strang, Sept. 5, 1850, folder 12, Strang Collection, Beinecke Library.

52. Amos Lowen to James Strang, Dec. 7, 1850, folder 420, Strang Collection, Beinecke Library.

53. Louisa [Sanger] to James Strang, Apr. 18, 1850, folder 159, Strang Collection, Beinecke Library.

Strang may have been able to dazzle the young and impressionable members of the congregation with the drama of his coronation, and he may have convinced Elvira Field and other women when he boldly proclaimed himself to be above the law, but a growing number of church members were not buying Strang's presumption of royal privilege, and the indignation among the gentiles was growing ever greater.

8

THE WRATH OF THE GENTILES
1850-1851

> *George J. Adams was viceroy at the time of the coronation & assisted in the ceremonies. He however soon left the Church in consequence of his corrupt heart in following after lewd women & also by the entreaties of his wretched wife Louisa. He tried to make havoc of the church and drew away some of the baser sort after him; and they devised lies, to get the United States, Enlisted against us in order to destroy us from off the face of the Earth: But the saints prospered, & the Kingdom prevailed.* —Warren Post, in "Record of the Apostles." [1]

While most of the Strangite Mormons had moved to Beaver Island, Benjamin Wright remained with his brothers in Voree, where a touchy situation developed in mid-July. A Strangite, Luther Prindle, was suspected of stealing a horse and was in jail at Mineral Point near the lead mines. Benjamin went to see what the matter was and succeeded in getting him out on bail. "It seemed he lost his presance of mind," Benjamin explained to Strang. "It has been an unpleasant time but it is over. I think Luther is sufficiently punished for his folly and will learn wisdom and will not be caught in another such scrape."[2]

Two weeks later, Benjamin wrote again to inform Strang that George J. Adams had been in Voree. "He has pseudoed," Benjamin reported. "He went to John E. Page and told him all about the organization that he could[;] he

---

1. Warren Post, "The Record of the Apostles of James, Written During 1854-1863, Relating to the Events of 1844-1856, James J. Strang, the Mormons, and Beaver Island, Lake Michigan," unpublished manuscript, 5, Clarke Historical Library, Central Michigan University, Mount Pleasant, Michigan; cf. *Record of the Apostles of James, 1844-1856,* facsimile ed. (Burlington, WI: John J. Hajicek, 1992).

2. B. G. Wright to James Strang, July 16, 1850, folder 540, James Jesse Strang Collection, Yale Collection of Western Americana, Beinecke Rare Book and Manuscript Library, Yale University, New Haven, Connecticut. Some of the Strangite men had continued to work in the lead mines, trying to earn money for their families and/or the church.

says Strang has t[w]o wives and his council was in like manner [of] corrupt men. I recon if you had given him t[w]o wives and then supported him he would have thought you was a clever fellow."[3] And so it was that Wright gave Strang an early warning that George J. Adams, viceroy in Strang's kingdom, was about to betray him. As the fall of 1850 approached, it became more and more apparent that Adams was unhappy with the church. Oddly enough, the source of Adams's dissatisfaction was Adams's own polygamy, not Strang's.

As early as 1847 Adams had written prophetically of Strang's coronation in a letter from Boston: "I have come to a firm conclusion. I shall unfurl the banner of the cross. Spread, by God's help, the glorious principles connected with it, and will never desert it until the kingdom is established; until I see the beautiful fabric raised in all its grandeur, majesty and simplicity; until I see the last stone brought up and raised before all the people with rejoicings and shouts of [hosanna] unto it."[4]

Adams had said he would not leave until the kingdom was established, so in that sense he had kept his word—it was done. "Now I wish it understood that as I am to go on a long and perilous mission. I want no man to go with me who will not stand by me—drunk or sober," Adams told the Strangites the night of July 3, 1850, before the gentiles' Fourth of July celebration, "for when I am sober I can take care of myself but should I be so unfortunate as to get drunk as Noah did I then want a friend who will stand by me right or wrong."[5] Few in the congregation that night would have realized how soon Adams would fall into transgression and that they would have to choose between him and Strang.

When Adams arrived on the island in early summer 1850, it was with a woman named Louisa Cogswell. Adams claimed his wife, Caroline, had died and that he had remarried, saying Louisa was a wealthy widow from a family in South Carolina. Adams stayed on Beaver Island for a few weeks after Strang was crowned, then left for a church mission on August 1. Louisa remained behind in St. James. She was a young woman in her late twenties and was said to be alluring. A reporter wrote in 1866 that "her face is oval, her neck is short, bust full as a prima donna's, her eyes dark blue and sharp, her

---

3. Wright to Strang, Aug. 1, 1850, folder 541, Strang Collection, Beinecke Library.

4. "Boston, September 8th, 1847," *Gospel Herald,* Oct. 7, 1847.

5. Remarks of George Adams, Tuesday, July 3, 1850, noted by James W. Greig, folder 187, Strang Collection, Beinecke Library.

voice pleasing, her tongue exceedingly voluble and her command of language ready. When not excited or angered by opposition her conversation is intelligent and ladylike and her tongue runs like a pepper mill."[6]

Adams disapproved of some of Strang's new converts, especially Hezekiah D. McCulloch, a surgeon from Baltimore who had arrived on the island in the spring. Perhaps a little jealous of the doctor's talent and influence, or even apprehensive because McCulloch had friends in the east who may have known of Adams's questionable reputation, he wrote to Strang shortly after leaving the island to complain that McCulloch had treated him in a way that was "damn mean, meaner than I was eaver treated by a Saint before." Adams cautioned Strang to watch out for McCulloch, while reassuring the prophet of his own loyalty: "All are not true men that appear to be.... Men will come to you with tales about me—yes! And women too—listen not to their Slander—you know I am a true man but you don't realize how true I am and what I will do to serve you ... All men and things will proove themselves. May my King live forever; yours in love, truth and everlasting fellowship."[7]

Adams had not been gone long when the true story of his "deceased wife" was received from church members in the east. Adams had taken an ailing Caroline to the home of a member in New Jersey and left her there for dead.[8] But Caroline did not die until July or August 1850, several months after the grieving "widower" had already remarried.[9] Strang learned Adams's new wife was, in fact, not a rich widow but a prostitute Adams had met in Boston. Not too long after this discovery, Strang had a disagreement with Louisa, although the cause and substance of it are unknown. Strang allegedly

---

6. Clarence Day, "Journey to Jaffa," 29, copy in the Doyle C. Fitzpatrick Collection of Strang Papers, Library and Historical Center, State Library of Michigan, Lansing, Michigan. The description of Louisa was written in 1866 by a reporter working for the *Portland Press*. Her weight in 1850 is not known, but sixteen years later she was considered "quite fat."

7. George Adams to James Strang, Aug. 1, 1850, folder 212, Strang Collection, Beinecke Library.

8. Depositions of Moses Chase, Katherine Hall, Franklin Johnson, Mrs. F. Johnson, Hezekiah McCulloch, Mrs. H. McCulloch, Edward Preston, David Whipple, and Mrs. David Whipple, *United States v. James J. Strang*, Burton Historical Collection, Detroit Public Library.

9. Amos Lowen to James Strang, Oct. 6, 1850, folder 419, Strang Collection, Beinecke Library. Lowen wrote that Carolyn Adams died at Brother Flagg's house in July or August.

threatened Louisa that if she did not leave Beaver Island, her life would be in peril.[10] Louisa responded by drawing out a bowie knife and threatening to put it into Strang's heart if she had the chance.[11]

When Adams returned to the island in the early fall, he was censured, but forgiven, for having abandoned his true wife and having taken up with a prostitute. But Adams was not pleased with the way Louisa had been treated while he was gone. During a church conference on October 13, the new Mrs. Adams was excommunicated. Vowing an "eternal war and a war of extermination," the couple left Beaver Island that same day.[12] They headed for Mackinac Island, where there were plenty of gentile ears willing to hear the stories they had to tell about Mormon atrocities.

Over the next few months, Adams instigated a number of legal actions against Strang, charging him with having threatened his and his wife's lives and of stealing the stage props Adams had used at Strang's coronation. As a result, Strang was imprisoned at Mackinaw on several different occasions, but the charges were dropped in each case.[13] A number of Strangites later testified that Adams tried to get up mobs against them and that he openly advocated burning Mormon houses, slaughtering the men, ravishing the women, and making a spoil of Mormon property.[14] This testimony is ironic because only a few months earlier while Strang was absent at Voree, Adams had held a secret council and plotted to "burn out and ruthlessly destroy" Peter McKinley's trading post on Whiskey Point. This was to be in retaliation for the Mormons having been beaten, assaulted, and robbed of their mail. Adams tried to keep the council concealed, but Strang heard of it and "condemned it strongly."[15]

Word of the division between Strang and his right-hand man spread

---

10. "Administration of Justice," *Northern Islander*, Feb. 2, 1854. Louisa claimed he told her if she did not leave the island, he would ride her out backwards on the back of a black ram.

11. Ebeneezer Page, deposition, *United States v. James J. Strang*.

12. Ibid.

13. "Administration of Justice," *Northern Islander*, Mar. 2, 1854.

14. Depositions of Marvin M. Aldrich Jr., Moses Chase, Alonzo Cheeseman, Samuel Graham, James Greig, Anderson G. Hopper, Franklin Johnson, Hezekiah McCulloch, George Miller, Edward Preston, and Phineas Wright, *United States v. James J. Strang*.

15. Depositions of Andrew Hopper and Franklin Johnson, *United States v. James J. Strang*.

quickly among the scattered Mormons. "The news of Adam's treason & der-eliction has not surprised us in the least—no, not if you-yourself had been assassinated & your wife made a Widow by [his] ruthless hands," James and Louisa Canney wrote prophetically from New York City.[16] In fact, one wonders how Mary Perce Strang reacted to the unfolding events and if she was concerned about her husband's safety, not to mention her reaction to her husband's coronation. But the record is quiet about her possible disposition. She and her children lived on Beaver Island from the spring of 1850 through May 1851. She was said to have been well respected in the community and "greatly loved by all those who knew her."[17] Mary may well have filled an important position in the community as a translator since she had studied French when she was in school in New York. Many of the nearby Chippewa Indians and Canadian traders spoke only French.

Mary enjoyed drama and was part of a thespian group on the island that sometimes performed in the tabernacle under George Adams's direction. On the night of October 8, 1850, Mary was playing the part of Cora in the play *Pizzaro* and became so ill she could not finish her performance. Nor could she be comfortably moved, so she spent the night in the building.[18] The Mormon surgeon, Hezekiah McCulloch, examined her the following morning. He described her as "extremely feeble, low, and in an extremely critical state." No one in the building was allowed to speak above a whisper as "Mrs. Strang was very sick." Her husband stayed by her side in constant attendance that evening. His other wife, Elvira, had not attended the evening performance but was in the tabernacle with James the following morning.[19]

It would be speculation to project the idea that Mary had become aware of Elvira's connection to her husband and what her reaction may have been, but Mary did contact her relatives in Illinois and Wisconsin to ask for help in getting off the island. By October, Elvira would have been about three months pregnant with James's child. Only four weeks after Mary's illness in the tabernacle, her brother, William Perce Jr., wrote to Strang asking if his

---

16. James and Louisa Canney to James Strang, Nov. 18, 1850, folder 278, Strang Collection, Beinecke Library. Canney's words would come true on July 9, 1856.

17. Elizabeth Whitney Williams, *A Child of the Sea and Life among the Mormons* (n.p.: by the author, 1905), 78.

18. Depositions of Asa B Field, Anderson Hopper, Hezekiah McCulloch, and Daniel Wheelock, *United States v. James J. Strang*.

19. Hezekiah McCulloch, deposition, *United States v. James J. Strang*.

sister and her children could come live with him in Elgin, Illinois. Perce said he was concerned because he had heard the Strangites would be short of food and supplies that winter.[20] Simultaneously, navigation on Lake Michigan was coming to a halt for the season and Beaver Island would soon be sealed off from the rest of the world until spring. Whether by choice or otherwise, Mary and her children remained on the island through the winter.

Oddly, Mary did not write to James's parents from the time she left their New York home in April 1850 until sometime the following year. Abigail Strang wrote to her son about Mary and the children in November, saying she was "very disappointed in not receiving a letter from Mary." She enclosed a note for James to deliver to his wife, in which she said, "I suppose your sickness last spring prevented your writing according to agreement?"[21]

Strang's parents and siblings were growing increasingly concerned about his change in profession from lawyer to cleric. "I cannot express to you the anxiety of our parents for your well being, the deepest longing of soul," his sister Myraette wrote to him early in his career. "When I think of my beloved brother in a far-off land, the propagator of strange doctrines; my heart sinks within me; & I know not how to address you. I have nothing to say in regard to the motives which may have actuated you—but I entreat—I beg you, in the name of all that is near and dear to you, all that is sacred; pause and think of the solemn and fearful responsibility you have taken upon you."[22]

By the fall of 1850, Strang's parents had learned about his split with George Adams and pleaded with him to make his own break with the Mormons. "We mourn on account of your confiding in & associating with men of his character & standing & most earnestly wish to see you clear from such company," his mother wrote. "We feel troubled about you, and fear that your life will be taken. I really desire to have you settle off with all with whom you have associated & return to private life where you may live free from your present toils and troubles, enjoying the blessing of life with your family, quiet

---

20. William Perce to James Strang, Nov. 10, 1850, folder 145, Strang Collection, Beinecke Library.

21. Abigail Strang to Dear Children [James and Mary Strang], Nov. 1, 1850, folder 188, Strang Collection, Beinecke Library. The illness Abigail speaks of is probably from the spring of 1850 in Buffalo, New York. Mary was ill so frequently, it is hard to know which illness is intended.

22. Myraette [Strang] Losee to James Strang, May 5, 1846, folder 120, Strang Collection, Beinecke Library.

& unmolested."[23] On another occasion, Abigail wrote that she would like to visit James but was afraid of traveling on the Great Lakes and did not want to leave her parents behind in New York.[24] Nevertheless, within the next three years, she and Clement would pack their belongings and make the long passage to Voree. It may have been an attempt on their part to convince their son to give up his religion and figure out why he had more than one wife.[25]

Propelled by the "treachery" of George Adams, the situation between Mormons and gentiles on Beaver Island gradually became worse. Each group accused the other of robbery, arson, illegal voting, and threatening the lives of citizens. In September 1850, Eri J. Moore, a trader on the island who had briefly joined the church and subsequently married a Mormon woman, wrote to the governor of Michigan complaining about the sect. He reported his Mormon neighbors were engaged in stealing and murdering, counterfeiting, illegal voting, and threatening people's lives. He said he was concerned he had not seen or heard from someone named Hall who had last been seen on Beaver Island and was believed to have been murdered by the Mormons.[26]

In a second letter to the governor, Moore reported that "there has been a larger body of their kin ordered by James J. Strang and his Privy Council to go in small bands out through the different parts of the Union and Burn Cities and Villages and to kill any person that may come in the way & to rob steal & plunder everything they can lay their hands on; and especially to Procure all Guns and Ammunition that they possibly can." Accusing the group of counterfeiting, he urged the governor to send men to take the "whole band" of Mormons into custody and usher them out of the state or send them to prison. "There will be blood shed in the North and the sooner there is force used the less Blood will be shed & if they can be taken it will save the Burning of Cities," he predicted.[27]

---

23. Myraette Losee and Abigail Strang to James and Mary Strang, Nov. 20, 1850, folder 124, Strang Collection, Beinecke Library. This letter also incidentally brought news to Mary of another death in her family, that of her Aunt Freelove, at whose marriage in 1834 James Strang had been a witness.

24. Abigail Strang to My Dear Child [James Strang], ca. Nov. 1850, folder 119, Strang Collection, Beinecke Library.

25. James Strang to David Strang, Nov. 10, 1853, Clarke Historical Library. James reports to his brother that their parents arrived in Burlington without mishap.

26. Eri J. Moore to the Governor of Michigan, Sept. 26, 1850, Detroit Public Library.

27. Eri J. Moore to the Governor of Michigan, Mar. 8, 1851, Detroit Public Library.

Strang, in turn, accused the gentiles of stealing letters from the post office at Whiskey Point, putting their mark into wood belonging to Mormons, and stealing staves from barrel makers.[28] He added a complaint about the plight of Native Americans, who were being taken advantage of. He explained that when they took their canoes to the spot where they were supposed to receive their annual government annuity, they ended up waiting for weeks. While they waited, they had to survive on credit from the traders. The Indian men spent their time drinking—on credit, of course. When the annuity finally arrived, it had already been spent and the Indians were more reliant on the traders than before.[29]

The traders and fishermen were making a tremendous profit by selling adulterated alcohol to the Native Americans, Strang explained. He said they called it "Indian Whiskey," made by diluting two gallons of alcohol with thirty gallons of water and by adding enough red pepper to make it fiery and tobacco to make it intoxicating. "Its cost is not above five cents per gallon," he elaborated in the *Northern Islander.* "Thousands of barrels have been sold every year, the prices generally being fifty cents per gallon by the cask, twenty-five cents a quart by the bottle and six cents a drink…. More than half the fish taken by the Indians for thirty years have been paid for this [way] and more than half their annuities … laid out in the purchase of it."[30]

In an effort to suppress the whiskey trade, the Mormons passed a law in 1851 that required traders to post a bond before they could sell intoxicating liquor. The bond was meant to ensure against property damage by the traders' customers, but it merely became another sticking point in the tense Mormon-gentile standoff. No trader on Beaver Island could afford to post the security bond, but all continued to sell alcohol.[31]

During February 1851, the Strangites heard that Eri J. Moore was on Garden Island selling whiskey to the Indians. Knowing the Indians would conceal and possibly defend the trader, the Mormon sheriff took along a posse of eleven men to help him take Moore into custody.[32] In actuality,

---

28. "Indian Payments," *Northern Islander,* Aug. 7, 1851; James Strang, *Ancient and Modern Michilimackinac, Including an Account of the Controversy between Mackinac and the Mormons* (1854; Ann Arbor: University of Michigan Library, 1987), 16.

29. "Indian Payments."

30. "Indian Whiskey," *Northern Islander,* Feb. 2, 1854.

31. Ibid.

32. Court records, *United States v. James J. Strang,* Detroit Public Library. The Mor-

Moore had been on Garden Island earlier in the day but had already left to go across the ice to Mackinac for supplies and to deliver the mail. He made the trip by dog sled, accompanied by his wife and several other men and Indians including a postal carrier. The Mormon posse reached the Indian village, searched until they were satisfied Moore was not there, then started back across the ice to Saint James. As they came around a point of land, they saw Moore and his party returning to Garden Island. Having run into broken ice, Moore had decided he could not continue to Mackinac. The Mormons chased after Moore, who escaped into the woods, assisted by the Indians and several white men.[33]

As soon as the ice broke up on Lake Michigan, Moore went to Mackinac to obtain warrants against the thirty-nine Strangites who had put him "in fear of danger," charging them with arson, robbery, and burglary. The sheriff of Mackinaw, Henry Granger, traveled to Beaver Island to execute the warrants. He was unable to do so because Strang and eleven of the men listed on the warrant had gone to Hog Island to try to rescue a yawl, a small boat they had found frozen in the ice. On April 11, Granger raised a well-armed posse of thirteen gentiles and thirty-two Indians and went to Hog Island in pursuit. When they arrived, it was dark and the Mormons had gone inland to camp. The posse stole the boat the Strangites had arrived in and chipped the yawl to pieces. A little past midnight, they fell upon the camp of Mormons with shouts and Indian war whoops. The plan was to surprise and capture them, but the Indians gave a war whoop a moment too soon and awakened the sleeping men.

The Mormons sprang to their feet and scattered. Finding their boat gone, they took to the woods. In the darkness, they felt their way through the trees and across a deep swamp, many of them without their boots. The men met up on the opposite shore of Hog Island where they found an old fishing boat filled with ice and snow. One of their number, David Bates, was missing.[34] It was cold; Lake Michigan was spotted with drifting ice. "With the boat preserved from sinking only by the frozen ice and snow, and without sails or oar locks and with three unsuitable oars, not half-clothed, no provi-

---

mon sheriff may have also tried to arrest Moore on a complaint issued by Samuel Graham, who claimed Moore's dog had bitten Graham's son.

33. "Indian Hostilities," *Northern Islander,* Mar. 2, 1854.

34. "War on the Mormons," *Northern Islander,* Mar. 2, 1854.

sions, without a line to tie their boat, nor any axe to repair the boat with, they set out on the broad blue water for a place of safety," Strang recalled.

Circuiting the neighboring islands at a distance in order to remain unseen, Strang and his men buffeted the lake's waves for nearly twenty-four hours before landing on Gull Island, which was uninhabited for the winter. The men had suffered so much from exposure, and their faces were so swollen, they could barely recognize each other. They found an abandoned fish shanty where they stayed for the next five days, surviving on provisions they found inside. Lacking an axe, they tore down nearby shanties to fuel their fire. They worried about the fate of their lost companion, but their biggest fear was that the gentiles had attacked Beaver Island.[35]

Strang and his men painstakingly repaired their boat sufficiently to be able to return to Hog Island to look for their missing man. To their surprise, they found him alive. Bates had subsisted for twelve days on rawhide intended for oar straps and about two quarts of frozen potatoes. The sheriff and his party had left on the assumption the stranded men would probably perish. Granger took possession of the Mormons' tools, provisions, cooking utensils, and blankets as "spoils of war," dividing up the loot among the posse. A chest of joiner's tools owned by Royal Tucker was referred to as a box of "burglar's tools."[36]

Granger hunted down as many as twenty of the thirty-nine men listed on the arrest warrants and took them to Mackinac where a judge ordered the men to prison; the charges against them were eventually dropped.[37] Furious that Strang had escaped his grasp, Granger placed a price on his head and solicited donations for reward money. The reward was set at $25 at first and soon raised to $300. For the next month, Strang was hunted by "bands of armed men, Indians and half-breeds, all seeking to earn this prize."[38] One of the Strangites commented that "many of those involved in the chase evidently believed the sheriff's advertisement would legally justify them in the killing of Strang. Others looked upon it as an easy method of getting rid of him."[39]

---

35. "Indian Hostilities."

36. Ibid.

37. Ibid.

38. "War on the Mormons."

39. Elvira Field Strang and Charles J. Strang, "Biographical Sketch of James J. Strang," unpublished manuscript, n.p., State Library of Michigan.

Several important events occurred in the spring of 1851. On April 6, the most holy day of the Mormon Church calendar, Elvira Field gave birth to a son. The child was delivered three days shy of nine months from the day of Strang's coronation. The April sixth date of birth was significant because Joseph Smith had organized the original Mormon Church on April 6, 1830. In addition, many members believed that Jesus Christ himself was born on April 6.[40] It is an odd circumstance that Elvira Field's birthday, July 8, fell on the same date Strang received a revelation in 1846 to develop his church, while her first child was born on the auspicious date of the original church's organization. It seemed to be a sign that God was pleased with Strang. In another odd twist, James and Elvira named their first child Charles, after his mother's pseudonym, Charley Douglass.

There is no way of knowing what Mary Perce thought about Elvira's delivery. Unfortunately, there are no known letters or manuscripts dealing with this issue. But Strang apparently continued to rely on his first wife, and she tried to live up to his expectations. Still in hiding, James wrote to Mary on May 19, 1851, asking her to send a barrel of fish to his father once the danger of starvation on the island had passed.[41] Strang had even given Mary an advisory position on his governing council in April. Before making this appointment, James discussed it for several months with Samuel Graham, the president of the Twelve Apostles and Strang's best friend.[42]

However, something happened in May to change Strang's opinion of Mary and caused him to banish her from the island. Graham wrote to James saying he thought the prophet was making a mistake to exile her. "The same facts were in existence when you made her a member of your council in April," he reminded James. It was Graham's opinion that "in no one thing was she your foe or the foe of the church in your absence, but she had her enemies and they had their influence."[43]

There is evidence of something more serious and ominous than a few personal conflicts with other members on the island. The tantalizing clue is

40. James E. Talmage, *Jesus the Christ* (Salt Lake City: Deseret Book Co., 1977), 104.

41. James J. Strang to M. A. P. Strang, May 19, 1851, folders 74, 74a, Strang Collection, Beinecke Library.

42. Samuel Graham to James Strang, July 20, 1850, folder 348, Strang Collection, Beinecke Library.

43. Samuel Graham to James Strang, July 10, 1851, folder 347, Strang Collection, Beinecke Library.

jotted down in the margins of a newspaper clipping—the serialization of M. L. Leach's "A History of the Grand Traverse Region," published in the *Grand Traverse Herald* in 1883. The published paragraph reads:

> Strang himself was the first to set the example of polygamous practices. In the early period of the settlement of the island, many conscientious Mormons were assured, at Voree, that he did not approve of polygamy or the 'consecrating' of property, but on arriving on the island found him preaching both. His lawful wife came with him to St. James, but returned to Voree when his open association with other women made her position no longer unendurable. His second wife was openly acknowledged as such only after the birth of her first child.

The note in the margin explains: "This is false. Elvira was acknowledged as a wife, but did not live in the house with Mary. Mary tried to kill Elvira's child, the writer of this [note], when he was an infant." The handwriting matches that of Charles Strang in his contemporary letters to historian Henry E. Legler and Strangite Lorenzo Dow Hickey.[44]

Although there is no corroborating evidence in other extant documents, there seems to be little doubt that at least Charles believed this was the motivation for Mary's eviction from the island. Charles accumulated a great deal of material about his father and made similar jottings in the margins of other articles.[45] If what Charles thought he had uncovered about his infancy was in fact true, it gives a plausible reason why James would suddenly order Mary to leave the island after having just made her a member of the church's governing council. It also explains why other Strangites held such animosity toward her and her memory. If so, why would Mary have done such a thing? It is possible she was chronically depressed or felt intensely threatened by the possibility of her own children losing their inheritance and standing. Unfortunately, the truth may never be known.

Samuel Graham may have been unaware of some of the details of James's decision and assumed the prophet would forgive his wife and rescind his order. "You say that you have lost all in Mary: this I cannot understand," Graham wrote. He said that since receiving the eviction order, she had "done

---

44. M. L. Leach, "A History of the Grand Traverse Region," *Grand Traverse Herald*, 1883, 88, Clarke Historical Library. I have substituted the bracketed word *note* for *paragraph* in the handwritten notation to differentiate from the published paragraph.

45. See note 19, chapter 7, of this volume.

as you told her to do. You fear that She has turned from you in heart[.] I do not believe it. I think She will yet meet you and be to you all that She ever was if you ever git on a place where peace reigns. I will not believe for a moment that She does intend more than a Short visit from you."[46]

Nevertheless, Mary Perce would never again return to Beaver Island. She lived for a time with her brother William in Illinois, where she was once again in ill health—perhaps disheartened over her behavior and subsequent separation from James. Mary and her children later returned to their own home in Voree, where they ran a sizeable farm.[47] James's parents did not know that Mary had left Beaver Island, nor were Clement and Abigail aware their son had taken a second wife, although there is no doubt they knew of it a few years later.[48]

Elizabeth Whitney Williams, in her book *A Child of the Sea*, said Mary Perce opposed both polygamy and her husband's absolutist rule on the island. She recounts a tale of how Mary secretly enlisted the help of Chippewa Indians to covertly assist a disenchanted family in leaving the island, which would have elicited James's wrath.[49] Unfortunately, there is no corroborating evidence to prove this story. Even with Mary gone, James continued to deny they were separated. He later claimed his wife spent her summers in Voree looking after his business interests and winters with him in Lansing, where he attended the Michigan state legislature.[50]

In the spring of 1851, the conflict between the gentiles and the Mormons took a new twist. The president of the United States, Millard Fillmore, received the allegations from George J. Adams, Peter McKinley, and Eri J. Moore that Strang and his followers were guilty of treason, robbing the mail, counterfeiting, and trespass on federal land. Vowing a "vigorous and sweeping prosecution," Fillmore ordered the United States warship *Michigan* to

---

46. Samuel Graham to James Strang, July 4, 1851, folder 346, Strang Collection, Beinecke Library.

47. Samuel Graham to James Strang, July 27, 1851, folder 348, Strang Collection, Beinecke Library.

48. Abigail Strang to "My Dear Children," folder 118, Strang Collection, Nov. 1, 1851.

49. Williams, *Child of the Sea*, 141.

50. "Beaver Island—Mormon—Strang the 'Saint,'" *Northern Islander*, Oct. 11, 1855; also Myraette [Strang] Losee to David Strang, Jan. 1, 1855, Clarke Historical Library. Losee wrote that James was taking Mary and six-year-old Hattie to Lansing, while the older children were staying with their parents in Voree.

Beaver Island to arrest Strang and take him to trial.[51] The *Michigan* was placed under orders of George C. Bates, district attorney for the state of Michigan, and Charles Knox, United States marshal. The ship arrived about two o'clock mid-evening on May 24. As Strang was still in hiding with a price on his head, one of the Mormon men arranged for district attorney Bates to talk to him.[52] James met with Bates, then walked with him to the *Michigan.*

Once on board, Strang was told he and thirty-eight others were charged with trespass on federal land and other crimes. Strang asked Bates for a list of the men and said they would come to the ship of their own accord within two hours if they heard from him. Strang wrote a note asking the men to turn themselves in, and within two hours, thirty-one men—all of those on the list who were on the island at that time—appeared at the ship and surrendered in response to Strang's plea.[53] Bates had a young man with him who claimed he had knowledge of the Mormons' counterfeiting activities. The youth reported he had been invited to join the business, which allegedly took place in an artificial cave in a nearby hillside, and that he had seen the work going on. He later admitted his tale was false.[54]

After a verbal investigation, Strang and twenty-three of the men were arrested for going out in armed force and obstructing the United States mail. This was in connection with the incident three months earlier when the Mormons had gone to arrest Eri J. Moore on Garden Island. Strang and two others were also charged with counterfeiting, and about a dozen men were indicted for trespass on public lands. Knox took Strang and three defendants to Detroit for further judicial proceedings while the others were temporarily left on the island.

As soon as Strang was gone, the gentiles stepped up their harassment of the Mormons, accusing the men of a multitude of offenses, for which they were arrested and taken to away to jail in Mackinac. Several gentiles plundered the property of those who had been arrested on the belief that Strang would be found guilty and the Mormons driven off of the island. Hezekiah McCulloch was robbed of 100 cords of wood. Other Mormons lost smaller quantities of lumber intended for use on houses and docks.

---

51. "United States Takes up against the Mormons," *Northern Islander,* Mar. 2, 1854.

52. The friend was reportedly Samuel Graham.

53. *Northern Islander,* Mar. 2, 1854.

54. Ibid.

On July 24, 1851, the *Northern Islander* apologized for its delay in publication, explaining that "a printer cannot be had" because, "for nearly a month, three-fourths of the men residing on the Island have been away, either as defendants or witnesses." The women were doing the best they could, the newspaper explained.

> The labor of the fields, even, has fallen upon the women. But—it has not been neglected—. The crops are well cared for, and in an excellent condition. Indeed, if arrests and prosecutions founded on false witnesses continue, we shall hand over the printing office also to them, and thus keep work moving. The workmen of the office were absent at Detroit three weeks as witnesses and previous to that time they were called from the office so much that they could not attend to the publication of a paper for more than a fortnight. We think we shall now be left at rest for a time. If not, it is harder on us than on our subscribers.[55]

The federal government seized large quantities of lumber from the Mormons, alleging it had been illegally cut on public land. The Strangites countered that most of the wood had been cut on private land and otherwise had been cut in accordance with the Commissioner of Public Lands. Strang presented an official note from George C. Bates, the same district attorney then prosecuting him, allowing the Strangites to cut the timber. The government restored the lumber, but not before four thousand feet of wood was thrown into the lake under the direction of Peter McKinley, whom the marshal had left in charge of it.[56]

A few days after Strang was taken to Detroit, Samuel Graham went to Whiskey Point to consult with Sheriff Granger and ended up being badly pummeled with a cane by two men. The Mormons claimed it was an unprovoked act and that Graham, who suffered a broken arm and fractured skull, had not so much as even spoken to the two men. Warrants for the arrest of Richard O'Donnell and James Hoy were issued by two Mormon judges, but Sheriff Granger would neither arrest them nor allow anyone else to interfere. It was said he took the two men into his custody until they were able to escape to the fisheries. The prosecuting attorney traveled to Beaver Island with an arrest warrant for the two men, which he gave to a Mormon constable, William Chambers. The constable went to the fishing grounds to carry out the

---

55. Ibid., July 24, 1851, [p. 2].
56. "General Oppression," *Northern Islander*, April 13, 1854.

arrest. On his way there, he had to pass by the home of Thomas and Samuel Bennett, who stopped Chambers at gunpoint and drove him away. Chambers returned with warrants for the Bennett brothers for resisting an officer in discharging his official duties. A posse of about thirty to forty men accompanied the constable.[57]

Exactly what happened next is hard to determine. According to the Mormon version, the Bennett brothers refused to surrender, retreated to their house, and fired on Chambers, who fell, seriously wounded in the head. The posse returned fire. A few moments later, Thomas Bennett lay dead—shot through the heart—and Samuel Bennett's hand had been nearly shot away. Calling it a "most atrocious murder," newspapers in the towns surrounding the Great Lakes claimed the Bennetts had been unarmed and had stood up against Mormon law. Rumors circulated that after the "blood thirsty" Mormons killed Thomas Bennett, they cut his body into pieces and horribly mutilated his brother. This derived from the surgeon's inquest and autopsy, which had been performed by Hezekiah McCulloch, the Mormon surgeon. Gentiles claimed McCulloch had cut out Thomas's heart and held it up for display. For miles around, people swore vengeance against the Mormons for the shooting.[58]

Samuel Bennett pressed charges against nearly all the men on Beaver Island for the murder of his brother. Twenty Strangites were arrested and taken to Mackinac, where fourteen of them remained for over two months before being brought before a grand jury.[59] The Mackinac prison at that time was a log building about eleven feet square, built into the side of a hill. It consisted of two rooms, one of which was used as a lavatory. The other room was "cold and damp, like an outdoor cellar," and contained "neither beds, chairs, benches or tables."[60]

The Mormons believed the gentiles intended for them to "perish of the confinement." According to one account, it was the prisoners' own resourcefulness and "Sheriff Granger's greed [that] saved them." At their own sug-

---

57. "Affair with the Bennetts," *Northern Islander*, April 13, 1854. This incident is also related in Strang, *Ancient and Modern Michilimackinac*, 33.

58. Ibid. The Mormon version of this story was that McCulloch had simply moved Bennett's heart out of the way during the autopsy, then as part of the inquest held it up to see which way the bullet had passed through.

59. Ibid., 34.

60. Ibid.

gestion, the prisoners were allowed to go out and work around town during the day as long as they gave their wages to Granger for board—even though the board was already being paid by the county.[61] Ironically, Granger utilized these men, who were being held for murder, in other ways, even asking them to serve as a posse on one occasion. They performed jury duty at an inquest and two of them gave appraisals on some property. After being detained for ten weeks, the men were discharged after a grand jury found no reason to hold them.[62]

Other arrests were made under various pretenses, but in every instance the parties were eventually set free. Elvira Field said "the threat was made publicly that the [gentiles] would take off all the men, and then drive off and destroy their families." She found it telling that "in the whole course of this, even with perjury and falsehood against us, not one has been found guilty ... These prosecutions have been carried on with the purpose (in many cases avowed) of destroying the settlement here, but we shall outlive them all, and live to remember the authors of them. The Lord reward them according to their works."[63]

When word of Thomas Bennett's death reached Detroit, there was such outrage it was assumed the Strangites would not fare well in court. Fearing the worst for himself and his people, Strang implored the governor of Michigan to protect the little settlements on Beaver Island. He wrote that

> Whites, Indians, and half-breeds; all the lawless of the upper region, were four or five days ago gathering against the devoted Mormon Colony on Beaver Island, to murder mere women & children, infant and suckling, for the crime of obeying a civil officer, in the execution of the plainest duty. I have the utmost painful apprehension that the Mormon settlement (some 700 souls) is already or will[,] before relief can reach them[,] be annihilated....
>
> Those who are arrayed against them are well armed and I speak from personal knowledge when I say that at the time I left Beaver Island there were not twenty guns and pistols of all kinds among the Mormons on Beaver Island.

---

61. Ibid., 35.

62. *Northern Islander,* Mar. 18, 1852. The following were charged with murder. All but Loomis and McCulloch were detained for ten weeks: Gurdon Brown, Geo. Brownson, Orson Campbell, Albert Field, Judson Linnell, Chauncey Loomis, H. D. McCulloch, Tobias McNutt, A. Parrish, G. T. Preston, Stratton Rogers, Murray Seaman, Saml. Shaw, Eli Steele, and John Whitlock.

63. Strang and Strang, "Biographical Sketch."

They have no means of self defense whatsoever unless it has since been provided.... You will forgive my anxiety. I left a wife and children there. I do not expect to ever see either [of them], this side of the grave. I know well the men who have got up this violence and unless resistance has been interposed which I do not anticipate, the vengeance which has so long sought me in vain, has been wreaked in the blood of the companion of my bosom, and the children God has given me.[64]

Strang's prosecution continued before the U.S. District Court at Detroit from the latter part of May until the first part of July. On July 9, 1851, a year and a day after Strang's coronation, an eleven-member jury found him and the other Mormons "not guilty" of obstructing U.S. mail.[65] The other charges were quietly dropped, and George J. Adams quickly departed from the scene.[66] Strang, on the other hand, took the opportunity to blast the trial. He said it had finally come out that there had not even been any mail in the dog train on the day in question. Even so, he found it remarkable that he and the others had been acquitted:

Thirteen persons were tried on the indictment for mail robbing and acquitted. It is well known that these [thirteen] men were prejudged and foredoomed, and that nothing but a defense beyond doubt or caviling could have produced their acquittal. The whole public expected their conviction.

It is important to note that the defendants were accused of robbing the mail on the 19th of February, however they were not arrested until 3 months afterwards. Testimony was taken of 300 witnesses, and not one man could be found

---

64. James Strang to the Governor of Michigan, June 12, 1851, Detroit Public Library.

65. Strang would die on this date in 1856; July 9 was also the date Strang received the letter of appointment from Joseph Smith.

66. George Adams may have departed from the Strangite scene but not from the historical record. In the 1860s, Adams founded the Church of the Messiah in Massachusetts and Maine, where he successfully convinced thirty-four families to migrate to Palestine to await the second coming of Jesus Christ. The colony was a disaster and many of the people needed assistance from the United States government to return back home. Adams was back in Philadelphia in 1873, once again establishing his Church of the Messiah. He sought membership in the RLDS church in 1878 but was rejected. He died in Philadelphia of typhoid-pneumonia, May 11, 1880. Louisa Cogswell stayed with him until after the failure of the colony in Palestine. Her subsequent whereabouts are unknown. Adams's son Clarence became a respected Baptist minister in Philadelphia. For addition information, see Peter Amann, "Prophet in Zion: The Saga of George J. Adams," *New England Quarterly*, 37 (December 1964): 477-500.

who had ever heard of it until after the arrest.... Not only that, but Peter Mc-
Kinley on the witness stand admitted that he [later] sent the same mail ... on a
vessel owned and navigated by the same men he was prosecuting for robbing it.[67]

In an issue of the *Northern Islander,* Strang boasted that

a few weeks ago every body, except a few of the faithful, believed we should be
obliged to leave this place immediately. Now the blindest can see that we have an
entire victory; in a word, [and] that the day of mobbing the Mormons here has
gone by.

Three months since sixty armed men were hunting the prophet, with the
openly avowed intention of shooting him wherever they could find him, at first
sight. Now he sits quietly in his own house, without keeping one of his trusted
friends by to assist him, and dispenses the law to these same men as a Justice of
the Peace; and when business requires goes alone and unarmed in the midst of
them, without molestation or danger.[68]

The triumph in Strang's tone is unavoidable, but also somewhat disingenuous since he must have suspected the calm would be short-lived. He
portrays himself as a man who is happy with a simple life centered around
hearth and home. In reality, it was not in his nature to be satisfied with little;
whether in the domestic sphere or in the outside world, he would soon be
reaching for more.

---

67. Strang, *Ancient and Modern Michilimackinac,* 32-33.
68. "The Gathering," *Northern Islander,* Aug. 14, 1851.

9

A HOME ON BEAVER ISLAND

1852

"There are many kinds of warfare,
but the object of all is the same, namely to destroy, waste and desolate. Now
the enemy did not there come out in the open field to fight us; but they re-
sorted to a sort of warfare which in the days of the rebellion was counted a
'guerilla warfare.' A warfare that was equally murderous as any other,
but of the most cowardly kind, so regulated by all. Now many Mormons
when they went on to those Islands, were a good deal to a loss to know what
to do. Some, Quaker-like, thought it was wrong to raise the sword after all
in self-defense. Others thought that the law should be executed, and this
was tried, but it turned out as in Missouri, that in going through the pro-
cess of the law that the very officers of the law themselves were the meanest
among our enemies. In such cases, what could honest and innocent men do?
They tried to bear it of course, but so menacing had this state of things be-
come that they resolved that they would bear such abuse and oppression
and outrage no longer. And would stand up in their own self defense."
—Wingfield W. Watson to daughter Grace. [1]

Even though Strang no longer had a price on his head and had been acquitted of obstructing the mail, the gentiles continued to harass the Mormons with the ultimate goal of driving them away from Beaver Island. The most common way to disturb the Strangites was to file legal complaints and have the men arrested. Not only did this take valuable manpower away from the island, the bond money required to keep them out of jail cut into the finances needed to establish businesses in the settlements and to buy property on the island. Between March 1851 and March 1852, ninety Mormons were arrested on more than 200 criminal charges. Strang was taken into custody forty times, sent to jail six times, and indicted fourteen times on crim-

---

1. Wingfield Watson to [daughter Grace], letter fragment, n.d., Clarke Historical Library, Central Michigan University, Mount Pleasant, Michigan.

inal charges. Hezekiah McCulloch was arrested on twenty charges, indicted on thirteen, and sent to jail five times. Those arrested were eventually cleared of all charges.[2]

Several Mormon families decided to leave Beaver Island. There were those whose opinion of Strang changed after his coronation. Others departed because the situation with the neighbors was too difficult. Most disaffected members were opposed to polygamy and became disenchanted after they saw it practiced on the island. One of the casualties in this sifting of wheat and tares was Samuel Graham, president of the Twelve Apostles and Strang's best friend. After being badly beaten by two gentiles in May 1851 and thrown into jail on Mackinac Island on trumped-up charges, Graham returned to his home in Parma, Michigan. This was during the time Strang was standing trial in Detroit. Graham wrote to the prophet informing him he did not intend to return to Beaver Island:

> I am worn out with persecution and confinement and have but little hope in the future. [I] would gladly seek retirement and spend a life of solitude rather than live as I have and yet I feel an unwavering attachment to my brethren on the Island. I am of [the] opinion that we must abandon that post and if so: the sooner the better....
>
> I think you had better counsel our brethren to leave the Island and establish themselves for a time in some good place and we had better go to some country where the blighting influence of Democracy or Whigery will not continuously curse us[,] where we can worship God as we think proper. I had rather go to Salt Lake then live in continual strife.[3]

Some of the Strangites called Graham an apostate and a coward for leaving the island. Among other insinuations, he received "a long exhortation from Br. Hickey, which I doubt not came from his heart, but in it I find some things that appear to come with an ill grace. Such for instance, as this," Graham wrote to Strang, "that I would wrong the poor Saints. I have taken on to that Island more than $2,500 and shall never take any part of it from there except my household stuff and my team[.] That I will take if I can and let those

---

2. "Prisoners of Hope," *Northern Islander,* Mar. 14, 1852.

3. Samuel Graham to James Strang, July 8, 1851, folder 346, James Jesse Strang Collection, Yale Collection of Western Americana, Beinecke Rare Book and Manuscript Library, Yale University, New Haven, Connecticut.

who say that I have wronged the saints have their say."[4] In his opinion, it was simply not wise for the church to remain in harm's way, although he also had some unflattering words for the members, saying he had been "growled at by lazy loungers as long as I will." Not that he was complaining, he quickly reassured Strang, "but James[,] we must have men that will work and not steal if we would build up a kingdom or church." He assured the prophet of their friendship. "You have in me a friend," he wrote, "when all our enemies are dead; if we cannot agree in policy we will not quarrel."[5]

Two weeks later Graham resigned his office as president of the Twelve Apostles. Within weeks, the friendship between the two men soured. There was a peculiar irony in this because at one time Graham had been one of the most respected leaders in the church and one of Strang's closest confidantes. He had assisted Strang with the translation of the sacred scripture called the Book of the Law of the Lord, which, like the Plates of the Rajah Manchou of Vorito, came from a set of ancient buried records. Exactly how, when, and where Strang received the hidden plates is uncertain, but their emergence was an important part of the establishment of the Strangite Church.

The first mention of the additional translation came in 1849-50 when Strang was on his mission to the eastern states. In order to prevent inquiries and protect his work from theft, Strang referred to the translation he was undertaking as his "Swedish work." Using this code word, he mentioned the project in an off-handed way to several people. Mary, in one of her letters, queried her husband: "On what subject is the Swedish work you are translating, and what is the object of doing it[?]"[6] James had also mentioned the translation to Amos Lowen, a follower in Philadelphia. "I have an uncle in

---

4. Samuel Graham to James Strang, July 10, 1851, folder 347, Strang Collection, Beinecke Library. Although he tried for many months, Graham never recovered the valuable horse team and household possessions he had taken to Beaver Island.

5. Ibid. After his departure from Beaver Island in the summer of 1851, Graham turned against Strang. In November 1851, Graham wrote to Brigham Young to inquire about moving to Salt Lake City, but was apparently rebuffed by Young. Graham then went on the lecture circuit speaking in Michigan about the dangers of Mormonism. In September 1861 at the age of forty-two, Graham joined Michigan's Ninth Infantry to fight in the Civil War, where he contracted tuberculosis. He died on January 19, 1863, at Jackson, Michigan. In the *Northern Islander*, April 13, 1854, Strang blasted Graham's character but acknowledged he had been a bosom friend.

6. Mary Perce Strang to James Strang, Jan. 9, 1850, folder 115, Strang Collection, Beinecke Library.

this city who is somewhat of an antiquarian," Lowen wrote to Strang, saying his uncle had "a keen scent for old records. I shall show him your account of the Swedish work you have discovered which will no doubt excite his curiosity."[7] George Adams was aware of the "Swedish work" and wrote to Strang in early 1850 "rejoicing" that the prophet was getting along so well with the translation of these new plates.[8]

According to Strang, the Book of the Law of the Lord was one of the lost books of the Bible and had been so revered in ancient times that it was kept inside the Ark of the Covenant. The book was supposedly too sacred to be placed in the hands of strangers, so when translations and copies were made of the other books of the Old Testament, the Book of the Law, as it was called, was kept separate, according to Strang. When the Jewish nation was taken captive into Babylon, they lost this holy book of scripture. Strang said the copy he had was written on plates of brass, taken from the house of a Jew named Laban in the days of Zedekiah, the king of Judah, and were called the Plates of Laban, as in the Book of Mormon. Strang had received the plates from an angel of God.[9]

Seven of Strang's apostles, Samuel P. Bacon, Samuel Graham, Albert N. Hosmer, Ebeneezer Page, Warren Post, Jehiel Savage, and Phineas Wright, testified to having seen and held the original brass plates. "The engravings are beautiful antique workmanship, bearing a striking resemblance to the ancient oriental languages," they wrote in a preface to the published book, "and those [metallic pages] from which the laws in this book were translated are eighteen in number, about seven inches and three-eighths wide, by nine inches long, occasionally embellished with beautiful pictures."[10] The "translation" took the form of divine revelations received by Strang about the original contents, divided into thirty-eight chapters in the published book. The

7. Amos Lowen to James Strang, Jan. 10, 1850, folder 417, Strang Collection, Beinecke Library.

8. George Adams to James Strang, Feb. 18, 1850, folder 210, Strang Collection, Beinecke Library.

9. *The Book of the Law of the Lord, consisting of an inspired translation of some of the most important parts of the law given to Moses, and a very few additional commandments, with brief notes and references* (Saint James, MI: Printed by command of the King at the Royal Press, 1851), testimony and preface, copy at the Library-archives, Wisconsin Historical Library, Madison, Wisconsin.

10. Ibid.

scripture offered explicit direction on such things as the organization of the kingdom of God, the responsibilities of the priesthood, the laws of inheritance, and setting up a municipal government. It also offered direction on clothing apparel and ornamentation, social order, household relations (including polygamy), payment of debts, and how to establish the "Law of God." At the end of each chapter, Strang wrote notes and commentary to further explain and enlighten the topics.

Strang continued to work on the Book of the Law translation during the winter of 1851 on the Steamer *Lexington,* which had wintered in Beaver Harbor.[11] His days were spent either on the ship or at the print shop where the *Northern Islander* was produced, "rising early and sitting up late and frequently missing his meals for want of time to eat."[12] Samuel Graham spent nearly two months assisting Strang. In fact, Graham was known to have the plates in his possession a good deal of that time.[13] He may have had them with him in Albany, New York, during the winter of 1849-50 when he was forced to put up at a hotel while he recovered from an illness. The hotel owner appropriated Samuel's trunk as security against the hotel bill. Graham was frantic when he wrote to Strang about getting his trunk back and asked for help with funds to pay the hotel owner. "There is some important things in it: more than clothing [if] you can guess what it is," he wrote, his anxiety level fairly transparent.[14]

Chauncey Loomis would later call the Plates of Laban a forgery and accuse Graham of being an accomplice, saying Graham confessed to helping Strang construct the plates from which the Book of the Law of the Lord was translated. "[They] prepared the plates and coated them with beeswax and then formed the letters and cut them in with a penknife and then exhibited them to the rest of the Twelve," this former Strangite alleged.[15] Samuel Ba-

---

11. Gabriel Strang to John Wake, June 23, 1932, Clarke Historical Library. Gabriel wrote: "Father translated them on a boat in the Harbor at Beaver Island that filled with water while resting on the ground and was left there through the winter." The Mormons held dances on the *Lexington* during the winter of 1851-52.

12. Court records, *United States v. James J. Strang*, Burton Historical Collection, Detroit Public Library.

13. "Samuel Graham," *Northern Islander,* Apr.13, 1854. By this date, Samuel Graham was giving lectures on the "evils of Mormonism" in Jackson County, Michigan.

14. Samuel Graham to James Strang, Mar. 13, 1850, folder 340, Strang Collection, Beinecke Library.

15. Chauncey Loomis, "Experience on Beaver Island with James J. Strang," *Saints*

con, who succeeded Graham as president of the Twelve Apostles, reportedly found evidence of the "forgery" while he was repairing Strang's house. Bacon told Loomis he had found "fragments of those plates which Strang made the Book of the Law from" behind the ceiling in Strang's house.[16] Bacon immediately lost faith in Strang's leadership, gathered his family, and "sneaked off the island" supposedly in fear of their lives, according to his report, and left most of their possessions behind.

Other Strangites might have left Beaver Island if they had been allowed to take their property with them. Under the Book of the Law, those who wished to receive an "inheritance" were required to pay tithing—ten percent of their possessions—in place of the more strict communal arrangement in Voree. Nevertheless, land and real estate were considered irrevocably "consecrated" to God since the island was intended for use only by God's people; one had to forfeit any claim to it on departure.

The John Cole family was among those who became disenchanted with Strang. According to family tradition, John and Anna Cole had moved to Voree by 1848 but became "dissatisfied" and sought an excuse to leave Beaver Island. "At the death of a member of the family, the Coles claimed the deceased had made a request to be buried on the mainland. So using this ruse to escape the island, they put on all the clothes they could wear and left the rest of their belongings behind."[17] The same was true for the Royal Tucker family. Daughter Sarah Wexstaff later recalled that her father's property was seized. "We could apostatize, but not our house and lot, or father's tools," which in Wexstaff's words were not allowed to leave the church.[18]

Despite the loss of Graham, Bacon, the Coles, Tuckers, and other fami-

---

Herald 35 (Nov. 1888): 718, copy in the Library-Archives of the Community of Christ, Independence, Missouri.

16. Ibid.

17. Family Genealogy of John Cole and Anna Eastman, unpublished manuscript, James Strang Papers, Doyle Fitzpatrick Collection, Library and Historical Center, State Library of Michigan, Lansing, Michigan. John contracted cholera while visiting the Michigan mainland and died there in 1850. Anna Cole and her children went to live on Beaver Island with Anna's daughter, Cynthia, who had married Gilbert Watson. The departure of the Coles from the island would have taken place about 1852. Gilbert and Cynthia apparently remained Strangite, however, until the RLDS church was organized in the 1860s. Gilbert became the head of a small branch of the RLDS Church in Wisconsin. He died in 1875. A young man by the name of Galen Cole remained on the island through 1856.

18. *Journal of History* 5 (Jan. 1912), copy in the Library-Archives, Community of Christ.

lies, Strang retained such stalwarts as Benjamin, Phineas, and Samuel Wright, who had finally given up the colony in Voree and come to Beaver Island to settle. There was also Lorenzo Dow Hickey, who after the incident concerning Charley Douglass in New York City never again doubted Strang. George Miller, a former member of Joseph Smith's inner circle at Nauvoo, had gone west with Brigham Young as far as Nebraska Territory, then turned around and traveled to Zodiak, Texas, where he joined Lyman Wight, another self-proclaimed successor of Joseph Smith. Once in Texas, Miller had become dissatisfied with Wight's leadership and began having dreams about James Strang.

Miller became convinced by these dreams that the red-bearded prophet of Beaver Island was the true successor. "I had frequent manifestations of brother Strang being called of God to lead his people, even as Moses to lead the Israelites out of Egyptian bondage," Miller wrote in his life history, "and I began to set myself earnestly to make preparations to gather with the saints" in Michigan.[19] When the group arrived at Beaver Island in September 1850, they consisted of twenty-three people: Miller, his two wives and their children; Miller's son Joshua, his wife and children; and Clark Lyman Whitney, who had three wives and numerous children. Clark was the younger brother of Newell K. Whitney, a prominent individual in Joseph Smith's inner circle during the Nauvoo period of Mormon history. George and Joshua Miller were soon called to fill important positions in the Strangite community, but Whitney was not long for this world. He became ill and died in the spring of 1851 in Voree.[20]

Another staunch supporter, Hezekiah McCulloch, had been baptized by George Adams in Baltimore. McCulloch was one of the two men, along with Strang, who was most detested by the gentiles and was repeatedly arrested and jailed in Mackinac during the winter of 1850-51. He was once held on $2,000 bond for taking a key and padlock from Eri J. Moore, with whom he had joint occupancy of a warehouse. The key and padlock were valued at sev-

---

19. "Correspondence," *Northern Islander,* Oct. 18, 1855. Also, H. W. Mills, "De Tal Palo Tal Astilla," *Historical Society of Southern California Annual* (Los Angeles: McBride Publishing, 1917). George Miller died in 1856, a few weeks after Strang, while he and his family were en route to California. Miller recounted the story of his experiences as a Mormon and a Strangite in the *Northern Islander.* The articles were serialized from August 9 to October 18, 1853.

20. Ibid.

enty-five cents. Half of the materials in the warehouse were McCulloch's.[21]

On September 20, 1851, Sheriff Henry Granger from Mackinac arrived to arrest McCulloch on yet another charge and was impeded by Strang and his men, who saw what was happening and rushed out of a meeting to prevent the arrest.[22] The Strangites surrounded Granger and told him they would not allow him to take one more person. The sheriff cited Strang for helping a prisoner escape but stopped short of arresting him. Strang traveled to and from Mackinaw several times during the next few months, but no further effort was made to apprehend him. However, the outstanding warrant would materialize again nearly a year and a half later at the Michigan state legislature.

After nearly two years of being harassed and falsely imprisoned, the Strangites were determined not to share the island. They turned from a strategy of self-defense to an effort of driving away the gentile residents, making their lives so "uncomfortable" they would leave—thereby rationalizing their own vigilantism. "From the time of the arrival of the colony in 1847[,] the former inhabitants, mostly fishermen, were gradually expelled," Charles R. Wright later recalled. "This was accomplished mainly by petty bickerings and by the Mormons making it uncomfortable in every way. They would steal one's chattels before his face and then laugh at his discomfiture. This was continued until 1852, when there were only two Gentile families left. Mine was one of them."[23]

Eri J. Moore wrote again to the governor of Michigan informing him of the Mormon "atrocities." Moore related an incident he said occurred at midnight on September 21, 1851, when Strang, wearing a sword at his side, ordered his men to throw stones through the windows of Moore's house. Several women and children were inside. Moore said his family was in constant

---

21. Unknown correspondent [probably Strang] to the readers of an unknown newspaper, draft copy, April 9, 1851, Detroit Public Library.

22. McCulloch and another Strangite, William Chambers, were accused of firing the shots that killed Thomas Bennett in June 1851. "The People of the State of Michigan vs. Hezekiah D. McCulloch and William Chambers—Indictment Murder. A True Bill," folder 1, Jacob Merritt Howard Collection of Documents and Letters Relating to the Strangites, 1851-1856, Beinecke Library; also deposition from Sheriff Jedidiah [Henry] W. Granger stating he was unable to take McCulloch because Strang and other men helped McCulloch escape, folder 2, Howard Collection.

23. "An American Principality with Two Kings," *Chicago Tribune*, Oct 13, 1895, Library-archives, Wisconsin Historical Society, Madison, Wisconsin.

fear and always on their guard. He claimed Strang continually harassed the gentiles with lawsuits, which the gentiles lost because they could not receive justice in a Mormon court. "Strang says either the gentiles or Mormons must leave the island and I have no intention of going," Moore wrote.[24] He eventually backed down, however, and followed his gentile neighbors into exile.

As their neighbors left the island, the Mormons often took possession of their property by citing some obscure township tax that had not been paid. In several cases a gentile's home or business was burned or destroyed to prevent the owner from coming back. There is evidence the Strangites planned to do even more than that. An extant letter addressed to "King James" outlined plans to take the island from the gentiles by force:

> The time has come to manifest our faith by our own works[,] for my faith is that the Dominion is to Be taken By force[.] Now Brother Strang how many can there Be Raised Between this and next December that will fight for the kingdom[?] [N]ow if you can get twenty or twenty five true men that will be as true as ste[e]l you can take the Kingdom and Establish Peace on this Island ... [I]t will Be [no] Difficulty for them to Rise up under A good Leader and bring the Rest in Subjection to the Law of God Because 25 men under Good Discipline can whip 300 anytime ...
>
> I assure you I do not look upon it to Be a lite thing to Establish the kingdom of God ... Now I will give you Some Reasons for saying that I Believe next December to Be the time to strike the Blow[.] I Do not consider it to be good Policy to Do anything this Summer to make any Stir or give our enemies any Suspicions of our intentions[,] [at least for] now[,] By Keeping the matter as Still as Possible until the time that Shall Be appointed arrives and all things Prepared for the occasion ... Brother Strang[,] lets Give the Pseudos and Gentiles there Desserts [?] this winter[.] [W]e can Do it if you will Be here with us[.] I Do Believe there can Be twenty five Boys that will obey your counsel[,] that can Be organized and Properly Disciplined By that time[,] which will Do executions[.]
>
> Another Reason I Will give that December is the time[.] [Y]ou are aware that at the Close of navigation that steamers of all kinds are laid in for six months.... We that are here are shut up from the Rest of the World for six months ... and it Seems to me that the Sooner the Blow is Struck after the close of navigation the Better for we want time to Prepare and fortify ourselves against those without.... and now I Do cinserly Believe that if we are to take a Bold and

---

24. Eri J. Moore to the Governor of Michigan, Sept. 26, 1851, Detroit Public Library.

Determined Desider [decisive] Stand and let our motto Be Victory or Death that the Government will yield to our Request and let us alone for the Present.[25]

There is no evidence Strang ever intended to follow the suggestions alluded to in this letter. The actions may not have been necessary as the gentiles basically left the island of their own accord.

By the spring of 1852, the Mormons were finally able to set up the island the way they wished. In April, Peaine Township was organized, with Strang as town supervisor, Hezekiah McCulloch as clerk and health officer, George Miller as treasurer, and Samuel Wright and George Preston as assessors. Anson Prindle and Warren Post were made school inspectors. Other men were elected commissioners of highways, justices of the peace, constables, and keeper of the pound.[26] A hospital was established to be kept in constant readiness. A new ordinance banned gunpowder inside the township unless it was in tight casks or canisters. Dogs had to be licensed and were required to wear a collar at all times with the owner's name on it, nor were any animals allowed to roam at large. The pound accommodated not only dogs but also horses, cattle, sheep, mules, asses, and goats. A law was passed to protect residents from the odors of rotting fish, requiring that fish be cleaned inland rather than in the harbor, and the offal had to be buried within twenty-four hours in a trench at least one foot deep and ten feet away from the nearest dwelling.[27]

Plans were laid for establishing additional settlements near the lighthouse at the southern end of the island and on South Fox (renamed Paros) Island and High Island. Benjamin G. Wright and a number of families prepared to settle at Cables Bay (renamed Galilee) to the south, while others settled on Lake Watonesa toward the western coast.[28]

"The discipline of the Church in the matter of temperance and morals was very strict," recalled Elvira Field. "The use of tea, coffee and tobacco, as well as liquors, was prohibited. The temperance laws of the state were strictly

---

25. Unsigned letter to "King James," n.d., folder 156, Beinecke Library. Dale L. Morgan, who catalogued the collection of Strang correspondence at Beinecke, tentatively identified the writer, based on the handwriting, as George J. Adams. As far as the language style, the letter is more suggestive of Lorenzo Dow Hickey. For instance, Adams is noted for underlining words, and none are underlined in this particular letter.

26. "Township Officers for 1852," *Northern Islander,* Apr. 22, 1852.

27. "Township Ordinances," *Northern Islander,* Apr. 22, 1852.

28. "New Settlements," *Northern Islander,* Apr. 22, 1852.

enforced with especially good effect among the fishermen and the Indians," she stated somewhat disingenuously. In fact, this would be a major point of contention with the fishermen and Indians. Nevertheless, Elvira continued to note that

> the seventh day was set apart as the Sabbath and every person physically able was commanded to attend church on that day. The saints were required to pay one-tenth of all they raised, earned or received [,] into the public fund, and the tithing was used for improvements, taking care of the poor, and paying State, county and township taxes. No other tax was levied. Schools were organized and flourished finely. A printing office with sufficient capacity to print all the papers, books, pamphlets, tracts, etc. needed for the church was maintained and became a strong arm in the association. No betting or gaming was permitted, but the rules were very liberal in the matter of amusements. Many improvements were made upon the Beaver, while small settlements were planted on neighboring islands.[29]

With the gentiles and unbelievers gone, the Strangites were becoming more aware and accepting of polygamy, although most still did not care for the practice. Outside newspapers reported rumors that the federal government was planning to move against the Mormons in Salt Lake City to halt the practice of plural marriage. Strang took the opportunity, probably ill-advised, to defend polygamy in an article in the *Northern Islander*:

> Polygamy is not forbidden as common law. It is not forbidden in the Bible, and the Brighamites, the citizens of Utah will not make a law against it, and for want of something else to make a fuss about, the judges have come home with this as the great complaint against the citizens of Utah. Had it been found that the Territory was overrun with brothels, as every city in the US is, with free quarters for public officers, no complaint would have been heard for such offenses.
>
> But when they are found regularly marrying wives, taking them home and providing for them and their children, as Jacob, David, Solomon and the Prophets and Patriarchs generally did; in this Christian land they are charged with immorality and crime, and a public outcry is raised against, and, an excuse got up for persecuting them. Nothing can be found in the common law against polygamy; nothing in the civil law: nothing in the Old or New Testament

---

29. "The King of the Saints," *New York Times*, Sept. 3, 1882. Elvira and her son Charles provided most of the information for the article. The sabbath was, and still is, observed on Saturday instead of Sunday.

against it. But it is forbidden by canon in all Catholic countries, and by statutes in all Protestant states: and the Brighamites who are so far behind the times, as to follow the example of God's chosen servants of the olden time, are, forsooth, dangerous and rebellious citizens.[30]

Whatever else could be said about this essay, it was timely. Just two months before it was written, Strang had taken another wife, Elizabeth (Betsy) Mc-Nutt, who became his third spouse in a growing royal household.

Betsy was born on her father's farm in Preble County, Ohio, on August 17, 1820, the youngest of ten surviving children of Alexander and Elizabeth Tillman McNutt.[31] Her grandfather was a Scottish nobleman who had immigrated to the United States in 1764 and settled in or near Roanoke, Virginia. His service in the Revolutionary War was repaid with 1,000 acres on the south side of the Big Twin River. In 1800, Betsy's father, Alexander, constructed a large brick home on the property about a mile and a half from Lewisburg, Ohio.[32]

Little is known about Betsy's childhood. However, it may have been quite interesting in such a large family. She and her sister, Rhonda, older than Betsy by two years, had eight older brothers.[33] Rhonda died when Betsy was eighteen, leaving Betsy as the only girl in the family.[34] In 1846-47, George J. Adams arrived in the Lewisburg area and introduced the McNutts to Strangism.[35] Adams was followed by James Blakeslee, another successful Strangite missionary.[36]

---

30. "The Salt Lake Settlement," *Northern Islander,* Mar. 18, 1852.

31. McNutt family genealogical records from personal correspondence with a descendant of Tobias McNutt, 1998; "The Diary of James Oscar McNutt, Elder of the Mormon Church at the Mormon Settlement, Jackson Co., Wisconsin; One Time Follower of James Jesse Strang," 1, State Library of Michigan; cf. "Reminisces of James O. McNutt of the Mormon Settlement, Jackson County [Wisconsin], and Warrens, Monroe County, Related by J. O. McNutt, and Recorded by his Daughter Miss Sadie McNutt," Wisconsin Historical Society, which is nearly identical except for the title page.

32. Ibid. The old homestead and the three lime kilns were still in existence in the 1930s.

33. McNutt genealogical records. Betsy's mother, Elizabeth, died at an unknown date. Her father later married Catherine Eichelberger.

34. Ibid.

35. James Oscar McNutt, interviewed by Milo M. Quaife, May 24, 1920, Clarke Historical Library.

36. "Cincinnati, Ohio, June 8th, 1849," *Gospel Herald,* July 5, 1849. Blakeslee later became a successful missionary for the RLDS Church.

In the fall of 1850, a large company of the McNutt family, including Betsy, her parents, and the families of her brothers John, Tobias, and Jacob, made a pilgrimage to St. James.[37] Betsy's father had not converted, so he and his wife stayed the winter, then returned to Ohio with their son Jacob. Betsy, John, and Tobias remained.[38] The two brothers established farms on the shore of Round Lake on the interior of the island, about three and a half miles south of St. James, where they built log homes.[39] No doubt, Betsy lived with one of her brothers, probably with John, until 1852 when she married Strang. John was eighteen years older than his sister and was more likely seen as a protector than a peer.[40] Tobias, on the other hand, was six years older than Betsy, and with his wife, Mary, had three young children—two daughters and a son, James Oscar. The diary James Oscar kept provides a candid glimpse into the everyday life of the Midwest Mormons.[41]

As related in his memoirs, James Oscar documented how he and others cleared their land for farming and cut timber to sell as cordwood for the steamers that docked at Beaver Harbor. Wood that was too hard to split was cut into lengths to await a "rolling bee," whereby men rolled the logs onto piles for burning. To transport a log to its pyre, the men drove long hard spikes into each end of the log. Neighbors helped lift and situate a log, usually requiring four to five men per log. After the fire was lit, it took about six to ten days for the pile to burn down. Someone stayed on hand to watch the fire, adjusting the pile to keep the logs burning. When the logs had been burned at one farm, the men gathered at the next neighbor's home and repeated the process. "This is the way all got their farms in the hardwood timber country," J. O. said.

The McNutt farms were plentiful in lumber and wildlife. Like other

---

37. Various McNutt family members are listed in the 1850 federal census for Preble County, Ohio, recorded in August 1850. Three of Betsy's brothers, John, Peter, and Tobias, married sisters from the Wantz (Vance) family. John later married Mary Jane Whitlock. In June 1851, Tobias and Alexander were among the men charged with cutting down trees on federal land.

38. McNutt diary, 2; see note 31 above.

39. James Oscar McNutt interview, May 24, 1920.

40. Ibid. Lorenzo Dow Hickey said John McNutt was fond of playing cards and dancing.

41. See note 31 above. James O. was two years old when his family came to live on Beaver Island and nine when his family left.

Strangites, the brothers brought their own cows, sheep, and chickens to their new home. Tobias bought a horse team and shipped it to the island in about 1854. The Mormons also made their own sugar from maple trees. "We raised ... everything we [needed to] eat and feed except flour," J. O. wrote. "In those days, mother carded the wool by hand and spun the wool on a little spinning wheel she run by treadle with her foot."[42]

An old maid at the age of thirty-two, Betsy was not considered particularly attractive. When she was teased about her marital status at a social gathering, she replied that there was only one man she would even think of marrying. "It appeared that she had Strang in mind, and when this was reported to him, he—out of supposed gallantry—offered to marry her," one member recalled, suggesting that Strang was "something of an easy mark in the matter."[43] Strang probably sent one of his apostles to propose to Betsy, as he never did so in person to any of his plural wives.[44] Elizabeth became his third wife on January 19, 1852, in a private ceremony.[45] Afterward, she was welcomed into the white frame home where Strang lived with Elvira and their baby, Charles. Mary and her children had long since left the island in late May or early June 1851.

Betsy was said to excel in cooking and homemaking. Her prized rolling pin, which she "used with such magic skill," one Strangite recalled, "was the handsomest piece of bird's eye (maple) I ever saw."[46] She also helped with such work as counting the words on each page of the Book of the Law, the number appearing at the end of each section, so no one could publish an unauthorized copy with alterations.[47] Without question, she appears to have been devout in her religion. Even so, something she said caused a rift between Strang and Samuel Graham. Graham wrote to Betsy on July 30, 1851, three days after he resigned as president of the Twelve Apostles and about five months previous to Betsy's marriage to Strang. Apparently, the two had been friends for a time and shared confidences, but in his letter, Graham accused Betsy of slandering him:

---

42. McNutt diary, 2-3.

43. Wingfield W. Watson, interviewed by Milo M. Quaife, Dec. 10-11, 1918, Clarke Historical Library. Watson said he found Betsy to be unattractive.

44. Clement Strang to Milo Quaife, Oct. 11, 1920, Clarke Historical Library.

45. James Oscar McNutt interview, May 24, 1920.

46. Clement Strang to Stanley Johnston, Aug. 13, 1939, Clarke Historical Library.

47. A. E. Ewing to Milo Quaife, Apr. 9, 1919, Clarke Historical Library.

I wish you to know that I have heard some of the slanderous tales that have been put in circulation on that Island since I left and were I the only injured one by the uttering of such base falsehoods I should now forbear to write and wate patiently untill the future might satisfy all those that I care any thing about satisfying. But I am not the only one that is made the subject of slander[,] one that your tongue was always first to press.... I am surprised that such can be the case and am slow to believe, but James has hinted some things to me and others have talked plain.

I now say as I ever have said and ever expect to say, ... (that is) that Mormonism is with me first, middle and last; last at the expiration of life; I may change in many things but in the [s]entiments of our holy religion I change not; and I am not likely to change towards my friends, friends that are friends and are likely to remain unless changed by the poisonous arrows of slander.

I am aware that with you and others with whom I dared I used more freedom than perhaps was always prudent, but in all God knows my heart and to him I appeal[,] And to you[;] and I am aware that with you I used more freedom than with any other one and I shall not now assign a reason but may at some future time and I have a great anxiety to come back soon and see the people that I love better than all the rest of God's people on earth. Well Betsy, I must close my letter for the present, give my love to all that in my absence don't slander me[,] and those that do may look forward to the day when shame will come to them and that not long first.[48]

Whatever deficiencies Betsy may have had in social skills, and she appears to have had a reputation for having a presumptuous temperament, her husband was very pleased with her. She bore him four children—Evangeline in 1853; David James, who only lived about ten days, on June 22, 1854; Gabriel in 1855; and Abigail on January 1, 1857. One of Strang's followers noticed how he grieved over the baby's death, "counting the days till they ran into months."[49]

While Betsy took care of the domestic chores for the household, Elvira served as Strang's private secretary and looked after his business correspondence when he was absent. At one time she had a file of more than a hundred letters from distinguished government officials. She also kept meteorological

---

48. Samuel Graham to Elizabeth McNutt, July 30, 1851, Clarke Historical Library. The other person Graham alludes to was probably his wife Leah, who died in 1856 at the age of thirty-three.

49. Eugenia Phillips to Stanley Johnston, May 24, 1938, Clarke Historical Library.

records on the island's weather. She observed the clearness of the sky, temperature, wind course, and wind velocity every day of the week at sunrise and other specified times: 9:00 a.m., 3:00 p.m., and 9:00 p.m. The results were published in each issue of the *Northern Islander* and later submitted to the National Smithsonian Institution.[50]

Elvira may have also taught school on Beaver Island. She felt it was important for children to be educated so they could occupy "honorable positions" in life.[51] She loved the "beauties of nature" such as her flower garden. She knew the botanical names of most of the common flowers and shrubs, as well as for many of the trees of the forest. She detested profanity and the use of tobacco and liquor in any form.[52] In addition to Charles, who was born on April 6, 1851, she gave birth to a daughter, Evaline,[53] on April 18, 1853, Clement on December 20, 1854, and James J. on January 22, 1857.

Elvira and Betsy set an example for other women on the island in many ways, including their adoption of bloomers in place of the traditional floor-length dresses of the period. Bloomers became a customary costume for women on Beaver Island. Strang thought this sort of attire was safer and more sanitary than long skirts that could get caught in the fireplace or dragged in the mud. Elvira was the first to make and wear the bloomer costume. It consisted of pantalets—long loose trousers made of calico that were gathered about the ankles, then covered by a skirt that came down to the knees. The calico overdress had no waistline but hung straight from the shoulders and was made without a single "tuck, ruffle or puff."[54] The portion of the bloomers below the skirt was made of the same material the dress was made of and was not longer than an ordinary shirt sleeve. It reached from below the top of the shoe to above the knee, where it fastened to the usual drawers either by hemstitch or lap seam.[55]

---

50. Elvira Field Strang Baker Memorial Book, State Library of Michigan.

51. Clement Strang to Chester W. Ellison, Oct. 10, 1941, Clarke Historical Library.

52. Baker Memorial Book.

53. Evaline was called. "Eva" with a short *e* to distinguish her from Betsy's daughter Evangeline, or "Eva" with a long *e* vowel sound.

54. "Saw a King Crowned: Woman Living at Fish Creek Recalls a Most Curious Incident," *Green Bay Advocate,* Feb. 7, 1905. Cecilia Hill called the bloomer outfit "hideous." Beads, jewelry, or any personal adornment was taboo. Hill said the women wore their hair slicked back and tightly braided.

55. Gabriel Strang to John Wake, May 8, 1929, Clarke Historical Library.

Most of the women on the island wore this outfit.[56] Elvira's mother, Eliza Field, and an older woman hated the costume but put up with it because they were "loyal to the king."[57] Gentiles thought it was a particularly strange garb. One man visiting the Beaver Islands for two days said he could tolerate polygamy but he did not like seeing the Mormon women wearing "pants." "I do not object to the number [of wives assigned to] each man, but the trousers I do not like," he wrote.[58] At least one Strangite said the women he knew preferred bloomers to the "long sidewalk sweeping" dresses worn by other women. Wingfield Watson asserted that the women were not compelled to wear bloomers if they did not wish to. "And dear me," he said, "I knew a good many who wore them long after the saints were driven from there, and said they would wear them in spite of any fashion to the contrary; simply because they had learned that they were easy healthful and convenient. No compulsion was necessary in this matter. The prophet of God taught them to wear those short and convenient dresses, and they willingly obeyed and found that there was a blessing in it like all other things taught by prophets of God."[59]

A Michigan judge, Samuel T. Douglass, wrote about seeing the fashion among Mormon women. "We stopped with Strang who lived in a log house with four rooms and two wives; rooms upstairs led us to believe that he slept with them on the other night plan," Douglass wrote. "All the women on the island wore the bloomer costume," he added. He was not the only outsider to take an interest, not only in the ladies' clothing, but the evident signs of polygamy on Beaver Island. Michigan district attorney George Bates, who prosecuted Strang in Detroit, claimed to have seen the evidence when he traveled to Beaver Island to arrest Strang for counterfeiting and obstructing the mail. However, his recollection was sensationalist. He wrote:

> The capturing party on arriving [about 2:00 a.m.] at the place where Strang usually slept, saw light gleaming from an upper window of a long hewn log building two stories high, with the gable end toward the path.... [T]he district attorney and the faithful deputy crept quietly upstairs, entered a long, low room

56. "The King of the Saints," *New York Times*, Sept. 3, 1882. Also Judge Samuel T. Douglass, interviewed by C. K. Backus, June 9, 1877, Clarke Historical Library.

57. Clement Strang to Stanley Johnston, Dec. 4, 1940, Clarke Historical Library.

58. J. C. Dousman to "Dear Sir," Nov. 16, 1855, Clarke Historical Library.

59. Wingfield W. Watson to unknown, n.d., letter fragment, 9-13, Clarke Historical Library.

where wide berths, heavily draped with stunning calico, shielded beds like the berths and staterooms of steamers, which proved to be occupied by Mormon women four in a bed.[60]

Bates's deficiency in observation or memory aside, his narrative showed the common gentile assumption about Mormons in the 1850s.

The actual practice of polygamy among the Strangites was strictly regulated according to the Book of the Law of the Lord. "At first it was talked of quietly and secretly among the leaders and afterwards publicly and openly among the people," Elvira Field recalled. "It was not looked upon favorably and there were never over 20 cases of plural marriage upon the islands. No man had more than three wives except Strang," she said.[61] In fact, a man had to show he had the means and ability to care for an additional wife before entering into a commitment. Any sort of lewdness or prostitution was disallowed. "Of course in dealing with those outside the Church it was necessary to resort to the civil law," Elvira explained in another carefree allusion to the imposition of Mormon standards on outsiders. Still, there were different standards for church members. "By-laws for the kingdom were adopted and published, and every household possessed a copy. They were very strict in all that regulated society, morals, and religious observances, and absolute obedience was enjoined."[62]

Wingfield Watson arrived on the island in 1852. He said that at first, "if anyone asked ... if we believed in [polygamy] we had to make an effort to prevent blushing, ... so strongly was our antiquated traditions riveted upon us."[63] He said that to the best of his knowledge there were only about eighteen polygamous families on Beaver Island. More would have entered into plural marriage if they could have afforded it and if there had been more women to go around, he ventured. He acknowledged the dampening effect in the community on those who remained opposed to the practice.[64] Still, because it was carried out in such a highly honorable fashion, according to Watson, few women raised objections. He said he and his wife discussed practic-

---

60. George C. Bates, "The Beaver Island Prophet," *Detroit News*, [July 10, 1877], Clarke Historical Library.

61. "King of the Saints," *New York Times*, Sept. 3, 1882.

62. Ibid.

63. Wingfield Watson to unknown.

64. Wingfield W. Watson interview, Dec. 10-11, 1918.

ing polygamy but were driven from the island before they felt they were ready to do so.[65]

In a letter from 1929, Gabriel Strang listed the men he knew to have participated in polygamy. Wingfield Watson's name was on the list. "Among those whom I know who had more than one wife in this dispensation," Gabriel wrote, "are Joseph and Hyrum Smith, John E. and B. T. [Ebeneezer or Finley] Page, James J. Strang, L. D. Hickey, Marvin M. Aldrich, Jonathan Pierce, Phineas, Samuel and B. J. [G.] Wright, A. N. Hosmer, Ludlow Hill, William Bickle, Jas. C. Hutchins, Wingfield Watson, and John Raymon, one of whose wives had been a wife of Hyrum Smith. Her daughter Ellen was born shortly after Hyrum was killed: I lived next door to them a couple of years in 1864-5."[66]

One of the men on the list, Benjamin G. Wright, married Rhoda Ballard Whitney, Adeline Ballard Whitney, and Nancy Richardson all on the same day. The three women were widows of Clark Lyman Whitney, George Miller's associate who died in 1851. Wright married the widows in order "to care for them and support them" and to "raise up seed" to their deceased husband, according to the tenets of the Book of the Law of the Lord.[67] Two of the women, Rhoda and Adeline, were sisters, and Nancy was their maternal aunt. Nancy was past childbearing age when she was sealed to Clark and she never changed her name from Richardson. Benjamin's legal wife, Margaret, never shared her home with these women, who lived in a separate home, according to a Wright family descendent.[68]

Many years later, Lorenzo Dow Hickey explained the importance of polygamy to the Strangites:

> Now with reference to us Strangite people, we generally calculate to marry for life everlasting; but if a man had lost his wife and wanted to have her [in the next life], he would have both of them [his wives] sealed to him. The [wife] that was living would not be piggish and say he could not have the [wife] that

---

65. Gabriel Strang to John Wake, May 8, 1929, Clarke Historical Library. Gabriel experienced a close familial relationship with Watson all his life and would have known Watson's marital situation. Aside from this one statement, however, there is no other evidence to support Gabriel's claim.

66. Gabriel Strang to John Wake, May 8, 1929.

67. Personal correspondence with a descendent of Benjamin G. Wright, 2002.

68. Ibid.

was dead, so he would have her sealed to him, and then have both of them.

Strang translated the plates that he claimed were genuine and found in them the [principle] of polygamy; and after the translation he published it, and then he indorsed the doctrine of polygamy after he was commanded to do so.... It was not part of the Strangite doctrine until after the translation of the Book of the Law of the Lord....

Strang never believed in polygamy until that time, and when he translated the plates and found out that they taught polygamy, he threw the whole thing on the floor and said he would not go any further with it ... and he did not believe in it then until the Lord knocked it into him.[69]

This apologetic is intriguing for its parallel to what was later said about Joseph Smith, that the prophet entered into polygamy reluctantly only after an angel drew a sword and threatened him with annihilation unless he complied.[70] In both cases, these vivid, dramatic stories and underlying assumptions are difficult to harmonize with the chronologies of events available to historians, but in whatever way polygamy was first initiated, it became established in the minds of the faithful as a sign of piety rather than a mark of a libertine.

---

69. Lorenzo Dow Hickey testimony, *Reorganized Church of Jesus Christ of Latter Day Saints vs. Church of Christ, et al., Independence, Missouri, 1891-94*, Detroit Public Library; cf. *The Temple Lot Case: Complainant's Abstract of Pleading and Evidence, in the Circuit Court of the United Sates, Western District of Missouri, Western Division, at Kansas City; The Reorganized Church of Jesus Christ of Latter Day Saints, Complainant, v. The Church of Christ at Independence Missouri* (Independence, MO: Price Publishing, 2003), 407-08. Hickey's obituary erroneously says he was a devoted Mormon who nevertheless rejected polygamy (*Coldwater Daily Reporter*, Apr. 26, 1897).

70. See, e.g., Lawrence Foster, "A Little-Known Defense of Polygamy from the Mormon Press in 1842," *Dialogue: A Journal of Mormon Thought* 9 (Winter 1974): 22n4, in which Foster observes that "accounts of the 'angel with a drawn sword' story are widespread, although manuscript evidence for such a story apparently does not exist from the period when Joseph Smith was alive."

10.

THE CHOSEN PEOPLE

1852-1853

Lord God! ... Look down from thy
holy habitation from heaven, and bless us this day, even all the children of
thy kingdom; and the land which thou hast given us, and establish us for-
ever....

We were a people, few in number; scattered among our enemies: they
killed our prophets, murdered our brethren, robbed us of our possessions,
and banished us from among them; but God has made us a kingdom; and
the fear of us is upon those who hate us.

When the gentiles evilly entreated us and afflicted us, and thrust us
out, we cried unto the Lord God of our fathers; the Lord heard our voice,
and looked on our affliction, and sorrow, and homelessness; and he gave us
this land for an everlasting possession; and hath made us a kingdom.
—The Book of the Law of the Lord [1]

T he fifteenth of June, 1852, arrived unseasonably hot on Beaver Island. Elvira Field took the temperature and found it to be eighty
degrees in the shade. The temperature had been 112 degrees at noon the day
before. The Mormon men had finished sowing their crops, including some
late oats and turnips, and the women had planted their vegetable and flower
gardens. Immigration was steady.[2] The fisheries around the island were not
as good as in previous years, but large quantities of fish were still being har-
vested from Lake Michigan and were selling for as much as seven to eight
dollars a barrel.[3]

---

1. *The Book of the Law of the Lord, consisting of an inspired translation of some of the most*
important parts of the law given to Moses, and a very few additional commandments, with brief notes
and references (Saint James, MI: Printed by command of the King at the Royal Press, 1851),
60-61, copy at the Library-archives, Wisconsin Historical Library, Madison, Wisconsin.

2. *Northern Islander,* June 17, 1852, [p. 2].

3. *Northern Islander,* July 15, 1852, [p. 3].

On the Fourth of July, the Propeller *Troy* made a visit to St. James.[4] A correspondent for the *Erie Chronicle* was on board and later reported a brief description of the island and history of the conflict between the Mormons and their non-member neighbors:[5]

> This Island is yet very little settled.... A few feet from the beach the shores rise very regularly to the height of 12 to 15 feet. On the margin of this bank stands the foundation of a temple—100 feet long by 60 feet wide—which has been abandoned for a while on account of the late difficulties. The Mormons say they have been persecuted, and no doubt they have. A good deal of prejudice exists against them among the surrounding people. Some of this prejudice has probably a foundation, and some of it none.
>
> Like John and James and Zebidee of old, most of them are fishermen; and like all other people rendered a little exclusive in feelings and interest by devotion to a despised religion, they don't like to have unfriendly Gentiles come from a distance to surround their Island with nets and deprive them of the means of substance. This was done. A little feeling was aroused on both sides; recrimination followed crimination; threat followed threat, until the consequences was more serious and terrible than could have been desired by either party in the beginning.
>
> The Mormons who participated in the proceedings referred to were undoubtedly culpable beyond all exemption; but evil doings of a few graceless scamps should not taint with infamy the good intentions and good behavior of any community of real or professing Christian people.
>
> It may be that I have been deceived by the outward appearance and professions of these Islanders, but my impression is, they are a community disposed to do well when let alone.[6]

Although they were living on the edge of the Michigan frontier and the island was still "very little settled," as the journalist reported, the Strangites nevertheless enjoyed some of the pleasures of civilization. A Mrs. Philmot lived next door to the Indian Mission Schoolhouse and gave daily piano lessons and classes in the German language. Roswell Packard had just opened a new store with a general assortment of dry goods, hardware, and groceries

---

4. The Mormon community of Troy was apparently named after this ship. The captain of the *Troy* was a friend to the Strangites.

5. "From the Erie Chronicle," *Northern Islander*, Aug.12, 1852.

6. Ibid.

one door south of the printing office. He preferred cash but would trade his goods for wood, fish, grain, or almost any kind of produce that could be raised on the island. E. H. Derby offered "gentlemen's garments of all description made to order," while another merchant, located one door south of the tabernacle, had a quantity of wool for sale for hosiery.[7]

Franklin Johnson's store offered "a full assortment of fresh goods," which were sold at "Buffalo and Detroit prices." Dry goods, groceries, fishing tackle, and various other supplies were sold, including kitchen stoves. For the women, Johnson offered shawls, bonnets, calicos in various patterns, and other fabrics for multipurpose use.[8] There was even a self-proclaimed scientist on the island, Moses Chase, who had invented the "common and improved single, double and triple complex, re-acting, galvano, electro-magnetic torpedo machine," which—whatever that may have designated—was offered for sale to those who "had a mind for science."[9]

The Strangites celebrated holidays and social occasions. Church services were held on Saturdays with classes at 9:00 a.m., followed by meetings at 11:00 a.m. and 2:00 p.m. Prayer meetings were held on Thursdays and Saturday evenings. The weekly newspaper, the *Northern Islander*, was published every Thursday during the navigation season and periodically the rest of the year. For a time there was also a debate club, a thespian group, and of course the secret society of Illuminati, which met one evening a week. There was a religiously based educational society called the School of the Prophets, as well.[10]

On July 8, the second anniversary of Strang's coronation, the church held a conference and special ceremony to commemorate the event. It opened at sunrise with a "most solemn sacrifice." Ninety-five families presented animals that day to be killed, cooked, and dismembered without breaking or cutting a bone. The tables were spread with a "splendid feast" and 488 persons sat down about 1:00 p.m. to eat.[11] After the meal, there were sermons and a baptismal service at Font Lake.

---

7. Ibid., July 15, 1852.

8. Ibid.

9. Ibid.

10. Gabriel Strang to Chester Flanders, letter fragments, July 7, 1919, Clarke Historical Library, Central Michigan University, Mount Pleasant, Michigan.

11. "Conference," *Northern Islander*, July 8, 1852.

By all appearances, the colony of Mormons was rapidly maturing into a peaceful and prosperous settlement. However, it was an illusion. The gentiles who had left the island had not gone quietly. In the *Green Bay Spectator,* it was reported that the Mormons had driven away residents and that the refugees were now destitute. Strang hesitated to admit any wrongdoing but suggested that if anyone had been driven from Beaver Island, it was because they deserved it. This was the beginning of the fulfillment of scripture, he wrote in the *Northern Islander,* to "reward her as she rewarded you."

> For we have not forgotten that 10,000 of these "Latter Day Saints" were driven in destitution, poverty and want from the State of Missouri, without so much as being accused of a crime.... And we ... remember full well that 25,000 of these Latter Day Saints have also been driven in destitution, poverty, and want from the State of Illinois leaving behind them the ruins of the most populous city in the State, and $5,000,000 worth of lands, of which they were robbed to enrich their spoilers.... If there are any persons who have been driven from here in poverty and want, they came to want by drunkenness, and by spending their time and money in trying to drive off the Latter Day Saints. The pit they dug for us have they fallen in to, and there has been no driving except by sending officers of the law to arrest them for their perjuries and their thefts. If this is driving men off, we intend to keep at it, and the editors of the *Spectator* are welcome to keep them company. Fit associates they are.[12]

In an article about piracy in the Great Lakes, the *Green Bay Advocate* noted that the crimes were generally attributed to "desperadoes from the Beaver Islands."[13] Strang countered in his newspaper that two years ago "the desperadoes" had stolen eighteen or twenty barrels of pork and lard from a Mormon store on Beaver Island. The items were later found buried in the sand at the front door of the home of one of the Mormons' enemies on the island. Strang related how his people had been blamed for taking a boat belonging to the keeper of the Isle-le-Galet (Skilagalee) lighthouse. The boat was later found on Hog Island just as the owner had left it, with clothing, provisions, nets, and spyglass undisturbed. "The people have itching ears to hear something against the Mormons," he accused the gentile newspaper. "No matter what occurs, if it is ill done it is laid to them. And there are fools enough who

---

12. Ibid., July 15, 1852, [p. 2].
13. "Anxious to Be Noticed," *Northern Islander,* Aug. 5, 1852.

will pretend to believe it if they know it false. In truth, the officers in this region need somebody to lay their blunders to."[14]

Several newspapers had blamed the Mormons for the theft of a lantern, a piece of chain, and some old irons from a wharf 120 miles east of Beaver Island. Strang denied the charges, replying tongue-in-cheek that 120 miles was really too far for the Mormons to go for a few shillings' worth of materials.[15] He speculated that the gentile fishermen who were unable or unwilling to repay the traders who had advanced them money for supplies were inclined to say the Mormons had stolen the items so the fishermen could default on their payments. When fishermen relocated to distant fisheries, the missing items mysteriously appeared again, according to Strang's interpretation.

A few months earlier during the November 1851 elections, the residents of Beaver Island had gained strength in the political arena. Prior to the elections, there was a reapportionment of voting districts and Emmet County, in which Beaver Island was located, was attached to the Newago district instead of the legislative district at Mackinac. Few in Emmet County realized the implications of this adjustment, and the Strangites used the general ignorance of the change to their advantage. Strang was nominated to run for state representative, but he chose not to announce his candidacy until election day on November 2.[16] Not even the four other candidates in the district knew Strang was a contender.

The canvassers, who met several hundred miles away in Newago, were shocked when a Strangite messenger arrived with the results of the Mormon vote. The messenger had to convince the electors that the Beaver Islands were part of their district, and when this was confirmed, Strang was shown to be the clear winner. He made preparations to travel to Lansing in January to appear in his responsibility as a new delegate to the Michigan state legislature. He wrote his brother David shortly after the election, setting down his feelings about the matter:

> You have doubtless learned already that I am elected to the House of Representatives of the State of Michigan. All circumstances considered[,] I regard my election a great triumph. The office I do not value. I would sooner resign today if I could get the same things done which I believe I can accomplish by be-

14. "Government Property Stolen," *Northern Islander,* Aug. 19, 1852.
15. "Stealing on the Fisheries," *Northern Islander,* Apr. 13, 1854.
16. "Mr. Strang in the Legislature," *Northern Islander,* Apr. 13, 1854.

ing in the House. But that after all the injuries I have suffered, and all the contumely I have endured, I should be elected to represent twenty six counties in the legislature, without a political organization to sustain me, and with religious prejudice, [and] vast local interests and great wealth to oppose, is certainly no ordinary triumph....

But I began early with some notion of improving the condition of the human race, of bettering my fellowmen; nothing, perhaps, [but will be] a little imperceivable; but nevertheless benevolent, and such as could be sustained only by those philanthropists who are willing to sacrifice and suffer for the sake of others; notions which[,] if they are never received among men, will be rejected because they are too heavenly.

And for having such ideas, and seeking to practice upon them[,] I have been set upon, maligned, and my footsteps dogged as a shadow from the days of my childhood til this day. They have caricatured virtues which they lacked; belied my actions, and misconstrued my motives, until I was nearly crushed beneath the load of infamy they heaped upon me. I was made the sinner and they the Saints who [claimed they] loathed all vice. And this is my revenge; —to triumph in the forums of the same publick where they sought and well-nigh accomplished my ruin. Beyond that I am near indifferent to either wealth or publick honours. I have twice as much of either as I know what to do with. Moreover, I am fully persuaded that my future fame depends upon the calling which God has put upon me, and not upon any office which men can bestow.[17]

The people of Mackinac were mortified by Strang's election and moved to keep him from taking his seat in Lansing. The old warrant for his arrest, when he had helped McCulloch escape, was conjured up. In fact, an ambush was set to catch the newly elected representative on his way to Lansing. Strang anticipated this and thwarted his attackers by traveling a different route. When he arrived in the Michigan state capitol, he discovered his certificate of election had disappeared from the files at the office of the Secretary of State and that a police officer was waiting to arrest him before roll call at the House. Strang had brought along a copy of his certificate of election and successfully convinced the House to examine the arrest charges against him. His case for election was accepted and he was allowed to take his seat.[18]

The Mormon prophet was a big attraction in the Michigan capitol. "Mr.

---

17. James Strang to David Strang, Nov. 25, 1852, Clarke Historical Library.

18. "Mr. Strang in the Legislature," *Detroit Advertiser,* Feb. 10, 1853, rpt. *Northern Islander,* May 10, 1853.

Strang's course as a member of the present Legislature, has disarmed much of the prejudices, which have previously surrounded him," reported the *Detroit Advertiser.* "Whatever is said or thought of the peculiar sect of which he is the local head, I take pleasure in stating that throughout this session he has conducted himself with a degree of decorum and propriety which have been equaled by his industry, sagacity, good temper, apparent regard for the true interests of the people, and the obligations of his official oath."[19]

The *Temperance Advocate* had equally high praise for Strang as a Michigan representative, reporting Strang to be the most talented and ready debater in the House:

> He seems equally ready on any subject, political, commercial, financial, judicial, educational, or anything else in the range of legislation. He is bold, decided, positive and often overbearing in debate, and sometimes reckless in his statements … and woe to him that provokes his satire and sarcasm, for his wit is as unmettled as it is ready in retort. He is ardent, passionate and rapid in his oratory, even to a fault, but is clear and forcible in argument, and never fails to make himself understood…. From his social position as 'King of Beaver Island,' he is the lion of the House, and is always pointed out to the ladies visiting the Capitol.[20]

Back home, the gentiles of nearby Mackinac Island were less than impressed with Strang's lofty orations and apparent benevolence. By virtue of their greater population and bloc voting, the Mormons had managed to elect several members to important township and county positions, making them a growing and immediate threat to Mackinac. This was not helped by the officiousness of the newly elected sheriff of Beaver Island, the Strangite George Miller, who announced his intention in May 1853 to arrest any trader or fisherman who sold alcohol on Lake Michigan. He was ostensibly responding to a new state law that required the licensing of alcohol vendors, but the fishermen and traders in the area reacted with animosity and malevolence.[21]

The *Northern Islander* reported that "there is a prevalent practice of sending out trading vessels to trade on the fishing grounds with a supply of liquors. We wish it understood," the editors stated, "that authority to sell intoxicating liquors in Mackinac does not carry with it the right to sell on Lake

---

19. Ibid.
20. *Temperance Advocate,* Feb. 10, 1853, rpt. *Northern Islander,* May 10, 1853.
21. "Sheriff of Mackinac," *Northern Islander,* May 5, 1853.

Michigan.... If the trade is persisted in, the Sheriff will go out with sufficient force and make arrests in all such cases. The law will be enforced whatever the cost."[22] In response, the gentiles accused the Mormons of robbing and committing depredations upon the fishermen of Lake Michigan. John W. McMath, a correspondent for the *Detroit Free Press*, wrote:

> It appears that the Mormons are becoming more daring than formerly. Heretofore, they were satisfied with robbing the poor fishermen of their boats, nets, and fish, stealthily, doing everything possible to avoid detection; but now seeing the almost utter impossibility of being brought to justice, they carry on their piratical trade with scarcely any regard to concealment. This, of course, arises from the fact that now all offenses committed upon the shores and waters of Lake Michigan ... must be tried on Beaver Island, by Mormon tribunals, with good Mormons for witnesses and jurymen.[23]

Mormons were accused of destroying fish shanties and stealing boats and nets from gentile fishermen, especially those near Gull Island and the mainland. McMath continued his report:

> There are quite a number of fisherman here [Mackinac] who are ready to commence business each with a stock worth from four to six hundred dollars, who dare not go to the fishing grounds for fear of the Mormons. The nature of their business is such that it is nearly impossible to keep anything like a guard over their property. Their nets when set for fish are often eight or ten miles from their dwellings with buoys attached which can be seen only a mile or two off. The Mormons soon learn the locations of these nets, and when the wind is fair, sail out to them in their small boats which move very rapidly, taking them up, [and] then[,] shifting their sails, are soon far away on the water, leaving no trace by which to be detected.
>
> In the night they make their descent upon the land, steal, rob and burn what they can find, then with oars and sail they glide away upon the watery element, and the fisherman wakes up in the morning but to find his boats, nets and perhaps all the property he has in the world stolen or destroyed. The only reason that can be assigned for these acts is (as they have openly declared) that they intend to monopolize these fishing grounds, and appropriate the same to the service of the Lord and his "Saints."[24]

---

22. Ibid.

23. "Mackinac Mob Administration," *Northern Islander,* June 30, 1853.

24. Ibid. Depositions signed by persons claiming to have been robbed by the Strang-

With such an agitated and politically charged atmosphere, decisive action on the part of one group or the other was perhaps inevitable. In fact, on May 16, 1853, a large number of people, including prominent citizens, met at the Mackinac Island courthouse to discuss how the fishermen and others could protect their property from the Mormons. They expressed sympathy for the fishermen who had purportedly suffered losses at the hands of the Mormons. They drafted a resolution pledging to cooperate in preventing the recurrence of such misfortune. "The high-handed pretensions and immoral courses of the people called Mormons are inimical to our republican institutions, subversive of the good order of society, and destructive of all security to person and property," the resolution read.[25]

Going so far as to anticipate bloodshed, the Mackinac residents vowed "to resist to the last extremity any and every attempt to commit depredations upon the persons and property of our citizens, whether committed by open violence or under the pretended sanction of legal authority." Five or six of the men in attendance were selected as a "safety committee" to appeal to the president of the United States and the governor of Michigan for assistance in stopping the Mormons, to call public meetings of the citizens when urgency required it, and to "take such measures as may seem conductive to the public safety."[26]

Strang published an article about the meeting in the *Northern Islander.* He countered by explaining that Mormons were only trying to enforce the state liquor laws in Emmett County. "The village of Mackinac has a larger proportion of its population engaged in the business of selling intoxicating liquors, particularly in retailing it than any other village of the same population in the State. And in the trade," he explained, "which Mackinac carries on in the fishing grounds, more profits are made upon the liquors probably than upon all other articles together. But of the ruin and moral desolation which this trade carries with it on the fisheries, no man can form any conception but he who has seen it."

Strang insisted that although charges had been made about Mormons

---

ites can be found in the Jacob Merritt Howard Collection, Yale Collection of Western Americana, Beinecke Rare Book and Manuscript Library, Yale University, New Haven, Connecticut.

25. Ibid.

26. Ibid.

stealing and robbing, no proof had ever been shown for any infraction of this kind. "Why is it that the temperance men throughout the State—with here and there an individual exception, join in this crusade of a liquor selling people, against the only municipality in the State where the liquor law is enforced; against the only county in the State in which no liquor is sold?" He wondered how far non-Mormons would push this. Will they "endeavor by bloodshed and civil war to force the trade upon us?" he asked. Provocatively, he answered his rhetorical question with this: "Our reply to Mackinac and her allies is 'let words cease and deeds begin.'... We prefer peace; but if war must come, let it be upon us and not upon our children. We shall not yield a step to the threats, and are ready for the blow."[27]

A group of about seventy-five fishermen and traders living in a settlement called Pine River, now the present day town of Charlevoix, on the Michigan mainland about thirty-five miles southeast of Beaver Island, had apparently written to the residents of Mackinac asking for protection against the Mormons. The Mackinac Safety Committee wrote back offering the residents support and advice:

> Friends: We have received your communications and very sincerely sympathize with you.... We feel that the time has come when something must be done, promptly &, energetickly; or else to submit, to abandon yo[u]r fishing grounds and to seek a home and a living elsewhere. There is no middle ground on which we can stand. To submit and surrender yo[u]r rights—to join the Mormons, or to resist their practices & pretentious, to punish their outrages and if need be to banish them from the land. It is a strife in which there can be no reconciliation, and no compromise; it may require violent measures, and may terminate in bloodshed, But there is no other alternative and you must count the cost and be prepared for the last resort. If such should unfortunately be the result at last, now is the time for action. These people are rapidly increasing and it will be easier to crush the serpent in its weak infancy than to wait until years add to his venom and strength.[28]

The Safety Committee provided a list of measures the people at Pine River should undertake to prepare to fight the Mormons. The recommendations included setting a signal to guard their boats and organizing reliable men

---

27. Ibid.

28. "Address to the Inhabitants of Pine River," May 19,1853, James Strang Papers, Burton Historical Collection, Detroit Public Library.

who could be depended upon in an emergency, whose guns should be loaded and conveniently available for immediate action.[29] Something was bound to happen—and it did.

In mid-July 1853, the Mormon sheriff of Emmet County, George Miller, went to Pine River to summon three people for jury duty for the approaching circuit court, which would be held on Beaver Island. The residents of Pine River had vowed they would not accept any legal process promoted by the government on Beaver Island and threatened violence against anyone who attempted it. In order to avoid potential problems, the Mormon sheriff took two boats and fourteen men with him, thinking this would avert trouble until he had announced his reason for being there. The fifteen men had a total of four guns with them.[30]

The women of Pine River were holding a quilting party that day in one of the homes at the mouth of the river. When they saw the two boats approaching, they spread the alarm. Before long, a large crowd had gathered at the beach to see what was happening. To avoid trouble, the Mormons left their guns in the bottoms of their boats. The sheriff assured the people he was not there to make trouble but wanted only to serve three men with summonses for jury duty. Two of the men summoned were Mormons who had fled Beaver Island under the guise of moving to Drummond Island, but who had gone to the Pine River settlement instead. The third was a gentile fisherman who had briefly joined the Mormon Church in 1849 or 1850.[31]

The Pine River residents believed the summonses were a pretext to get these men back on the island to punish them for leaving. The residents stood by the ex-Mormons and told the sheriff and his party the best thing they could do would be to leave immediately or they would be "made to go." The Mormons headed for their boats. What happened next is not exactly clear. The residents of Pine River claimed that when the Mormons shoved off, one of the them fired his gun and wounded a small boy in the leg. The enraged fishermen jumped into their boats and began chasing the Mormons, firing at them as they paddled. The chase continued for about twelve miles into Lake

---

29. Ibid.

30. James Strang, *Ancient and Modern Michilimackinac, Including an Account of the Controversy between Mackinac and the Mormons* (1854; Ann Arbor: University of Michigan Library, 1987), 40-41.

31. M. L. Leach, "A History of the Grand Traverse Region," *Grand Traverse Herald*, 1883, 94-95. The three men were David Moon, William Savage, and one named Hull.

Michigan. Six of the Mormons were wounded as more than fifty balls passed through their boats and rigging. Just as the gentiles were about to catch up, the Mormons came upon the bark *Morgan* and begged for sanctuary.[32]

Captain E. S. Stone was having dinner in his cabin when he heard "a great firing of guns." He and his crew rushed to the deck to see a small fleet of rowboats coming toward them from the south shore. "They were evidently in a fierce battle, and viewing them from my spyglass, I saw that there were three [actually two] Boats filled with men fleeing from some larger barges, double banked with oars, that were rapidly gaining on the smaller boats, and firing on them as fast as they could load and fire." Stone recalled that "when the smaller boats got near enough to hail us, they asked us for God's sake to take them on board and save them from being murdered, as they were completely exhausted and could pull no longer and were being shot to pieces."

Stone granted their request. The bullets flew thick around the Mormon boats as they pulled alongside, some shots striking the bow of the *Morgan*. "The men in the boats in chase hailed me, demanding that I should drive them off, as they were Mormons, robbers and thieves, and they wanted to kill everyone of them; and if I did not do so they would fire into my vessel, which threat I knew they did not dare carry out," Stone recalled.

"In taking the Mormons on board, I found all of them armed with rifles, and the first one as he stepped on board turned and said: 'Now we will give it to them.' I caught and disarmed him and all the rest as they came over the rail. When they were all onboard I asked the fishermen from Pine River to come nearer and talk with me, which they did, but not near enough to be recognized, as there were some on both sides that knew me and called me by name."[33]

The fishermen claimed the Mormons were the aggressors. The Mormons denied this, saying they had not fired a shot. They showed Stone their guns to prove that all were fully loaded and not a shot was missing. Of the fifteen Mormons, six were severely wounded; their boats were riddled with bullets and bespattered with blood. The water in the bottom of the boats was full of blood. "It seemed almost a miracle that none of them were killed. An oar

---

32. Ibid.

33. Henry E. Legler, *A Moses of the Mormons: Strang's City of Refuge and Island Kingdom* (Milwaukee: Parkman Club, ca. 1897), 165-68.

pulled by one of the men was struck by three bullets, yet the man was unhurt," Stone recalled.

The fishermen lay on their oars for some time watching the Mormons on the ship. They finally got tired of waiting and pulled their boats back to their homes at Pine River. The crew of the *Morgan* dressed the wounded men's injuries as best they could and then fed their guests. That night, under the cover of darkness, the Mormons returned to their boats and pulled the best they could for their homes on Beaver Island.[34] A few days later a rumor reached Pine River that over a hundred Mormons were making preparations to retaliate. The fishermen "knew there could be no hope of successfully resisting such a force," so they abandoned the settlement. The little steamer *Columbia* came in and took most of the fishermen and their families to Washington Island at the mouth of Green Bay, Wisconsin, but some went to other locations.[35]

In a circuit court hearing held on Beaver Island, several of the gentiles were indicted for attempted murder, but almost a year later none had been apprehended. "Since then there has been no attempt to interrupt the due course of legal administration in Emmet," Strang wrote. "The population is rapidly increasing. Though as yet it has no rich men, it has no paupers. There are schools for all the children. No liquors are sold," he boasted, "and the population are contented, prosperous and happy." Even the "Indian population are superior in moral and material progress to any others in the State."[36]

---

34. Ibid.

35. Leach, "History of the Grand Traverse," 94-96

36. Strang, *Ancient and Modern Michilimackinac*, 41.

11

TENSIONS MOUNT

1854-1855

"You might easily have divided the colony into two classes. There was one division as peaceable as any community, ... honest and hard working. Sincere believers in the Mormon faith, they had come to their new homes at the behest of Strang to earn an honest living and to lve in peace. They were not polygamists and did not believe in that doctrine. When polygamy was introduced in 1849, many of them would gladly have got out. But Strang had them bound in bonds of steel. Any deserter of Mormonism lost all his property, according to the laws of the church, and if a man left the island he was compelled to leave everything he had.... Strang had his trusty lieutenants see that such laws were executed—[one] could not get away. This class [of sincere, hard-working people] was largely made up of industrious farmers, who made some of the best farms on the island. The second class were a tough lot. They were neither honest nor truthful. They would stoop to anything to abet their selfish and devilish ends. Between these two classes, Mormon troubles began."
—Charles R. Wright to the *Chicago Tribune*.[1]

For many of the Strangites, Beaver Island was a land flowing with milk and honey. Wingfield Watson, who arrived with his wife in June 1852, described the "refreshing breezes, pure water, splendid grass, ... cedar swamps for fencing, shingles, etc." Beyond the forests were "inland lakes [that] abounded with fish of many kinds" and "pleasant streams for cattle to quench their thirst and to run sawmills and gristmills." For emigrants from the prairies, the landscape was "trying and forbidding" at first, but they grew accustomed to it. "The Eastern people," by contrast, "got along with it very well from the first," according to Watson. Another advan-

---

1. "An American Principality with Two Kings," *Chicago Tribune*, Oct. 13, 1895, copy in the Library-archives, Wisconsin Historical Library, Madison, Wisconsin.

tage was that the colony was "free from the contamination of Gentile vices such as drunkenness, swearing, fashions and foul language."[2]

Three other families accompanied Watson and his wife inland about midway up the island and built cabins and began to clear the land for farms. When they needed provisions, they would simply "walk 6 miles and chop wood," sell it, purchase supplies, and return home with about "70 pounds of flour on our backs and a chunk of pork for the families." They would harvest lumber "til we got a little ahead," then "work away on our own places again." Watson said the road to Beaver Harbor was still just a cow path through cedar swamps and intermittent highlands covered by creeping hemlock.

Near their cabin, the Watsons "planted potatoes and corn, and squashes and pumpkins, rutabagas, turnips, and cabbage and various other things, among the logs." Wingfield reported that "they grew fine. Potatoes needed only a hole made and the sets put in, and covered up and they needed nothing more done to them till ready to harvest, and finer potatoes never grow; and so everything else. A hoe and a good ax were all that a man needed at the time to start with." A curiosity to Watson was that there was not a cemetery on the island that he knew of. In fact, he said, he knew of only two deaths during the period the Mormons lived there. "One was J. M. Greig, and the other a little infant child of Mr. Strang's. One man [,] noted for a little drollery [,] said the Island was so healthy that nobody died there, and that if a grave yard must be started they would have to get a corpse from Chicago."[3]

The colonists devoted their winters to cutting cordwood and hauling it to the docks for sale to the steamboats when summer arrived. A road called the King's Highway ran from the harbor at St. James up through the rest of the island. Other roads branched off from this highway and led to the various

---

2. John Cumming, "Wingfield Watson: The Loyal Disciple of James J. Strang," *Michigan History*, Dec. 1963, 315. Watson lived on Beaver Island but was not considered an important leader at that time.

3. Wingfield W. Watson, interviewed by Milo M. Quaife, Dec. 10-11, 1918, Clarke Historical Library, Central Michigan University, Mount Pleasant, Michigan. There were more deaths than Watson mentioned. For instance, Jonathan Pierce, George Preston, and two other Mormons were lost at sea on November 25, 1855, transporting goods between Pine River and Beaver Island. The boat washed up near the mainland shore, but the men's bodies were never recovered. This incident is noted in the *Northern Islander*, Jan. 24, 1856, and in M. L. Leach, "A History of the Grand Traverse Region," *Grand Traverse Herald*, 1883, Clarke Historical Library.

Mormon farms.[4] A log tabernacle sat on a bluff overlooking the harbor at St. James. This was one of the first construction projects initiated by the Mormons, but the work had slowed and was unfinished because of the frequent arrests and imprisonment of the Strangites. They did make progress on their houses, which were built of hewn logs and painted with whitewash.[5]

In April 1854, Strang announced that they would establish Strangite colonies on the Michigan mainland. Pine River was mentioned as a place with good farm land and water connections, with the further advantage that the gentiles who had lived there were now gone. It was said to be the best location in the region for building up an extensive farming community. Settlements were also begun on Drummond Island and other islands in Lake Michigan and Lake Huron. Drummond Island was relatively large, twenty miles long and thirteen miles wide. It was located in Lake Huron, about fifty miles east of Mackinac and therefore about ninety miles east of Beaver Island. It offered several harbors and numerous rocky bays. The major benefit in that part of the country was there were only a few settlers and no opposition to Mormons.[6]

Meanwhile, the Strangite towns on Beaver Island—St. James, Troy, Galilee, and Enoch—were progressing well. New converts arrived every summer and there was room for more. The *Northern Islander* gave an update for readers thinking of immigrating. "Every kind of business is prosperous at this place. Money was never as plenty as at this time," so the newspaper said. "Seventy-five cents per cord is freely offered for cutting wood in any quantities ... and yet the supply is far short of the demand. Fishermen are taking more than the usual quantities of fish, for which they are realizing good prices." The newspaper allowed that imported goods were unusually expensive, but were said to be tempered by the equally high prices the colonists were able to obtain for their exports. It was said that the crops were doing well, also that "several span of horses and numerous horned cattle, pigs, poultry, etc, have been brought [onto the island] this season, so that now the supply of stock is good. Large quantities of feed are produced for their winter supply." Although "occasionally" someone decided to leave the island for "employ-

---

4. Testimony of J. O. McNutt, Dec. 12, 1924, Clarke Historical Library.

5. Stanley L. Johnston to Mr. Ray, Oct. 5, 1960, Clarke Historical Library.

6. "Drummond Island," *Northern Islander,* Aug. 9, 1855. Drummond Island soon became the base for a large copper mining operation run by non-Mormons.

ment somewhere else, every kind of business here is seeking more hands than can be obtained. Two hundred additional hands would find constant employment," the article stated.[7]

At the same time, Mackinac Island was in decline after once having been the center of the fishing industry and political power in the northern Great Lakes. Fewer and fewer steamships were stopping to refuel at Mackinac because the island had been nearly depleted of lumber. As the wood and fishing trade declined there, business shifted to Beaver Island, creating even more resentment against the Mormons. What little trade had existed between the Mormons and gentiles all but dried up. "The trade between this place and Mackinac amounting a few years ago to $8,000 or $10,000 a year, has entirely run out," the *Northern Islander* reported. "We are quite warranted in saying that in 12 months past it has not amounted to $5.00."[8] Matters were so bad that the mail between Beaver and Mackinac, a distance of thirty to forty miles, went by way of Detroit.

Some of the Mackinac merchants were trying to rebuild trade relationships with the Strangites, but the Mormons resisted their overtures. As explained by the *Northern Islander:*

> Aside from any objection to patronizing particular men, there are strong reasons why we cannot do business with Mackinac at all. If there is trade between the two places, the advantages must be reciprocal. Now, it is well known that citizens of this place cannot go to Mackinac without going armed, or subjecting themselves to danger of personal violence.... The only terms on which we can consent to have any intercourse with them are, that, they will cease their warfare against us, and produce such a state of affairs there that we can go to Mackinac in our own boats with our property, without danger to person or property. And as this is the undivided feeling of the whole people here, and we are not dependent on Mackinac for anything whatever, they might as well talk against the east wind as undertake to break through it.[9]

While the Strangite newspaper propagated the immoralities of the gentiles, other publications were quick to relate stories of Mormon atrocities, which seemed to sell newspapers. Even the most unsubstantial rumor spread

7. *Northern Islander,* Aug. 17, 1854.
8. "Trade with Mackinac," *Northern Islander,* June 1, 1854.
9. Ibid.

quickly from ear to ear and often found its way into the newspapers. The story was told about Strang and a companion catching two gentiles, John and James Martin, in a small boat, robbing them of everything—even to their coats and oars—and setting them adrift on the lake. The story had a fortunate ending in that the wind later brought the two men to shore to tell their tale. A former Strangite said the Mormons were horse thieves, that at one time there had been thirteen double teams on the island and that eight of those had been stolen. He said the sheriff of Oakland County, Michigan, came to Beaver Island on one occasion after some stolen horses and Strang lent him every assistance, even furnishing the thieves themselves to join in the posse searching for the horses. At Strang's direction, the sheriff and posse searched one-half of the island the first day and the other half the next day. The horses were supposedly moved from one end of the island to the other during the night.[10]

A Milwaukee newspaper, *Yenowine's Illustrated News,* later reported that the Mormons were guilty of murder, saying that persons "obnoxious to Strang" were frequently summoned to sit on a grand jury in St. James in order to get them into the Mormon capital for intimidation. The "victim" usually made haste to leave the country, which was what the Mormons wanted. A warrant would be issued against the delinquent juror and placed in the hands of Mormon deputies for service. "If the victim was caught he had short shrift. Occasionally, the deputies shot their victims without ceremony when found." The newspaper claimed two fishermen named Sullivan were supposed to have been disposed of in this manner.[11]

Another story told of a man from Kentucky who was traveling up the lakes one summer and was leaning over the handrails as the ship lay moored to the dock at Beaver Island. A team came up with a load of wood and the Kentuckian recognized the horses as his. "Those two horses belong to me," he said to an officer standing beside him. "For God's sake, don't say so on shore," was the quick reply.[12] According to the gentiles, the Mormon web stretched far and wide, and very few fishermen got out of Strang's "clutches" with possessions intact if confronted by a Mormon boat, which was said to be

---

10. "History of Grand Traverse," 92-96; "King Strang's Reign of Terror on Beaver Island," *Yenowine's Illustrated News,* Milwaukee, June 24, 1888; John Hajicek, *Mormons in Wisconsin: A Closer View of the Early Settlements* (Burlington: by the author, 1992).

11. "King Strang's Reign."

12. Ibid.

the fisherman's greatest terror. A fisherman who "escaped alive" from the Mormon king told his story to *Yenowine's News*:

It was early in the spring of 1855, as near as I can recollect, when my partner and I started from Mackinac for Gull Island with $700 worth of supplies. It was storming when we started and we were glad enough to make the shank [local jargon for the Waugoshance lighthouse] that night. We started early the next morning, but lost our course in the fog. After boating about all day we made Beaver Island. Hardly had we landed before we were surrounded by Mormons who made us walk up the beach. In a short time, King Strang came down, issued a few orders, and twelve men separated from the rest. Six of them began to examine their guns in a manner that sent cold chills galloping up and down my back.

They had been appointed to kill us. The others were to bury us. Then Strang placed a double barreled shot gun to my breast, asked me more questions in regard to our intentions, issued new orders, which proved to be to clear away the boat, remove all the sails and oars and cast us adrift. We did not wait for the expiration of the ten minutes which we were allowed to get away in. Luckily for us one of the crowd, more humane than the rest, had secretly thrown in some oars, but the boat was aground on a rock and we couldn't budge it.

I then went back to the group and asked some of them to help us off. One whispered in my ear to get away as soon as possible. There was no use, besides a storm had come up and I didn't believe any boat could live in the sea. I went to Strang and begged to be allowed to stay. He told me coldly that unless we went we would be in h—l before daylight. On this we thought we might as well be drowned as shot and managed to get off. It was intensely cold and we were obliged to run for Mackinac, nearly forty miles away. Our chances were very slight and our sufferings were intense, but thanks to good constitutions we both recovered from the effects of the exposure, and had the pleasure a year later of taking part in the banishment of the Mormons from the island.[13]

The Strangites were accused of murdering the entire crew of the brig *Robert Willis,* which disappeared during a snowstorm in 1853. According to gentile reports, the brig was loaded with flour, pork, and provisions, and immediately after her disappearance, the Beaver Islanders were found to be well supplied with these articles. The report spread that the *Willis* had gone ashore at Beaver Island and that those members of the crew who were not drowned were "put out of the way by the Mormons." The *Northern Islander* denied in-

---

13. Ibid.

volvement with the ship's demise.[14] Strang argued that it did not make any sense for the Mormons to steal wheat when there wasn't a flour or a gristmill within 150 miles. "At the time the piracy was alleged to have been done," Strang wrote, "there were fourteen large vessels and three steamers lying here manned by some two hundred and fifty men. The population of the island is some two thousand. Whoever believes that pirating can be done in such a community and kept secret for months is lacking in common sense."[15] The *Northern Islander* also bemoaned the claim of Mormons having stolen a trunk during its transfer from one steamer to another. The contents were later discovered in the hands of three crewmen, who had a store of disguises. The point was that the boats did not always have honest crew members—they hired whomever they could.[16]

By the summer of 1855, stories of Mormon thievery and piracy had expanded up and down the Great Lakes. In July, five or six horses were stolen near Pontiac, Michigan, and the *Pontiac Gazette* was strongly inclined to believe the Mormons had taken the horses.[17] They were later found in Milwaukee and recovered.[18] In another case, a Mormon accused of stealing a span of horses had to produce a bill of sale to prove he had purchased the horses in Ohio.[19]

In Grand Traverse, Michigan, a town fifty-five miles from Beaver Island, the Strangites were accused of having abducted children. "A few days since, two of the Mormon fraternity visited the house of a Mr. Ladd, and ... took his child, telling his mother they would make a king of him," the *Chicago Journal* reported. "Mrs. L. called for help, when a plaster was put over her mouth. Three Indians, however, hearing her cries, proceeded to the house, when the Mormons decamped." The article went on to relate how four persons were seen prowling about the house again at midnight. The prowlers were shot at and one of them, "supposed to be a Mormon," fell to the ground. "The inhab-

---

14. "Painful Rumor," *Northern Islander,* Nov. 2, 1854. "At the time of her loss, the *Willis* was bound from Chicago to this port with a cargo of wheat and was last seen by the schooner *Lansing,* on the 22 November, off Sheboygan, bound up the lake in very heavy northeast gale."

15. Ibid.

16. "Stealing," *Northern Islander,* Nov. 2, 1854.

17. "Pontiac Gazette Again," *Northern Islander,* July 25, 1855.

18. "Daring Wholesale Robbery," *Allegan Record,* rpt. *Northern Islander,* Nov. 1, 1855.

19. "After Blackmail," *Northern Islander,* Sept. 13, 1855.

itants of Grand Traverse are greatly excited, and intend holding a meeting to invoke the aid of the government. If denied them, they will take the responsibility, and drive them [the Mormons] out from among them," the paper reported.[20] Strang responded in the pages of the *Northern Islander*: "The Indian farmer at Grand Traverse informs us that the child stealing was a mere joke, arranged by two squaws on a neighboring white woman," he wrote. "The night attempt was [made by] a few specimen of young Americans, genuine Grand Traverse growth, out stealing watermelons in a neighbor's garden."[21] Strang may just as well have saved his breath rather than try to convince a skeptical public that Native Americans had kidnapped a child as "a mere joke," but the claim that Mormons were stealing children was nevertheless absurd.

In actuality, most of the claims of piracy leveled against the Mormons were due to the actions of a real band of pirates then operating in Lake Michigan. The *Allegan Record* gave an idea of the scope of the pirates' operations:

> The people along Lake Michigan, from here north to the Manistee, have been thrown into a state of the most intense excitement by the operations of a gang of marauders, who are reported to be Mormons from Beaver Island, and who have carried on in their operations with a boldness, coolness and desperation rarely equaled in the records of highwaymen. They are reported to have burned saw mills and robbed stores north of the Grand River. At Grand Haven they made repeated attempts to break into stores and shops.... There is said to be upwards of 20 in the gang. They sail one small schooner of 20 or 30 tons, and two Mackinac boats.... There seems to be no question as to the identity of the robbers or their hailing place. They are emissaries from King Strang's Realms, and the whole power of the State should be lent to ferret out and bring to justice the perpetrators of such bold crime.[22]

The irony was that the Mormons themselves had been victims of these pirates, according to Strang. "In 1853 a statement went the rounds of the papers generally that the Mormons had stolen six or seven hundred barrels of fish, salt, &c. from the northern shore," he wrote. "Investigation showed that the theft was forty or fifty barrels instead of six or seven hundred, and that it was done by the sloop *Mary Clark*, of twenty or thirty tons, built in Chicago for a yacht, but then owned and sailed by members of this gang, with the

---

20. *Chicago Journal*, rpt. in *Northern Islander*, Sept. 20, 1855.
21. "Child Stealing," *Northern Islander*, Nov. 1, 1855.
22. "Daring Wholesale Robbery."

name painted off, and 'Defiance' painted on over it. This sloop has been refit-
ted as a schooner."[23]

Whoever the pirates were, they had struck terror into the hearts of the
residents along the coast of Lake Michigan. The *Lansing Republican* surmised that it was probably not an authorized campaign directed by Strang
himself, but that a few renegade Mormons must be the cause of it:

> Almost every mail brings us accounts of depredations along the coast of Lake
> Michigan. They are confined principally to the Northern portion of the Lake,
> but here, we believe, reached as far south as the Kalamazoo, and have been occa-
> sionally committed on the coast of the upper part of Lake Huron. So frequent
> and so extensive have been these robberies, that the people at many points on the
> Lake shore have been highly excited, so highly, indeed, that we should not be
> surprised to hear of serious conflicts and bloodshed....
>
> Stopping recently for a few days at Mackinac, we had ample opportunity to
> feel the public pulse, and we must say that we are really surprised at the deep and
> determined feeling which has taken hold of every person in that community. We
> met with several gentlemen from Grand Traverse and other places in that por-
> tion of the State, from whom we ascertained that the same spirit pervades the en-
> tire region of the country.
>
> "But who are the depredators?" the *Republican* asked. "Where is the pirati-
> cal retreat?" The citizen of Mackinac says, "It is at Beaver Island." The resident
> of Grand Traverse also cries "Beaver Island." And the men of Detour and
> Cheboygan, with one voice approve the assertion.... We are told on all hands
> that the Mormons are the authors of all these robberies and crimes; and whether
> it is so or not, such is the firm belief of the entire "Gentile" population of that
> section of the State. And the evidence which they address does seem to show
> conclusively, that whatever the character of the Mormons may be as community,
> there are some among them who often forget that important clause in the
> Decalogue which says, "Thou shall not steal." ...
>
> The northern portion of the Peninsula is rapidly settling, and unless the
> unfortunate differences existing between the Mormons and the "gentile" popu-
> lation are soon amicably arranged, the most serious and deplorable conse-
> quences will unquestionably be the result. We counsel our friends to be cool, de-
> liberate, forbearing. Punish wrong doers, but do it legally. Make no aggressions,
> but defend your homes and your property as is your right.[24]

---

23. Ibid.

24. "Piracy on Lake Michigan," *Lansing Republican,* rpt. *Northern Islander,* Dec. 6,
1855.

The Strangites were appalled and enraged that the charges of piracy leveled against them appeared in so many publications. After a group of privateers was apprehended, Strang asked in the *Northern Islander* where a newspaper could be found that had spoken in their defense. "Not one," he retorted. "When the thieves were actually pursued two hundred miles, and some hundred dollars of booty recovered, and by that fact the Mormons exonerated from suspicion," the newspapers remained "as silent as the house of death. That will not make a readable article for a newspaper. We have ceased to take to ourselves any trouble about these matters. We have known for years what the editors seem so anxious to impress upon us, that when the public vengeance is waked up the law will not protect us, and that among an angry people innocence is no shield."[25]

The followers of Strang were constantly aware they could lose all they had on Beaver Island. It would not have been the first time they had been driven away from their homes for religion's sake, as they saw it. They lived with that reality every day, and lest they forget, they were constantly being reminded of it in the *Northern Islander.* An article undoubtedly written by Strang recalled the exodus from Missouri in 1838 when the Mormons were treated as "foreigners and enemies," their crops, lands, and cattle taken. "Many were killed and some hundred made prisoners. And ten thousand driven at the point of a bayonet from the State and the Legislature appropriated $100,000 to pay the expense," Strang fumed. He spoke briefly of the Mormon exodus from Nauvoo, then added how the Mormons had been fully exonerated from blame by a committee of the Illinois senate, which had investigated the "Mormon difficulties."[26] Strang associated the past persecutions in Illinois with the present ones in Michigan, writing:

> We live in the consciousness that if any of us were murdered in any of the surrounding counties, no matter how publicly, the murderers would never be punished. Our property has frequently been taken from us without legal process, but we have seldom been able to get redress, and never without it costing more than the original injury. Mormons residing here have [had] large judgements [rendered in their favor] in Mackinac, on which the wealthiest men in that place are liable; but the power behind the law is so much above the law [itself] they have never been able to collect them. No sir, all protection has been

---

25. "Criminal Intentions," *Northern Islander,* Dec. 6, 1855.
26. *Northern Islander,* June 14, 1855.

withheld from us, and we have been treated as foreigners and enemies for years. That threat carries with it no terror.

As for civil war, we know its terrors better than those who talk of it at a distance. But we have contemplated it, till we do not dread it. If it must come, let it come upon us, and not upon our children. We suffered it when we were few and our enemies were many. We will not fear it now that the tables are turned. War is an inconvenient neighbor, and if it comes again, we shall endeavor to carry it into the enemy's country. And if we suffer in it[,] we have the Savior's assurance that if any man shall lose houses or lands, or wife or children for his name's sake and the gospel, he shall receive a hundred fold in this world, and in the world to come life everlasting.

We have no other place to flee to. If we had, we still remember the warning, 'He that will save his life shall lose it, but he that will lose his life for Christ's sake shall find it.' We are not men of blood, but suffering has given us a patient courage, that will endure when all else fails and wrings victory out of defeat.

There is something terrible in the encounter of men who have been injured so deeply, suffered so much, contemplated death so long that they neither wish to live nor dread to die; who have treasured up the memories of a life of unrequited injuries, all to be avenged in that struggle of life which takes persecuted and persecutors in the same hour to the judgement of God. Who would not relinquish the hope of yielding his life for the loved ones behind, to lengthen out its span twenty years, and die quietly between his sheets, with his family and friends around. You do not understand such men, and had better let them alone.[27]

The Mormons found themselves in an odd situation in the wake of the recent reversals of fortune in the islands, whereby they were elevated to position of economic strength and even a limited amount of political clout. Yet, the radius of hostility continued to increase—due, Strang said, to no fault of their own. The prophet pled his people's innocence through the pages of his newspaper. But what was interpreted at home as humility and even resignation appeared to outsiders to be obfuscation and saber rattling. His rhetoric seemed to confirm to outsiders what one would expect from an eccentric, self-proclaimed king, and Strang's presumed ambition and anti-Americanism implicated him beyond doubt in the minds of Michigan residents in the behind-the-scenes plundering and pillaging along the state's coastline. And so it went from year to year, Strang constantly trying to quench the flames of prejudice he was inadvertently continuing to fan.

---

27. Ibid.

12

THE PROPHET
MARRIES TWO COUSINS

1855

> *"From this time to the summer and*
> *autumn of 1855, matters progressed comparatively smooth for the Mor-*
> *mons, but polygamy gradually became more unpopular, and was the cause*
> *of much dissatisfaction. During this year Mr. Strang took his fourth and*
> *fifth wives, and some of the elders also took another, to give the thing popu-*
> *larity. But this action did not satisfy the mass of people and give them suffi-*
> *cient confidence in their opposition to and disobedience of the civil laws of*
> *the land in regard to the taking of more than one wife."* —Elvira Field, in
> "Biographical Sketch of James J. Strang." [1]

I n early July 1855, a group of about fifty Strangites left Beaver Island to attend a church conference on the Michigan mainland. They made passage across the lake in fishing boats and camped on shore near the place where the Battle of Pine River had occurred two years before. The following day they traveled up Pine River, through a lake they renamed Lake Mormon, to Holy Island, where they camped and made preparations for the conference. Many of the Mormons who had settled in the area joined the group.

On the day after the conference concluded, the men and women went together to the mouth of Pine River and erected a gallows where they hung in effigy the gentiles who had made the "murderous attack on two boatloads of unarmed Mormons" at that spot two years before. "Had the men been in hand instead of the effigies, they would have doubtless shared the same fate," the *Northern Islander* quipped. The following day the Strangites put up a synagogue as a future place of worship.[2]

---

1. Elvira Field Strang and Charles J. Strang, "Biographical Sketch of James J. Strang," unpublished manuscript, n.p., Strang Manuscript Collection, Library and Historical Center, State Library of Michigan, Lansing, Michigan.

2. "Conference at Lake Mormon," *Northern Islander,* July 19, 1855.

James Strang returned from the conference revitalized. He had a new wife, his fourth, and plans to marry a fifth. The two women were cousins, the teenage daughters of Phineas and Benjamin Wright. Over the previous eleven years, these two men had remained unswervingly faithful to the prophet, Phineas serving as one of the Twelve Apostles and Benjamin as a member of Strang's Privy Council. The young woman Strang had just married was Sarah Adelia "Delia" Wright,[3] seventeen-year-old daughter of Phineas Wright and Amanda Finch, born November 25, 1837, in Leeds, Ontario, Canada, as the oldest of four children.[4] She was just a baby when her parents joined the Mormon Church. In 1840 the family moved to Nauvoo and then to Potosi, Wisconsin, where Phineas worked in the lead mines with his brothers. Sarah was probably baptized into the Mormon Church when she was eight years old, according to church practice.

The Wright families converted to Strangism in 1844, moved to Voree three years later, and were among the first to join the Associated Order of Enoch, whereby members held everything in common. Sarah would have grown up as a participant in this communal organization. In addition, the three Wright brothers ran their separate families as one unit, each brother taking on a specific role. Benjamin was said to be the "business head," Phineas the "preacher," and Samuel, who kept the "home fires burning," was the "heart of the family." A Wright family descendent described the three brothers as handsome, kindhearted, intelligent men with bright blue eyes. Family members were also said to be very musical.[5]

Sarah's mother, Amanda, had died on January 1, 1848, after suffering an illness for five days, at only twenty-six years of age. "By this bereavement a most affectionate husband, 4 young children, and a large circle of brothers, sisters, and near friends, together with all the Saints, were cast into mourn-

---

3. Clement Strang to Milo Quaife, June 17, 1921, Clarke Historical Library, Central Michigan University, Mount Pleasant, Michigan.

4. A distant relative gives an alternative birth year of 1835, but Sarah told Milo Quaife she was seventeen when she married Strang, which would mean she was born in 1837.

5. "Autobiography of Benjamin Wright," unpublished manuscript, Beaver Island Historical Society, Old Mormon Print Shop, St. James, Beaver Island, Michigan; also personal correspondence with a descendent of Benjamin Wright, 1999. The three brothers were descendants of loyalists living in Canada. Their grandmother, Zilpha Downer, was an educated midwife and daughter of a physician. Sarah Wright later became a doctor, as well.

ing," her obituary read. She was buried the next day in the Mormon cemetery at Voree. Her obituary included an eleven-stanza poem about the sorrow of death and the joy of being reunited with a departed loved one, probably written by James Strang.[6]

The loss of their mother at such a young age must have deeply affected Amanda's children. Sarah had just turned ten years old. Elizabeth Jane was six, Zenas eight, and Phineas Jr. only two. The following year, Sarah's father married Rebecca Wagener, a young woman of nineteen years. The family moved to Beaver Island in the fall of 1850, where Phineas, at thirty-eight, worked as a cooper making barrels fishermen packed their fish in for salting and shipping. He was also a farmer and had the responsibility of making maple sugar for the islanders every spring.[7]

Like the other young people on the island, Sarah and her cousins worked hard helping to clear the land, raise the crops, and build the wood-framed homes. There is a chance Elvira Field was their schoolteacher for a time in Voree. Another teacher, who occasionally took his turn instructing the children in his communities, was James Strang. However, the principal schoolteachers on the island were Warren Post and Anson Prindle.

The year Sarah turned fourteen, ninety-nine Mormon men, including Phineas and Benjamin Wright, were arrested and taken off Beaver Island on "trumped up criminal charges" pressed by their hostile neighbors. Others were taken away on compulsory service as witnesses—all departing in the spring of 1851 and leaving only twenty-four Mormon men on the island. This meant the women and children had to cultivate the fields and produce the crops that saved the settlement from starvation the following winter.[8] They also had their routine household tasks to perform such as gathering and hauling firewood and caring for their animals. Most of the women kept sheep, then collected the wool and spun it into thread on spinning wheels. The Strangites raised almost everything they consumed on Beaver Island except for flour.[9]

---

6. Amanda Finch Wright obituary, *Gospel Herald,* Jan. 6, 1848.

7. Zenas Wright, interviewed by Milo M. Quaife, May 25, 1920, n.p., Beaver Island Historical Society; also the 1850 federal census for Mackinac County, Michigan.

8. James Strang, *Ancient and Modern Michilimackinac, Including an Account of the Controversy between Mackinac and the Mormons* (1854; Ann Arbor: University of Michigan Library, 1987), 35.

9. "The Diary of James Oscar McNutt, Elder of the Mormon Church at the Mor-

In the summer of 1855, Strang made preparations to solidify his relationship with the Wright families by proposing marriage first to Phineas's daughter Sarah, then to Benjamin's daughter Phoebe, who was a year and a half older than Sarah. As with his proposals to Elvira and Betsy, Strang would have sent an emissary to negotiate the transaction.[10] Phineas was initially opposed to his daughter marrying Strang. Despite the fact that Phineas was one of the apostles, he was apparently not a supporter of polygamy. The "Beaver Island Record," in which important events of the Strangite Church were recorded, shows only two marriages for Phineas.[11] In contrast, Benjamin took three additional wives. Samuel married at least one more woman while his legal wife was still alive.[12]

Much later in life, Sarah recalled talking to her father "about marrying James Strang" and remembered "he did not forbid me but said, 'My daughter I would almost as soon See you buried [than] marry in to polygamy. I am afraid you will not be happy.'" But Sarah, in her own words, "took the chance. I thought [Strang] was the Lord's chosen prophet & all would be right," that it was an honor "to be chosen as a plural wife of the prophet."[13] Zenas Wright, Sarah's younger brother, was about sixteen years old at the time and was upset by the prospect of his sister being a polygamous wife. For that reason, he decided not to attend his sister's wedding.[14]

The event nevertheless took place on July 15, 1855, immediately following the church conference on Holy Island. One of the twelve apostles conducted the ceremony. Sarah was seventeen, while her new husband was forty-two. She told Milo Quaife that Strang "had three wives when I married

---

mon Settlement, Jackson Co., Wisconsin; One Time Follower of James Jesse Strang," State Library of Michigan; cf. "Reminisces of James O. McNutt of the Mormon Settlement, Jackson County [Wisconsin], and Warrens, Monroe County, Related by J. O. McNutt, and Recorded by his Daughter Miss Sadie McNutt," Library-archives, Wisconsin Historical Society, Madison, Wisconsin.

10. Clement Strang to Milo M. Quaife, Aug. 13, 1920, Clarke Historical Library.

11. Zenas Wright interview, May 25, 1920. Gabriel Strang recalled that Phineas Wright was one of those who participated in polygamy.

12. "Beaver Island Record, A History of the Church of Jesus Christ of Latter Day Saints (Strangite) of the City of James, Beaver Island, State of Michigan, From 1848 to 1855," typescript, 53, Clarke Historical Library.

13. Sarah Wing to Milo Quaife, Spring 1920, Clarke Historical Library.

14. Zenas Wright interview, May 25, 1920. Zenas said his father, Phineas, was not a polygamist.

him, Elvira Field and Betsy McNutt besides his first wife. If he had any concubines," she continued, "I did not know it. He was a very kind husband and father. The Strangites believed in marriage for time and eternity."[15] Elsewhere, she elaborated:

> There was a rumor that we [Sarah and Phoebe] were married at the same time[,] but there was a five-month [four-month] difference. You ask how we got licenses to marry. People who believe in polygamous marriages do not get any licenses—they think the church authorities have a right to say the ceremony and pronounce you married. I was married by one of the twelve apostles. We did not consider we needed any other papers except what the church gave us.[16]

Strang's fifth wife, Phoebe Wright, was born in Leeds, Ontario, Canada on July 25, 1836, as the fourth of Benjamin's and Margaret's thirteen children. Her childhood would have closely mirrored that of her cousin Sarah since the Wright brothers had combined their families together. Not only were the girls cousins through their fathers, they were first cousins through their mothers, the three Wright brothers having married sisters Amanda, Margaret, and Rebecca Finch. Phoebe's father, Benjamin, was said to be "a man of broad intelligence and extensive knowledge ... who possessed the courage of his convictions," a granddaughter later recalled.[17] Benjamin was responsible for the stake at Voree for a time and later became a trusted member of Strang's Privy Council. Phoebe's mother, Margaret, was "greatly loved" and said to be of a "sweet and gentle nature and disposition, but very quiet and retiring. She had a sweet smile, but never laughed," her granddaughter remembered.[18]

---

15. Sarah Wing to Milo Quaife, n.d. [1920], Clarke Historical Library.

16. Sarah Wing to Milo Quaife, spring 1920, Clarke Historical Library.

17. Clement J. Strang, "Why I Am Not a Strangite," *Michigan History*, fall 1942, 479. This article includes a letter from Eugenia Phillips, Phoebe Wright's daughter. Benjamin stood about five foot ten and had black hair and blue eyes. He was slender and energetic. His brothers may have been similar in appearance, according to Eugenia Phillips to Milo Quaife, July 15, 1920, Clarke Historical Library.

18. Perhaps Margaret never laughed because she had seen too much sadness in her life. Both her parents died before she was thirteen years old. She lost six of ten siblings and three of her own children before she was thirty-five. One of the deceased sisters was Sarah Wright's mother, Amanda. Margaret said Amanda had been "full of life and laughter, very different than" Margaret herself. Eugenia Phillips to Mrs. N. A. Williams, in Genealogical Correspondence of Mrs. N. A. Williams, microfilm 1597819, item 17, Family History Library, Salt Lake City, Utah.

After leaving Voree, Benjamin and a number of other families settled at the southern end of Beaver Island, also known as the head of the island, at a community called Galilee. The men put up a dock and were soon doing a considerable amount of business providing cordwood for visiting steamships. Benjamin's brother Samuel built two sawmills at Galilee and had a third mill under construction in 1855.[19]

The common trait in Strang's wives was that they were all unusually intelligent women. Phoebe was no exception. She was energetic, ambitious, witty, and took great interest in civic affairs both locally and nationally. She was also considered to be attractive. People who knew her said she had a clear, fair complexion, black hair, and bright blue eyes.[20] She married the prophet-king on October 21, 1855, in a private ceremony in St. James when she was nineteen and her husband was forty-two. Her father was opposed to the match for the same reasons her uncle had objected to her cousin's marriage to Strang. Like Phineas, Benjamin thought his daughter would not be happy in polygamy.[21] Although she remained devoted to her husband all her life, Phoebe confessed years later that she became dissatisfied during the short time she was a plural wife.

In a letter to Milo Quaife, Sarah Wright described some of the logistical arrangements and daily routines within the prophet's polygamous household.

> You ask if we all lived in the same house. We did but had separate rooms. All met in prayer—ate at the same table. We had no quarrels, no jealousies that I knew of. He was a very mild-spoken kind man to his family although his word was law. We were all honest in our religion and made things as pleasant as possible. There were four of us living in one house.
>
> Mr. Strang's first wife never came to Beaver Island and I did not know much about her, but the church owned property [where she lived] in Voree. I don't know how it was managed. I think my father did, but I never asked[.] His first wife's name was seldom mentioned.... [H]e certainly supported her and [her] family. I don't think she ever had any divorce. I was acquainted with her when a child. She was very kind to me.[22]

---

19. "New Mill," *Northern Islander*, Oct. 18, 1855.
20. Eugenia Phillips to Milo Quaife, July 15, 1920.
21. Ibid.
22. Sarah Wing to Milo Quaife, Spring 1920.

It was Strang's habit to assign duties to each wife according to her particular taste and talents. Elvira continued as his private secretary and traveled with him to Lansing when he was a state representative.[23] Betsy's work was in the kitchen. Sarah and Phoebe cared for Betsy's two children and Elvira's three children, who stayed behind when Elvira left the island. The cousins were soon pregnant themselves and would have had additional children to care for.[24] Sarah was appointed through religious ordination to be a teacher in the Strangite Church, and one of her duties was to keep a list of proxy baptisms for the dead in the Beaver Island Record, a Strangite book of conference minutes and other church events.[25]

The calling of a teacher was, and still is, a priesthood position in the Strangite Church. Several women were called to this office, in contrast to the Utah church, where the position is held only by males fourteen years of age or older. According to the Strangite Law of the Lord, a teacher must be educated in letters and science in order to instruct others. Teachers of eminence were set apart to become doctors, a career Sarah would have later in life, although the Law of the Lord probably meant doctors of education. In short, the women Strang chose for himself were women of substance and ability, in keeping with his own advice, as he reported in the *Northern Islander* in 1854: "The best qualities to look after in a wife are industry, humanity, neatness, gentleness, benevolence and piety. When you find these, there is no danger. You will obtain a treasure, and not regret your choice."[26]

The house where Strang lived with his wives was large and surrounded by a good garden, flowers, and vines. It was neatly kept and attractive, as were most Mormon residences. The houses in St. James all had the same general appearance, the simple log cabins the people had lived in when they first settled the island having been gradually replaced by whitewashed, wood-frame houses. Strang's home was near the harbor and was surrounded by a thick grove of trees. A hillside behind the house gave a nice view of the harbor and lake. There were two "good sized log frames" to the back of the house, con-

23. Sarah Wing to Milo Quaife, n.d. [1920], Clarke Historical Library.

24. Clement Strang to Jack G. Boon, Jan. 26, 1941, Clarke Historical Library.

25. "Minutes of the Conference, held at Enoch Grove, Saint James, Beaver Island, July 7th, 8th, 9th, 10th and 11th 1855," *Northern Islander,* Aug. 9, 1855; also the *Book of the Law of the Lord,* 1851 edition, chapter XXIV, "Teachers."

26. *Northern Islander,* Nov. 2, 1854, [p. 4].

nected to the main structure by a "covered way." The nearest neighbor was about 600 feet away. They were about 200 feet from the lake.[27] A short distance further back on the hillside stood the tabernacle.[28]

By 1855 the gentile community was well aware polygamy was being practiced in the Great Lakes. In 1846 the State of Michigan imposed a fine of $500 or up to five years in prison for polygamy, a development followed closely by Strang and his people.[29] Outsiders read articles in newspapers about Beaver Island that mentioned polygamy, one article purporting to be the story of two gentile girls who were brought up on the island to become plural wives but committed suicide rather than allow themselves to marry Mormon elders.[30] There is no evidence the story was true.

When a newspaper admitted the number of polygamists on Beaver Island appeared to be small, it ascribed this to a limited supply of available women. If a young girl were averse to polygamy, she was said to be the subject of "urgent offers of marriage," sometimes with encouragement from the girls' own parents, according to the reports. In one instance, the story was told of young Henrietta Baxter, whose widowed mother felt she had been tricked into converting only to find her property held fast in the clutches of the church. Henrietta was employed by a gentile family, but she worried she would have to enter polygamy. To avoid that possibility, she loitered around the steamships and finally boarded one, taking with her only the clothes on her back. She went to the Old Mission settlement where the Bower family, former Mormons, took her in, and eventually came to live in Traverse City with the Austins, also formerly of Beaver Island. In fact, Eri Moore, the Austins' son-in-law, was one of Strang's archenemies.[31] Henrietta's name, in fact, appears on a list of Mormons who signed the Oath and the Covenant before Strang's coronation.[32] She is listed in the 1850 federal census as the seventeen-year-old daughter of Delana Baxter.

---

27. "The Pontiac Gazette Again," *Northern Islander,* July 25, 1855.

28. Geo. A. Whitney to the *Green Bay Globe,* Sept. 4, 1877. Whitney had recently visited Beaver Island and said nothing remained of the tabernacle or temple except a few charred logs but that the ruins of some of the other buildings could still be seen.

29. "The Pontiac Gazette Again," *Northern Islander,* July 19, 1855.

30. George R. Fox to Milo Quaife, Jan. 7, 1919, Clarke Historical Library.

31. M. L. Leach, "A History of the Grand Traverse Region," *Grand Traverse Herald,* 1883, 55-56, Clarke Historical Library.

32. "Book of the Covenant," folder 188, James Jesse Strang Collection, Yale Collection

Another girl supposedly made it on board a boat docked at Beaver Island and locked herself in the stateroom. The Mormons detained the boat until she gave herself up, according to the story.[33] There is no evidence to support this account. One of the newspapers that published the rumors about polygamy was the *Rochester Daily Democrat*:

> This Island has an excellent harbor, and is 12 miles long and 8 broad. Its exports are wood, potatoes and fish. Its imports, Mormons, from all parts of the globe—mostly females. If they bring chastity with them, it is soon lost, for polygamy is an article 'in the creed' here as well as in Utah.... Some come here with considerable funds[,] some are runaway daughters—some have rid themselves of their husbands, and got here in some manner. It is a good place to find absconded wives, if they are worth looking after.

The newspaper mentioned that Strang himself had a first wife who resided in Wisconsin, as well as "the particular favor of two women on Beaver Island, by whom he had children."[34]

Strang was actually preparing to marry his fifth wife, but this did not prevent him from chastising the *Daily Democrat* for dragging his private life before the public. "I am nevertheless quite willing your readers should believe, that I have particular [sentiments] for two, four, or ten women; whom I provide for, and who bear children to me, and whom I would marry if the law permitted me," he wrote. "If they imagine that in this I violate any law of this State, they are mistaken."[35] He obviously meant that his marriages were not legal in the eyes of the public or strictly according to the law, but they were in the eyes of God.

In his own newspaper, Strang took the additional step of extolling polygamy as beneficial to women in that it allowed them to have a choice in husbands rather than forcing them to accept whatever marriage offer came along. For some women, the chance of getting a good husband was about equal to that of drawing a capital prize in a lottery, he asserted. Polygamy was

---

of Western Americana, Beinecke Rare Book and Manuscript Library, Yale University, New Haven, Connecticut.

33. M. L. Leach, "A History of the Grand Traverse Region," *Grand Traverse Herald*, 1883, 89, Clarke Historical Library.

34. "Beaver Island—Mormon Bloomers—Strang the 'Saint,'" *Rochester Daily Democrat*, rpt. in *Northern Islander*, Oct. 11, 1855.

35. Ibid.

a way for women to have a wider range for the selection of husbands and amiable children of excellent moral worth. "Selfish and mean men, and quarrelsome scolding women, are underrated by polygamy," he continued. "That is the sum of its discovered evils. Among its benefits are a higher estimation of physical, social and intellectual excellence; more of human happiness, a more numerous posterity, and a better race."[36]

As to the feelings of Mormon women on the subject of plural marriage, Strang published a letter from a woman in Utah to her sister in New Hampshire. Belinda Marden Pratt, plural wife of the Brighamite apostle Parley P. Pratt, laid out the plurality of wives as inspired by God and in the tradition of the ancient prophets. Belinda said she had a good virtuous husband whom she loved and that they had four children. Besides that, she explained, her husband had seven other living wives and upwards of twenty-five children. Even so, all the wives and children were united by kindred ties—by mutual affection, patience, long suffering, and sisterly kindness. She said she was as fond of her husband's other children as she was of her own. In her estimation,

> it is not only God's law, but also nature's law. The great object of marriage relations is the multiplying of our species—that is the rearing and training of children.... Polygamy, then, is practiced under the patriarchal law of God, tends directly to the chastity of women, and to sound health and morals in the constitutions of their offspring. The polygamic law of God opens to all vigorous, healthy and virtuous females a door by which they may become honorable wives of virtuous men, and mothers of faithful, virtuous, healthy children.[37]

Once again, Strang did not seem to have a well thought out plan in mind for responding to bad publicity. His equal doses of indignation and equivocation in his letter to the *Daily Democrat* were too transparent, especially against the backdrop of his high praise for plural marriage in the *Northern Islander*. More importantly, his claim that his privacy had been violated did nothing to alleviate suspicions about abuse of young women on the island—or at least about competition for women who were still of tender years. The ages of the prophet's most recent wives, seventeen and nineteen, compared to his forty-

---

36. "Mormon Polygamy," *Northern Islander*, Mar. 2, 1854.

37. Belinda Marden Pratt to Mrs. Lydia Kimball of Nashua, New Hampshire, in "Defense of Polygamy," *Northern Islander*, June 8, 1854. Apostle Parley P. Pratt was murdered three years later by the estranged husband of Pratt's seventh wife.

two years, would have provided an extra shock for readers of the *Daily Democrat*. Even among the church membership itself, the disparity in age between the prophet and his most recent wives gave reason for pause. Two of Strang's most loyal followers, the fathers of the brides, were less than enthusiastic about this particular honor from their king.

13.

BETRAYAL AND CRISIS
1856

"In the spring of 1856 a number of seceders determined to break up and drive from the island the whole organization. A confederacy with the fishermen and Indians was easily formed, because the inducements were large. The ostensible object was to break up polygamy, and they therefore obtained the sanction and protection of the government; but the real object was to get possession of the rich homesteads, on many of which were valuable and permanent improvements." —Elvira Field Strang[1]

January 1856 started out merrily for the Saints on Beaver Island. Isolated from the rest of the world for the winter, they spent eight days feasting between Christmas and New Year's Day. "One splendid party danced out the dying year, and three [parties] gave a spirited welcome to the new one," the *Northern Islander* reported.[2]

The winter was unusually cold, and those who had to move about had to use sleighs. The ice in the harbor was close to two and a half feet thick and the lake was frozen over completely for forty miles around. The Mormons took the opportunity to drive their teams to Pine River to get supplies.[3] The previous fall the schooner *Hope,* which was loaded with wheat, had wrecked at the entrance of the harbor, so the Strangites salvaged considerable quantities of wheat for cattle feed and dried a small quantity for grinding.[4] Some individuals crossed the ice to Bear Creek, where there was a large gristmill and they could get the wheat ground.

---

1. Elvira Field Strang and Charles J. Strang, "Biographical Sketch of James J. Strang," unpublished manuscript, n.p., Strang Manuscript Collection, Library and Historical Center, State Library of Michigan, Lansing, Michigan.

2. "Amusements," *Northern Islander,* Jan. 24, 1856.

3. "Spring Opening," *Northern Islander,* Apr. 3, 1856; also Feb. 14, 1856, [pp. 2-4].

4. *Northern Islander,* Jan. 24, 1856, [p.3].

Strang was once again gone to Lansing, preparing to participate in the Michigan state legislature. He was re-elected to the office in November 1854 despite widespread opposition from gentiles. The state representative from Mackinac Island was trying to get Emmet County divided into two parts with the intention of limiting Mormon political power to the Beaver, Fox, and Manitou Islands.[5]

Following his return to St. James in the spring of 1856, Strang announced his intention to publish a daily newspaper in addition to the weekly *Northern Islander*, issued on Thursdays. The *Daily Northern Islander* was to commence publication with the opening of navigation. Knowing the paper was being read by outsiders, he used the pages of the weekly to discourage general immigration, although he camouflaged a call for additional settlers of a particular type:

> Among emigrants, those who wish to learn right ways are desirable.... We did not choose this as our place of dwelling, but God chose it for us. Those who don't think so had better choose one for themselves somewhere else....
>
> Those who expect to astonish the Islanders by a display of furniture, apparel or supercilious manners had better remain where they are.... Above all persons, those who use intoxicating liquors had better stay away, till they make up their minds to quit once and forever.... No amount of talent or industry will compensate for this pernicious habit; and the man who occasionally goes on a boat to take a drink at the saloon, is regarded as a disgrace to the community.[6]

Strang was serious about convincing a small number of Mormons who lived in the mission field to gather to Beaver Island and assist their brethren. He was specifically looking for a bookbinder, three or four good boat builders, six to eight journeymen, a painter, three to four printers, and qualified schoolteachers. He also wanted a baker; a provisioner; someone to make cedar pails, tubs, and wooden dishes; two good chair makers; a bedstead maker; a brick maker; and three or four brick and stone masons and plasterers.[7]

The various Mormon settlements away from Beaver Island were also preparing for the opening of navigation, which gave every expectation of being a profitable endeavor. Strangite Reuben Nichols wrote from Pine River to

5. "The Compromise," *Northern Islander*, June 21, 1855.

6. *Northern Islander*, Apr. 3, 1856, [p.2].

7. Ibid., Feb. 14, 1856, [p.2].

inform Strang of the condition of that colony. "We have had a pleasant and happy winter here," he reported. They had "held common school and Sunday school; chopped wood for a saw mill, made a canoe and some sugar." At a meeting at his house on the first Tuesday in April, Evangeline Township had been fully organized. "We have had a number of visits from the Indians and they appear to be very friendly," he added.[8]

Benjamin Wright gave notice in the *Northern Islander* that he had extended his wharf at Galilee and was prepared to open trade in the spring. He already had 3,000 cords of beech and maple piled up on the wharf and would be able to provide thirty cords of wood per day during the navigation season.[9] In the *Northern Islander,* Strang bragged about Mormons' market position. He seemed particularly proud of the wood trade and sent along a challenge to whomever might read the newspaper: "George Kidder of this place has cut during the past winter, 447 cords of steamboat wood, all hard wood but 3-½ cords. 70 cords of this was culled timber and has been realized by $51.25 per month, all cash. If this is beat by anyone between Buffalo and Chicago, send along."[10]

The Mormons were looking ahead to other markets that might benefit from the island's abundant wood supply, as well. Sharp-eyed and demonstrating a keen business sense, Strang realized that railroads were to be the transportation of the future. One Strangite, Isaac Pierce, on returning from a mission to Nebraska, had been a passenger on the first train to cross the Mississippi River on a new railroad bridge at Rock Island, Illinois.[11] Strang foresaw the need for wood in maintaining the trains themselves, such as the great number of railroads concentrating at Chicago, which would require an immense supply of fuel. Lumber would be needed for extensive buildings and fencing as the wood-scarce prairies in Illinois were settled. "They can get their wood as cheap from here as from any place," he wrote. "For many years no other place can successfully compete with this [island] in the [lumber] business. There is no other point near here, on the steamboat line, furnishing an abundant stock of standing timber, near an accessible harbour, with a back

---

8. "Correspondence," *Northern Islander,* May 22, 1856. Evangeline Township was named after Strang's and Betsy McNutt's daughter.

9. *Northern Islander,* Mar. 13, 1856, [p. 3].

10. "Hard to Beat," *Northern Islander,* May 1, 1856.

11. Ibid., [p. 2].

country to support the men and teams employed in getting the wood."[12]

By May 1856, immigrant companies led by Strangite missionaries, including Phineas and Samuel Wright, were beginning to arrive at Beaver Island. On May 21, the Strangites gave a reception for the returning missionaries and their converts. According to the *Northern Islander:*

> It was a most happy ingathering of cheerful and believing spirits, congratulating one another on past blessings and future hopes, while they praised God in the dance and with the musick of stringed instruments. The assembly was very large and the capacious rooms were all filled to overflowing, but the universal cheerfulness, native politeness, and genuine kindness, made all pleasant when with a little stiffness of manners half the number would have lacked room. The joyousness of the scene extended to all. Old men and young maidens danced together, mothers in Israel and their grandsons kept time in the maze. With what pride did the Elders[,] returned from their toils[,] look on the happy faces of those who had heard their testimony, as they met and passed in the intricacies of the dance.[13]

Hopkins Whaley, one of the converts dancing at St. James Hall, said he had never seen the like before—"no liquor, no swearing, but all seemed to breathe the spirit of friendship. The party commenced about 7 P.M. At 9[:00] they were called to order; a solemn silence pervaded the assembly; at which time a portion of God's law was read.... At this meeting (or party) the old and young all took a part, and I must say that the children were patterns worthy of imitation. It closed about midnight."[14]

As summer approached, the town resumed work on the tabernacle for the first time in five years. Started in 1849, the building had one room, thirty feet by sixty feet, but only a temporary roof due to the suspension of work in 1850 when so many Strangites were being prosecuted at Mackinac Island. The Saints intended to build a structure that would accommodate 4,000 people standing or 2,500 seated.[15] They also endeavored to improve the appearance of the downtown area by whitewashing the buildings. "There is a gratifying appearance of white paint showing itself along Water street," the

---

12. "Wood Trade at Beaver Island," *Daily Northern Islander,* May 19, 1856.

13. "The Welcome," *Northern Islander,* May 22, 1856.

14. "Correspondence," *Northern Islander,* June 5, 1856.

15. "The Tabernacle," *Northern Islander,* June 5, 1856.

Northern Islander reported. "Saint James Hall looks really domestick. Greatly may this improvement be extended."[16]

George Leslie, a correspondent for the *Chicago Daily Tribune,* noticed the efforts. "We called yesterday at the Mormon settlement on Beaver Island and had the pleasure of meeting with Prophet and High Priest Strang as well as other dignitaries of the place," he wrote.

> They gave the population at 1,500 and state that it is rapidly increasing. The whole settlement, so far as we could see, has an aspect of thrift and neatness about it, which shows that the community must be industrious. They have got three piers at the harbor with several thousand cords of wood got out for the purpose of supplying boats. They possess one grist and one saw mill, but no vessels although they are making an attempt to get some. They print a daily and weekly paper, made up principally with doctrinal discussions in the various elements of the Mormons faith. In the paper, the doctrine of polygamy is not openly avowed, but only defended with very mediocre ability. We have heard it reported that Strang has got nine wives: a statement which, if true, would go far to prove that his practice is even more distinct and [efficacious] than his profession. The agricultural capabilities of the Island are reported to be good and the soil produces all the smaller cereals, as also all kinds of vegetables in the highest perfection.[17]

Despite the appearance of prosperity, Strang felt pessimistic enough about the colony's future that he may have been making covert preparations to leave the island for a new colony in Texas or Canada. He had previously considered Texas but was dissuaded by the likelihood of a civil war and wanted the Saints to be as far away from the conflict as possible. According to Strang's son Gabriel, writing in 1929, this is why his father had chosen Beaver Island as the gathering place of the Saints in the late 1840s. Gabriel said the Saints were called to Voree as a test of their ability to dwell together, and when they proved they were able to do so, the Lord was ready to establish the kingdom in a more permanent location. Accordingly, Strang had sent two missionaries to investigate Texas, and from what Gabriel had been able to piece together, it had continued to remain a serious option. Gabriel wrote:

> A site of 10,000 acres near the coast in Ft. Bend and Matagorda counties Texas,

---

16. Ibid.

17. "News from the Straits," rpt. in *Northern Islander,* June 5, 1856. The Mormons actually had five docks—three on the harbor at St. James and two more at Galilee on the south end of the island. I have substituted the word "efficacious" for the article's "eflication."

was procured from the state of Texas which had been annexed to the United States.... That was in 1847 during the War between the United States and Mexico. Owing to the attempts that were being made at that time to extend the Slavery Zone, a strong prejudice was growing against northern people in the South. Soon there was a sure indication that there would be a war between the sections of the country over the question of Slavery, ... as the plan for the establishment of God's kingdom could not be a success unless the anti-slavery faction should win, it would not be best to start where the war would be fought; [therefore] ... by living on Islands away from Opposition the danger would be less, so Beaver Island was chosen from the start....

The first [Strangite property] inheritances were given on the mainland [of Michigan] Sept. 10, 1855 just after Anson Prindle and [James] C. Hutchins had been sent to Texas to look for another location near the new border line which had been changed after the Mexican War from the Nueces River to the Rio Grande, about 200 miles farther south. Brother Prindle returned to Beaver Island with their report just before Father was shot.[18]

Once again there were rumors the gentiles were trying to get up a mob to run the inhabitants of Beaver Island off the island. According to the *Northern Islander*, John S. Dixon, a new inhabitant of Pine River, was trying to get the Indians from around Little Traverse Bay to sign a paper asking for the removal of the Mormons from the Lake Mormon vicinity—but no one signed it. "We believe that he made the most untiring efforts to raise a mob from Grand Traverse, to drive them out; but entirely failed. It is said that some ill advised men went to assist him in arson and murder, but backed out for want of numbers and whiskey," the *Northern Islander* speculated.[19]

But the most pressing threats in 1856 came from within Strang's own community. There were rumors of church members using alcohol and the visible fact that some women refused to wear bloomers. One Strangite man was flogged—some said for adultery; others claimed he had violated an unwritten order of confidentiality in the community. "We learn with mortifica-

---

18. Gabriel Strang to John Wake, May 8, 1929, Clarke Historical Library, Central Michigan University, Mount Pleasant, Michigan. Strang, in fact, carried on a correspondence with Lyman Wight, a would-be successor to Joseph Smith who had taken a group of Mormons to Zodiac, Texas. Lyman Wight's son, Orange Wight, was married to George Miller's daughter and lived on Beaver Island. Strang sent two missionaries to the Wight settlement during the winter of 1855-56. See Lyman Wight to James Strang, July 1855, Clarke Historical Library, and the *Northern Islander*, June 5, 1856, [p. 5].

19. "Up North," *Northern Islander*, Apr. 3, 1856.

tion and sorrow, that intoxicating liquors were furnished for the entertainment of a party of young people, at the house of a respectable lady of this place," Strang had earlier disclosed in the *Northern Islander.* "Of the numerous and respected company there assembled, not one was found to remonstrate against, or resent such an insult." Strang was incredulous that "the thoughtless freak of a woman" could "undo in an hour the labor that a hundred strong men have been years in accomplishing." Strang's opinion was that every pseudo who "sips tea, pours down coffee, chews and smokes tobacco, or indulges in intoxicating drinks" indicates by his actions that "she did right" and condone by example the corruption of youth.[20]

In addition to members drinking alcohol, Ruth Ann Bedford and Sarah McCulloch were among those refusing to wear bloomers.[21] Strang had preached to the women during conference in August 1855 about the necessity of conforming their apparel to the pattern God had given them.[22] "The Mormon ladies have their own style of dress, convenient and very beautiful," the *Northern Islander* now reported. "But there is now and then, a lady who deems it beneath her dignity to wear a Mormon dress. Who are these dignified ladies? What has been their past life, that they will not demean themselves by stooping to Mormon styles?"[23]

Ruth Ann's husband, Thomas Bedford, was the unnamed individual in the newspaper article who was flogged thirty-nine times for some undis-

---

20. "Scandalous," *Northern Islander,* Aug. 24, 1854.

21. Ruth Ann's brother, Harrison "Tip" Miller, was a Mormon "renegade," while her sister Mary Jane was married to Elvira Field's brother, Albert. Ruth Ann's mother, Elizabeth Bouten Miller, may have been a plural wife of George Miller. However, Ruth Ann's father, according to *Past and Present of Eaton County, Michigan* (Lansing: Michigan Historical Publishing Association, n.d.), 304-306, was Walter K. Miller, a shoemaker from Westchester County, New York. Walter was said to have died in Westchester prior to 1851. Elizabeth died on Beaver Island the same year at the age of thirty-four. The Millers' five children were Ruth Ann Bedford, Mary Jane Field, Lewis, Charles, and Harrison, the latter known as the keeper of the life-saving station at Point Betsy, Michigan. Sarah McCulloch's husband was Hezekiah McCulloch. It is interesting to note that a Walter K. Miller, "late an inmate of the Connecticut State Prison, not a Mormon, ... was dropped from a boat here last year, and obliged to stay through the winter, for want of money to leave with" (*Northern Islander,* June 6, 1850). "Here" meant Mackinac. It is unlikely Strang would have written about Walter K. Miller if the man was simply an itinerant sailor.

22. "Minutes of the Conference Held at Enoch Grove, Saint James, Beaver Island," *Northern Islander,* Aug. 9, 1855.

23. "Mormon Dress," *Northern Islander,* May 1, 1856.

closed transgression. "A man not far from here was called to account this week, and after careful and fair examination as to the facts, condemned to thirty nine lashes with a beech for lying, tale-bearing, and endeavoring to incite to mischief and crime," the report read.[24] Thomas, a small dark-complexioned man, was an inveterate smoker who occasionally took a "little more liquor than a strict teetotaler would sanction." A fisherman by trade, he had joined the church after marrying a Mormon woman but had never been a "true believer."[25]

Sarah Wright heard that Bedford was staying with his fishing partner, David Brown, when Brown went into town on business one day and returned to find Bedford in bed with his wife. "Soon after, I heard that some men, Dave with the rest, caught Tom and tied him up and whipped him." Bedford, who suspected that Strang had ordered the whipping, threatened to kill the prophet in retaliation. "Of course I did not believe all I heard," Sarah added.[26]

In an interview with the *Detroit Evening News* in 1882, Bedford denied the whipping was over a "woman scrape," saying it was because he had disclosed what he knew about some organized theft among the Mormons. He said he had joined the Mormon Church because it was the only way to be able to stay on the island—something he and a few other gentile friends had done, pretending to convert out of necessity. "After a few years Strang saw fit to declare from the pulpit that all women must wear the bloomer style of dress and none of the men should smoke tobacco. If they disobeyed him they must walk over his dead body." This angered Bedford and his wife, both of whom by now rejected Strang's religious claims. Together, they declared they would no longer obey Strang's law. As a result, Bedford said, the Mormons had stolen from him a "fine span" of horses, ninety gill nets, and two fishing boats and their rigging.

Bedford explained he had incautiously told someone that the Mormons had stolen a boat from the gentiles and was overheard by some Strangites. "That evening after dark," about "the first of March 1856," a messenger came to Bedford's house, saying "Brother Strang wants to see you down at the printing office." When Bedford arrived, "the office was full of men, but

---

24. "Flogging," *Northern Islander*, Apr. 3, 1856.

25. "King Strang's Murder," *Detroit Evening News*, July 1, 1882; "Some Errors of a Magazine Article Corrected," *Detroit Evening News*, July 7, 1882, Clarke Historical Library.

26. Sarah Wing to Milo Quaife, Spring 1920, Clarke Historical Library.

James Strang was not there. Dennis Chidester reportedly told Bedford, 'You've been betraying us, telling about stolen property and we're here to make it right. We have been ordered to shut you up by giving you 40 stripes save one.'" The men had a horsewhip and eight hickory rods said to measure an inch in diameter at the heels. As they proceeded to dispense the punishment, Bedford promised revenge.[27] Some of the men later claimed that Strang was aware something might be done with Bedford but that he did not know the details and had not issued the command. Contrary to this, Wingfield Watson recalled hearing Strang say, "Whatever you do, let it be done quickly."[28]

Besides the controversies over bloomers and the flogging of Thomas Bedford, there was also dissension over the presence of alcohol on board the steamboats that anchored in the harbor. At least two Strangites had been seen frequenting the on-board bars. "If no other mode can be found to shut the bars of the boats visiting the harbor," the *Northern Islander* reported in May 1856, the Strangites would put a stop to it by having "no further business" to do with such boats. Strang reasoned that because there were "in all communities, men who cannot resist temptation; society owes them protection as far as in its power."[29]

The Strangites seen frequenting the bars were Thomas Atkyn, a daguerreotype artist at St. James, and Hezekiah McCulloch, a surgeon and once one of Strang's staunchest supporters. Atkyn had come to the island in 1850 when a steamboat dropped him off there for refusing to pay passage. According to the *Northern Islander,* he subsequently left the island to offer his services to gentiles who wanted to spy on the Mormons. When he returned in 1852 in poor health, he called upon Strang as a fellow mason in distress. Strang nursed him for three weeks until Atkyn recovered his health, then Strang gave him money for passage off the island.[30] Atkyn returned again in the summer of 1855 as a daguerrian portrait artist, well dressed and professing to have financial wherewithal but saying he had been recently robbed of his money. James M. Wait, a St. James merchant, agreed to provide capital for Atkyn to set him up in a portrait studio in St. James. Wait acquired the

---

27. "Some Errors of a Magazine."

28. Wingfield W. Watson to Milo Quaife, [June 10, 1920]; Wingfield Watson, interviewed by Milo M. Quaife, Dec. 10-11, 1918, Clarke Historical Library. Watson said Bedford had been acting as a spy for the gentiles.

29. "Intoxication," *Northern Islander,* May 22, 1856.

30. "Sunday, June 8, 1856: Messengers of Revenge," *Northern Islander,* June 19, 1856.

necessary equipment from Buffalo, along with the regular goods he imported to the island, and Atkyn promised to repay his benefactor as soon as he could. The studio was set up in Saint James Hall on Water Street, one door south of Strang's printing office.

By early winter, there was trouble between Strang and Atkyn, the latter boasting about what a "friend" he had in the prophet and the former rebuffing the artist for his heavy drinking. In fact, Atkyn was so frequently drunk, he was considered to be a general nuisance. In the spring, when navigation resumed on the Great Lakes, Atkyn renewed his personal store of liquor and started billing customers five to six times higher than previously. His investor sued him to recover the funds he had expended for photographic equipment. Atkyn was unhappy with this and attributed his troubles to Strang.[31] Strang took to calling Atkyn, a self-acclaimed doctor, "Dr. Ache-inside."

The *Northern Islander* went a step further and called Atkyn a "universal deadhead and sponge" who had "bored" everyone all winter with his inebriation. "In the stirring up of muddy waters, the filthiest will sometimes rise to the top"; the newspaper said Atkyn had come from "the filthiest depths below."[32] Taking a hint, Atkyn decided to sell his studio and equipment to Franklin Johnson, but instead of repaying Wait "ran away from the island" in the company of McCulloch. The captain of the steamer Atkyn boarded claimed the "little dark man" drank so much alcohol they "didn't even have enough left to light the lamps."[33]

Hezekiah McCulloch had stood in prominent positions in the Mormon Church and had been engaged in all its undertakings for six years. He held the public confidence and had wielded a great deal of influence. College educated, talented, and from a "respectable" family in Maryland, he had converted to Strangism in the spring of 1850, closed his business as a surgeon and apothecary in Baltimore, and started a mercantile business on Beaver Island in partnership with Franklin Johnson. Soon McCulloch was a judge on the church's highest tribunal and a member of Strang's confidential council. He was elected Emmet County coroner, county clerk, and register of deeds. He also "received many other testimonies of public confidence."[34]

---

31. *Northern Islander,* June 5, 1856.
32. "Messengers of Revenge."
33. *Northern Islander,* June 5, 1856, [p. 2].
34. "H. D. McCulloch," *Northern Islander,* June 19, 1856.

"Enemies showed [him] a great deal of malice," according to the *North-ern Islander*: "He was one of the first two men thrust in jail on charge[s] of the murder of Thomas Bennett and one of only two who were indicted.... [He was released] when it was shown that he acted in the matter ... as a pub-lic servant. Yet they dogged him like a shadow to get him to prison." McCulloch had been jailed twice in Detroit and once dragged through the streets of Mackinac in irons, but he now "betrayed" the Strangites by "going on steamboats, drinking to excess and becoming quarrelsome."[35]

Strang had intended for McCulloch to succeed him as state representa-tive in the election of 1854 but had now grown to fear the "disgrace" the doc-tor might bring on the Strangites. Very early in his business, McCulloch had been accused of using false weights and measures and of using fraud in set-tling accounts, especially with former church members. Reports of this kind had become more and more common over the years. It had been whispered for some time that he was no longer a believer; he was simply holding out for the chance to make a pile of money off the Mormons before being "off to dis-tant parts." The *Northern Islander* claimed McCulloch had refused to hand over the books, papers, and documents he used as a public officer, that he had falsified public documents and failed to record land titles. "For all this we shall not turn about and say there never was any good in him," Strang noted in the *Northern Islander*: "We believe he was a sincere man, seeking to lead a righteous life. Moral shortcomings he doubtless always had. Temptations have overcome him, and he has fallen."[36]

During the winter of 1855-56, Strang pulled McCulloch from his duties as county clerk after it was found he had defrauded some of the Saints in un-der-measuring their wood placed on his dock. He was found guilty of intoxi-cation and dropped from the Quorum of the Twelve Apostles. The "public's trust in him was lost," the newspaper now reported. By this time, McCulloch wanted to leave the island; but there was a problem—if he did so, under the laws of consecration he would forfeit everything he owned, and he had brought a great deal of merchandise with him to the island. It was about this time that he and Atkyn became drinking buddies. Strang took the two to task and embarrassed them in the pages of the *Northern Islander*. Vowing revenge for their public scolding and other offenses, the two began to plot Strang's

---

35. Ibid.
36. Ibid.

demise, assisted by other disillusioned Mormons such as McCulloch's partner in the mercantile business, Franklin Johnson. Alexander Wentworth, Johnson's son-in-law, and Thomas Bedford soon joined the conspiracy.

Wentworth, twenty-three, was said to be fine looking and intelligent but very quiet in his manner. He was married to Johnson's daughter, Phoebe.[37] For years rumors had circulated that Phoebe had been enamored with Strang's young nephew, Charley Douglass; other gossip reported that Strang had wanted to make Phoebe one of his wives. Apparently it was something else which had soured Wentworth against Strang—the prophet's slur against his family. This offence happened at a time when Wentworth had been talking loudly against polygamy. Strang heard about his remarks and countered them during a meeting, pointing out they came from a man "whose father was his grandfather, and whose mother was his sister."[38]

On May 6, 1856, McCulloch left the island with Atkyn, "breathing out threatenings and slaughter" against Strang and spreading ill will about the Mormons. When they returned a couple of weeks later, McCulloch brought back several revolvers and put them into the hands of Strang's enemies.[39] The conspirators spent several days practicing shooting at targets. With his "usual bravado," Strang scoffed at the reports of threats against his life even when the news came from reputable sources. "Captain Steele says that Dr. McCulloch has devoted his life to revenge on the Prophet for removing him from his Council, or some want of respect and confidence, and is bound to get him shot," Strang wrote boldly in the *Northern Islander* on June 5. Strang ridiculed the idea, saying "they who fear the assassination of the Prophet, may as well reserve their tears for awhile."[40]

In late May or early June, an anonymous "friend" sent Strang a package of forty-five letters written by various individuals warning and threatening Strang that he would be murdered and his followers swept from the islands. Strang's son, Gabriel, later recalled: "Parties [of Strang's enemies] were to be sent to all places where there was any prejudice, to tell the people that the

---

37. Zenas Wright, interviewed by Milo M. Quaife, May 25, 1920, n.p., Beaver Island Historical Society, Old Mormon Print Shop, St. James, Beaver Island, Michigan.

38. Wingfield Watson to Milo Quaife, [June 10, 1920].

39. Wingfield Watson, remarks on Elizabeth Whitney Williams's *A Child of the Sea and Life among the Mormons,* as given to Milo Quaife, June 20, 1919, Clarke Historical Library.

40. *Northern Islander,* June 5, 1856, [p.1].

Govt. was going to take a hand in the affair, and would be pleased to see that they [the Mormons] were driven away for good, and help from all would be gladly received."[41] The following Sabbath, as part of Strang's sermon in the tabernacle, he referred to the letters and instructed the congregation that if their enemies attempted to drive them from their homes, his instructions to them were to fight.[42]

In early June the U.S. warship *Michigan,* the same boat that had taken Strang to Detroit for trial five years earlier, arrived at St. James. The island was one of many stops the ship made every summer on a routine patrol of the Great Lakes, so the inhabitants did not think anything was unusual. During this particular stop, however, Captain Charles H. McBlair met secretly with several disaffected individuals from the Mormon community. The *Michigan* then left Beaver Island for Chicago. McBlair wrote to the Secretary of the Navy after the ship arrived in port:

> I found at Beaver [Island] some disturbance arising from the secession of members of the community from Mormonism and the mal-practices of James Strang the Leader and prophet. I felt it my duty to receive the depositions, under oath, of some of the citizens of Michigan belonging to that remote-settlement, charging Strang with robbery and other crimes, to lay before the Governor of the State.... I propose leaving here in a few days for [Lake] Erie, stopping at Beaver Island and other intermediate ports, and rendering such assistance to those citizens threatened by the hostility of Strang ... with a cautious regard for the laws of that State.[43]

McBlair sent the depositions to the governor of Michigan, telling him they had been made under oath by "certain citizens of Michigan belonging to the settlement at Beaver Island implicating James Strang and others in seri-

---

41. George Sage [Gabriel Strang] to A. E. Ewing, October 2, 1910. Clarke Historical Library. Gabriel said most of the letters were to and from civil and military officers, the rest being from enemies who had once been friends. In another letter, he said the package contained thirty-six letters, all of which were from "free Masons." Gabriel Strang to John Wake Jr., April 10, 1929, Clarke Historical Library.

42. Gabriel Strang to John Wake Jr., Apr. 10, 1929.

43. Captain C. H. McBlair to J. C. Dobbin, Secretary of the Navy, June 6, 1856, Clarke Historical Library. The depositions can be read in the Jacob Merritt Howard Collection of documents and letters relating to the Strangites, 1851-56, Yale Collection of Western Americana, Beinecke Rare Book and Manuscript Library, Yale University, New Haven, Connecticut.

ous crimes and misdemeanors." He said he had "every reason to believe that the greater part of the community has been for a long time engaged in a system of plunder upon the property of fishermen and others who may arrive at the island, and such as may be within reach of boat expeditions to the Michigan and Wisconsin shores." He accused Strang of establishing church law in place of secular law and exacting tithing as his due for "profits arising from trade and from the booty acquired by felonious practices." He stated that Strang's followers were generally bound to him, either by common interest or religious zeal, and were prepared to carry out all his measures.[44]

Strang had made false census returns, McBlair suspected, based on the testimony he had received—overstating the Mormon population nearly fourfold in order to get a larger proportion of the state's school fund. He told the governor there were between ten and twelve persons on the island who had more or less seceded from the church and were "exposed to all the consequences of Strang's resentment."[45] In addition,

> there are a number of others, who at heart are opposed to Strang but suppress their feelings from fear. The firm of F. Johnson & Co., consisting of Franklin Johnson and Hezekiah McCulloch from Baltimore, together with their families are at open variance with Strang, owing to their secession from the Faith and the desire of the firm to wind up their affairs and quit the island. They have in consequence incurred the wrath and ill will of the sect to a degree which they think threatens not only their property but their lives, and are deeply solicitous that some prompt and vigorous measures of protection be extended to them by the state. Strang is a man of uncommon ability and ... through his pretended mission and superior intelligence and energy of purpose has established a complete ascendancy over the minds of most of his ignorant and deluded adherents.[46]

About one o'clock on the afternoon of Monday, June 16, 1856, the *Michigan* reappeared in St. James Harbour and hauled up to McCulloch's dock. The Strangites were at a loss to know the reason for her return, as the ship had left only a few days before. Two men having the appearance of sub-

---

44. Captain C. H. McBlair to Governor Kinsley S. Bingham, June 6, 1856, Clarke Historical Library.

45. Ibid. McBlair said Christopher Scott and Franklin Johnson had counted ninety-five Mormon families on Beaver Island and eight on Gull Island for an estimated total of 515 inhabitants.

46. Captain C. H. McBlair to Governor Kinsley S. Bingham, June 6, 1856.

ordinate officers made a short trip on horseback into the interior of the island, then returned to the boat. In preparation for the events to come, McCulloch made a secret visit to the boat and reportedly signed over his property to one of the officers in order to prevent the Saints from collecting damages of any sort against him. McCulloch had already given the ship's officers the names of the leading men on the island "for the purpose of having them arrested, that if possible, there might be a complete overthrow of the Kingdom," according to later accounts.[47]

Someone called Strang's attention to the ship and Strang went to the window to see what boat it was. "They are not coming back for any good purpose," he predicted.[48] About seven o'clock in the evening, the captain sent one of his officers, Alexander St. Bernard, to find Strang and bring him on board. "I was well acquainted with the king, for he often came on board the ship," St. Bernard remembered. "He was a fine looking, sociable sort of a man; but he was not very popular among the Gentiles.... I went to the temple first, where I was told that he had just gone home. I found him sitting in his room, with four of his five wives, where he received me very cordially, and when I told him of my errand, accompanied me willingly." Strang put on his hat and left with his military escort. The two men walked along together talking pleasantly and even linked arms. Strang was in "particularly good spirits," telling jokes and stories.[49]

Meanwhile, Thomas Bedford and Alexander Wentworth joined about forty other men, including a number of marines, on the porch of Johnson's store at the foot of the pier. Strang and his escort stepped onto McCulloch's dock and started to walk down the narrow passageway between piles of

---

47. Warren Post, "The Record of the Apostles of James, Written During 1854-1863, Relating to the Events of 1844-1856, James J. Strang, the Mormons, and Beaver Island, Lake Michigan," unpublished manuscript, Clarke Historical Library; cf. *Record of the Apostles of James, 1844-1856*, facsimile ed. (Burlington, WI: John J. Hajicek, 1992).

48. Gabriel Strang to John Wake Jr., Apr. 10, 1929.

49. This sequence of events was compiled from several sources, including Wingfield W. Watson's account of the shooting in "Persecution," unpublished manuscript, Burton Historical Collection, Detroit Public Library; "The Murder of King Strang," *Detroit Free Press*, June 30, 1889, Detroit Public Library; "Interview with Thomas Bedford," *Detroit Evening News*, July 7, 1882; Post, "Record of the Apostles"; Gabriel Strang to John Wake Jr., Apr. 10, 1929; and a recollection by Alexander St. Bernard in the *St. Clair Republican*, Mar. 8, 1882, James Strang Papers, Clarke Historical Library. Some witnesses say St. Bernard stepped away after the first shot and Strang fell immediately to the ground.

cordwood. Bedford and Wentworth stepped behind them and followed for about fifteen or twenty feet, just far enough to clear the crowd, then simultaneously fired at Strang. One shot struck the king in the left side of the head behind his ear and traveled up through his high silk hat. As Strang turned to see where the shots were coming from, another shot struck him in the back on the left side, penetrating one of his kidneys. A third bullet glanced off his right cheekbone about an inch under the eye. Strang staggered, hanging onto St. Bernard, while Wentworth ran full speed for the *Michigan*. Bedford took his horse pistol and hammered Strang in the face with the butt until the pistol was broken. Strang clung to St. Bernard's arm for a moment and then let go and fell onto the gangplank leading to the *Michigan*. St. Bernard was covered with blood from head to feet.

As Strang lay wounded, Bedford ran to the vessel and gave himself up to the ship's captain. Some witnesses said the captain had watched the entire transaction himself. Safely on board the ship, Wentworth made the remark that they had got rid of the "damned rascal." Someone asked "Who?" and Wentworth replied, "Strang, the damned Son of a Bitch." Some of the deck hands reportedly lifted the gangplank where Strang lay bleeding until his body slid back onto the wharf, then pulled up the gangplank. St. Bernard and some crew members who had witnessed the shooting picked up the prophet and carried him off the pier.

Wingfield Watson, who had been working on the roof of the tabernacle nearby, rushed to Strang's side within minutes and stood there "lest the enemy, thinking he was still living, might rush in upon him to finish him." Watson put his own finger upon the wound on Strang's head to stop the bleeding and held it there for seven hours until the wound closed up again. Before long, the news had spread through town and a "howling mob of men, women and children gathered around their dying chief," St. Bernard recalled. If the assassins had not escaped to the safety of the ship, he added, "the mob would have pulled them in pieces if they caught them. Of course, suspicion fell on me, many thinking I had led him to his death, and I received several friendly warnings to be on my guard, but I was not molested."[50]

Strang was taken to the nearest dwelling, the home of one of the Prindle brothers, and the surgeon from the *Michigan* was called in to assist. The sur-

---

50. Ibid.

geon pronounced the wounds mortal and told Strang he would not recover from them.[51] The officers and surgeon of the boat "feigned" sorrow over Strang's condition and rendered a small amount of assistance.

Strang's subordinates gathered together to counsel on what course to take. The sheriff immediately demanded that Captain McBlair turn over custody of the two shooters and anyone else who could have been an accessory to the crime, but McBlair refused. He replied that the prisoners would be carefully kept until they could be delivered into the hands of the first civil authority in Mackinac.[52] Although it was true that Bedford and Wentworth were in custody, they were nevertheless allowed to roam the ship at will. McBlair sent a file of soldiers to protect other Mormon conspirators, including Hezekiah McCulloch and Franklin Johnson and their families, who were brought to McCulloch's home to spend the night under guard to protect them from the infuriated Mormons. The next morning the conspirators and anyone else who wanted to join them were escorted aboard. The ship headed for Mackinac, where the captain planned to deliver Strang's attackers to law officials.[53]

McBlair wrote to the Secretary of the Navy justifying his actions. "As well as I can learn," he wrote, "Strang has provoked his fate by numerous acts of persecution against the seceders from his faith, belonging to the settlement. The two men who attempted his life are said to have been among the greatest sufferers from this cause. I gave passage to Mackinac to seven families, including those of the prisoners and numbering about thirty persons, who thought their lives in jeopardy from the Mormons."[54] At about 10 o'clock the morning after the incident and before leaving the harbor, McBlair visited Strang, who was conscious and lucid, to express sorrow such a thing happened while his ship was in port. Strang demanded custody of the men who had shot him and the captain once again refused.[55]

The Strangites back on Beaver Island had expected as much. "Our opinion is that they will be set at liberty; as soon as they reach Mackinac, & instead of that punishment being inflicted upon them, which their crime mer-

51. Ibid.

52. Post, "Record of the Apostles."

53. "Interview with Thomas Bedford," *Detroit Evening News,* July 7, 1882.

54. Charles H. McBlair to J. C. Dobbin, Secretary of the Navy, June 19, 1856, Clarke Historical Library.

55. Watson, "Persecution"; Post, "Record of the Apostles."

its, they will be applauded & extolled for the celebrity of the Act," Wingfield Watson wrote in his journal. "But if such fiends in human shape can go unpunished of Men; the [y] cannot escape the punishment of the Eternal. The word of God is, 'Touch not mine Anointed, and do my Prophets no harm.' ... [B]ut God is the avenger of blood and will render unto all men according to their deeds."[56]

Five hours later, when the *Michigan* pulled up to the pier in Mackinac, Bedford and Wentworth were turned over to Sheriff Henry Granger, who joyfully showed them the way to the jail. The prison was "immediately filled with sympathizing citizens, one of whom brought the prisoners a bed and some tobacco and pipes, while another brought a bottle of sugared brandy." After one of the citizens said something to the sheriff in French, everyone stepped out of the jail, including Bedford and Wentworth. Apparently, the Frenchmen had told the sheriff if he locked the prison doors, the citizens would tear the jail down. "Being of an economical turn of mind," the sheriff concluded to save the building. He escorted the "prisoners" and their families to his own boarding house, where he kept them for a week without charge.[57]

After three days of loose "confinement," Bedford and Wentworth were brought before a mock court that heard testimony for less than an hour and then discharged the prisoners. The judge solemnly announced he would have to charge them $1.25 each for court costs, but even that was never paid. One day in Mackinac, a man on the street gave Bedford five dollars without saying why. Bedford claimed this was the only money he ever received in connection with the shooting of James Strang.[58]

Gabriel Strang later explained the logistics of the legal proceedings. Initially it was claimed that "the crime took place over the water and consequently not in the jurisdiction of the state," so the matter was referred to federal court. Once there, it was determined that "when the fatal shot was fired[,] the men were on the wharf[,] which was connected with the land[,] which was under state jurisdiction." To avoid double jeopardy, it was reasoned, the prisoners could not be returned to state court, "so that was the end of the farce" and the prisoners were discharged.[59]

---

56. Watson, "Persecution."

57. "Interview with Thomas Bedford," *Detroit Evening News,* July 7, 1882.

58. Ibid.

59. Gabriel Strang to John Wake Jr., Apr. 10, 1929.

14.

DEATH AND EXILE

July 1856

*"The saints rendered every assistance
unto their King, which was in their power, & often called upon the Lord
to speedily restore him in health unto them. By the blessing of the Almighty
& the faith and works of the Saints, the Prophet's life was lengthened out
marvelously. The saints believed God would heal him, even if 'his visage
was marred more than that of any man, and his form more than the sons of
men.' We hoped he would remain alive on the earth until the coming of Jesus Christ, in the Clouds of heaven with power and great glory.... It was,
advised for ... [the Saints] to keep out of [the] way until the excitement
was over, & 'until the prophet recovered his health so he could prosecute
our enemies, and bring them to justice according to the law.'"* —Warren
Post, "Record of the Apostles of James."[1]

Although Strang was not dead, he was badly wounded. He spent
two days at the home of the Prindles and was then transferred to
his own home, where he was lovingly cared for by his followers. The leading
men on Beaver Island held a council, where they determined it would be
better for the colony if Strang were taken to Voree to recuperate. The biggest
worry was that gentile vigilantes would descend on Beaver Island and the
prophet would be the first to be killed. Only two weeks earlier Strang had
told his followers he wanted them to fight if attacked.[2] But the strategy had
changed since then. Perhaps fearing what would happen if his people were
engaged in a full-scale battle with the gentiles, the prophet suddenly reverted

---

1. Warren Post, "The Record of the Apostles of James, Written During 1854-1863,
Relating to the Events of 1844-1856, James J. Strang, the Mormons, and Beaver Island,
Lake Michigan," unpublished manuscript, Clarke Historical Library, Central Michigan
University, Mount Pleasant, Michigan; cf. *Record of the Apostles of James, 1844-1856,* fac-
simile ed. (Burlington, WI: John J. Hajicek, 1992).

2. Gabriel Strang to John Wake Jr., Apr. 10, 1929, Clarke Historical Library.

to the previous philosophy of non-violence he had recommended to the Saints in Nauvoo twelve years earlier. He told his followers not to resist.[3]

Gentile friends told the Mormons that arrest warrants had been sworn out against most of the church leaders in an attempt to get them off the island. The men believed the charges might be dropped if they were already gone. This would leave the rest of the inhabitants unmolested and able to leave the island at their own speed. "The better way for them to [respond], would be to scatter over the country in small bodies that would not attract too much attention or opposition until a way was provided for the work to go on and the warrants were outlawed," a mortally wounded Strang advised his apostles.[4]

On Saturday, June 28, twelve days after he was shot, Strang was carried onto the propeller *Louisville*. A number of the Mormons, those considered to be the most offensive to the gentiles, and their families accompanied him. The plan was for the rest of the colony to follow as soon as they could get their possessions ready to go and ships came into the harbor. In the meantime, however, they were left virtually leaderless and unprotected. Among those who accompanied Strang were his apostles Lorenzo Dow Hickey, George Miller, and Benjamin Wright, as well as Strang's wives Betsy McNutt and Phoebe Wright, and Betsy's two young children. Edward Chidester, postmaster, apostle, and co-publisher of the *Northern Islander,* was also on the *Louisville* and kept a brief account of the journey in his diary.[5] The voyage to Voree with the wounded prophet was unusually long and hazardous because of bad weather. The *Louisville* was forced to lay over at South Manitou Island for two days and did not arrive in Racine until Tuesday, July 1, four days after the ship had left St. James.

---

3. Sarah Wing to Milo Quaife, June 28, 1920, Clarke Historical Library. Sarah said the people were helpless because there were not more than fifty firearms on the island at the time.

4. Gabriel Strang to John Wake, May 8, 1929, Clarke Historical Library. Although he was paralyzed from the waist down due to the shot he took to the spine, Strang was conscious and cognizant and assisted in making plans with his leaders for the defense of the people.

5. Edward Chidester, Diary, n.p., copy in author's possession from the original in private hands. Edward Chidester was born in Milford, Otsego County, New York, in 1826. He was mild, quiet-spoken, and studious, and his ecclesiastic labors seem to have been mostly in the area of writing. In 1848 he moved to Voree with his brother Dennis. After Strang was shot, Edward hid the type from which the Book of the Law of the Lord was printed; he later moved to his father-in-law's farm in Comstock, Michigan.

At Racine, the men loaded Strang into a railroad baggage car for the next leg of the journey. It was a "rough ride" as the tracks to Burlington had been only recently completed. The Strangites arrived later that night.[6] On arrival, Strang was taken to the home of his parents, who had moved to Voree three years earlier. He was then moved next door to a home that was owned by the church.[7] Legend asserts that Strang repeatedly asked for his first wife, Mary, that in a "pang of conscience" he wanted his "true" wife to be with him when he died. It was claimed that Mary came to him and forgave her husband for his misdeeds. The first part of the story may be true, that Strang asked for Mary, but the second part was not. Far from coming to his side and forgiving him, Mary was not even in Voree, but rather in Elgin, Illinois, where her brother lived.[8]

It is interesting that even though Strang's parents lived in Voree at the time their son was shot, only Strang's mother, Abigail, is spoken of in Chidester's diary as attending to her son. Her husband, Clement, was known to be a loving, caring father and, as far as can be determined, had experienced no falling out with his son. The probable reason for his absence is that he went to Elgin, a distance of about fifty miles, to fetch Mary and her children back to Voree.

At Beaver Island, two days after Strang's evacuation, several families left for Voree on the *Iowa*.[9] Strang's fourth wife, Sarah Wright may have been among them or she may have left a few days later. In any case, she traveled from Racine to Voree to visit her husband, but was not able to stay long. Financial necessity forced her to return to Racine with her father, Phineas Wright.[10] Elvira Field and her three children probably did not leave the island until early July, arriving in Voree on July twelfth.[11]

Strang seemed to rally from his injuries, but there was not much hope for a full recovery. The wounds on his head and under his eye had nearly healed,

---

6. Ibid. Chidester wrote that a dishonest clerk stole his trunk while he was making the arrangements for the trip from Racine to Voree.

7. Sarah Wing to Milo Quaife, n.d., Clarke Historical Library. The residence may have been Strang's own house.

8. Ibid.

9. Post, "Record of the Apostles."

10. Sarah Wright to Milo Quaife, June 28, 1920.

11. Elvira E. Baker to "Dear Friend" [Wingfield Watson], Mar. 22, 1883, Clarke Historical Library.

but the ball in his back had lodged near his spine and caused paralysis.[12] However, he was conscious enough of his situation to realize that death was near. On July 7, Strang confided to Edward Chidester he knew the "active part of his life was at an end, that the bearing off of the kingdom must devolve upon others; he felt that his ministry as chief was done." Despite his impending death, Strang refused to name a successor. Nevertheless, as Chidester recalled, "his eyes brightened, and his countenance was lit up, and it was observed by all, that he was a great deal better." On "King's Day," July 8, Strang took another turn for the worse and "began to run down." From then on, "it seemed as though he just wilted away."[13] Chidester sent for Caleb P. Barnes, Strang's former law partner, to settle Strang's business affairs. In the meantime, Chidester recorded,

> I asked him if he was going to leave us. He said he was. I then asked him if we were to have a successor appointed through him: a tear started in his eye, and he said, 'I do not want to talk about it.' ... Brother Hickey & Adeline [Hickey] were with me that night to assist me.... I helped turn and fix him comfortable about break of day, and lay down for a nap. I lay about one hour and a half at the foot of his bed. When I awoke there was no one in the room but him & myself. I immediately arose and discovered that he was dying. I nursed him very attentively for about an hour and saw no hopes of recovery, when I sent for some of the neighbors. I asked if there was anything he wished to communicate. He replied 'Yes,' which was the last word he spoke.[14]

Gabriel Strang was a toddler at the time but remembered his father's death with some clarity. Perhaps his mother, Betsy McNutt, reminded him of it as he was growing up, but his reminiscence seems credible.[15]

> All the other children were kept out. I can remember Dr. Cooper coming to dress the wounds so well I recognized him 18 years afterward when I next

---

12. Post, "Record of the Apostles."

13. Edward Chidester Diary; also Post, "Record of the Apostles."

14. "Part of a Record by Edward Chidester, Apostle," unpublished manuscript, Strang Papers, Clarke Historical Library; also Post, "Record of the Apostles."

15. Although Gabriel was only about eighteen months old, it is possible he possessed his father's famous photographic memory. The prophet had a vivid recollection of incidents from his childhood, which were later reaffirmed by his mother and aunts. See Elvira Field Strang and Charles J. Strang, "Biographical Sketch of James J. Strang," unpublished manuscript, n.p., Strang Manuscript Collection, Library and Historical Center, State Library of Michigan, Lansing, Michigan.

s[aw] him. I used to sit on the floor in a corner near the bed and [from there I] watch[ed] the operation. I can remember that someone in the room would speak to me and once they called me over to the bed. Dr. Cooper, Edward Chidester, and [Sarah] Adelia, the daughter of Phineas Wright were there. I was standing by a window. I was timid and did not start quick so Adelia came over and carried [me] to the bed. They all spoke to me but I do not remember what they said. When the Dr. left, Bro. Chidester and Adelia stepped out of the room with him perhaps to get private instructions from the Dr. I was still standing by the bed when they returned and father was lying with his eyes shut as if asleep. Adelia took me by the hand and led me to the other side of the room. Afterwards they left the room and after what seemed to me a long time father opened his eyes and seeing me standing by the wall called me over and talked to me awhile.

I cannot remember all he said. But I remember very distinctly that he said he was going away and he was not sure that any others of his family would have the patience to endure the trials that would befall those who would come to him; but he felt sure I would have the patience, and he wanted me to always remember that day, and that he asked me to be sure and follow him. It was not long before several persons came into the room and I went out. I do not remember whether he died that day or not but I am quite sure I did not see him again.[16]

Edward Chidester, Lorenzo Dow Hickey, Sarah Hickey, George Miller, Betsy Strang, Evangeline Strang, Gabriel Strang, Mother Strang (Abigail), and Phoebe Strang were all at the prophet's bedside when he died about 9:45 a.m., July 9, 1856.[17]

The funeral was held at 2:00 p.m. the following afternoon. Some of the prophet's strongest supporters attended the service, including Edward Chidester, Lorenzo Dow Hickey, Chester Linnell Sr., George Luther, George Miller, Lorenzo Tubbs, and Benjamin Wright, along with their families.[18] A "respectable congregation of gentiles from Burlington also attended." Edward Chidester wrote that

---

16. Gabriel Strang to Mr. Chester Flanders, letter fragments, July 7, 1919, Clarke Historical Library.

17. Edward Chidester Diary; also Post, "Record of the Apostles." It appears that July 9 was an important date to Strang. Exactly twelve years previously, he had received the letter of appointment at the Burlington post office, and it was five years to the day that he was cleared of all charges in the trial at Detroit.

18. Edward Chidester Diary. A "Sister Townsend" listed among those attending the funeral may be the woman of that name who was said to be one of Strang's concubines.

Bro. Hickey opened the meeting by prayer, & such a prayer I never heard except from the Prophet himself. It seemed as though the earth trembled, the wagon where he stood did at any rate, he had the Spirit to such a degree that he never had it before, at least he says so. Brother B. G. Wright then attempted to preach, but it was only an attempt, Brother Hickey had the Spirit. He [Strang] was buried in the burying ground at Voree, in as good a style as that part of the country could afford. I paid twenty dollars for his coffin, and it was said to be worth $35.00, his shroud was of the finest silk flannel at a cost of $4.77. I considered him worthy of the best, and therefore I gave it to him.[19]

The prophet was buried in the Mormon cemetery near the Hill of Promise with a simple wooden marker commemorating the spot.[20] A few years later, as the Strang estate was settled, the cemetery was sold to a gentile farmer who chose to situate his hog lot in the middle of the burial ground, then built a barn and located its doorway over top of one particular grave so that entrance to the barn necessitated treading on it.[21] The farmer's view of the prophet stood in stark contrast to Apostle Warren Post's panegyric: "Thus ended the life of James, the beloved of the Lord. He was 43 years, 3 months, and 18 days old. He bore his sufferings with great patience, & as far as we know as innocent as a lamb, and had patience like Job, & meeker than Moses, and the wisdom of Solomon. Since the days of Jesus Christ upon the earth, there has been none to excel him."[22]

As Strang lay dying and his followers were leaving Beaver Island for good, his assassins, Thomas Bedford, Franklin Johnson, and Hezekiah Mc-Culloch, "exalted" in their victory as they traveled to Green Bay, Wisconsin, to recruit sixteen men to "begin the work of finishing up the history of Mor-

---

19. Post, "Record of the Apostles," 16.

20. Clement Strang to Stanley Johnston, Aug. 13, 1939, Clarke Historical Library. There were several graves in the cemetery, including those of little Mary Strang, James's daughter, and Amanda Wright, Sarah Wright's mother.

21. Ibid.; also "The Diary of James Oscar McNutt, Elder of the Mormon Church at the Mormon Settlement, Jackson Co., Wisconsin; One Time Follower of James Jesse Strang," State Library of Michigan; cf. "Reminisces of James O. McNutt of the Mormon Settlement, Jackson County [Wisconsin], and Warrens, Monroe County, Related by J. O. McNutt, and Recorded by his Daughter Miss Sadie McNutt," Library-archives, Wisconsin Historical Library, Madison, Wisconsin; "Old Newspaper File Tells Voree Story," *Racine Journal News,* Jan. 20, 1931.

22. Post, "Record of the Apostles."

monism on Beaver Island."[23] The three returned to St. James on the commercial steamship *Michigan*—not the warship of the same name—and landed at several points on the island to forcibly "collect" Mormon hostages for questioning about a burned building. They took the hostages to Mackinac Island but failed to get the information they desired and let the hostages go.[24]

On July 3, 1856, a correspondent for the *Green Bay Advocate* proudly informed his readers that he, "on behalf of the citizens of Green Bay and Washington Island," was planning to participate in driving the Mormons off Beaver Island. "The plan is to return this week if possible, with at least 150 men, properly armed and equipped, and just clear every Mormon from the island—peacefully if possible—but if they won't do that, than at the range of a rifle. God help them … if half their wrongs and grievances be true. The Mormon Kingdom then richly deserves such a fate."[25]

Giddy with having shot Strang, whom his followers had thought was invincible, the gentiles were enthusiastic at the prospect of finally driving the Mormons off the island. Not only were they going to rid the world of what they considered an annoying counter-culture, they knew there were tremendous properties to be acquired on the island. The instigators suspected that the United States government would not come to the support of the Mormons. After all, it had done nothing to punish Strang's assassins or those who had driven off Mormons in Missouri and Illinois.

As soon as the *USS Michigan* had left the harbor on June 16 with Bedford and Wentworth, boats loaded with armed men had already begun to land on Beaver Island at out-of-the-way places, temporarily keeping their distance and waiting for reinforcements. The steamers running between Lake Michigan and the lower lakes called at St. James and told the Mormons it looked like there would be trouble, that they had better send away the women and children and what property they could get together as quickly as possible.[26]

The news of the shooting and the mobilization of opportunists was carried swiftly around Lake Michigan. When the men on St. Helena Island

---

23. "An Interview with Thomas Bedford," *Detroit Evening News,* July 7, 1882, Clarke Historical Library.

24. Ibid.

25. Charles O. Burgess, "Green Bay and the Mormons of Beaver Island," *Wisconsin Magazine of History,* Autumn 1958, 46; *Green Bay Advocate,* July 3, 1856.

26. George Sage [Gabriel Strang] to A. E. Ewing, Nov. 5, 1910, Clarke Historical Library.

found out Strang had retreated to Voree, they determined to reclaim the property of those who had been driven off Beaver Island in 1851. Their leaders were Archie, Wilson, and Obediah Newton and a French fisherman from Cross Village, John Wagley. They were soon joined by fishermen from Washington Island, as well.[27]

On July 3, six squads of ten men each landed quietly on the back side of Beaver Island about a mile from the St. James harbor. The sheriff was with them, intending to arrest any leaders who might still be on the island. The men expected resistance, but the Strangites followed their prophet's advice to avoid armed conflict. Discovering that the people were docile and leaderless, the invaders began their work of "robbery and general destruction" throughout the island. "They came marching through the streets of St. James ordering all Mormons to leave and giving them only 24 hours to do it or be shot," Elvira Field noted. "Those individuals who tried to oppose the mob and defend themselves were thrust into the street and their houses burned. The Mormon tabernacle on the hill was torched, as were storehouses, businesses, valuable dwellings and the Mormon print shop."[28]

Pleased with the arson the pillagers had initiated, Thomas Bedford proudly announced that "it would have been cheaper to buy a new printing office than to attempt any work of publication at the one left by Strang."[29] The prophet's house and property were especially targeted for plunder and ransacking. His household goods and extensive library were thrown into the street and trampled in the mud. To show their hatred of Strang, the attackers shot at everything on the premises. Strang's large poultry yard with the rare Plymouth Rock chickens John C. Bennett had sent as a coronation gift was "made a shooting-mark for all."[30] The mob went looking for Strang's wives. "My friends advised me to keep out of sight," Sarah Wright recollected. "I was told some rough had said he would like to find Strang's young wife—but I was not found." She explained that the Mormons were helpless because

---

27. Marion Morse Davis, "Stories of St. Helena Island," *Michigan History* 10 (1926): 429.

28. Strang and Strang, "Biographical Sketch."

29. "Interview with Thomas Bedford," *Detroit Evening News*, July 7, 1882. Charles Strang, in a letter to Wingfield Watson, July 22, 1882, asked: "Did you see Tom Bedford's confession in the Detroit Evening News of July 7th? My brother who is studying law, thinks we can use it against him and bring him to grief yet before he dies."

30. Sarah Wright to Milo Quaife, June 28, 1920.

they did not know if Strang was still alive and had been told not to resist.[31]

Wingfield Watson was walking from his home to the port town about six miles away to see what the disturbance was about when he met Archie Newton and another vigilante, both of whom were armed with rifles and bowie knives. They asked Watson where he lived and he replied he lived about half-way down the island. Newton cursed Watson and told him to get his things down to the harbor by six o'clock the following evening or his house would be burned over his head. Watson asked to be permitted to stay a little longer since his wife had just given birth and was in no condition to travel but was answered with more curses. The two men threatened to tie him to a cherry tree and whip him. Watson noticed they were armed as well with whiskey as fire power and decided to acquiesce, telling Newton it would be difficult but that he and his wife would do the best they could.[32]

Watson's brother-in-law, James Smith, acquired an ox team and driver to take some of the Watsons' belongings to the harbor. The next morning Wingfield and wife, Jane, set out on foot for St. James. He carried their two-day-old baby girl while she walked beside him with their other daughter and her young son from a previous marriage. They made their way slowly along a road that was still just a path that wound in and out of stumps and through the cedar swamp.[33] They arrived at the harbor at about one o'clock in the afternoon. It was the Fourth of July. "The beach around the west side of the harbor seemed here and there like an open fair, or market-place," Wingfield said, "with cattle, tents, fires, smoke, furniture, and household goods of every description; all waiting, according to the dictates of the mob, to be off on the boat's arrival, chartered or hired for the business."[34]

Strangite apostle Warren Post was off the island at the time serving a mission in New York state. His two wives, Deborah, eight months pregnant, and Sarah, were alone with five children, the oldest one seven and the youngest five months. The intruders pounded at the door, then gave the two women one hour to get out and take their families to McCulloch's pier.

---

31. Ibid.

32. Wingfield Watson, interviewed by Milo M. Quaife, Dec. 11, 1919; M. L. Leach, "A History of the Grand Traverse Region," *Grand Traverse Herald,* 1883, 114-20, Clarke Historical Library.

33. Ibid.

34. Ibid.

Deborah ordered her seven-year-old son to get the wheelbarrow, then she and Sarah gathered what they could in blankets and bags. Shooing the older children ahead of them, the women took turns pushing the wheelbarrow containing the youngest children. After a time, some young Strangite men, who were also headed for the dock, took over.[35]

Most of the unbound copies of the Book of the Law of the Lord had been boxed up and taken away before the assault, but other pamphlets were in the printing office when the gentiles arrived. The manuscripts were "hurled into the street, and lay fluttering in the wind, all about the printing office door, in the eyes of all passing that way." Some of the gentiles took control of the printing office and struck up a manifesto of their "grievances," which they circulated to the Mormons and gentiles. Over 1,600 rare and expensive books in the office fell into the hands of the anarchists and many of them were later discovered to be in community libraries and schools throughout the state of Michigan.[36]

The steamer *Buckeye State*,[37] which Hezekiah McCulloch had chartered to take the people off the island, was delayed until the evening. When it arrived, "a general bustle and flurry commenced among the people, with here and there a 'G-d d--n ye, get yer things aboard,'" as Watson recalled. His friend, James Smith, had planned on leaving a few days later on the *Iowa* and had not yet packed up his belongings. Someone "slapped Smith around and at the point of a gun aimed at his chest ordered him to get on board the Buckeye State." Smith told the man that McCulloch had said he could stay until the *Iowa* came in, but the gentile replied, "G-d d--n McCulloch, ... we'll play hell with him pretty soon."[38] Watson continued:

> I got what few things I [had] ... aboard, but my poor brother-in-law got next to nothing of his large property. The industry of 30 years with him was mainly swept away in an hour. He had ... come onto the island from Pittsburg[h], P[ennsylvani]a, and built a large saw mill, bringing machinery of various kinds with him, from blacksmith's shop, turning lathe, and belting ... yet all was pos-

---

35. Jerry L. Gorden, "Warren Post: Beaver Island Too," *Journal of Beaver Island History* 5 (2002): 29-30. Gorden is a descendent of Warren and Deborah Post.

36. Wingfield Watson interview.

37. Ibid. Watson incorrectly identified the *Keystone State*, a sister ship to the *Buckeye State*, and was a day off in his chronology.

38. Leach, "History of Grand Traverse," 113.

sessed by the mob, innocent as he was and without charge of any kind being laid against him. Plead as he might and did, he never got a penny of the thousands he had invested there. He was a damn Mormon you know.[39]

Aldrich's dock on the southwestern side of Beaver Harbor was the first stop for the *Buckeye State.* The gentiles drove the unfortunate people on board "like so many sheep destined for the shambles." Their property was seized as "lawful booty." More than 100 head of choice cattle, horses, and mules were taken, as well as boats, nets, fish and fishermen's supplies, and large quantities of provisions, furniture, and household goods. Three stores and a printing office were rifled and their contents added to the plunder.[40] When all the people were loaded at Aldrich's dock, the ship went to McCulloch's dock in St. James where the scene was repeated. Everything was a mass of confusion. The Strangites boarded, expecting their belongings to be loaded after them, but far from loading any luggage, the gentiles searched everyone, even children, to see that no one carried away anything of value. The gentiles "drove them on the steamboats and loosened their lines from the dock[,] and they had to leave on the ship," Gabriel Strang recalled.[41]

Wingfield Watson's wife was the last to get on board the ship. Wingfield walked ahead of her with the baby while she feebly stumbled toward the boat, an armed gentile walking behind her. Because she was not moving fast enough to suit him, he cursed her to move faster.[42] As the *Buckeye State* left the harbor, the 350 exiled men, women, and children realized this would probably be the last time they would ever see their island and their homes again, nor did they have any idea of what the steamer's destination was. It arrived the following morning at the small settlement of Green Bay, Wisconsin, and unloaded ninety Mormons. "They are all in the most destitute circumstances, having neither money nor provisions, and not even clothes, save the shabby [clothing] on their backs," the *Green Bay Advocate* noted. "All their movables, except a scant supply of bedding, they were compelled to leave behind them … and it is one of the most pitiable cases we have recorded in a long time."[43]

Another 150 Mormons were deposited in Milwaukee, leaving about

---

39. Ibid.

40. Ibid., 114.

41. George Sage [Gabriel Strang] to A. E. Ewing, Nov. 5, 1910.

42. Leach, "History of Grand Traverse," 118-19.

43. Burgess, "Green Bay and Mormons," 46.

100 still on board when the ship arrived in Racine on its way to Chicago. At Racine, Benjamin Wright's son delivered the news that the prophet had died that morning. The Saints were thunderstruck; most had expected Strang to recover. Wingfield Watson and his family were among those who remained on the ship as far as Chicago. "Thus we were left in destitution and landed in a couple of days and left on the dock at Chicago to go where we pleased and find a home now where we could," Watson recollected. "Here we were left without shelter, the sun beaming down at fever heat. Here we were made a gazing stock for all kinds of people to stare at. One man began to swear at the mob for sending the people there and robbing them; and with some manly feelings he shoved the large warehouse doors apart and said, 'here, ladies and gentlemen, come in here out of the sun and stay until you can find places.' This was the first kind word that we had heard from any one during the whole proceedings and indeed we could appreciate it."[44]

The *Buckeye State* was at least allowed to dock. Other Mormons were not so lucky as various communities refused to let any of the Mormons come ashore. "The suffering of the saints in consequence of the cruelty of the mob [was] beyond the power of description," Gabriel Strang recalled, the refugees finding it nearly impossible to get settled anywhere along the lakes where the boats had left them. After being refused entry to a port, ships carrying Strangites headed down the lake and put a few people ashore at a time, landing them on the beach with small boats or putting a few here or there wherever there was a dock. The stranded refugees walked to where they could get help. Some stayed in deserted fishermen's shanties along the beach until they could build boats and travel up to Green Bay and the Fox River, across the Portage Canal to the Wisconsin and Mississippi Rivers. Many of them had previously lived in that area of the country and had friends who could assist them. Some went back to the places where they had settled after Joseph Smith's death before they were driven out of Illinois.[45]

The exiled Strangites who were forced to disembark in Milwaukee found themselves soon joined by an unlikely compatriot, according to accounts. If correct, this was the last person they would have expected to find in such a condition—Hezekiah McCulloch. According to Watson, McCulloch

---

44. Wingfield Watson to A. Chaney, Aug. 18, 1877, [p. 35], Clarke Historical Library.

45. George Sage [Gabriel Strang] to A. E. Ewing, Dec. 4, 1910, Clarke Historical Library.

had thought he would stay on Beaver Island, but the mobocrats had confiscated his home, store, and dock and banished him as well. He is said to have arrived in Milwaukee only three days behind the rest of the Strangites.[46] It may be that the story is incorrect because McCulloch's name was on the ballot in the fall of 1856 as a candidate to replace Strang as a state representative. McCulloch lost the election.[47]

While the band of about sixty armed men were making their initial assault on Beaver Island, another group paid a hostile visit to the settlements at Pine River. The Mormons had been notified of the danger and many had left, which infuriated the gentiles. A widow by the name of King was suspected of having helped many of the settlers to escape, so her house was burned down in retaliation. The mob ransacked and broke up the rest of the settlement and allowed only a couple of families to remain.[48]

Reuben T. Nichols, who had settled at Pine Lake during the summer of 1855, was "compelled by mob power" to leave without any compensation for his property. "On the 1st of July a mob visited the woods some fifty or sixty rods from my shanty, and fired some guns or revolvers rapidly," Nichols recounted. "After this I was informed that they intended to arrest me for stealing a chest of carpenter and joiner tools, then drive my family away, and banish us out of the country. In order to save my family from further abuse, on the 8th of July I took my family down to the foot of the lake in a boat, towing my cow with a bed cord hitched from her horns to the stern of the boat. We followed the shore of the lake and got down all safe."

But the family's troubles had just begun. The Nicholses were able to secure passage on a boat to Manistee, then board another vessel and work their passage to Milwaukee, where they arrived on July 20. A few days later Reuben got a job hewing timber but lost the job when his employers found out he was a Mormon. Lacking the basics of life, his wife was taken sick with typhoid fever. Reuben recounted what happened in his diary: "On the 13th [October] her breasts became dry, the infant child took sick, and on the 21st, my wife continuing unwell, the infant died, age 9 months and five days. Our

---

46. Leach, "History of Grand Traverse," 118-19.

47. Roger Van Noord, *King of Beaver Island: The Life and Assassination of James Jesse Strang* (Urbana and Chicago: University of Illinois Press, 1988), 268. Bedford and Wentworth were also on the ballot, Bedford as fish inspector and Wentworth as county treasurer, but both lost the election.

48. Leach, "History of Grand Traverse," 119-20.

daughter ... was sick also, with typhoid fever; both mother and daughter were senseless and helpless, and I was actually reduced to beggary."[49]

Not all of the Strangites had left Beaver Island as the attackers had demanded. Betsy McNutt's brother Tobias was not at home when the mob came to his house, but they warned his wife and took all the cows, sheep, and horses. "When Father got home he went over to Uncle John [McNutt]'s and they and another big Welshman, Lewis Thomas, decided they would not go and they did not; but the others all left," James Oscar McNutt recalled.[50] After "the excitement died down," the three families moved down to the bay into some of the vacant houses in St. James. "There were a good many Gentile families came onto the island and fisherman, including the families of Thomas Bedford and Alexander Wentworth," he wrote. Some Chippewa Indians also arrived. "The Mormons had left all their crops in, so those families that came to the island had a picnic, for they could go where they pleased and get the crops for nothing.... There were also some chickens around and some cattle that had been out in the fields when the mob came," McNutt added.[51]

Having gotten rid of Strang and the "undesirable" Mormons, Thomas Bedford and Alex Wentworth once again settled in. Wentworth had a potato wagon with which he sold potatoes up and down the mainland. Bedford's gentile companions gave him a span of horses to replace those allegedly stolen from him. Both men were glad they had killed Strang and said they would do it again.[52] The gentiles who took over vacant houses claimed they had not

---

49. "The Ministerial Labors of Reuben T. Nichols in the Church of Jesus Christ of Latter Day Saints," unpublished manuscript, 7-10, Clarke Historical Library. Nichols was born in Johnston, Montgomery County, New York, in 1807. He joined the LDS Church in 1833 and served many church missions, joined with Strang in the spring of 1846, and was one of the Strangites who acquired more than one wife.

50. McNutt diary.

51. Ibid. McNutt does not mention Hezikiah McCulloch.

52. Ibid.; Van Noord, *King of Beaver Island,* 270. One day Wentworth had his little daughter with him as he drove the wagon. She fell off and, before Wentworth could stop the wagon, the hind wheel drove over the little girl and killed her. He and his family moved to Janesville, Minnesota, to live with his wife Phoebe's parents. During the Civil War, Alexander enlisted in the Northern Army and died in Mississippi on August 31, 1863, of chronic diarrhea. He was thirty years old. Thomas Bedford lived on Beaver Island until 1864, when he was taken into custody for the murder of Thomas Gallagher. He apparently jumped bailed and enlisted in the Union Army to avoid further prosecution. Although his wife continued to live on the island, he moved after the war to Eaton Rapids, Michigan, and died there on July 5, 1889.

prevented the Strangite people from taking their personal property off the island. In their grief over the loss of their king, the squatters said, the Mormons deliberately left their property behind. The eviction order, they said, was met with submission and the people endured no particular hardship while they waited for the *Buckeye State* to arrive. Many insisted there had not been any physical violence because so many of the Strangites, held captive on the island by the king, were glad to get away. The gentiles claimed the presence of books from Strang's library in the state's schools showed "the damage must not have been as severe as the Mormons claimed."

At least two of the displaced Mormon families settled on St. Helena Island and worked for Archie Newton, the man who had led the raid on Beaver Island. One of the Mormon men had two wives, but the gentiles tolerated this because the women needed someone to take care of them. Many of those who had taken part in the mass raid on the island later held respectable positions in the St. Helena community. Newton became the first president of the village of Cheboygan.[53] The editor of the *Green Bay Advocate* wrote a fitting obituary for the Beaver Island colony: "Collisions and trouble ... became so common in that vicinity that they lost their novelty, and came to be regarded as the ordinary state of things there.... [And now] the stronger side, whether right or wrong, have driven out the weaker."[54]

53. Davis, "Stories of St. Helena Island," 440.
54. Burgess, "Green Bay and Mormons," 47.

II.

The Prophet's Wives and Children

15

MARY ABIGAIL PERCE STRANG
SETTLING HIS AFFAIRS

"We lived in the first house across the White River bridge and Mary lived in the next, which set farther back from the road, and Grandfather [Strang] lived ¼ mile farther toward where the road went up on the Prairie from the river bottom. When Romeo and Willie would drive in from the fields, they would unhitch in the lane near where we lived and would let Clement and I on the horses and let us ride back to the barn at their house. There were two girls at Mary's…. We all left when the property was sold. Mary went to Illinois and we went to Western Wisconsin." —Gabriel Strang to "Edith."[1]

Mary Perce and her children were not at home in Voree when their husband and father was brought there wounded on July 1, 1856. The family was visiting Mary's brother, William Jr., in Illinois, no doubt seeking consolation in the wake of a family death—that of James and Mary Strang's five-week-old granddaughter. The baby was born on April 3, 1856, to Myraette, who at sixteen was the oldest child in the Strang family. When the infant died on May 10, it must have been disheartening for the grandmother and devastating to the young parents.[2]

There is more to the story. Myraette had fallen in love with the improbably named Romeo D. Strang, her nineteen-year-old first cousin—the son of James's brother David. The young couple married on May 20, 1855, over her father's objection. James had made no secret of his disapproval of the match, but the young couple went to the Baptist Church in Voree and married each other anyway. One Strangite said it was well known James would not even "loan a team of horses" to Romeo. Although he made no attempt, at

---

1. Gabriel Strang to "Edith," n.d., Clarke Historical Library, Central Michigan University, Mount Pleasant, Michigan.

2. Perce Family History, unpublished manuscript, n.p., Library and Historical Center, State Library of Michigan, Lansing, Michigan.

least overtly, to break up his daughter's marriage, James considered Romeo to be a thorn in his side.[3]

Romeo apparently arrived in Wisconsin from New York in 1853 with his grandparents, Clement and Abigail Strang. The older couple obtained a farm in Voree near Mary Perce, which Romeo helped them manage. The young man also worked for some time in the stone quarry at Voree.[4] Clement and Abigail thought James might help Romeo get settled on a farm of his own, but for some reason, James would not assist him.[5] Although the Strangite book of scripture, the Book of the Law of the Lord, encouraged young marriages—Myraette was fifteen, and Romeo had just turned nineteen—the Law of the Lord prohibited marriage to a first cousin. There is no proof that Myraette ever joined the Mormon Church, but Strang definitely tried to get his new son-in-law to convert.

Romeo wrote to his father, David, in November 1855, laying out his situation in Wisconsin after the marriage:

> Uncle James arrived here from Beaver on Friday last and left yesterday. I had made a bargain with Grand Father in reference to some land which I propose working another year on shares. He [Uncle James] raised no positive objection to it, but refused to let me the quarry another year, and said that he might want some other person to work the land next spring.... [James] said that his children, to enjoy his favor, must become Mormons.... I see plainly that I must be a Mormon, or leave here, and as I do not cho[o]se to become one, nor engage with them in stealing and destroying the Gentiles, I must not depend on business here and consider myself thrown out of business.[6]

A few weeks later, Romeo went to Racine to try to get employment on the railroad. He talked for some time with the conductor and was confident of success. "He asked my name, and to my surprise, that broke it all up and he would hardly converse with me," Romeo wrote to his father. He attributed his failure to prejudice due to his name's association with the Mormons even

---

3. Stanley L. Johnston to John Cumming, May 15, 1976, Clarke Historical Library.

4. Myraette Losee to David Strang, Sept. 22, 1855, Clarke Historical Library.

5. Abigail Strang to David Strang, Feb. 14, 1856, James Jesse Strang Papers, Yale Collection of Western Americana, Beinecke Rare Book and Manuscript Library, Yale University, New Haven, Connecticut.

6. Romeo Strang to David Strang, Nov. 18 [1855], Clarke Historical Library.

though he was not a church member himself.[7] The couple considered moving back to New York, but Myraette was pregnant and Romeo did not want to take the risk of having her travel.

He wrote to his father again in February.

> When Uncle James was here last fall he said to me some things that they [his grandparents and Mary] do not know. He said that if I had any chance here I must be a Mormon.... These were not his words, but their simple import, and said in so firm a manner that was no mistaking it.... He wants me to go from here to Beaver Island. He is determined to make a Mormon of me at any rate & I think that he thinks if I cannot live here, he will get me to go to Beaver, and from appearances I think he intends to manage so that I cannot live here.[8]

Romeo and Myraette continued in Voree following Strang's death, living close to Mary and her children, eleven-year-old William and eight-year-old Harriet or "Hattie." For a time, two of Strang's other wives, Elvira Field and Betsy McNutt, also lived close by.[9] It would have been an uncomfortable time for Mary since Elvira and Betsy were both pregnant. James's father, Clement, helped support the three widows.[10] Clement and Abigail, who were Baptists, never approved of Strang's conversion to Mormonism, but being unable to prevent it, they resigned themselves and chose not to quarrel with him. Eventually they returned to Chautauqua County, New York, to live with James's sister, Myraette Losee.[11]

On July 21, 1856, Mary Perce Strang petitioned the probate court in Walworth County, Wisconsin, to appoint her administrator of her husband's estate. When she returned on March 8, 1858, to report the condition of the estate, she listed as outstanding debts $30 owed to Edward Chidester for nursing her husband through his last sickness, $36.27 to her father-in-law Clement for the coffin and other funeral expenses, and $16 to Dr. Edwin

---

7. Ibid.

8. Romeo Strang to David Strang, Feb. [1856], Clarke Historical Library.

9. Clement Strang, interviewed by Milo M. Quaife, Feb. 12, 1921, Clarke Historical Library.

10. Ibid.; also Gabriel Strang, in his letter to Edith (Clarke Historical Library), recalled that "Romeo is the only one of Uncle David's children I ever saw. He was with Grandfather Strang when he had charge of the Voree property."

11. Strang's father, Clement, died on Dec. 31, 1880, in New York. His mother, Abigail, died sometime after that. Myraette Strang Losee died about 1890.

Dyer for providing medical services. The estate fell $902.26 short of funds to pay creditors.[12] Curiously, James had owned up to 640 acres of land in Voree, which included land his wife Mary had inherited from her uncle Benjamin Perce and other family members, but much of it had been mortgaged, including his house, and there were unpaid taxes on the land and home. The court decided that because there were insufficient personal assets to pay the outstanding debts, the house and most of the property would be sold at a sheriff's auction.[13]

When the auction occurred on Christmas Day, 1858, at the house of Lemuel R. Smith in Spring Prairie (Voree), once again Mary's family came to her rescue. The buyer ended up being her brother, Samuel Y. Perce.[14] Other relatives purchased some 200 acres sold at a sheriff's sale in August 1859. A year later, Mary sold land to Caleb Barnes, Strang's former law partner. The 560 communal acres Strang had held in trust for the Associated Order of Enoch were divided among the church members who had contributed to it. They were all given title to their land, but most of them later sold it.[15]

Mary and her children continued to live in Voree for a time. The 1860 federal census for Walworth County listed her at forty-two years of age, living with Ellen M. [Myraette] at twenty; William J., fifteen; and Harriet J., eleven. She had property worth $3,150 and a personal worth of $300. Absent from the listing was Romeo, Myraette's husband. One individual said Myraette and Romeo had separated or divorced,[16] but another mentioned that Romeo had gone to Pike's Peak at the start of the gold rush and had been killed in Colorado.[17]

Sometime before 1870, Mary and her family moved to Terre Haute, Indiana, where their life continued to be filled with some sorrow. Mary's brother William L. Perce Jr., who had provided so much support for her, died in 1861

---

12. James Strang, Probate Record Books, 1856, 3:175-76, 215; 11:25, 27, 144, 149, 173, 176; 12:48, 98; 13:11, 13, 17, 100, 105, 121, 123, Walworth County Court House, Elkhorn, Wisconsin.

13. Ibid.

14. Ibid. The real estate sold for $1,350 and the household goods brought in another $600.

15. Mr. and Mrs. Theron Drew to Mark Strang, June 20, 1956, Clarke Historical Library.

16. Stanley L. Johnston to John Cumming, July 23, 1963, Clarke Historical Library.

17. Gabriel Strang to John Wake, June 23, 1932, Clarke Historical Library.

at the premature age of thirty-nine. Mary's father and sister had also died by this time.[18] Harriet Anne, the youngest child of Mary Perce and James Strang, passed away on August 16, 1868, when she was only twenty.[19] The cause of her death is unknown. Myraette lived with her mother and brother, taught school and music in Terre Haute, and served in the Civil War as a nurse for the Union Army. She never remarried or bore another child. In 1925, she died in Colma, California.

Mary's only son, William, also served in the Civil War, then worked for the railroad before opening a jewelry store in Terre Haute. He married Emma E. Flowers on June 25, 1871, at the Methodist Episcopal Church in Centralia, Illinois. The couple had thirteen children; however, eight of them died before they reached adulthood.[20] Mary lived with William and his family until her death on April 30, 1880, at the age of sixty-two. She never remarried.[21]

William felt bitter about his father's involvement with other women and the fact that he had sired other children by these wives. Because of his sensitivity to the topic, Myraette stopped writing to her half brothers and sisters, although she had previously been friendly toward them.[22] Clement Strang, Elvira's son, tried at one time to strike up a correspondence with Myraette, who he learned from an aunt was "a very attractive young woman." He wrote to her "from Dowagiac in 1882, and received a nice letter from her.... I received a second letter, also good, and longer, and filled with interesting facts about the family.... Finally a third letter came, a very brief one; stating that her father [brother] was very much opposed to having any interchange [with] living relatives with any of the polygamous connection. And that he had made the demand so strong that she could not live with him if she made any recognition of any of us."[23]

---

18. James Strang, Probate Records, Sheriff's Deed, Aug. 13, 1859; also Perce Family History, State Library of Michigan. William Perce died on June 3, 1855, at the age of sixty-two. Harriet Newel Perce, who was two years older than Mary, died sometime before 1859, probably in the late 1840s. She was married to Adam Hughes and had one child, Elizabeth H. Hughes.

19. Perce Family History, State Library of Michigan.

20. Ibid. William's and Emma's first three children all died before they were one day old.

21. Ibid. The place of Mary's death is unknown.

22. Clement Strang interview, Feb. 12, 1921.

23. Clement Strang to Stanley Johnston, May 6, 1939; Clement Strang to Milo Quaife, Apr. 28, 1931, Clarke Historical Library.

It was Myraette who had Strang's body exhumed from the "cow pasture" in Voree and moved to the Burlington cemetery. Myraette's baby daughter and her sister, "little Mary," who had been buried in the Mormon cemetery, were also relocated.[24] Clement was present in Voree the day his father's body was transferred to the new cemetery. "I went with the man who helped to remove father's bones—that is all that was left from the pasture lot—to the cemetery—and he showed me the spot of the old temple, the spot of the old grave and the place of the new one," Clement wrote. He said his father, his father's "little daughter Mary, and little granddaughter [Myraette's baby]," were "all that occupy the lot."[25] Arthur Smith, a nephew of Moses and Aaron Smith, was also present and said he recognized Strang from the "peculiar shape of the head and other distinctive marks."[26]

Myraette paid to have the bodies moved but could not afford to purchase headstones, so the graves remained unmarked and overgrown until sometime after 1931 when historian Milo M. Quaife took up a collection for a monument. "Mr. C. M. Burton of Detroit and Dr. Otto L. Schmidt of Chicago provided the major portion ($50 each)," Quaife explained in 1950. "Clement Strang contributed $25. The daughters of Wingfield Watson $25 and I contributed the final $25. If there were any other donors than these I have now forgotten them."[27]

In 1898 Myraette thought about what she had heard of her mother's marriage to James Strang and decided it had been appropriate that the wedding day was "ushered in by rain, and sleet and snow, and November wind and gloom—a fit precursor for the tragic life of Mary Abigail Content Perce. Who could have imagined, as they walked up the aisle to the altar that Sunday morning, the sorrow and trouble, the heartache, and woe and pain the years were holding for her?"[28] Before their nuptials, Mary had promised her father she would be an obedient wife and make home pleasant for her husband.[29] The evidence is she tried to do her best despite the pull of intellec-

24. Stanley Johnston to John Cumming, May 15, 1976, Clarke Historical Library.

25. Clement Strang to Wingfield Watson, April 28, 1931, Clarke Historical Library.

26. "Old Newspaper File Tells Voree Story," *Racine Journal News*, Jan. 20, 1931.

27. M. M. Quaife to the editor, *Wisconsin Magazine of History* 34 (Winter 1950): 2, 124. Quaife wrote to correct a previous piece, "Adventures in Old Voree," wherein Strang's descendants were credited for the grave monument.

28. Perce Family History, State Library of Michigan.

29. See chap. 1, n. 22.

tual interests outside the home and her frail health, which eventually seemed to place a wedge between her and her husband.[30]

Not that James Strang was the ideal husband. One wonders whether, if Mary had known what the future held, she would have allowed herself to marry him. She probably harbored reservations about her husband's visionary claims since she was not immediately baptized into his church and did not have her children baptized.[31] Still, James seemed to prize her intelligence and even, to some degree, her independence.[32] In return, he expected her to be understanding of his own imperfections and eccentricities and grant him the liberty to marry whomever he wished. Mary may even have been somewhat tolerant or even indifferent to James's polygamous tendencies. The breaking point seems to have come when the "other woman," Elvira Field, who had pretended to be James's young male secretary, became pregnant.[33]

Even considering the melodramatic events surrounding the unveiling of "Charley Douglass" as a plural wife, one should not assume Mary and James had been incompatible or had not enjoyed a time of great happiness and contentment in each other's company. James's diary is a good indication of how taken he was by Mary during their initial engagement.[34] However, it is true that Mary's life, on balance, included its share of heartache and tragedy. The complexities of her situation, which tempered whatever hopes she had for the future, continued to plague the next generation. Myraette seemed as well adjusted and optimistic as any of the children, but she and her husband were opposed on all sides by family as well as by outsiders and could not escape the stigma of their association with the very man who had all but disowned them.

With the exception of James himself, it was a life none of them would have chosen. James was the cause of their misery, for his expectation that they live extraordinary lives outside the norm of American society. His endeavor ended with his assassination, while the family spent the rest of their days living with the weight of that event on their shoulders. Mary found safe harbor among her own family, the Perces, but that refuge was rocked by numerous

---

30. See chap. 1, nn. 32, 34, 36.
31. See chap. 4, nn. 45, 46.
32. See chap. 12, nn. 19, 25.
33. See chap. 8, nn. 20, 44.
34. See chap. 1, n. 19.

deaths. For her offspring, the resentment of past events was so strong, even correspondence with other family members was difficult. Yet, the most telling piece of information of all is probably the fact that Mary chose not to remarry or have additional children, revealing a window into the depth of her regret and grief.

16

HARVESTING BLUEBERRIES

"After Mr. Strang's death the church
in Michigan had no leader and its members soon scattered. A few of the
most faithful went to Utah, while the majority returned to their former
houses. Strang's own family went first to Wisconsin, but afterwards scat-
tered. He left 5 wives and 12 children." —Elvira Field Strang[1]

After Strang was shot, his wives Betsy and Phoebe accompanied him back to Voree. Elvira and Sarah left Beaver Island a few days later. Sarah, five months pregnant, visited her husband on his deathbed for only a short while and then, for financial reasons, left with her father's family.[2] A pregnant Phoebe Wright also went to live with her parents following Strang's death on July 9, 1856.

The Strangite Mormons scattered, some returning to the communities where they had lived before joining with Strang, others leaving to live on the charity of friends and relatives. A few traveled to Utah to join the Mormons under the direction of Brigham Young. All were tremendously grieved and shocked at their prophet's death. Most had expected him to survive and complete the "work" Joseph Smith had started. Some even expected he would soon resurrect.

A few of the diaspora, including Elvira Field and Betsy McNutt, stayed

---

1. Elvira Field Strang and Charles J. Strang, "Biographical Sketch of James J. Strang," unpublished manuscript, n.p., Strang Manuscript Collection, Library and Historical Center, State Library of Michigan, Lansing, Michigan. Strang fathered fourteen children by five wives. Mary Perce had three living children, Elvira had four, Betsy three, and Sarah and Phoebe one each; Mary lost a daughter and Betsy lost a baby son.

2. Sarah Wing to Milo Quaife, June 28, 1920, Clarke Historical Library, Central Michigan University, Mount Pleasant, Michigan. Sarah wrote that she left Beaver Island with "only the clothing [she] stood up in." She did, however, manage to take with her the letter of appointment, which she later gave to her father for safe keeping. In the 1880s, Phineas Wright gave the letter to Anson Prindle, who gave it to Charles Strang, unless Phineas gave it to Charles directly. From there, the letter passed to Milo Quaife and Yale University.

for a time in Voree as part of a penniless, scattered flock that had no shepherd. Since the land the church owned was held in Strang's name, some of the members may have remained until his estate was settled, hoping to regain the property they had consecrated to the Order of Enoch. Others simply had no other place to go. Several families would have lived together in the houses formerly owned by the Order of Enoch. When Strang's estate was finally settled, everyone had to leave.

In 1883, Elvira Field sent Wingfield Watson a brief sketch of her life after the Mormons were exiled from Beaver Island:

> At that time my faith was strong, I expected a great deal. In fact, I did not think it was in the power of the wicked to destroy the life of James[;] when I got to Voree and found him dead, I felt as if I had nothing to live for any longer. After he was shot, he never told us anything what to do, what was to be done, he fell back on medical aid the same as anyone would. When they started to take him on to the boat, he never bid us good by—those of us which were to stay. I was around busy, expecting before he started he would have a regular parting; but the first I noticed, they were gone; nearly halfway down to the dock. Then I felt deserted, forsaken, but not half as much as I did when he was dead.
>
> The next week I went to Voree, [having] heard nothing from him, and when I got there he had been buried two days. Betsy and Phoebe [whom] he took with him, said he did not tell them much, said they must do the best they could. In regard to short dresses and keeping Sunday; they would have to conform to custom for a little while. I just thought he would be raised from the dead, I had that faith.[3]

Both pregnant, Elvira and Betsy lived together in Voree with support from Strang's father. They lived in a small house about a quarter mile away from Strang's parents, next door to Mary. Betsy gave birth to a daughter, Abigail, on January 1, 1857, seven months after Strang's death. Three weeks later, on January 22, Elvira gave birth to her fourth child, a son she named James.

In June 1857, Betsy's brothers, John and Tobias McNutt, and their families moved into the little house with Elvira and Betsy. The brothers had refused to be forced off Beaver Island and remained there until Tobias became seriously ill; in August, Tobias died of "yellow jaundice." John McNutt buried his brother in the Strangite cemetery along the White River and built

---

3. Elvira E. Baker to "Dear Friend" [Wingfield Watson], Mar. 22, 1883; punctuation and paragraphs added.

a "nice" picket fence around his grave. Tobias's young wife and four children soon returned to Lewisburg, Ohio, for a time to live with family members.[4] John McNutt became the official provider for Strang's two widows and their seven children, as well as for his own wife and five children. Strang's father, Clement, assisted the best he could.

In October 1857, a visitor to Voree said he saw the unusual sight of three women all dressed identically in calico, with sunbonnets on their heads, working with hoes in a garden attached to a small house in Voree. The visitor, Joseph E. Chamberlin, later a Boston journalist, said he was told the women were the widows of "Strang, the Mormon King, who had been killed on Beaver Island in Lake Michigan shortly before." Chamberlin was astonished because he "had never before seen women working in the field."[5] The unusually dressed women were probably Elvira, Betsy, and John McNutt's wife, Mary Jane, who continued to wear the Mormon "bloomer" costume.[6]

One by one, the Strangite families left until, by the beginning of 1858, there were less than ten Strangite households struggling to hold on to their land in Voree. As they left, the community reverted back to its old name, Spring Prairie. Most Strangite houses were by now missing their windows and doors. Similarly, the windows of the unfinished temple had been pilfered, and the temple was now used to store hay. The heavy oak doors to the Tower of Strength had been removed and placed on a barn.[7] Elvira and Betsy joined the Strangite exodus in 1857, moving with John McNutt to a sparsely occupied portion of Marquette County, Wisconsin. They all lived there together in one small log house.[8]

4. "The Diary of James Oscar McNutt, Elder of the Mormon Church at the Mormon Settlement, Jackson Co., Wisconsin; One Time Follower of James Jesse Strang," 8, Library and Historical Center, State Library of Michigan, Lansing, Michigan; cf. "Reminisces of James O. McNutt of the Mormon Settlement, Jackson County [Wisconsin], and Warrens, Monroe County, Related by J. O. McNutt, and Recorded by his Daughter Miss Sadie McNutt," Library-archives, Wisconsin Historical Society, Madison, Wisconsin. Tobias died on August 3, 1857. His widow returned to Preble County, Ohio, to be near her own family, but then relocated to Black River Falls, Wisconsin, in 1863 to be with other Strangites.

5. "Voree History Is Told By Former Voree Child," *Elkhorn Independent*, Feb. 14, 1929.

6. James Oscar McNutt to Sister Willis, Mar. 7, 1929, Clarke Historical Library.

7. Ibid.; also "Voree History Is Told," *Elkhorn Independent*, Feb. 14, 1929.

8. Clement Strang to Stanley Johnston, Dec. 4, 1940, Clarke Historical Library.

In the spring of 1859, the group moved to Jackson County, Wisconsin, where they built another log house near the settlement later known as Warren's Mills. At that time, the settlement was new and had no mill or any other features of village life.[9] Some of the Strangites were already there—Lorenzo Dow Hickey, James Hutchins, Anson Prindle, the Wright brothers, and the Alvord, Bickle, and Kidder families. Elvira, Betsy, Mary Jane, and their children picked blueberries for a living while John McNutt made baskets to sell.[10]

Elvira's parents and brother had gone back to Eaton Rapids, Michigan. They wrote to Elvira asking her to come home, informing her that her father, Reuben, was ill and was not expected to live. In late 1859 or early 1860, Elvira had saved enough money to make the journey back to Eaton Rapids. Having lived together as sister-wives for nearly eight years, Elvira and Betsy had become close friends, so it must have been hard for them to make the decision to part. On the other hand, there seemed to be no other way for them to support their children.

In February 1860, Absalom Kuykendall wrote a sympathetic letter to "E. and E. Strang," meaning Elizabeth and Elvira: "We were glad to heare from you, but sorrow to learn that you have had bad luck in farming or raising the nesaryes of life. I think you are doing for the best to leave that part of the country and go to your people and do the best fore yourselves you can and pray God for deliverance from among the weaker generation."[11]

Twenty years earlier a delegation of Mormons had gone to the Black River Falls area of Jackson County, Wisconsin, to procure lumber for the temple at Nauvoo. The first birth in the area occurred in 1841, and some of the Mormon women who had gone up river to the "pineries" with their husbands had assisted the mother.[12] However, most of the Mormons had left the

---

9. Clement Strang to Stanley Johnston, Sept. 2, 1938, Clarke Historical Library.

10. McNutt diary, 12. Most of the Strangite families arrived in Black River Falls in 1858-59. John McNutt put up a small log cabin in the woods, identified as Section 6, Township 20, Range 1 West. See also Clement J. Strang, "Why I Am Not a Strangite," *Michigan History*, fall 1942, 467.

11. Absalom Kuykendall to E. and E. [Elizabeth and Elvira] Strang, Feb. 5, 1860, folder 408, James Jesse Strang Collection, Yale Collection of Western Americana, Beinecke Rare Book and Manuscript Library, Yale University, New Haven, Connecticut.

12. Jackson County Historical Society, *Jackson County: A History* (Dallas: Taylor Publishing, 1984), 95.

pineries after Joseph Smith was murdered in 1844. The Strangite refugees who returned to lumbering in the fall of 1856 found this area in the northwestern part of Wisconsin to be much as it had been a decade earlier. It was sparsely inhabited and remained rich in natural resources. There were numerous swamps, which could be adapted to hay growing, a sandy loam soil well adapted to agriculture and blueberry growing, and extensive cranberry marshes. The culture of the wild cranberry meant money to early pioneers.[13] Eastern Jackson County was heavily timbered, primarily with pine, providing logs for markets down the river as far as New Orleans. The northern part of the county between the Yellow and Black Rivers provided excellent hardwoods. Yet, the area was still very unsettled. Wild game was common and wolves were occasionally captured.[14]

Unfortunately for the Mormons, the human beings who inhabited the area were living nearly as close to nature as the animals. The Wisconsin lumber camps in the 1850s were like the fishing settlements of Lake Michigan, where "inebriety was the rule, and sobriety was the exception. The man who refused to drink was an enemy to the human race and room made for him as for a leper. Card playing supplemented this vice and large sums of money were nightly lost."[15] Attempting to start over again in the same type of environment where they had lost their prophet and all their possessions, the Strangites, probably wisely, decided to hide their identity. Once again, they faced problems associated with alcohol. There was also another complication. Many of the Strangites had more than one wife.

No more polygamous marriages occurred after the Strangites left St. James, but the ones that had been consummated on Beaver Island needed to be concealed. Gentiles would often harass a man known to have more than one wife. "People had to practice concealment and subterfuge and would move often. In some cases, children were taught to call their father "uncle" so their neighbors would not understand the true arrangement," Wingfield Watson noted.[16]

---

13. Ibid., 5. By 1909, cranberry growers in the marshes near Millston hoped to raise fifty barrels per acre. A total of 5,294 bushels of blueberries were shipped from the area in 1893.

14. N.a., *History of Northern Wisconsin, Containing an Account of Its Settlement, Growth, Development, and Resources* (Chicago: Western Historical Company, 1881), 395.

15. Ibid.

16. Wingfield W. Watson, interviewed by Milo M. Quaife, Dec. 10-11, 1918, Clarke Historical Library.

For safety as well as religious reasons, many of the faithful gathered to the small settlement of Knapp, located southeast of Black River Falls near the town of Millston. For many years Knapp was known as the "Mormon Settlement" because of the large numbers of Strangites who lived there. Early families lived off the land with only a few cows and chickens. They canned their garden vegetables. Blueberries and potatoes were among their most important crops. "The only time we had any money was during blueberry season when we lived in the swamps and picked for two months and we got $3 a crate," an old settler recalled.[17]

The swamps around Knapp were also good for cranberries if one had the stamina to harvest them. In 1861, six members of the William Bickle family cut and put up nine tons of hay and picked fifty bushels of cranberries in one week. All told, "Brother Wright ha[s] picked three hundred bushels," Bickle wrote to Wingfield Watson.[18] Located in the vast pine forests of Wisconsin, Knapp later became Jackson County's most progressive sawmill area. At one time the community had over 1,000 residents, most of whom were Mormons.

James Oscar McNutt, son of Tobias McNutt, moved to Knapp in 1863 and recorded much of the history of the Mormon settlement in his diary. He and his extended family, including his mother and siblings, found other Strangites already living in Knapp when they arrived, including James's Aunt Betsy and Uncle John. That summer, sixteen-year-old James and his family picked and sold $80 worth of blueberries, a large sum in 1863.

The Mormons worked cooperatively to help newcomers construct homes. At their house-raising parties, they built log cabins without one nail or spike in them. "Our door hinges were wood and pinned on with wooden pins, our floors were so heavy that the tongue held them in place. This may sound like a big story, but it is the truth. Many a poor family ... has done the same thing" in other areas of the frontier, James McNutt knew. In their case, "if it wasn't for the berries, I don't know what we would of done." He praised the "marsh hay," as well, which they "cut for our cattle with scythes and raked it with hand rakes." Several Mormons combined their money to build a sawmill, but the mill burned down at least twice.[19]

Other Strangites, including Phineas, Benjamin, and Samuel Wright,

---

17. Jackson County Historical Society, *Jackson County*, 33.
18. William Bickle to Wingfield Watson, Nov. 2, 1861, Clarke Historical Library.
19. McNutt diary, 18-19.

gathered at Black River Falls to set up their own lumbering business. Like most Mormons exiled from Beaver Island, the Wrights made the move to western Wisconsin in stages, stopping first in Racine for a short time. Phineas and his son Zenas worked on the Racine and Mississippi Railroad while the others worked harvesting crops.[20] Not able to improve their circumstances, the families purchased horses and wagons and struck out for the lumber country of Wisconsin. There is some indication the men may have previously worked in the lumber region before they went to the lead mines in Potosi. Phineas had been a lumberman in Canada before he joined the Mormon Church.[21] In any case, the Wrights reached Black River Falls in September 1856.[22]

One member of the extended family did not make an appearance in Wisconsin. Phineas's second wife, Rebecca Wagener, and her children stayed behind on Beaver Island with her brother-in-law, a man whose last name was Scott. He reportedly was not a Mormon and was on friendly terms with the gentiles.[23] He could have been Christopher Scott, who was one of the disgruntled signers of the depositions solicited by Captain McBlair on the *Michigan* before Strang was shot.

Phoebe Wright gave birth to a daughter, Eugenia, on October 28, 1856, in Black River Falls, and her cousin, Sarah Wright, delivered a son, James Phineas Strang, on November 11. In order to avoid further persecution for her religious beliefs, Phoebe changed her last name from Strang to Jesse. Their families earned a living near Black River Falls cutting and selling cordwood and doing some farming. They named their town Alma after the Book of Mormon prophet by that name. Within a few years, the Wright brothers had acquired a large amount of timberland about nine miles from Black River Falls and relocated their families to a settlement that soon became known as Wrightsville.

Before long, Wrightsville included a flour mill, lumber mill, boarding house, and five smaller structures that provided shelter and plenty of work for

---

20. Zenas Wright, interviewed by Milo M. Quaife, May 25, 1920, n.p., Beaver Island Historical Society, Old Mormon Print Shop, St. James, Beaver Island, Michigan; copy also at the Clarke Historical Library.

21. Ibid.

22. *Badger State Banner,* Sept. 6, 1917; also Zenas Wright interview, May 25, 1920.

23. Zenas Wright interview, May 25, 1920.

all. "Men with families were hired and houses built for them and no rent charged, though the best wages of the times were paid. A schoolhouse was built, and roads improved leading to their village, which was given a post office," a Wright family member recalled.[24] In spite of these efforts, and their determination to hide their religious identity, people began to surmise who they were. Like so many times in the past, the information elicited ridicule. One of Strang's apostles, Warren Post, advised the members to continue to exercise caution in their dealings with non-Mormons in order to avoid bad situations. "Let your actions towards those out of the church, be of that kind that best accords with the law, that you may bring no unnecessary trouble upon yourselves," he reasonably advised them. "As for me," he continued, "I wish to live so that I bring no reproach upon myself, or the Church of God.... It is better not to be too hasty in matters that require great caution, and wisdom, as well as righteousness and power."[25] Despite Post's good advice and everyone's best effort to follow it, there was nevertheless trouble between the Strangites and the gentiles. It was said that James Hutchins's son was killed for the sole reason that he was a Mormon, as an example of the tension and bias.[26]

Elder Post wrote to Wingfield Watson on May 5, 1867, with news of additional persecution. "It is not for want of respect to you, or Bro. Hickey that I have been silent so long," he wrote. "Our troubles in this valley have been sufficient excuse for not making names and P.O. addresses too familiar.... It is sufficient to say we have passed through a fiery ordeal and had not the Lord delivered us, we should have been numbered with the dead & our property divided among outlaws." Confirming that they had not tried to draw attention to themselves and had not instigated any trouble—"we have often wished ourselves away in some quiet place where we could feel secure in per-

---

24. Clement Strang, "Why I Am Not a Strangite," 476-77. Clement read this article to the Algonquin Club of Detroit on March 13, 1942, and Eugenia Phillips added a postscript when it was published in *Michigan History*.

25. Warren Post to [Wingfield Watson], letter fragment, n.d., Clarke Historical Library. Warren was away on a church mission to New York when the Strangites were banished from Beaver Island, and he subsequently had a difficult time locating his two wives. He finally found them in Aurora, Illinois. His second wife left him and went to live with her parents in Michigan. Warren and Deborah Post continued on and settled in the Mormon settlement at Knapp, Wisconsin.

26. John Hajicek, *Mormons in Wisconsin: A Closer View of the Early Settlements* (Burlington: by the author, 1992).

son and property—Post regretted the "time and money" repeatedly spent in "defending ourselves against the ravages of a mob."

Post said the previous fall, he, along with Frank and Lorenzo Tubbs, had been arrested as accessories to arson in the destruction of a neighbor's property. "Sister Tubbs" was also arrested on another warrant. "But the Lord delivered us from that dilemma—and our reputation is such this spring that I was elected justice of the peace," he added with some satisfaction. Still, a lawsuit was pending against Brother James Lee Hutchins, filed in county court by the State of Wisconsin, for setting fire to the neighbor's house. "Lee will get clear and Wantz will be proved a perjured wretch," Post predicted. "We hope for the safety of the settlers in this valley, that there will be no more violence.... For it matters not who does the deed, our enemies are determined to make all Mormons guilty of the crime."

Post articulated what every faithful Strangite had probably felt at one time or another: "I sometimes feel as though God had determined our utter destruction, both remnant & issue.... We have hard times here for food for ourselves & cattle & feel as though famine was near ... [W]e are destitute of money or we should have remitted it to you for our indebtedness long before this."[27] For all the Mormon settlers strung out across Wisconsin, life was difficult. Not only were they impeded by prejudice and with having to start over again without an economic foundation, many felt greatly disillusioned by the promises of their religion. Some felt utterly forsaken, especially by the prophet. Many "lost heart" and quit their allegiance to Strang's church altogether. Others held out for a "new prophet." Nearly all missed the camaraderie and feeling of community they had experienced on Beaver Island, as Elder Post wrote in another missive to Brother Watson:

> Dear Brother in the Lord; it is a long time since we have lived near each other where, we could see each other's face in a large Congregation of Saints, every Sabbath day, and hear the word of the Lord as it fell from the lips of his Prophet. That was a pleasure worth living for—I often look back to that day when the Law of God was kept upon Beaver Island. It is yet to me the most hallowed spot I ever dwelt upon—there were God's Officers and Judges to see that God's Laws were respected and obeyed—that justice & judgment were well administered—there the rich and the poor could meet before the Judges and have their cases tried impartially without cost, and justice rendered without fear—

---

27. Warren Post to Wingfield Watson, May 5, 1867, Clarke Historical Library.

there we could dwell upon inheritances given us by the Lord through his Servant the Prophet. There we could lawfully strive to perpetuate our names upon our inheritances without derision, or molestation. There we could gather the true riches both for time and eternity.... [We are] praying earnestly for that day when all things shall be restored again to us, even as at the beginning.

We do not expect our Prophet James, to be restored to us again as a Prophet (we trust he has passed into glory), but we expect one in his stead—and if not our former inheritances (which the most of us were not found worthy to enjoy), we shall have inheritances far better, if we do not esteem the gifts of the Lord contemptible, and his work a thing of nought.[28]

Ten years after Strang's death, the faithful were still waiting for the Lord to anoint a new prophet and lead them to some particular gathering place. One of Strang's apostles, Lorenzo Dow Hickey, had moved from Wisconsin to Coldwater, Michigan, and was trying to convince others to relocate in Boyne City, Michigan. "I cannot think of settling down alone.... [T]o dwell alone or scattered abroad is not good," he wrote. He enticed the Saints with reports of livestock prices and prospects for crops, repeating that he didn't "want to go alone. Still I don't know but I shall. I have thought of going back to Wisconsin. But Sara likes it here and thinks we can do better in Michigan than Wisconsin. But, O, My Soul, Brethren. I cannot think of dwelling separate from any of my brethren. Pray that I may be prospered and guided right."[29]

In another letter, Hickey complained of his enduring loneliness:

If you don't come and dwell near us I don't want to stay here alone.... Pray what shall I do here alone? When I look ahead for years to come it seems that we had better go to this land. But when I think of the toils and hardships of settling in timberland I hardly know what to think. But the land will cost us nothing and it is bound to be valuable and it is not far from our island home. Again in all these streams there are plenty of fish and I am told wild game abounds. I felt it my duty to come here and I am not sorry I came. I shall hunt up the few saints and wait until I get a letter from you.[30]

---

28. Warren Post to Wingfield Watson, Nov. 26, 1865, Clarke Historical Library.

29. Lorenzo Dow Hickey to Wingfield Watson, July 15, 1866, Clarke Historical Library.

30. Lorenzo D. Hickey to [his brethren in Wisconsin], 1866, Clarke Historical Library.

One of the Strangites who decided to move to Boyne City was Wingfield Watson, who similarly encouraged his fellow church members to move to the area. To Reuben Nichols, he wrote: "I think Bro. Nichols that it is not only your duty but the duty of all the saints to get as near (if not on) as possible to their inheritances. God is, and will favor the gathering of all who wish to gather to these lands."[31] Nichols heeded Watson's recommendation, but he was one of the few to do so. Even Hickey himself changed his mind and decided to stay in Coldwater. In either case, in Boyne City or Coldwater, they re-encountered prejudice and hardship. Watson wrote to Nichols that he had "received your letter giving an account of your past persecutions. I infer that some mobocrats took your cow the same as they did mine, and they took other things besides just as they did from the rest of us."[32]

The Strangites who remained in Wisconsin persisted in seeking compensation for their property loss on Beaver Island. A good example is a letter John C. Comstock wrote to the governor of Michigan about 1870. "I have many times cried unto the King of Kings for redress for the outrages which have been committed by insurrectionists or mobocrats in this ... state," he wrote. "I have also appealed to the governors who have preceded your honor in the office of Chief Magistrate of this state since the time of that outrageous proceeding in Peaine County in the summer of 1856." He continued:

> As one individual alone, I could not withstand the force of an armed power of three bands with a Captain of each band—who brought no [court] order, claim or demand before me [other] than that they had assumed the reigns of government, and as such, ordered me from my own dwelling with threats of burning my house and my [belongings]. For these outrages I have had no redress from the government nor from any soul. I am now in my 70th year without any home or the means to buy one for myself or wife. My own judgement would be that no amount short of ten thousand dollars, due fourteen years ago ... with all its lawful interest ... would satisfy the demands of justice.... Nevertheless a lesser amount will be thankfully made until the day of final doom when all wrongs will be righted.... O Hear my prayer and send relief.... For the justice of an offended God will soon rule all nations with his iron rod.[33]

---

31. Wingfield Watson to Reuben Nichols, Aug. 15, 1877, Clarke Historical Library.

32. [Wingfield Watson] to Reuben Nichols, letter fragment, Dec. 23, 1875, Clarke Historical Library.

33. John C. Comstock to Governor of Michigan, ca. 1870, Clarke Historical Library.

Of course, there would be no compensation for the refugees' losses and no rationale would be advanced for why the settlers had been evicted from their land. From a humanitarian standpoint, the government's indifference constituted an additional insult to the sufferings already endured. From a historical standpoint, an inquiry would have shed light on what transpired on Beaver Island, not only during the eviction of the Mormons but also previously when the gentiles were evicted from their homes. One is left to speculate where the record is silent and to sympathize with those who made their hardships a matter of record.

17

ELVIRA FIELD STRANG BAKER

TYPHOID AND ORCHIDS

"The brethren were good to us, fur-
nished us with money, and father Strang's folks helped us that we got along
through the first hard year. We stayed at Voree nearly two years, lived in
Marquette [County] a year, then went to Jackson Co[unty, Wisconsin].
There were several families gathered, Hickey, Post, Hutchins, Alvord,
Bickle, John McNutt. But they wanted to go on without a head and usurp
authority, and I became disgusted and came to Mich[igan]." —Elvira
Field Baker to Wingfield Watson.[1]

I n 1859, Elvira Field was living with Betsy and John McNutt in
Jackson County, Wisconsin, when she received several letters from
family members asking her to come to live in Michigan. Her father, Reuben,
was ill and wanted to see her. Unfortunately, he died before she was able to
make the arrangements to travel to Eaton Rapids.[2] The cost of the journey
was "somewhat of a problem" for the young widow, as she also needed funds
to transport her four young children. Her Strangite friends donated some of
the money for the trip, as did her relatives in Michigan; she packed several
carpetbags with items the family would need during their journey and prepared a large chest of goods to be sent by freight.[3]

"My mother parted company with Betsy and her family, and the family
of her brother, whom we called Uncle John McNutt, and with whom we

---

1. Elvira E. Baker to "Dear Friend" [Wingfield Watson], Mar. 22, 1883, Clarke
Historical Library, Central Michigan University, Mount Pleasant, Michigan.

2. Clement Strang to Chester W. Ellison, Oct. 10, 1941, Clarke Historical Library.
Both Reuben and Eliza Field had relatives living in the Eaton Rapids area. Reuben died on
August 13, 1859.

3. Clement Strang to Stanley Johnston, Sept. 2, 1938, Clarke Historical Library.
These items included several hundred letters addressed to and from James Strang, along
with other correspondence.

spent most of our days after the mob drove us from the Island," her son Clement recalled. John McNutt took them by horse-drawn wagon to the nearest train station, Tunnel City, about twenty miles away. The plan was for the young mother and children, ages nine, seven, six, and three, to take the train to Chicago, where they would change cars, then take the Michigan Central Railroad to Marshall, the closest station to Eaton Rapids.

The rail trip from Tunnel City to Chicago was uneventful, but the family ran into trouble when the car arrived at the station in Chicago. Clement recalled what occurred:

My brother Charley (named for Charley Douglass) ... carried a satchel and sister Eva (short for Evaline) had a bit of hand luggage neatly wrapped. I was directed to follow close to mother, Eva next, and Charley to bring up the rear; Mother of course taking the lead. The plan was good, but the trouble began as soon as people began to move toward the open door to leave the car. James ... was being carried on mother's left arm, so that [her] right hand would be free to attend to opening and closing doors, or whatever else needed manipulation.

As she approached the door of exit, a man who seemed to be ahead of her dallied and blocked the passage. As she attempted to move forward, he stood in her way; then she stepped back to let him move on, but he also stepped back, as if he were politely saying "ladies first" in behavior language; then she started forward, but he moved forward, again blocking the way. At this the Field quality of impatience expressed itself. Then she said, "Mr. If you wish to leave the car, please do so; and if not please give me a chance for I wish to go." He said, with a bow, "Excuse me Madam!" and passed quickly from sight.

When we were seated at the station and preparing for continuing the journey by the train that would soon pull in, mother left us together while she went to the ticket office. On arriving there she reached into her pocket for her purse, and found it was missing. Then she understood the behavior of the rogue who took advantage of her condition to rob her of what might have been the last cent she owned; but by what I call inspired caution. We children observed her sad countenance; and Charley spoke the word for us all: "Mother, what has happened?" Her reply was, "That rogue who blocked my way took my pocketbook. I should have hid it in my clothing. He could not have done that if my hands had not been full."

But she quickly mastered her emotions and stated her purpose to go to the retiring room and take money from a place [where] it had been sewed into some undergarment. When she returned her hand held a twenty-dollar gold piece, with which that journey was finished and our Eaton County, Michigan life began.[4]

The Field family reunion in Michigan was one of "great happiness" even though life would continue to be difficult for Elvira and her family. With Reuben dead, Albert Field, Elvira's brother, was left to care for her and her four children, as well as for his mother, Eliza, and his own family consisting of his wife, Mary Jane (called Jane or Janey), and their three children. The household included seven children under the age of nine.[5]

Clement again provided a vivid account of what transpired.

> Our Brookfield home was in close proximity to the "12-mile swamp," which is characterized by marsh grass, cat-tail flags, some willow clumps here and there; and in animal life by the snakes, muskrats, pollywogs and mosquitoes. The compound family, Field and Strang, began "coming-down" [with fever] late in summer and increasing in number and severity of attack, until by late autumn, nine out of eleven of us were stretched out on beds of sickness. Those suffering from ague … [had] chills [that] lasted about an hour on the average, as I remember, then the fever took its turn; and which was worse, the chills or the fever, I could not say for I dreaded them both and equally. The attacks in my case began every other day. Then it began coming every day, and finally I was taken twice a day, forenoon and afternoon. And this continued till the frost came and killed the flies and mosquitoes.[6]

Mary Jane Field and young Eva, seven years old, were the only ones to escape the affliction. Between spells of *ague,* the family took care of the domestic animals and the garden. "Aunt Jane bossed the affairs the best she could, and Eva was inspired to do her utmost to help wherever she was di-

---

4. Clement Strang to Chester W. Ellison, Oct. 10, 1941.

5. Clement J. Strang, "Why I Am Not a Strangite," *Michigan History* (Fall 1942): 468; *The Past and Present of Eaton County, Michigan* (Lansing: Michigan Historical Publishing Association, n.d.), 304-06. Albert Field married Mary Jane Miller on March 22, 1851, on Beaver Island. When Albert and Reuben arrived in 1856, they purchased eighty acres of land in Section 34 of Eaton Township and cleared about twenty-five acres before Reuben died. In 1863, Albert traded this property for eighty-three acres with a frame house and barn in Section 24 of the township. Clement Strang said they were located about four miles from Eaton Rapids. Reuben died on Aug. 13, 1859, Eliza Granger Field on Oct. 1, 1862.

6. Clement Strang to Chester W. Ellison, Oct. 10, 1941. This happened in the fall of 1860.

rected to go, or whatever she was directed to do," Clement remembered.[7] He continued:

> The illness among us children was mostly ague. Mother had typhoid fever, Uncle Albert had malarial fever; and Grandmother had worked herself nearly to death taking care of the rest. The regular doctors were kept busy attending the families who were able to pay; and besides this, our people had no faith in the medical practice that always began with bleeding the sick as the initial treatment for whatever the disease, or possibly a feature of the diagnosis.[8]

For many years, Elvira's mother had gathered information regarding the medicinal value of roots and herbs and acquired quite a reputation in the community as a healer. Yet, she was not able to heal her own daughter. "Grandmother Eliza, Uncle Albert and mother began to suspect that [mother's] death was just ahead. Mother did not care so much how soon she was called, except for her children. She prayed, and tried to win faith, but the situation was such that she decided—live or die—she must do all she could to find homes for her children," Clement recalled.[9]

Elvira decided to place an ad in the weekly newspaper in the nearby town of Charlotte asking neighboring residents to take in her children. Remarkably, people responded. A farmer came and made arrangements to take Charley, Elvira's oldest child, then about nine years old. Charley was considered a "good boy" who would not cause his new guardians much trouble. A physician in Charlotte, whose wife was still grieving over the death of their own young daughter, came to get Eva, seven. There was a marked resemblance between Eva and the couple's lost child, so "they were happy to take her to their beautiful home facing the courthouse from the north."[10]

"The next to go was James J. Strang, just a baby," Clement remembered. The newspaper notice attracted the attention of Mr. and Mrs. David A. Grier who, because Mrs. Grier was unable to conceive, were considering adoption. Apparently they did not stop to ask the child's name when they saw little James but, coincidentally enough, began calling him Charley. "When they learned what his real name was," they kept "the J. for a middle letter,"

7. Ibid.

8. Clement Strang, "Why I Am Not a Strangite," 469.

9. Clement Strang to Chester W. Ellison, Oct. 10, 1941.

10. Ibid. The doctor's name was Walter Waltersdorph.

Clement explained. The baby would have been about three years old at the time. Clement was five and was passed around from one person to another to stay for a week at a time.

"After placing her children, mother's mind seemed to rest more easily," Clement wrote. "Her prayers for restored health were answered. Her reputation as a teacher of district schools stood her in hand. She could look after places for my temporary home and clothe me, and thus I was kept in close touch with her so her mother love remained in full function."[11] Elvira worked as a housekeeper and tailor, as well as a teacher, to save enough money to gather her family back together if she could.[12] By the spring of 1864, three years after her catastrophic illness, the young mother finally returned to normal health.[13] Her first priority, now that she could see a future for herself, was to try to retrieve her children. With the guardians of her three oldest, she was successful; but the couple that had adopted her youngest, James—or Charlie, as they called him—considered him their own. Even so, since Elvira lived nearby, the adoptive parents allowed the mother and siblings to visit freely.[14]

Strang's widow next acquired a small log house on five acres of land two miles east and a half mile north of Charlotte. She and her children farmed that property, along with three acres of land they rented in Windsor Township, Eaton County. "My sister was eleven years old, and she stayed in the house and got the dinner when we were working on the place we rented. We had five sheep and mother carded and spun the wool and made our socks, mittens and winter shirts," Clement wrote.[15] Elvira was so accustomed to the bloomer costume from Beaver Island that she still wore it whenever she worked outside. In the harvest season, she proved useful cutting and binding three acres of wheat a day alongside two other field workers.[16]

In the summer of 1865, Elvira, now thirty-five years of age, met John Baker, a forty-six-year-old widower whose wife had died the previous April. John had five children, one only four months old. The two married on No-

11. Clement Strang, "Why I Am Not a Strangite," 469-70.

12. Elvira Field Strang Baker Memorial Book, Library and Historical Center, State Library of Michigan, Lansing, Michigan.

13. Clement Strang, "Why I Am Not a Strangite," 469-70.

14. Ibid.

15. Clement Strang to Stanley Johnston, Dec. 4, 1940, Clarke Historical Library. Elvira rented the land from a man named Laberty.

16. Ibid.

vember 26, 1865, and their families lived together near Dimondale, Michigan. Two years later they moved to Onandaga, Michigan, where John did farming.[17] In 1874 they moved to Lake County, Michigan, where John worked both in farming and lumbering. Lake County was a still a primeval forest in 1874 and there was no transportation system, which meant he had to convey his goods by wagon for twenty miles to the nearest railroad.[18]

John was "the kindest of men and he never scolded," according to one account. He had a "cheery" smile, a knowledge of medicine, and was active in the county fair where he won many prizes. He was fond of flowers and occasionally brought home rare specimens of orchid, water lily, or meadow lily. He also held numerous township and school district positions in the communities where they lived.[19] Like Elvira, he was opposed to tobacco and liquor. He was a Universalist. In later years, when he lived too far away to conveniently attend a Universalist church, he chose not to affiliate with any other denomination. A memorial booklet written at the time of his death claimed "his temperate habits and uniform good nature made him friends wherever he was known." John and Elvira both loved to hunt. For many years they had an ongoing tradition of a Thanksgiving Day hunt.[20]

The couple had two children together—Emma, born April 22, 1868, and May, born in October 1874.[21] As the mother of eleven children, six of her own and five of John's, Elvira tried to make her home a place of cooperation and learning. "It was her ambition that her children should be educated, and occupy honorable positions in life, and her home instruction was always with the purpose of lifting up to higher ideals of living."[22] She was equally concerned about the moral environment of her home. She detested profanity, and "her influence was always against the use of tobacco and liquor in any form." Like John, Elvira was "a great lover of the beauties of nature. She al-

---

17. John Baker Memorial Booklet, State Library of Michigan; also Clement Strang to Stanley Johnston, Sept. 2, 1938. John Baker's farm was on the Lansing-Eaton Rapids Road in Windsor Township, Eaton County, where the road crosses the Grand River a couple of miles upstream from Dimondale.

18. John Baker Memorial Booklet. Baker was born in 1819 in New York and died in Courtland, Kent County, Michigan, in 1911.

19. Ibid.

20. Ibid.

21. Ibid.

22. Elvira Field Strang Baker Memorial Booklet.

ways had her flower garden and could call by the botanical name most of the common flowers and shrubs, and many of the trees of the forest. In her younger years, when her children went out for themselves, her admonitions were always for the clean honorable, industrious life, and scarcely a week was allowed to pass without writing to them a long letter of encouragement," a memorial booklet about her life stated.[23]

In 1868, Elvira wrote to Betsy McNutt:

> I have a kind husband and we are getting along very well, but we don't own a farm, and working farms on shares takes off the profits. I have a pretty large family this winter, seven all the time and more part of the time. Charlie and Clement are gone to school. Charlie boards away ... and Eva is studying at home.... James was here last summer and made a visit. He lives 20 mile[s away]. He has got a good place and they think as much of him as though he was their own.... They have no child of their own. I think they do better by him than I can.... I have not heard from Father Strang['s] folks in a long time.... It has been so long since I had a letter from them."[24]

Fifteen years later, Elvira wrote to Wingfield Watson to update him on her life and religious condition, explaining that the first year with her brother in Michigan, all had become sick with the *ague* and she "got discouraged and scattered my children."

> My youngest ... I let go to Mr. Grier's, two mile[s] from Charlotte. He makes his home there yet & they call him Charlie Grier. He is a lawyer, admitted to the "bar" 3 years ago. My oldest Charlie, the one at Lansing, went to Mr. Perkies, a farmer in Eaton, but he could not make a farmer of him and [Charlie] stayed only three years. Where my daughter went, the woman died in about 6 weeks.
>
> I went to teaching school, Managed to clothe myself and two children for the next 3 years. Then I took three of them and went to keeping house.
>
> In about a year and a half I saw Mr. Baker, concluded to marry and since then I have had a house. That very act shows I was weak in the faith. Mr. Baker is not much of a religious man. He claims to be a "Universalist," a very good man in his way.
>
> There are times when I have almost given up the thought of there ever be-

---

23. Ibid.

24. Elvira E. Baker to "Dear Friends," Jan. 27, 1868, Library-Archives, Community of Christ, Independence, Missouri. This letter was probably written to Betsy McNutt because of references to her children Abigail, Evangeline, and Gabriel.

ing a renewal of the church. But when these members of the reorganized church came and lived four mile from us and began to preach, it aroused a desire for a head of the church. It makes me want to have a place to go to meeting, and none of these other denominations will satisfy that longing.

I have never taught my children anything of the doctrine of the church, but kept my books and when they were men I let them read for themselves.

There was one thing James did which always caused me to wonder: He never tried to bring his own relatives into the church. Nor did he have his first (Mary's children) join the church, be baptized [,] and he allowed Nettie his oldest daughter to Marry her cousin, a Gentile, a year before he died. He gave her money to attend a dan[c]ing school at Burlington before they left Voree. All these things come up and fill me with wonder.[25]

For the rest of her life, Elvira involved herself in "Christian work," attending church and participating in activities alongside people of other denominations, without joining another church. Some of Strang's followers attempted to persuade her sons Charles and Clement to take their father's place at the head of the Strangite movement. Both refused, but the two sons were instrumental in preserving most of the valuable letters and manuscripts used today in studying their father.[26] "Mother never joined any other church because the early teachings of her parents had been to count the Christians about us as apostates from the real church of God," Clement explained. "But the teachings of Jesus made such an appeal to her that she respected every person who was trying to put these teachings into the daily program of life. We enjoyed going to Sunday school at the schoolhouse and were taught to enjoy reading the Bible and listening to all the good things that Christian people uttered in our hearing.[27]

Elvira remained active in her later years caring for her flowers and preserving the produce from her garden. One day in 1897, she went hunting near her home in Lake County and shot a buck. When she returned to the house, the men were incredulous. In was, in fact, an amazing feat for a sixty-seven-year-old woman.[28] Like her sons, who preserved letters and remi-

---

25. Elvira E. Baker to "Dear Friend" [Wingfield Watson], Mar. 22, 1883.

26. *The Detroit News,* Aug. 22, 1882.

27. Clement Strang to Stanley Johnston, Sept. 2, 1938.

28. Clement Strang, interviewed by Milo M. Quaife, Feb. 12, 1921, Clarke Historical Library. Elvira also shot a hawk on the wing in Voree after Strang died.

niscences about their father, she also preserved many of the documents that form a part of her husband's legacy. She had served as his secretary, and when Beaver Island was invaded, she was able to quickly locate and secure much of his personal correspondence.[29] She kept it safely guarded, eventually giving it to her son Charles, who in turn passed it on to his brother Clement. Other items Elvira had saved, including pictures, were consumed when the Baker home in Lake County, Michigan, went up in flames in the late 1890s.[30]

After the fire, the Bakers lived with relatives, first with Elvira's brother Albert in Eaton Rapids, then with her stepson Warren Baker near Rockford, Michigan.[31] Until the last few years of her life, she enjoyed good health for a woman of her age. A booklet published at the time of her death revealed that "in the past three years her physical strength has been failing fast, yet her determination was such that she was up and dressed and about the house and yard every day until the Friday evening preceding her death ... making but two days confinement to her bed." She died of bronchitis at one o'clock on the morning of Monday, June 13, 1910, at her stepson's home. She was just one month shy of eighty years, survived by her husband, John Baker, ninety-one years old, and by six children, twenty-one grandchildren, and twelve great-grandchildren.[32] Her husband, the man who brought orchids when Elvira suffered "a sickness of the soul," died the following year.

As Elvira's children grew older, they gradually became acquainted with the name of Thomas Bedford, their father's assassin, and came to realize the part he had played in the intense hardship and suffering their parents and grandparents had endured. "All this [language] would be tinged with sorrow and the ... latent hope that God would in some way bring good out of all this evil, and punish those who were the real offenders," Clement recalled. "I have in later life come to think this covering of inward bitterness was partly due to the relationships of the family. It must be remembered that Uncle Albert's wife, Jane Miller was a sister of Tom Bedford's wife Ruth Ann Miller. They were daughters [sisters] of Harrison Miller [Beaver Island light keeper and later ship captain]. The murderous act of Tom was felt more keenly because it

---

29. Clement Strang to Dorothy Strang, Aug. 3, 1939, Clarke Historical Library.

30. Clement Strang to Stanley L. Johnston, Dec. 4, 1940.

31. Charles Strang to Wingfield Watson, May 23, 1907, Clarke Historical Library.

32. Elvira Baker Memorial Booklet. Clement Strang said Elvira was living with Baker's daughter Helen Baker Paine at the time of her death.

was the act of one to whom the sufferers were closely bound by family ties."[33]

In 1866 Bedford made a call to visit the family, notably alone, without his wife, and made a gesture of apology to Elvira to show a spirit of changed enmity. "This much I remember," Clement remarked. "Bedford had asked about the hardships mother had endured in her widowhood, and she told him.... With a sort of sad, shamed face look," he acknowledged his role in her troubles. "The words I do not remember," Clement added, "but the impression remains that while he was sorry for her, he had no regrets to express for having done this deed."[34]

In 1867 or 1868, Bedford had moved to Eaton Rapids, where he and Albert Field went into business together cutting cat tails from the swamp and supplying them to Jackson State Prison for the inmates to use in bottoming chairs. "Bedford and Uncle Bert got into an argument and Bedford said, 'I have killed three men and can kill another if I get mad enough,'" according to Clement Strang. "Uncle Bert could not endure this and told him to get out of the neighborhood and stay out or he would be reported to the officers on this threat. Witnesses persuaded Bedford to take his wife and go to some other place to live." Clement did not know where the Bedfords had gone after that incident, but he knew that "Aunt Jane and mother kept up the correspondence as long as they both lived."[35]

Clement had heard stories about Bedford killing someone else on Beaver Island after the Mormons left. The incident was apparently over a game of cards, and Bedford was said to have hidden the victim's body under a milk cupboard. Bedford was arrested and incarcerated awaiting trial, but was allowed to enlist, whereupon he was sent to the front lines in the Civil War. He allegedly ended up killing a fellow soldier before he deserted. "His wife hid him away and he was never brought to jail for either murder," Clement explained.[36]

Before the death of James Strang, Elvira had believed his claim to succeed Joseph Smith as leader of the Mormons was superior to Brigham Young's. Later in her life, however, she seemed to have harbored some mis-

---

33. Clement Strang to Stanley Johnston, Sept. 2, 1938.

34. Ibid.

35. Ibid.

36. Ibid. Roger Van Noord, in *King of Beaver Island: The Life and Assassination of James Jesse Strang* (Urbana and Chicago: University of Illinois Press, 1988), identified the man killed on Beaver Island as Thomas Gallagher.

givings. Even so, she never doubted the "excellence of Strang's moral worth." "He was intelligent, a fascinating speaker, his character was the best ... He was generous, kind, and very thoughtful of others," she wrote in a biographical sketch of his life.[37] Clement commented on his mother's persistent devotion to Strang and believed his mother to have been "a very good woman." Elvira had given Strang "her complete devotion as a wife; and mother to his children; and served him as secretary—the family of four wives dividing the household chores as agreeably as if they were born sisters in the same human family."[38] However, "Strang's death, and ... his change of attitude toward life while he was on his death bed, led Elvira to adopt a waiting attitude. If God approved of his career, he would make it known and appoint his successor. If not, she would live according to the precepts of Jesus and the dictates of a clear conscience. And this she did faithfully," Clement confirmed.[39]

From her early childhood on, Elvira had been taught that God had inspired Joseph Smith, and that everything Joseph commanded should be strictly obeyed. She believed the same faith and obedience was due James Strang as the legitimate and divinely inspired successor. "I am sure this was the state of mother's mind after the tragedy that scattered the followers of the King of Saint James to the ends of the earth. Her problem was: if James was what he claimed to be, why did not the God he served so faithfully overthrow those who opposed him instead of overthrowing his faithful followers?" "To cap the climax," Clement's analysis continued, when James was asked about his successor and "his only answer was, 'take care of your families,'" there was little for his followers to hold on to.

Elvira told her children she could not understand why God had allowed the prophet to die. She even speculated that it must have been for some sin her husband had committed. "Father's wife Betsy ... verily believed Father would rise the third day, and [she] really prepared to meet him," Clement had been told. "Mother admitted to us children that she hoped it, but [she] really could not generate in her soul the faith to do anything but wait until God did something to show his mind in the matter."[40]

---

37. Elvira Field Strang and Charles J. Strang, "Biographical Sketch of James J. Strang," unpublished manuscript, n.p., Strang Manuscript Collection, State Library of Michigan.

38. Clement Strang to Dorothy Strang, Aug. 3, 1939.

39. Ibid.

40. Clement Strang to Stanley Johnston, Jan. 6, 1942, Clarke Historical Library.

Elvira's oldest son, Charles, grew up following in his father's footsteps to some extent as the publisher and editor of a newspaper in Charlevoix, Michigan. He wrote to Wingfield Watson telling him of the persecution he had suffered because of his name. "Only those who previously knew my father treat me with decent respect after they learn that I am a natural son of 'King Strang.' Some shallow-pated people have tried to discredit my family and injure my girls by calling them 'good for nothing Mormons,' but I have tried to so educate them that there is no cause for shame or humiliation, and yet these things are sometimes annoying." Charles died in February 1916.[41]

Elvira's daughter Evaline married Martin C. Baldwin, a prosperous farmer in Onandaga, Michigan, in 1872. She died in September 1926.[42] Like Charles, Clement Strang also followed the path of a newspaper publisher for a brief period of time in Black River Falls, Wisconsin, where he lived with his father's fifth wife, Phoebe Wright. Eventually Clement went on to become a Congregationalist minister and then a schoolteacher. He died in 1944.

Like his father and namesake, Elvira's fourth child, James Jesse Jr., whose name was changed to Charles J. Grier when he was adopted, became a lawyer in partnership with an attorney in Charlevoix. The partnership went well until the two attorneys were asked to defend some white men who had killed an Indian. Grier thought it was a clear case of cold-blooded murder and said he would not be party to such a case. In court, the assailants were acquitted. Grier went on to briefly edit his brother's newspaper, the *Charlevoix Journal*, and then to serve as commissioner of the U.S. circuit court. He died in the autumn of 1934.[43]

When the children were still young, Elvira apparently confided her unsettled feelings about her late husband, as Clement remembered:

> When she talked with us children when I was nine years old she expressed a slight doubt about the mind of God being expressed in these things. She sometimes feared that James had been over tempted to self-glorification; and that the calamities were his punishments. I think that when we visited her parents in their home after father's death, they told her of his behavior before his death,

---

41. Charles Strang to Wingfield Watson, July 15, 1909, Clarke Historical Library.
42. *Strang Family Newsletter,* La Canada, California, Apr. 2, 1980, 2.
43. Ibid.

and that he repented of the whole affair; and best of all that he seemed to be at peace when he passed away.[44]

Clement reiterated that in his mother's view, "God would never have permitted [Strang] to be assassinated" if he had not stumbled in some way.

> She never would name any particular items as the one she thought might have been misfavored by the heavenly father, but she named three or four things any one of which might have been contrary to God's will, but positively refused to name one for herself. The t[hings] she named were such as other people had mentioned to her. I think her love for father stayed with her to her dying day; though her faithfulness to her second husband was perfect, even though she realized that he was far inferior to her first love.[45]

In 1849, Elvira Field had cut her hair, dressed as a man, and traveled with her "husband" on a great adventure. Compared to the wise and wizened matron she became in the 1890s, the contrast is so stark it is difficult to comprehend how they could be one and the same person. An interesting aspect of Clement's perspective is that his mother's relationship with James transcended the respect of an adherent and may have constituted a real and enduring love affair. Clearly, James had been distracted during his east-coast trip when he took Elvira with him, involving the total neglect of his first wife. Perhaps with the benefit of hindsight, Elvira wondered if this had been right in God's eyes. She also mentioned her husband's pride, which now appeared to her to have been more of a problem than it had seemed at the time. Other issues, to be discussed in a subsequent chapter, involved less than strictly ethical behavior, which had seemed right under the circumstances, when they had enemies on all sides, but looked less noble in retrospect. In the presence of James Strang and at his bidding, Elvira had been compliant; but after he was gone, she wondered if she may have in fact erred, an uncertainty she passed on to her children. Clement came to understand that his father had been a man of great talents and equally serious flaws, among which were probably an impractical idealism and, ironically, a growing indifference about and short-sightedness with regard to the future.

---

44. Clement Strang to Stanley Johnston, Jan. 6, 1942, Clarke Historical Library.
45. Ibid.

18

ELIZABETH "BETSY" MCNUTT STRANG

THE LAST TO DENY HIM

"I cannot remember all he said, but I remember very distinctly that he said he was going away ... and that he asked me to be sure and follow him.... One thing that served to impress this request on my mind [was] that about the same time he had told mother that she would be one of the last to deny him.... [F]or more than 30 years afterward it seemed impossible to her that She ever would. She was always worried about what he said and often mentioned it. Each time I heard her speak about it, it reminded me of what he had said to me."
—Gabriel Strang to Chester Flanders.[1]

Alfter the Strangites had been driven from Beaver Island, they began to search for a new place where they could gather together and "there would be no enemies to murder and rob them." Many of them went to Voree at first, but other groups scattered throughout the Midwest, some traveling in covered wagons pulled by ox teams, in search of a new location.[2]

Betsy remained with her children in Voree for two years in a house they shared with Elvira Field and Betsy's brother, John McNutt. Betsy gave birth to a daughter, Abigail, on January 1, 1857, seven months after Strang's death. In the spring of 1858, Betsy and Elvira accompanied John McNutt's family to Marquette County, Wisconsin. Lorenzo Dow Hickey and Basil Young helped them settle on a farm Betsy purchased about seventy miles north of Madison. She sold that farm a year later and in the spring of 1859 the group continued northward to Jackson County, Wisconsin.[3]

---

1. Gabriel Strang to Chester Flanders, July 7, 1919; also a fragment of another letter presumed to be from Strang to Flanders, n.d., Clarke Historical Library, Central Michigan University, Mount Pleasant, Michigan.

2. George Sage [Gabriel Strang] to A. E. Ewing, Dec. 3, 1911. Clarke Historical Library.

3. Gabriel Strang to John Wake, May 8, 1929, Clarke Historical Library.

Two years later, the two sister-wives, Betsy and Elvira, said their good-byes to each other. They had lived together for eight years, sharing the same husband for four of those years. They had probably assisted each other in child birth and raising children. Their parting would have been a momentous event, not only because they would miss each other but also because the separation implied that the gathering of the Saints was not likely to occur. The Strangite Church had become broken and scattered and would presumably never unite again.

While Elvira and her children returned to her family in Michigan, Betsy prepared to join her relatives in Ligonier, Noble County, located in northern Indiana. Several of her relatives already lived there, including her brother Jacob, who had lived briefly on Beaver Island in the early 1850s, and her sister-in-law, Mary, the widow of Betsy's brother Tobias. Tobias had died of yellow jaundice in 1857 and was buried in the Mormon cemetery in Voree.

John and Betsy and their families traveled the 550 miles from Jackson County, Wisconsin, to Indiana with two ox teams. Once there, John purchased forty acres of land next door to Jacob McNutt, who gave Betsy an acre of his own land. The neighbors pitched in and helped build log houses for the new arrivals. The Elkhart River ran along one side of the McNutt properties, over which a bridge was built for the AirLine Rail Road. The McNutt family group planted apple orchards, hay, corn, oats, and wheat.[4]

Although most of the people in Ligonier were McNutt relatives, those who had once been Strangites were considered "curiosities." Partly for this reason, Betsy and her brother John decided to move back to the wilds of Wisconsin where there were other members of their church. Another consideration for making the move—one that was important to some members of the group—was that the Civil War had started and a few of the boys were approaching draft age. Therefore, the ten families hitched their oxen to their covered wagons and left Ligonier in September 1863.[5] Betsy's sister-in-law

---

4. "The Diary of James Oscar McNutt, Elder of the Mormon Church at the Mormon Settlement, Jackson Co., Wisconsin; One Time Follower of James Jesse Strang," 12, Strang Manuscript Collection, Library and Historical Center, State Library of Michigan, Lansing, Michigan; cf. "Reminisces of James O. McNutt of the Mormon Settlement, Jackson County [Wisconsin], and Warrens, Monroe County, Related by J. O. McNutt, and Recorded by his Daughter Miss Sadie McNutt," Library-archives, Wisconsin Historical Society, Madison, Wisconsin.

5. Ibid.; also George Sage [Gabriel Strang] to A. E. Ewing, Dec. 3, 1911. J. O. McNutt said there were over 100 people in the company leaving Ligonier.

Mary McNutt and her children joined the company. Mary's son, James Oscar, was fifteen years old and wrote of the move west in his diary.[6]

> Everything went smoothly, and [we] had a nice time until we got to Chicago. We were on State St. and driving those loose cows, them running here and there and us boys after them and one dray (wagon) run against Irvin Vance and knocked him down.... [Irvin] picked up a stone and was going to hit the drayman and a policeman told him if he threw the stone, he would lock him up. The policeman told us we had better go [a few streets] further west where the travel was not so thick.... [W]e did and ... got onto a street where the railroad run along one side. This was worse than State St., so we went several streets farther west and got thru alive, but I never want to try that again![7]

The month-long trip took them not only through the urban jungle of Chicago but also across a wild, sparsely populated area south of Jackson County, Wisconsin. Gabriel Strang, Betsy's son, who was eight years old at the time, remembered how the group stopped to cut hay for the stock near Tomah, Wisconsin, then traveled on to the Mormon settlement at Knapp where about forty Strangite families had settled.

> We ... built log houses in the woods, splitting 'shakes' for the roofs and punchens, smoothed with an adze for the floors. It was several days drive to any [other] settlement. Some of the men[,] on going out after supplies, found several men looking for a good place to hunt until the war was over, and brought them back with them. Before spring we had more than a hundred men there who had run away from the draft, mostly from St. Louis and Chicago and our teams were kept busy hauling deer and bear to the nearest shipping point.[8]

In 1867, Betsy's daughter, Evangeline, married John Denio, and Betsy and her other two children moved in with the newlyweds, all of them squeezing into Denio's backwoods cabin. Evangeline was only thirteen or fourteen years old when the marriage took place. Denio was a Strangite widower who

---

6. McNutt diary.

7. Ibid., 12-13. The McNutts had seven or eight head of cattle; others in the company also had cattle.

8. George Sage [Gabriel Strang] to A. E. Ewing, Dec. 3, 1911. The exact location of this settlement cannot be determined, but James McNutt said it was south of Tomah, Wisconsin. Gabriel mentioned that the settlers had to keep an eye out for Native Americans, some of whom were hostile, but this was probably an exaggeration.

had lived on Beaver Island and was forty years of age.[9] At forty-seven, Betsy was actually closer to her son-in-law in age than her daughter was. Elvira Field had a daughter the same age as Betsy's daughter, Evangeline, and wrote to her old friend gently chastising her for letting Evangeline marry so young. "It don't seem that Evie is old enough to be married. I would not have Eva marry the best man in the world" at that age, Elvira wrote.[10]

In the spring of 1868, twelve years after James Strang's death, Betsy moved again, this time to the site of a former Strangite colony on Drummond Island in Lake Huron, only a few miles from Canada. Betsy and her children, including the Denios, lived for a time with the Isaac Pierce family. Pierce had been one of Strang's most trusted friends and supporters. Several Strangite men and boys, including Nephi Hutchins, James Oscar McNutt, Dave Post, and Frank Tubbs, helped Betsy make the move, driving her cattle from Black River Falls to Milwaukee. From Milwaukee they loaded the cattle onto a boat headed toward Drummond. They stayed on the island most of the summer to help Betsy get settled.[11]

Like his father, Betsy's son Gabriel was precocious—far beyond the norm in his intellectual ability, intuitiveness, and memory. He demonstrated these abilities at a young age.[12] "I heard much talk about the latter-day work, and many things that various persons had heard father say," he recalled. "Such subjects were always discussed when any of them [Strangites] visited us. I had good opportunity to hear because I was always at the table reading." In other words, instead of playing with marbles or joining friends outside, Gabriel was always at the table reading or studying. "Before I was seven years old I had read the Book of Mormon and had a very clear conception of the principles it enunciated," he wrote. "We had a large collection of books from the library on Beaver Island.... Mother read the Bible and the Book of the

---

9. The 1880 federal census for Jackson County, Wisconsin. James O. McNutt gave the wedding date as 1866, which appears to be about right. However, since Denio's second wife died in 1867, the wedding probably occurred that year. RLDS Church records give John Denio's birth date as July 15, 1826, in Jefferson County, New York, while Evangeline was born in 1853 or, according to RLDS records, 1854. Denio's first wife died in 1856.

10. Elvira E. Baker to "Dear Friends" [Betsy McNutt], Jan. 27, 1868, Library-Archives, Community of Christ, Independence, Missouri.

11. McNutt diary, 21.

12. On the other hand, Gabriel was also prone to exaggeration, as seen in some of his letters.

Law frequently, but none of the other children ever read anything.... Mother never talked familiar with us children, neither did her brother who lived near us part of the time, so the only companions I ever met with whom I could talk on any subject was the old man who lived 25 miles away—Samle [Samuel] Seaman, the oldest son of Murray Seaman," he remembered.[13]

Murray Seaman had settled on Drummond Island back in the days when James Strang was still alive. Strang had told Seaman he might send him on a mission to South America where "a great work would be performed." Gabriel learned that "Seaman believed this so much he had a large boat built that could go through the St. Lawrence [River] and down the coast to the Amazon to the foot of the Andes. He died shortly after it was built."[14]

Betsy wrote to her friends, telling them she was living in poor circumstances and complaining about not being treated well by Strangite Isaac Pierce and his clan.[15] A mutual friend, D. R. Whipple, wrote back to her, offering verbal support and praising her for remaining strong in the faith.

> I am glad that there are some honest faithful Saints remaining that have not thrown away hope and made a shipwreck of Faith.... It appears so strange that Isaac [Pierce] should do by you and your children as he has. I think your conclusions about going to the [Bruce] mines in the spring to live, are good and I wish I was able to tender you some assistance.... I am in hopes that the saints will not remain in their present scattered and downtrodden condition, but will be gathered in truth and righteousness, where they will keep and abide by the Law of the Lord which they did not do when he gave them dominion.[16]

In 1870, apparently still unhappy, Betsy moved to St. Joseph's Island in Canada, about eight miles north of Drummond. She wrote to Wingfield

---

13. Gabriel Strang to Chester Flanders, July 7, 1919. It is particularly interesting that Gabriel mentions books from the library on Beaver Island. Some accounts of the banishment claim the books were destroyed or taken by the mob.

14. Ibid.

15. Lorenzo Dow Hickey to Charles Strang, n.d., State Library of Michigan. There is some indication that Betsy slandered Isaac Pierce and his family. Letters to and from Isaac Pierce discussing the slander are nearly illegible. The dates on the letters are also difficult but appear to be 1861 or 1868, most likely the latter. See folders 462, 462a, James Jesse Strang Collection, Yale Collection of Western Americana, Beinecke Rare Book and Manuscript Library, Yale University, New Haven, Connecticut.

16. D. R. Whipple to [Betsy McNutt Strang], Mar. 29, 1869, folder 523, Strang Collection, Beinecke Library.

Watson in June, encouraging him to move there and giving him an account of her personal situation.

> We live 12 miles from Detour (a small village in the United States) and about the same distance from the Bruce Mines in Canada, a town of about 2,000 inhabitants. Both of these places are visited by steamers and vessels. We live in a small bay that runs into the land about a mile and a half. A river road runs into the head of the bay on which one of our gardens is situated. The other is in front of the houses about half way up the way.... The land is better than it was on Beaver. You have to go in small boats to get to town....
>
> I would like to have you and Robert come up here, but I don't want you to come up here and be dissatisfied and blame me.... You wanted to know who lives here. There is no Mormons lives here but us and John. There is two families of Canadian French lives on the point and that is all that lives on the bay.[17]

Betsy mentioned that Watson could get a job teaching school on the island if he and his son Robert would settle there. John Denio was engaged in fishing and coopering, she related. Denio may have also worked in the Bruce Copper Mines.[18]

Three years later, unsuccessful at convincing other Strangites to come to St. Joseph's Island, Betsy and her family once again moved back to Jackson County, Wisconsin, this time to the town of Millston, where John Denio worked in the lumber mills to support the extended family.[19] That same year, 1873, Betsy's daughter Abigail married her cousin Ferdinand Juan McNutt, the son of Tobias McNutt.[20] It was the second time one of Strang's daughters married a first cousin—a union prohibited in the Strangite book of scripture, the Book of the Law of the Lord. Mary Perce's daughter Nettie had married her cousin, Romeo Strang, in 1855.

Betsy wrote to Watson again in 1877, apprising him of her family's condition and offering advice.

> My health has been poor all winter & I did not have no ambition to hardly

---

17. Betsy McNutt to Wingfield Watson, June 2, 1870, Clarke Historical Library.

18. Ibid.

19. McNutt diary, 23.

20. Ibid., 4. Ferdinand had suffered an infection in one of his thigh bones when he was ten weeks old, stunting the growth of the infected leg by two inches and leaving him to walk with a limp. James Oscar McNutt, Tobias's other son, married Alma Pierce, the daughter of Isaac Pierce, the Strangite who lived on Drummond Island.

moove around. John [Denio] has broke his arm. It has been broke over two months. He is able to do a little work. Now you spok about Sending me some money. You take your money and use it, for i have plenty to live on at present, & if i ever should come to want it & you had any[,] then you can lend a hand....

[I] am glad to hear that those [Beaver] islands is going to be cleansed [Strang had prophesied that God would cleanse the island of gentiles,] as for my part i do not think it is the place for the Saints till it is Scourged. As for my part i think that if we would all Seek for a prophet it would not be long till there would be a head to lead[;] but i am afraid there will not be many to lead[,] the way things is running now.... In the future i want you to teach your Family to live & not die. That is what i teach mine. I think that the end of tim[e] is near at hand.[21]

Betsy's mention of poor health may have had to do with asthma. "My grandmother was unable to lie down and sleep for more than 65 years," Gabriel Strang reported in 1929. "My mother for 45 years and I in common with many of my relatives on the Tillman side have been a great sufferer from the same cause (asthma)."[22]

Like Elvira, Betsy took responsibility for the important Strangite records that had fallen into her possession, carrying these heavy items with her when she moved on at least eleven different occasions. She concealed the small plates of Raja Manchou of Vorito at the time the wounded prophet was taken off Beaver Island.[23] At one time her family possessed Strang's diary and unbound copies of the Book of the Law of the Lord. "Mother had 1,500 [unbound] copies when I was small," Gabriel Strang recalled. "It was decided at a [church] conference in Hixton [Wisconsin], Christmas 1863, to divide them up among interested members of the church.... Several families took a hundred copies or so, and mother kept the rest."[24]

"Mother had a large chest filled with letters and papers that she was careful to have taken from the island before they should get into the hands of the mob," Gabriel wrote.[25] The chest was full of manuscripts and other arti-

---

21. Betsy Strang to Wingfield Watson, May 23, 1877, Clarke Historical Library, terminal punctuation added.

22. Gabriel Strang to John Wake Jr., Apr. 10, 1929, Clarke Historical Library.

23. A. E. Ewing to Milo Quaife, Apr. 9, 1919, Clarke Historical Library.

24. Gabriel Strang to Chester Flanders, July 7, 1919.

25. Charles Harris [Gabriel Strang] to Wingfield Watson, Jan. 3, 1915, Clarke Historical Library.

cles of interest to the church, "including the plates found in the Hill of Promise ... and over a thousand letters."[26] Included with the other documents
were "the Essays of the Illuminati and the Charlie Douglass letters of
Elvira." Explaining what had become of this trove, Gabriel continued:

> I wrote to Eva and asked her if she would not send them to Charlie Strang so we
> could look them over and see just what there was.... Abbie was very sick while I
> was at St. Joseph and one day she got a little penitent and told me that years be-
> fore, Eva had given the papers to the [Joseph] Smith [III] family. And they had
> taken everything out that could be used against us in argument or ridicule and
> that she had told them all the inner workings of the "Kingdom" on the Island.[27]

According to Gabriel, there had been other treasures in the chest Betsy
owned, including Strang's correspondence in the Michigan legislature and a
manuscript translation of the Voree plates. Betsy had possession of the small
brass plates for years but lost them in her old age. "All I can learn about the
Voree plates is mother loaned them to a stranger one Sunday when there was
no one else home," Gabriel wrote.[28]

Heman H. Smith of the Reorganized Church of Jesus Christ of Latter-
day Saints (RLDS) said Betsy McNutt had the plates with her in Lamoni until she loaned them to Charles Hall, a Hedrickite who wanted to use them in
connection with the temple lot lawsuit in Independence, Missouri. Hall's wife
took custody of the plates about 1898. Two years later, his wife loaned them to
two elders from the Mormon Church in Utah and they were not returned.
The Voree plates, according to Hall's wife, were "four in number, about six
inches by four inches in dimension," and "very evidently made from a copper
kettle." "The figure of the crowned boy on one of them, and the hieroglyphics
were crude enough to have been scratched thereby by a child," she claimed.[29]

One of Betsy McNutt's grandsons loaned James Strang's diary to
Heman Smith. The latter part of the diary contained a copy of the secret

26. Gabriel Strang to Chester Flanders, July 7, 1919.

27. Charles Harris [Gabriel Strang] to Wingfield Watson, Jan. 3, 1915, Clarke Historical Library. Gabriel said he had written to Eva to enquire about the documents about "6
or 7 years ago."

28. Ibid.

29. Heman Hale Smith to Milo Quaife, June 9, 1920, Library-Archives, Community
of Christ. The temple lot suit dealt with ownership of a plot of land in Independence, Missouri, claimed by both the Josephites and Hedrickites.

Oath and Covenant of the Illuminati, documents relating to the Order of Enoch, original signatures of those who took the covenant, and materials relating to the secret passwords, signs, and tokens of the Illuminati. Betsy's grandson said he loaned this material to Smith because he trusted him, rather than because of affiliation with the RLDS Church.[30] When historian Milo M. Quaife later met with Heman Smith, the RLDS official still had the diary and other documents and allowed Quaife to make copies of them. Betsy may have also saved some of the books from Strang's extensive library on Beaver Island. One of Strang's grandsons said he saw a few of them in the RLDS library in Lamoni, Iowa.[31]

By 1880, John and Evangeline Denio had five children and Betsy still lived with them. She is said to have "helped in the house" as much as she could, considering her poor health.[32] In 1883 the Denios moved yet again, this time to Davis City, Decatur County, Iowa, where they joined the RLDS Church, since renamed the Community of Christ. Betsy's daughter Abigail and her husband had preceded them to Davis City the year before. The Denios later moved to Leon, Iowa, and finally to Lamoni, where the RLDS Church was headquartered.[33]

John Denio became a strong proponent of the RLDS Church and presided over the branch in Leon for four years. He received his confirmation directly from church president Joseph Smith III, after which Denio returned to Wisconsin for a short proselyting mission. When Denio died in June 1897, Joseph III assisted in the funeral service. "His life was one of great integrity and faithfulness without stain or reproach of any kind," his obituary read.[34]

The RLDS Church would count many former Strangites among its membership even though, under the direction of Joseph Smith III, the

---

30. Heman Hale Smith to Milo Quaife, June 7, 1920, Library-Archives, Community of Christ. Smith met Quaife in Chicago or Madison with the diary, a copy of the Book of the Law of the Lord, and notes from an interview with Betsy's daughter, Abigail.

31. Charles W. Brown to Wingfield Watson, Apr. 4, 1917, Library-Archives, Community of Christ.

32. The 1880 federal census for Millston, Jackson County, Wisconsin, lists Betsy Strang as "Elizabeth Strong," fifty-nine years old, living in the Denio household and "helping in the house."

33. McNutt diary, 28. Evangeline's daughter, Melvinna, also joined the Reorganized Church, but Evangeline's four sons did not.

34. John Denio obituary, *Saints' Herald*, 420; also RLDS membership records, B215, Library-Archives, Community of Christ.

church was radically opposed to polygamy. Those who had left the Strangites because of polygamy found the reorganization appealing, but it was also becoming clear to others that the Strangite Church was not going to be rebuilt. It was two former Strangites, Jason Briggs and Zenas Gurley, who set the reorganization in motion. Briggs and Gurley called a special conference in June 1852 for any and all Mormons scattered throughout northeastern Illinois and southern Wisconsin. It was decided at the conference that these adherents would reaffirm the doctrine and authority of the original church under Joseph Smith and await the emergence of a direct descendent of the slain prophet, Joseph Smith Jr., before consolidating their disparate congregations. Those who accepted this premise came to be called the "Josephites" as opposed to the "Brighamites," who followed Brigham Young.[35] Joseph Smith III stepped forward to assume leadership of the church at Amboy, Illinois, eight years later. By 1866, church officials had moved to Plano, Illinois, and in 1881 to Lamoni, Iowa.[36]

It is not certain whether or not Betsy McNutt ever joined the reorganization. The RLDS Church records list an Elizabeth Strang, baptized on August 12, 1879, but the brief entry does not have a birth date for the woman or a place of baptism. This could have been Strang's wife, Betsy McNutt, but her Denio grandsons later claimed Betsy never joined the church.[37] However, whether as a courtesy or because she was a member, her obituary was printed in the *Saints' Herald*, the official RLDS publication.

The Strangite apostle Lorenzo Dow Hickey was furious at Betsy and her children for "moving into RLDS territory." He wrote to warn her that if she moved in among the Josephites, she would be "used as a prostitute."[38] This allegation reached the attention of Joseph III, who responded angrily to

---

35. Interestingly, Brigham Young was careful never to refer to himself as the prophet or successor to Joseph Smith, but rather as a caretaker until Joseph Smith's son David, whom Young considered the likely heir, stepped forward to assume his father's role. See *The Essential Brigham Young* (Salt Lake City: Signature Books, 1992), xii; D. Michael Quinn, "Joseph Smith III's 1844 Blessing and the Mormons of Utah," *Dialogue: A Journal of Mormon Thought* 15 (Summer 1982): 84-5; Roger D. Launius, *Joseph Smith III: Pragmatic Prophet* (Urbana and Chicago: University of Illinois Press, 1988), 32.

36. *Restoration Trail Forum* 3 (May 1977): 2. This was a publication of the RLDS Church.

37. Milo M. Quaife's notes, Clarke Historical Library.

38. Joseph Smith III to W. H. Kelley, Jan. 14 1884, William H. Kelley Papers, Library-Archives, Community of Christ.

Hickey. "You offered a gratuitous insult to the body which I represent," he wrote, "and told what you knew to be false when you wrote to Sr. Betsy Strang, that if she came down among the Josephites that she would be 'used as a prostitute.' For so dastardly a lie I despise you. Mrs. [Abigail] McNutt can assure her mother of better treatment."[39] Hickey apparently mended the breach, at least with Betsy's children, because in 1893 he delivered a sermon at an RLDS Church in Leon, Iowa. He later gave his impression of the family, saying he found that Eva Strang was "glad to see me and I think she will come out alright. But Betsy is not liked—only by the Whitmere School," in reference to another branch of Mormonism.[40]

Betsy McNutt never remarried. When she died on September 22, 1897, at seventy-eight years of age, it was at the home of her daughter Evangeline in Lamoni, only three months after the death of her son-in law John Denio. Betsy's life was "eventful in one of the historical scenes of the latter-day work," her obituary read. Funeral services were held in Evangeline's home, and she was buried in the Lamoni cemetery.[41]

Evangeline and Abigail were devout RLDS Church members for much of their adult lives. By contrast, Gabriel kept in close association with the Strangite leaders Lorenzo Dow Hickey and Wingfield Watson, even proposing to build up a Strangite colony in Mexico or trade his Mexican property for land in Belize. He thought a colony would be workable in Belize because of its lower population, recognizing that "there are so few of us in the world."[42]

In 1904, Evangeline Denio wrote a sketch of her father's life for the RLDS Church publication *Autumn Leaves*. She said she hesitated to do so because people might suspect her motivation and accuse her of injuring her father's reputation. "But such is not my desire," she insisted, "and I want the readers of this article to understand" that it was written only "for the benefit

---

39. Joseph Smith III to Lorenzo Dow Hickey, Jan. 23, [1884,] Joseph Smith III Letter Press Book, Library-Archives, Community of Christ.

40. Lorenzo Dow Hickey to Wingfield Watson, June 22, 1893, Clarke Historical Library.

41. *Saints' Herald* 44 (1897): 628.

42. Gabriel Strang to Wingfield Watson, Jan. 28, 1915, Clarke Historical Library. In a letter to Watson dated January 3, 1915, Gabriel said his sister Eva never cared for much more than "dancing" and "getting out of work." He said she was twenty years old when she acquired "the drug habit" and that "her life since has been mostly day dreams." Apparently the drugs were for sleeping, but Gabriel also mentioned that it "has been a fight for her all that time to keep out of the asylum."

of the Church."[43] In what proved to be a mixed review of her father's legacy, she began by rehearsing the major events in his life, then added what she believed she knew about the early Strangites.

> When they went to the world to preach, they taught the gospel, just as we do; but when converts came to the island they found it quite different. First they were taught to obey counsel. The members had no privileges that the leaders were bound to respect. The women were compelled to dress in bloomers, against their wishes; and the young men were taught to leave the island and seek wives and leave the young women of the island to the old men.
>
> They were taught to steal from the gentiles—which they were pleased to call consecration—and if one turned traitor he must look out for his life. Strang taught them also that the leading men should be princes and have others joined to their households—the greater the household, the greater the glory in eternity. He taught that Jesus Christ was not begotten of the Holy Ghost, that Joseph was his father. He taught that Christ came to earth to set up the kingdom but could not do it so the Lord sent him [Strang]. He taught that he was the Holy Ghost and had been given a body to finish the work that Christ left; and mother said he told her his glory would be greater than that of Christ. He taught Spiritual Wifery and the raising of seed for one's brethren....
>
> My father was very ambitious and loved power and honor. He was very kind, yet very firm; when he told one to do anything, one knew that he meant it. He served four years in the Michigan legislature. The later years of his life were spent at St. James, the capital of the kingdom which he founded on Beaver Island."[44]

The article is interesting because it was written by a woman who was born on Beaver Island to Strangite parents, grew up in Strangite settlements, and married a man who had been a devoted follower of her father. With her mother and husband deceased, Eva had little left to connect her to this strange past, much of which must have seemed like a distant memory by then. She was an example of many other Strangites who had come to feel at home and comfortable with the teachings and practices of the reorganization. She died in Lamoni, Iowa, on April 7, 1915. Her sister, Abigail Strang McNutt, died in May 1921 in St. Joseph, Missouri.

Betsy's son, Gabriel, believed his mother never really lost her faith in

---

43. *Autumn Leaves* 17 (Sept. 1904): 9, 392-93.
44. Ibid.

James Strang. "I had not seen mother for a long time before she died," he wrote to Elder Watson. "I think she joined the Josephites like L[orenzo]. D[ow]. Hickey did[,] but [like Hickey,] she soon see the Hypocr[is]y of the leaders and dropped out and was with the Whitmer people awhile only because they were opposed to the Josephites. [Betsy's] girls and their families were very bitter against her [for it]."[45] It seems that Gabriel's mother never forgot what her husband had said to her on his deathbed, that she would be the last to deny him. That seems to have been truly the case.

---

45. Charles G. Harris [Gabriel Strang] to Wingfield Watson, Mar. 5, 1916, Clarke Historical Library.

19

SARAH WRIGHT STRANG WING

PLURAL WIFE AND PIONEER DOCTOR

> *"When the mob drove us from the Is-*
> *land we landed in Racine, but James Strang had been taken to Voree.... I*
> *went from Racine with my father to Voree. I saw James, but could not stay*
> *there, for my father left Voree immediately after.... I had no other way to*
> *live, only with my father."* —Sarah Wright Wing to Milo M. Quaife.[1]

F ive months pregnant with her first child, Sarah Wright left her dying husband and prophet in Voree and moved with her father,
Phineas, to Racine, Wisconsin. Phineas and his son Zenas worked temporarily on the railroad while the other men in the Wright families went to work
harvesting crops.[2] When the 1856 summer harvest season was over, the
Wrights set out for the Black River pineries in wagons conveyed by ox teams.
They arrived in September 1856. For the winter they moved into a shanty, all
three families living together under the same roof.

During the next few years, Phineas and his brother Benjamin built up
the prosperous lumbering communities of Alma and Wrightsville. Phineas
later sold his share of the business to Benjamin and moved his family to
Trempealeau County, Wisconsin, near what is now called Coral City. He and
his sons built a flour mill there that gained a reputation for being the best in
the county.[3]

Sarah and her family had few possessions. "I was driven" off the island ·
"with only what I stood up in," she told historian Milo Quaife.[4] Of the few

---

1. Sarah Wing to Milo Quaife, [Spring] 1920, Clarke Historical Library, Central
Michigan University, Mount Pleasant, Michigan.

2. *Badger State Banner*, Sept. 6, 1917; also Zenas Wright, interviewed by Milo M.
Quaife, May 25, 1920, Clarke Historical Library.

3. "A Visit to Wright's Mills," *Jackson County Banner*, Feb. 22, 1868.

4. Sarah Wing to Milo Quaife, June 28, 1920, Clarke Historical Library.

items she did manage to rescue was the original letter of appointment from which Strang had claimed authority from Joseph Smith. A few years later, she gave the letter to her father for safekeeping.[5] She gave birth to a son four months after Strang's death, on November 11, 1856,[6] and named the baby James Phineas after his father and grandfather.[7] A portrait of the new mother holding her young son on her lap, probably taken in 1857 or 1858, shows Sarah to be an attractive, sad-eyed woman with dark hair and fair skin.[8]

Within three years, Sarah married for a second time. By coincidence, her new husband, Joseph Smith Wing, was not a Mormon and was not named after the prophet Joseph Smith but rather after a doctor by the same name who had delivered Wing. Joseph Wing was a self-taught doctor who partnered with his brother in a mercantile and lumber business in Black River Falls. He was twenty-seven years old when he married Sarah.[9] The exact date of the marriage is unknown, a detail not unexpected since such events often went unrecorded in the Wisconsin backcountry. In any case, Sarah and Joseph were probably united by 1859 because Sarah gave birth to their first child late the previous year.[10] Wing's nephew, Samuel Wing, also lived in Black River Falls, where he kept the books for the Wright family's lumber company. Samuel married Sarah's sister, Elizabeth Jane Wright, in 1860.[11]

When Brighamite missionaries came through the area, Phineas Wright often allowed them to preach and hold meetings in his home. Samuel Wing and his uncle, Joseph Smith Wing, attended these religious discussions and were baptized into the Utah church in 1862, upon which they decided to join their fellow Mormons out west. In the spring of that year, the Wing party, which included Sarah and her sister, started out for Florence, Nebraska, to join a company headed for the Rocky Mountains. Sarah's son, Phineas, and her two-year-old daughter, Elizabeth, were part of the company, and Sarah

---

5. Gabriel Strang to John Wake Jr., Apr. 10, 1929, Clarke Historical Library.

6. Sarah Wing to Milo Quaife, [Spring] 1920.

7. Mark Strang to Russel Nye, May 12, 1960, Clarke Historical Library.

8. Special Collections, Clarke Historical Library.

9. Correspondence with a descendent of Joseph Smith Wing and his first wife, Rebecca Davis, 1999. Joseph S. Wing was born in Mecca, Trumball County, Ohio, on Sept. 18, 1830.

10. "LDS Church Records of Springville, Utah," *Record of Members, 1851-1892*, microfilm 0026459, Family History Library, Salt Lake City, Utah.

11. Ibid. Samuel Wing was the schoolmaster where Sarah's sister was teaching.

was pregnant with her third child. Joseph Wing's sixteen-year-old nephew, John, stowed way and remained hidden until the group was far enough along that he could not be sent back to Wisconsin.[12]

As the emigrants passed through Illinois, Sarah underwent an experience that must have badly shaken her confidence in her new husband. She agreed to accompany him on a visit to a family he said he knew in Clayton. They were greeted at the door of the house by a twelve-year-old girl. After questioning the girl and determining she was the only one at home, Wing slyly asked the girl if she would like to go riding with them, then picked her up and put her on the horse with him. The surprise for Sarah was that he never returned the girl to her home. He took her all the way to Salt Lake City.[13]

Sarah was appalled at her husband's actions, figuring he had kidnapped the young woman. When she demanded to know the reason for this action, she learned that Joseph S. Wing had been married previously and that the house they had visited belonged to his first wife. The young girl, Adelia, was his own daughter. Joseph had apparently intended to take both Adelia and her ten-year-old brother, Byron, to Utah, but the boy had not been at home.[14] Until this time, Sarah was unaware of the previous marriage. There was more to learn. Wing had not only married and divorced his first wife, but had married and abandoned two subsequent women before meeting Sarah. It dawned on the incredulous hearer of this news that she was in fact not his first wife as she had supposed—she was his fourth![15]

There is no way of telling how Sarah felt about this. She was twenty-four years old, pregnant, and had two children under six years of age. She was on her way to the Rocky Mountains, far away from her family's support system.

---

12. Wing family documents, "Joseph Smith Wing in Utah," *The Wing Family Website* (http://members.aol.com/lynnash911/Wing.html).

13. Ibid.

14. Ibid. Wing may have had a court order giving him custody of his children. Later on in her life, Adelia's mother traveled to Utah to see her.

15. Ibid. His wives were Rebecca Davis, Frances (unknown last name), and Signa Anderson, in that order. A descendent of Signa wrote in 1990 that his father maintained two households while married to Sarah Wright. Signa, living in a neighboring county, bore Joseph Smith Wing a son in 1858. Sarah bore him a daughter on Nov. 17, 1858, and married him two months later on January 1, 1859, according to Glen V. Smith, "Joseph and Signa: A Clash of Cultures," *Ancestors of the Smith Family of Wisconsin* (online at http://members.aol.com/Pionear504).

There was nothing she could do except proceed with the journey. The next stop on their trek was Florence, where they joined the Lewis Bronson Wagon Train Company headed for Salt Lake City. The Bronson company consisted of 212 people, 48 wagons, 75 yoke of oxen, 17 horses, 10 mules, and 68 cows. Joseph Wing served as one of the clerks and captain of the guard. The group left Florence on June 17, 1862.[16]

In May 1862, in either Florence, Nebraska, or on the plains of Wyoming, Sarah gave birth to her third child—a girl she named either Mary or May.[17] She carried another prized possession with her across the Great Plains—a small portrait of James Strang that he had given her at the time of their wedding in 1855.[18] The portrait was probably taken by Thomas Atkyn, one of the men who later conspired to have Strang killed.

The Bronson company arrived in Salt Lake City on August 29, 1862, thankfully without any "accident worthy of note" during their long journey. The *Deseret News* published the immigrants' names and belongings, including "Joseph Smith Wing, born in Ohio, age 31, doctor of medicine: one wagon; 2 oxen; 2 cows; no horse, mules or calves. Sarah A. Wing, born in Canada West, age 24; Adelia Wing, born Illinois, age 18; James Phineas Strang, born Wisconsin, age 5; Elizabeth Wing, born Illinois, age 2; Mary Arminta Wing, born New York, age 1 year; and Mercy Ross, born in England, age 21, died June 22, 1862."[19] According to Wing family descendants, Joseph listed his daughter's age as eighteen so he could not be arrested for kidnapping. The new baby was inaccurately recorded as having been born in New York a year earlier.

Sarah and Joseph moved first to the town of Lehi in Utah County and then farther south to Fairview in Sanpete County, but eventually settled down in Springville, about five miles south of Provo. Sarah taught school to help make ends meet. She also learned the medical profession from her husband and aided friends and neighbors with their health problems. She may have had some prior familiarity with medicine since two of her ancestors had been physicians.[20] While she lived in Springville, she gave birth to four more chil-

---

16. *Deseret News,* Sept. 3, 1862.

17. Wing family documents; also "LDS Church Records of Springville, Utah."

18. Zenas Wright interview, May 25, 1920.

19. *Deseret News,* Sept. 3, 1862.

20. Eugenia Phillips to Mrs. N. A. Williams, "Genealogical Correspondence of Mrs. N. A. Williams," microfilm 1597819, item 17, Family History Library.

dren—Joseph Smith Wing Jr. in 1864, Sarah (Sadie) in 1867, Benjamin in 1869, and Amanda in 1872.[21]

Joseph Wing grew somewhat restless over time and began making forays into the surrounding mountains to prospect for gold. He had some success at it as the first to extract gold in 1865 from the Marysvale area of Paiute County. He later discovered the famous Flagstaff mines in Cottonwood Canyon, east of Salt Lake Valley and realized a "considerable fortune" for this discovery. When he sold out his claims, he received $40,000, a considerable amount in the 1870s.[22]

Two years after the Wing family arrived in Utah, Joseph was asked by church officials to participate in polygamy. Sarah must have found this to be disturbing, having renounced polygamy after James Strang's death in 1856. Nevertheless, within the next four years, Sarah stood by while her husband married six more women.[23] Wing's nephew Samuel, who married Sarah's sister, also participated in polygamy.[24] Gradually finding that she was unhappy in her marriage and particularly disturbed by polygamy, Sarah separated from Joseph sometime in the late 1860s or early 1870s.[25] In 1872 she set up her own medical practice inside her home in Springville, Utah. She was thirty-six years old and had seven children. Her oldest, James Phineas, was only sixteen. Joseph paid for Sarah's house with his earnings in the gold field. "I bought city lots and the best of land in and around Springville, Utah, and built my families, four in number, good new houses, bought them stock and house furnishings amounting to over twenty thousand dollars," Wing later wrote.[26] A few years later, the doctor and prospector tried to renew his relationship with Sarah, but she refused to have anything to do with him.[27]

According to a legend maintained by the Wing family, Joseph became bitter toward the Mormon Church in 1890 when it renounced polygamy. For

---

21. Wing family documents; also "LDS Church Records of Springville, Utah."

22. Wing family documents.

23. Ibid.; also Ancestral File database, Family History Library, on-line at *Family Search* (www.familysearch.org). Joseph Smith Wing's plural wives were Mary Josephine Allen (married 1864), Anena Sophia Bohne (married 1866), Amelia Hendricksen, Ellen Larsen, Elizabeth Marshall, and Frances Anna McCurdy.

24. Wing family documents.

25. Ibid.; also Zenas Wright interview, May 25, 1920.

26. Wing family documents.

27. Zenas Wright interview, May 25, 1920.

refusing to follow church council about selecting one of his plural wives to settle down with, the church excommunicated him. The seventy-year-old man told his family he had only one request when he died: "Bury me far enough away from those damn Mormons, so I don't have to be around them." His wish was granted. Joseph Smith Wing was buried by himself in the Kingston town cemetery, situated on a hill in remote Paiute County. An iron railing surrounds his grave.[28]

At a time when it was unusual for women to work in a profession, Sarah Wright became a respected physician in Springville, earning as much as $2,500 a year.[29] She officiated at the birth of hundreds of children, including her own grandchildren. "She pulled hundreds of adults through the prevalent diseases. She was known as Dr. S. A. Wing and was generally respected and revered," recalled Sarah's grandson Mark Strang.[30]

Although she lived and worked in the Mormon community, Sarah and at least two of her seven children became disenchanted with the Mormon Church and left it.[31] Nor did Sarah remain true to her Strangite beliefs. Her thoughts on this, as she communicated them to Quaife, were unequivocal:

> The people who were more strong in their faith looked to the lord to send a successor to Strang to lead them aright, but no successor ever came. I made up my mind in time that my husband was like some other men who sought to build up a kingdom in the midst of a republic. I got fearful that my son [,] [who] of course ... was not born when his father died, [might] find his father's books and writings. Try to follow in his footsteps. I thought if the lord wanted my son to do any work, he was abundantly able to tell him so without any old books or manuscripts of his father's. So when I was very sick, the doctors told me I could never recover. I told my people to gather up all James' books and papers and burn them up.[32]

Until Sarah's son James was nearly grown, he was unaware of who his true father was.[33] "She raised him, under the name Wing along with her other

---

28. Wing family documents.

29. Milo M. Quaife's notes, Clarke Historical Library, Dec. 11, 1919.

30. Mark Strang to Manilla Brown, editor, *Springville Herald*, July 9, 1961, Clarke Historical Library.

31. "LDS Church Records of Springville, Utah." Sarah's daughter, Elizabeth Wing, was excommunicated on March 1, 1878.

32. Sarah Wing to Milo Quaife, June 28, 1920.

33. Ibid.

children, and until he was about to be married, she guarded the secret of his name and lineage—not from shame, but for fear the enemies of Strang among the leaders of the Utah church might wreck their rage on the son, and perhaps the mother," her grandson explained. After their marriage, James P. Strang and his wife joined the Presbyterian Church in Springville and raised their family of seven children in that faith. Their children were educated in Protestant schools.[34] In the 1890s the Strangite apostle Lorenzo Dow Hickey appeared at James's door and tried to convince him to take his father's place at the head of the church. "He spent several weeks with us in 1894. I was 10 years old at the time," recalled James's son, Mark, "and [Hickey's] sincerity and dedication to James Jesse Strang made a lasting impression." In fact, Hickey referred to the prophet as "St. James" and "his account of a life consecrated to the service of mankind placed my grandfather alongside the holiest of the Bible Saints," Mark wrote.[35]

For Hickey, the reunion with the son and namesake of the prophet was a moving experience. "James P. Strang of Springville is a fine man; the very picture of his father," the disciple wrote. "I met him in tears of joy and he received me in gladness! He told me in plain words that he was glad I found them as he had not heard nor seen any man to speak a word in defense of his honorable father." James told Hickey he would give Strangism "an honest investigation and do it with due care." He even spoke of dreams he had experienced in which it appeared the same spirit that had fallen on his father would fall on him.[36]

Hickey spent several weeks in James's home trying to persuade him to take up the leadership of the Strangite Church, but James finally refused. "My father," Mark Strang wrote, "knew he did not have the necessary education. He did not decline for lack of admiration and respect for his father." Mark said he found Lorenzo Dow Hickey likeable. "Even in his advanced age his mind was keen and alert and his enthusiasm was inspiring," Mark remembered.[37] "I was pulling for him in his effort to persuade my father to accept leadership of the Strangite movement. But my grandmother Sarah was

34. Mark Strang to Russel Nye, May 12, 1960.

35. Excerpts of letters copied by Mark Strang, dated Dec. 17, 1956, Clarke Historical Library.

36. Ibid.

37. Mark Strang to Russel Nye, May 12, 1960.

against it and father remained adamant in his rejection of the offer," he later wrote.[38] Although Sarah had loved the prophet James Strang to the point of adoration when he was alive, she could not bring herself to advise her son to assume the risks, according to another account of her cautionary advice.[39] In 1904, James P. Strang and his wife, Lydia Houtz, moved to Claresholm, Alberta, Canada.[40]

Living in Utah most of her adult life, Sarah Wright had little contact with James Jesse Strang's other wives and children. The exception was her cousin, Phoebe Wright, whom Sarah visited in Salt Lake City in 1896. However, Sarah disliked talking about her experiences on Beaver Island and what had happened to the Strangite people.[41] "I have always refused to give magazine writers any information on the subject. So many of them exaggerate and write things that are not true," Sarah told Quaife in 1920.[42] She carried on a lengthy correspondence with Quaife, who visited her in Utah two years before her death. "I had faith that James was a prophet of God and would not do wrong. I don't believe today that God ever speaks to any men," Sarah asserted to Quaife. "When the lord has done nothing for our church in 63 or 64 years we think differently."[43] Sarah died in Boise, Idaho, at the home of her daughter Amanda on August 18, 1923. She was eighty-seven years old.[44]

"It is true that she did not embrace the Utah Mormon faith," Mark Strang wrote of his grandmother. Nevertheless, he detected she had "remained faithful to Strang's underlying religious convictions and high moral standards and lived very much by his philosophy. Regardless of material gain," he added, "she helped wherever help was needed with her medical skill and profound wisdom." Mark had come to accept the view of his grandfather's life as dedicated to the betterment of the world, and so, too, that of his grandmother. "She, too, devoted her life to the service of mankind. She admonished me always to think of my grandfather as a good man and reiterated time without number, 'He was a good man.'"[45]

---

38. Mark Strang to Stanley Johnston, June 3, 1955, Clarke Historical Library.
39. Excerpts of letters copied by Mark Strang.
40. Mark Strang to Manilla Brown, July 9, 1961.
41. Mark Strang to RLDS Church archives, Oct. 15, 1952, Clarke Historical Library.
42. Sarah Wing to Milo Quaife, June 28, 1920.
43. Sarah Wing to Milo Quaife, [spring] 1920.
44. Eugenia Phillips to Mrs. N. A. Williams.
45. Mark Strang to Russel Nye, May 12, 1960.

Mark repeated on another occasion that his grandmother "never had anything but the highest praise for James Jesse Strang." In Mark's view, "her unhappy second marriage to a Dr. Wing" was probably what "soured her on religion in any form." As Sarah Strang was approaching the end of her life, Mark "asked her what she thought about life beyond the grave. She replied, 'I don't know. But I have always done the best I could and I am sure that if there is a reward after death I shall receive mine and if not, I won't know anything about it.'"[46] It was a more cynical eschatological view than might have been expected of the wife of a prophet—not a view she would have developed on Beaver Island. But time and adversity had found a way of forcing Sarah and other Strangites to think deeply about their faith, each one coming to his or her own conclusions and for reasons known more-or-less only to themselves.

---

46. Mark Strang to Stanley Johnston, June 3, 1955.

20

PHOEBE WRIGHT STRANG JESSE

A LIFETIME OF DEVOTION

> *"My mother, Phoebe Wright, was*
> *the last woman he [Strang] married and I, her only child. She never*
> *married again. We lived with her parents until I married. She then lived*
> *with me. We seldom talked of father, though she loved him sincerely."*
> —Eugenia Jesse Phillips.[1]

Phoebe Wright was at James Strang's bedside in Voree when he died on July 9, 1856. Five months pregnant, she moved with her parents and other family members to Racine, Wisconsin, then to Black River Falls, where her daughter, Eugenia, was born on October 28. Phoebe may have named Eugenia after a baby sister who died in 1849 when Phoebe was thirteen years old.[2]

In order to "appear less conspicuous before the world" when they reached Black River Falls, Phoebe dropped her last name, Strang, and used her husband's middle name instead, thereby becoming Phoebe Jesse. She thought it would not be long before the Saints would be gathered together and she could again assume the name Strang, but that time never came.[3] For the rest of her life, she lived either with her parents or her daughter. In Wrightsville she taught school for about four years, then took charge of her parents' home when her mother, Margaret, became an invalid.[4] She wrote letters for her mother to keep track of scattered family members, especially

---

1. Eugenia Phillips to Stanley Johnston, Oct. 31, 1936, Clarke Historical Library, Central Michigan University, Mount Pleasant, Michigan.

2. *Gospel Herald,* July 12, 1849. Eugenia Wright died before she was two years old.

3. Eugenia Phillips to Mrs. N. A. Williams, Genealogical Correspondence of Mrs. N. A. Williams, microfilm 1597819, item 17, Family History Library, Salt Lake City, Utah.

4. Eugenia Phillips to Milo Quaife, July 15, 1920, Clarke Historical Library.

her mother's sister, Rebecca, the wife of Samuel Wright, with whom Phoebe herself was exceptionally close.[5]

Phoebe's daughter, Eugenia, wrote about Benjamin and Margaret Wright that "no one could have loved a father and a mother more than I loved my grandparents, whose home was my home till the day of my marriage." She was impressed with her grandfather's "greatness of spirit, his kindness and generosity to the many men he employed in the large business he built up after a few years in the lumbering business while pioneering in Wisconsin. He with his two brothers and their families constituted a small community in themselves. He, the eldest and leader of the three in all matters of importance."[6]

One of the responsibilities Benjamin assumed was the protection and care of the unbound copies of The Book of the Law of the Lord which the Strangites had managed to bring with them from Beaver Island. Just before the outsiders tore out James Strang's printing press and forced the Mormons from their homes, Benjamin had boxed and shipped the unbound signatures to Racine. For a time, he may also have had possession of the small brass plates Strang translated in 1846, although the Voree plates later ended up in Betsy McNutt's possession.[7]

At least two of the Wright brothers, Benjamin and Samuel, practiced polygamy secretly while they lived in Alma and Wrightsville. Benjamin had three wives in addition to his legal wife, Margaret Finch. The other three wives were the widows of Clark Lyman Whitney who had died in Voree in the spring of 1851. Rhonda Whitney, Adeline Whitney, and Nancy Richardson married Benjamin in a triple wedding on July 9, 1853, on Beaver Island. Rhonda and Adeline were sisters, Nancy their maternal aunt.[8] Samuel Wright had one plural wife, Edna Chidester, to whom he was sealed on October 12, 1851. His legal wife was Rebecca Finch.

From the perspective of plural marriage, it is interesting Eugenia referred to her grandparents as two rather than five individuals, whom she also compared to a father and mother. Census records for Jackson County portray

---

5. Eugenia Phillips to Mrs. N. A. Williams.

6. Clement J. Strang, "Why I Am Not a Strangite," *Michigan History* (Fall 1942): 476-77.

7. Lorenzo Dow Hickey to Charles Strang, Mar. 2, 1879, Clarke Historical Library.

8. Correspondence with a descendant of Benjamin Wright. Benjamin may also have been married or sealed to Elizabeth Enoch, probably posthumously.

each wife in her own home, living nearby but not next door to each other. "When the Wrights got to Jackson County, they did not talk to their neighbors regarding their personal affairs and many simply did not know that they had been members of the Mormon Church," one modern-day descendent noted.[9] The children from these polygamous marriages were trained to keep the relationships secret. In fact, since the children were young when they arrived in Jackson County from Beaver Island, many of them may not have even known about these marital alliances.

On February 22, 1858, Frank Cooper, editor of the *Jackson County Banner*, paid a visit to "Uncle Ben," as Benjamin Wright was affectionately known. Few people who read Cooper's article would have known that the prosperous Wright family and most of the men who worked for them were former Mormons. Nor did they know that Cooper himself was a Mormon and an exile from Beaver Island. His article is particularly informative about the business interests of the Wright brothers.

> About 11 years ago B[enjamin]. G., Phineas and Samuel C. Wright and a family named Whitney, came to this country and located on homesteads near Black River Falls. After arriving here, they paid out their last dollar for something to live on. Being in possession of good health and stout hearts, they were just the kind of people for the life before them.... Phineas, Samuel and Uncle Ben's boys commenced cutting wood while Uncle Ben drove a yoke of oxen to haul the same to town, where they found a ready sale for it at $1.25 per cord....
>
> In a year or two they had comfortable homes in town, owned several span of horses and were doing a thrifty business hauling goods from Sparta and La Crosse for the village merchants.... Eight years later ... they purchased land, gristmill and sawmill on Halls Creek.... [T]he first payment took almost all the property they had amassed since locating here. By the following spring they had earned enough to pay off the old score....
>
> All hands went to work with a determination to succeed.... (Let us say here that it is the remark of all who know the Wrights that they never saw a more harmonious and intelligent and pleasant family in the west.) They continued to purchase pine lands and extend their lumbering operations just as fast as their means would permit ... several miles up and down the creek....
>
> In 1867 Uncle Ben commenced building a flouring mill ... 32 x 60 feet, four stories tall ... That mill, like the whole Wright family is solid and substantial, and will do its work well. They have a blacksmith shop, a grocery and provi-

---

9. Ibid.

sion store, several comfortable dwellings, and excellent stable rooms for their teams.... The majority of the family work there ... with about 60 men. Let us sum up a little—Uncle Ben and his "boys" as he calls them, own three first-rate saw mills, which are each capable of cutting 1,000 feet of lumber per hour, a grist mill, ... over 3,000 acres of pine lands, eight good mill sites on Hall's Creek, a thrifty village and in the course of time will have a railroad at their doors. Their property today is worth no less than $150,000.... Our party left Mr. Wright's pleasant home entirely satisfied with the visit and wishing that Jackson County had scores of such enterprising families."[10]

Benjamin, Phineas, and Samuel Wright became three of the most respected and influential men of Jackson and Trempealeau Counties. It was probably of some use that they regularly interacted with the editor of the newspaper, who met secretly with other Mormons for fifty years. Other former Strangites such as Anson Prindle also became prominent businessmen and community leaders. In all cases, they kept the secret of their past so well concealed that not even many of their descendants knew their parents had been affiliated with the Strangites on Beaver Island.[11]

In 1876, Phoebe's daughter, Eugenia, twenty years old, began teaching school in Black River Falls and made a home there for herself and her mother. When she married Thomas Phillips, an area businessman, Phoebe continued to live with them in Black River Falls. For a short time, Elvira's son, Clement Strang, also lived with Phoebe and the Phillipses while Clement published the *Independent*, another local newspaper. The *Independent* folded when it endorsed the prohibition of alcohol, much to the displeasure of the lumber town's work force.[12]

In July 1880 the determined former apostle of James Strang, Lorenzo Dow Hickey, paid a visit to the Strangites in northwestern Wisconsin. A conference was held for three days in the Mormon settlement of Knapp, after which Hickey visited his old friends, including Frank Cooper and Phoebe and Eugenia Strang. He wrote that he enjoyed this visit.[13]

In 1892 Eugenia's husband became the manager of a bank in Duluth, Minnesota. Phoebe accompanied them to Duluth and continued to live with

---

10. "A Visit to Wright's Mills," *Jackson County Banner,* Feb. 22, 1868.
11. Clement Strang, "Why I Am Not a Strangite," 476-77.
12. Clement Strang to Stanley Johnston, May 23, 1940, Clarke Historical Library.
13. Lorenzo Dow Hickey to Charles Strang, July 18, 1880, Clarke Historical Library.

them. Interestingly, the family relocated to Salt Lake City four years later for a two-year stint before moving on to Tacoma, Washington.[14] Over the more than two decades since Eugenia and Thomas married, Eugenia bore six children, two of whom died young.[15]

Phoebe Wright was considered to be a woman of "ambition" and "energy," according to her daughter. She had a "clear and vigorous" mind and took a great interest in city, state, and national affairs. When she was about sixty years old, she injured her hips in a fall and thereafter walked with a cane. "She was an ardent admirer of Theodore Roosevelt and once went leaning on her crutches to hear him give an address in Wright Park, Tacoma," Eugenia mentioned.[16] On November 9, 1914, at her daughter's home in Tacoma, Phoebe died at the age of seventy-eight.[17]

According to Eugenia Phillips, her grandfather Benjamin Wright gave up Mormonism entirely after James Strang died. Wright felt he had been deceived and "desired that father's name never be mentioned in his presence." On one occasion when he "talked to me of father," Eugenia reported, her grandfather said her father had been "a man of brilliant mind and a wonderful public speaker, holding his audience in rapt attention for hours at a time, and felt he might have aspired to the highest office our country could give him, had he staid by his legal practice and the interests of his country and kept away from Joseph Smith and his followers."[18] Although Benjamin may have renounced what he considered to have been religious pretension, he apparently did not renounce religion altogether. "I used to listen when a very small child to my grandfather converse with an occasional proselytizing Mormon calling on him," Eugenia recalled. "He quoted the bible profusely to show them their mistakes. Sometimes one of the orthodox types of religion called and he would 'lay them out' equally well. He was weary of man made doctrines.... He was particularly well versed on theological subjects, though not a professor of religion."[19]

Through a series of misfortunes, Benjamin Wright lost his extensive

---

14. Eugenia Phillips to Mrs. N. A. Williams.
15. "Looking Back: Jackson County's Ghost Towns," *Banner Journal*, Jan. 6, 13, 1993.
16. Eugenia Phillips to Milo Quaife, July 15, 1920.
17. Ibid.; also Eugenia Phillips to Mrs. N. A. Williams.
18. Eugenia Phillips to Stanley Johnston, Oct. 31, 1836.
19. Clement Strang, "Why I Am Not a Strangite," 478-79.

property in northwestern Wisconsin and ended up living with his children for a number of years. When he died in 1900 at the age of ninety-one, his obituary read, "He was a man of broad intelligence and extensive knowledge, and possessed the courage of his convictions."[20]

A living descendent of Benjamin Wright believes the Wright family continued to privately hold to their beliefs and "simply ceased to belong to any organized religion." According to this woman, "the principles of Mormonism continued to be taught to the Wright children, long after Strang." She gives herself as an example, saying she was taught Mormonism at her grandmother's knee, her grandmother being Louisa Wright's daughter. At the time, she did not know it was Mormonism, the woman relates. Now a member of the Utah church, she believes the teachings that are still being taught in the family today are those that were treasured by her forefathers.[21]

---

20. Benjamin Wright obituary.
21. Correspondence with descendant of Benjamin Wright.

THE EARTH AND ITS FULLNESS

> *"Albert Field says polygamy had lit-*
> *tle to do with driving the Mormons from Beaver Island; that 'consecra-*
> *tion' did the fatal work. 'The flocks that feed on a thousand hills are the*
> *Lord's and we are the Lord's people. The Lord's flocks are to feed the*
> *Lord's people, and all that is necessary is for the Lord's people to help*
> *themselves.' 'Thou shalt not steal,' but you may help yourself (consecrate)*
> *to anything that belongs to a Gentile."* —Charles J. Strang.[1]

For the past 150 years, historians have debated whether or not the Mormons on Beaver Island were guilty of the atrocious acts of theft and piracy that were attributed to them. The descendants of the gentiles who were driven away and then returned to evict the Strangites have answered with an unqualified "yes" and offered proof—newspaper articles and personal recollections passed down over the years. They say the Mormons were thieves and pirates and deserved what they got. The descendants of the Strangites offer up another set of documents as proof their ancestors were not guilty of the multitude of acts attributed to them. They point out that the Mormons were the ones who were attacked and thousands of dollars worth of their property was seized and never returned. Indeed, the sheer number of claims and the distances involved make it highly unlikely the Strangites could possibly have been involved in all the acts they were accused of.

The truth probably lies at both ends. If the Strangites were not guilty of all these crimes, neither were the gentiles. Unscrupulous fishermen undoubtedly stole from both groups. Northern Michigan was the hinterland of civilization in the 1850s. Like frontiers everywhere, it attracted its share of lawless men who were hiding out not only for crimes they had committed elsewhere but from life in general. There were opportunists in every settlement looking for easy money and who were willing to do anything to get it.

No, the Mormons on Beaver Island were not guilty of everything, but

---

1. Charles Strang memo or diary entry, Dec. 26, 1898, Clarke Historical Library, Central Michigan University, Mount Pleasant, Michigan.

they were probably guilty of some of the criminal deeds. The evidence is in the historical record—the letters, diaries, and personal recollections of both gentiles and Strangites who were on or near Beaver Island at the time. The residents of Mackinac Island and other settlements in the Great Lakes were convinced that some of the Strangites were thieves. M. L. Leach, author of a history of the region, interviewed a number of people, gentile and Mormon, for his 1883 serialization in the *Grand Traverse Herald*. He wrote that Strang's "subjects consisted of several classes":

> The most numerous class, but not the most influential in the affairs of the church or the commonwealth, were the sincere believers in the original and fundamental doctrines of Mormonism, and in [Strang's] divine mission and office as the successor of Joseph Smith. To them, he was really prophet, priest, and king. His advice was sought and followed in all matters, temporal and spiritual. His word was law. No sacrifice was too great to be made if the prophet advised it; no crime too revolting to be committed if the king commanded it. In their view it was no crime. Not only could the king do no wrong, but an act of obedience to his authority could not be wrong, no matter how cruel or unjust it might be to a 'Gentile,' or how wicked, judged by 'Gentile' standards of morality.
>
> Another class, comparatively small in numbers but in influence more potent than the former, consisted of unprincipled men, whose adherence to Mormonism rose, not from conviction of its truth as a religious system, but from the opportunities it afforded for unbridled license under the pretended sanction of religion. These men were the willing tools of Strang. Without being themselves deceived by his profession of having a divine commission, they helped to fasten the deception upon others. The most important trusts were sometimes committed to persons of this sort, and they were usually chosen for leaders in the execution of projects likely to be distasteful to persons of tender conscience and large philanthropy.
>
> A third class, neither numerous or influential, consisted of those who were at first sincere believers in Mormonism, but whose faith had been shaken or wholly destroyed by the doctrines and practices taught by Strang and his followers, and who remained upon the island from inability to get away. An apostatizing or dissatisfied Mormon might leave, but he was not allowed to take away his property. That was 'consecrated,' that is, confiscated, for the benefit of the church.[2]

---

2. M. L. Leach, "A History of the Grand Traverse Region," *Grand Traverse Herald*, 1883, 87-90, Clarke Historical Library.

Leach said the "consecrating of Gentile" property, or "robbing of those who were not Mormons," was an established practice from the earliest settlement of the island until the time of Strang's death. "It was the natural and legitimate sequence of the doctrine that the Mormons were God's peculiar people, who alone had a right to the earth and were eventually to possess it, and that the 'Gentiles' were to be 'stricken with a continual stroke,'" Leach wrote.

The Strangite "plundering operations" were supposedly conducted with utmost organizational discipline by officers called "destroying angels." The outside world knew this group by the harmless name of deacons. "Brothers were generally chosen for destroying angels, as they were more likely to stand by each other in times of danger," Leach continued.

> Every Mormon was under obligation to go on a thieving or marauding expedition when ordered to do so by a destroying angel. The destroying angels were under the direct supervision of Strang himself and the expeditions were always done under his supervision. When any party or individual discovered a good opportunity for obtaining plunder it was reported to him, but nothing was done without his approval. When booty was brought in it was usually taken to the residence of some one participating in the expedition, where a division was made, one tenth being set apart for the use of the church. The remaining nine-tenths became the property of the plunderers....

Leach said that for the practice to be carried out with ease and safety, a network of "forts" was set up in lakeside towns. A fort was usually the home of someone who professed to have renounced Mormonism in order to gain the sympathy of the gentiles. The home became a safe haven for spies and emissaries of the deacons. At one time there were no less than twelve of these forts in the city of Chicago alone. According to the people Leach talked to, immense quantities of "consecrated" goods—dry goods, leather, fishing nets, horses, cattle—were periodically delivered to Beaver Island to be used by the Mormons. The author claimed to have testimony from some of the earliest Mormons on the island who said they saw plundered goods and used them themselves. "It is not probable that the Mormons were guilty of every case of wrong charged to them," Leach wrote. "On the other hand, it is not probable that their worst deeds, in all of their enormity, have been brought to light."[3]

The Strangites and their descendants vehemently denied there were ever

---

3. Leach, "History of the Grand Traverse," 89-92.

"destroying angels" or secret forts where plundered goods could be taken. In fact, it is significant that piracy continued unabated in the Great Lakes after the Mormons were driven from the island. But statements made by Strangites who lived on the island seem to indicate that some sort of stealing or "consecration" did take place. Samuel Graham wrote to James Strang in 1851 after leaving Beaver Island: "I have stayed there and been growled at by lazy loungers as long as I will and in Saying this to you, I don't want you to think that I complain of anything that you could have done and have not, so I do not complain: But James we must have men that will work and not Steal if we would build up a kingdom or church."[4]

Stephen Post, a Strangite who left the church because of polygamy, wrote to his brother, Warren, an apostle, giving another indication that forced consecration was practiced on the island. "You know [Strang] gave license to his followers to go out and rob the gentiles and received part of the plunder. At whose hands shall the blood of those be required whose ship was sunk in the harbor or near by?" he wrote. "Oh, how the heart sickens to call up the dark and damning crimes of those calling themselves saints. Heaven weeps and the earth was turned back into its old silence and the sound of the gospel scarcely heard in her for its very weakness."[5]

The concept of consecration had its roots in the Bible. In its purest form, consecration was the dedication of personal property to the Lord for the benefit of his church. But already during the early days of the Mormon Church, it had become synonymous with stealing. The practice was mainly associated with taking possessions belonging to gentiles to make up for the items Mormons had lost at their hands. In 1837-38, a highly secretive society of Mormon men called the Danites, or "Sons of Dan," was organized in Missouri, mainly to "convince" dissenting and excommunicated members of the church not to fraternize with gentiles and to leave areas where "faithful" Mormons were living. The Danites were bound together by secret oaths and signals and were sworn to uphold the church and each other to the point of death. They later expanded the purpose of the organization to wreak vengeance upon the enemies of the Mormons under the premise that stealing from gentiles was

---

4. Samuel Graham to James Strang, July 10, 1851, folder 347, James Jesse Strang Collection, Yale Collection of Western Americana, Beinecke Rare Book and Manuscript Library, Yale University, New Haven, Connecticut.

5. Stephen Post to Warren Post, Feb. 15, 1857, Library-Archives, Community of Christ, Independence, Missouri.

sanctioned by God as recompense for loss. Although the Mormon prophet Joseph Smith claimed to have no connection to such activities, he has been implicated by association in the research of some recent historians.[6]

It is not known whether the Danite organization, as such, continued along similar lines on Beaver Island, but several Strangites, including brothers Finley and Ebeneezer Page, had been Danites in Missouri or Illinois. Finley was one of five Mormon men from Monmouth, Illinois, found guilty of stealing from the gentiles in 1841. Finley was excommunicated for his actions but was rebaptized two years later.[7]

Elvira Field discussed the doctrine of consecration with her children as they were growing up. Clement Strang, Elvira's son, said there were some who acknowledged having taken gentile property such as fishing outfits and other items with the purpose of getting the gentiles to leave. "I know that this 'consecration' was not considered stealing. It was 'justified' by Bible passages," Clement explained. "Many of the saints could not reconcile it with the teachings of Jesus; and it took a special discourse on the subject, in which the King's word was exalted as the highest authority.... In this way James made himself supreme in the thought of all the people, and they did God service by obeying him. It was the same as using the enemy's goods to support the army in time of war."[8]

Elvira's oldest son, Charles, recalled a conversation with Lorenzo Dow Hickey. Charles lamented the adoption and practice of polygamy, which he felt had been the cause of their troubles, culminating in their dispersal in 1856. Hickey responded by telling Charles that polygamy was not the cause. "What then, was the cause?" Charles asked. Hickey's answer was evasive. "At that time I did not fully comprehend the meaning of 'consecration' as I have since learned it," Charles wrote, "but I had heard the word, and asked if that [had] anything to do with it. Hickey's "answer was not direct, but was a

---

6. See, e.g., D. Michael Quinn, *The Mormon Hierarchy: Origins of Power* (Salt Lake City: Signature Books and Smith Research Associates, 1994), 92-103.

7. William Shepard, "Stealing at Mormon Nauvoo," a paper presented at the John Whitmer Historical Association conference, Sept. 30, 2005, in Springfield, Illinois, copy in author's possession. In a list of known or suspected Danites, Quinn (*Mormon Hierarchy: Origins,* 479-85) includes early Strangites Daniel Avery and Jared Carter. It is possible that other Strangites were Danites in Missouri and Illinois, especially if Quinn is right that Nauvoo's police and militia officers were Danites.

8. Clement Strang to Stanley Johnston, July 17, 1938, Clark Historical Library.

strong defense and justification of the practice and was truly a surprise to me. From that [,] I began to look up the word and the practice and find that it meant much more than he dared to tell me."

Charles felt "such a reply from one in his position, who should have been able to deny and dispute all dishonest charges, did much to convince me that the charges were true, and that under the guise of consecrating property" they "were actually guilty of stealing." In Charles's view, you can "call those actions by whatever name you will; justify by whatever philosophy or logic; in the plain common language of common people it is nothing but thievery."[9]

Elvira told her sons the natural instinct of the people was to refuse this teaching, "but their confidence in their King and prophet, led them to try his way and demonstrate his statements of divine truth." According to her son Clement, it was for this reason many of the Strangites believed God had become displeased with Strang and allowed him to be taken from the earth.[10]

Clement said that when he was small, he overheard his mother talking about consecration to her brother and his wife:

I knew it was something that had hurt their consciences, and that they bore it because they had been brought up to believe the words and follow the instructions of the King and Prophet to the last detail. If Father had not quoted scripture in support of the practice, which began with the taking of the fish and nets of the Islanders, they would have felt different about it. But he quoted Moses in his instruction to the people on leaving Egypt instructing them in the method of "spoiling the Egyptians." The object of course was to drive them off the Island. And if they could have accomplished that they would have gone on with their living on the Island; and among themselves they would have been as brotherly as were the people when the Christian Church was founded.[11]

The Strangites took what was theirs by virtue of being God's peculiar people, Clement wrote on another occasion. "They called it consecration: which means to them the gift of God, used for the glory of God in the affairs of his peculiar people."[12]

Clement said his mother and her brother, Albert, were reluctant to talk

9. Charles J. Strang to Wingfield Watson, Sept. 29, 1895, Clarke Historical Library.

10. Clement Strang to Stanley Johnston, Oct. 1, 1938, Clarke Historical Library.

11. Clement Strang to Stanley Johnston, Mar. 3, 1940, Clarke Historical Library.

12. Clement J. Strang, "Why I Am Not a Strangite," *Michigan History* (Fall 1942): 471-72; also Clement Strang to Stanley Johnston, Jan. 6, 1942, Clarke Historical Library.

about what had transpired on the island, but when they did, it was with an air of sadness and deep regret. Elvira answered her children's questions with honesty. She told them the principle of consecration seemed "strange" to her—so different from the teachings of Joseph Smith, with whom her family had associated themselves when she was a child.[13] Clement wrote:

> We children began to hear the incidents of the past talked over in the family; and while there was much we could not understand, the way these "deep" items were spoken of showed us that the past was full of regrets, and problems that demanded, and sometimes disturbed faith. We realized that there was not perfect agreement as to steadfastness in the Mormon Faith. Sometimes Uncle Albert would become very angry and make the room resound with swear-words, swinging his fist and pounding the table; and continue in this fit of anger for many minutes. We children were afraid. But when the better things of life were under discussion he seemed to have fairly good judgement.[14]

Albert Field claimed polygamy had had little to do with driving the Mormons from Michigan, that it was the practice of "consecration" that did the "fatal work." This was according to his nephew Charles Strang, after having visited "Uncle Bert" and "Aunt Jane" in February 1879. "Had a long talk about father and matters on Beaver Island," he wrote about his visit. "Bert claims that father was either crazy on the subject of religion or was willfully and maliciously leading these people along to glorify his own name and raise up a nation or kingdom to be entirely free from every other government," which would then be "entirely under his control. As for [Strang] being God's servant to rule the people," Charles wrote, "Bert did not believe he was ever called except by his own volition."[15]

The trio talked over the issue of consecration, and Albert revealed the *modus operandi* for building God's kingdom on Beaver Island:

> Men who were unwilling to work as honest industrious men should were "consecrated" to go on certain missions. The principle work of these missions was to bring to the island everything which the saints could make use [of,] which they could get hold of, no matter by what means—in other words: Stealing. The doctrine of "consecration" was publicly preached by Strang, and men who were

---

13. Ibid.

14. Clement Strang to Stanley Johnston, July 27, 1942, Clarke Historical Library.

15. Charles Strang diary entry, Feb. 23, 1879, Clarke Historical Library.

most successful in consecrating the property of the Gentiles were rewarded by offices in the church.[16]

Albert told his nephew about one incident when two gentiles were punished for some offense against Mormons by being cast adrift in Beaver Harbor. The men's hands were tied and they were put in an open boat without oars or paddle. A strong wind was blowing across the lake. "The men finally landed at Mackinaw and organized the mob which broke up the community in 1856 and killed Strang," Albert claimed. Charles added that "in a conversation with Warren Post and Frank Cooper about this affair, Post and Cooper both expressed the opinion that no matter what their belief had been, this affair made them skeptical."[17]

Uncle Albert continued by telling his nephew that "Strang was elected to the legislature by the most unblushing fraud. Hundreds of names were voted who never had seen existence in that county or district." Charles was reminded of a story Albert had told Clement two years previously, "that at some polls small boys eight and ten years old voted without challenge and thus helped to swell Strang's majority."[18] Charles concluded his narrative by pointing out that this was "Uncle Bert's story. Until it is corroborated by other reliable witnesses, it will be well to make large allowances for deviation from truth. Not being friendly to the doctrines, and many times having trouble with members of the society[,] he cannot be considered an impartial judge. He is also a very violent man in expressing his opinion, especially when he dislikes any person or thing."[19]

Charles's brother Clement maintained that some of the Strangites continued to practice "consecration" long after they were driven from Beaver Island. Clement related how the Strangite apostle Lorenzo Dow Hickey and two of his sons, along with Betsy McNutt's son, Gabriel Strang, operated a business stealing horses and buggy outfits. Hickey himself told Clement some of the details of their activities during a visit Clement made to Hickey's home in Coldwater, Michigan, in the early 1880s.

---

16. Ibid.

17. Ibid. Albert told Charles "it was also regretted that Elvira (mother) was not with [Strang] when he died to know if he would make a will and for whose benefit." According to Albert, "Strang's mother Abigail did not think James was in his right mind on religious subjects."

18. Ibid.

19. Ibid.

One of Hickey's arguments, put forward with the most appealing enthusiasm, was this practice of consecration. Knowing that he had sons in the larger figures of the teenage, or possibly old enough to vote, I asked him as to their whereabouts. After some hesitation he finally revealed to me that they had been doing a very prosperous business in consecrating.... He related that they and Gabriel Strang were doing time in the Ohio State Prison. He stated that a mere accident led to their capture; but that on the whole, they were wise and skillful, and the blessing of God had followed them.[20]

Hickey allegedly said the three young men would go to various towns looking for particularly "fine-looking" horses and buggies. When they found one and determined the owner had left and would not return for awhile, the young men would unhitch the conveyance and take off with it. Their first stop was usually Hickey's barn in Coldwater, twelve miles from the Indiana state line, where the horse and buggy would immediately be hidden away in the barn. The following night, the three young men would drive the horse and buggy to Comstock, Michigan, just east of Kalamazoo, where another apostle, Edward Chidester, would assist in the "consecration business." The two young Hickeys and Gabriel Strang would put up for the day at Chidester's home, then continue to Grand Rapids, fifty miles north, to another Strangite "horse and buggy barn." After a night's rest there, the young men would complete their journey to a "thriving village north of Grand Rapids, Michigan," where for a discount price the people were "providing themselves with the best in family conveyances."

"After the horses and buggy were sold, the young men would separate and return to Coldwater by train using different routes. The three young men would then rejoin and bring the proceeds of the sale to Lorenzo Dow Hickey. Hickey would divide the 'spoils,' which were so great a blessing from God that the young men's best service after a brief rest would be to get up and at it again," Clement explained.[21] He offered his opinion of the affair.

Hickey had previously told me of the wisdom and consummate skill these consecraters had exhibited in their line of divine service; and how the blessing of God had followed them. When I failed in the response he anticipated, he seemed to think me devoid of common sense and good judgment....

---

20. Clement Strang, "Why I Am Not a Strangite," 475. Another informant in Coldwater also told Clement about the Hickey boys and Gabriel Strang being in prison.

21. Ibid.

Hickey really wanted me to be baptized and receive his apostolistic blessing, and join with them in "building up the kingdom." … He said he laid hands
on the heads of the boys, and sent them forth with the divine blessing; and then
he related how God protected them.[22]

In an attempt to show Clement the wisdom and skill these young men
had shown in their consecration trips, Hickey told him about one adventure
he was particularly proud of. The young Strangites observed a splendid
young horse and new buggy standing at the hitching-post and saw that the
owner had gone several blocks away. They had plenty of time to get away before the owner would know his property was gone. "But it chanced that this
new buggy with its new style thimble-skein had not been lubricated recently,"
Hickey said. "They observed that one wheel was sliding, leaving a distinct
mark in the road that could be easily followed." Being resourceful, the three
found a small, but strong fence rail, and used that to make the wheel turn.
The mechanism proved strong enough to get them through to Coldwater
where repairs could be made for the remainder of the journey.[23]

When Clement Strang related this story to Hickey's youngest son, Joseph, who had been only about three years old at the time the events were said
to have occurred, Joseph called the story a lie. He criticized Clement for waiting to tell such tales until all the people who could deny them were already
dead. Another Strangite who had not lived on Beaver Island, Stanley Johnston, claimed he had written to the Ohio State Prison and found there was no
record of the Hickey boys or Gabriel Strang ever having been in prison there.
"Then I regretted that I had not explained that a part of the wisdom of these
consecraters was the making of their adventures under an assumed name,"
Clement wrote.[24] In fact, "Hickey himself, told me that they worked under assumed names for the safety of the family in case they were caught." Clement
mentioned that he had corroboration from Edward Chidester, who "talked
the same [matter] over with me after he had quit."[25] Continuing, Clement
wrote:

---

22. Clement Strang to Stanley Johnston, Apr. 23, 1937, Clarke Historical Library.

23. Clement Strang, "Why I Am Not a Strangite," 475.

24. Clement Strang to Stanley Johnston, May 9, 1937; also his "Why I Am Not a
Strangite," 477.

25. Clement Strang to Stanley Johnston, July 17, 1938. Clement said Edward Chidester's mother admitted the family had participated in consecrating horses and buggies.

I had no desire to report these people for I knew they did not have regular criminal feelings in their hearts. They felt that they had been robbed by gentiles, and that God did not wish them to take all this hardship without opposition. I said nothing because I knew God had a plan by which to make evil reveal its own nature and bring its own punishment. Moreover I have heard my mother explain it [consecration] to all us children, after we attained age to understand, and [told us] to avoid talking about it to people where harm would come to anybody. I have heard my Uncle Albert tell of his share in a few of these consecration expeditions and how they came out.[26]

A letter from Charles Strang to Eugenia Jesse in 1879 provides additional evidence that Clement had spoken the truth about Gabriel Strang. In the letter, Charles denounced the teaching of "consecration" and told his half-sister he had learned their brother Gabriel was then in prison "for doing that which father taught."[27] Other evidence comes from the historian Milo Quaife. In his notes, Quaife wrote that Gabriel Strang, under the alias 'James Hartley,' served a term in the Ohio State penitentiary for 'consecration' in 1880.[28] Quaife discovered that Gabriel actually served two prison sentences for stealing horses. The second conviction occurred on January 28, 1910, in Grand Rapids, Michigan. Under the alias George Sage, Gabriel was sentenced to three to ten years.[29]

Quaife obtained the correspondence between Gabriel and his attorney, A. E. Ewing. Gabriel and Ewing became good friends and corresponded regularly during the four years Gabriel was incarcerated in the Michigan Reformatory in Ionia. Ewing said that at fifty-one years of age, Gabriel was a quiet, harmless appearing man, "the very last [person] one would pick out as a robber of horses." Ewing said Gabriel "was very intelligent and much traveled.... He thought people would not give him a chance once they learned his name was Strang and felt from childhood that his people had been persecuted."

---

26. Clement Strang to Stanley Johnston, July 17, 1938.

27. Charles Strang to E. E. Jessie [Eugenia Jesse], Dec. 1879, Clark Historical Library.

28. Milo M. Quaife's notes, Clark Historical Library.

29. A. E. Ewing to Milo Quaife, Apr. 9, 1919, Clarke Historical Library. The writing in this letter is very faint. The date of Gabriel's conviction could have been Jan. 18 instead of Jan. 28. For an account of Gabriel's arrest and conviction, see the *Grand Rapids Press,* Jan. 3, 1910, and *Detroit Journal,* Friday, Jan. 28, [1910]; also C. A. Engelbracht to Milo Quaife, Apr. 5, 1919, Clarke Historical Library.

In a series of letters he sent to Ewing during the years 1910-14 while he was incarcerated, Gabriel, as George Sage, outlined his life story and the history of the Strangites. He recounted his father's shooting. "Gabriel was a small boy when the murder, as he termed it, was committed. He was not old enough to realize the full import of it but could remember the grief of his mother, and how they were afterwards driven from pillar to post," Ewing wrote to Milo Quaife.[30] Gabriel recalled how his mother, Betsy McNutt, had carried the small brass plates to Wisconsin after the Saints were banished from Beaver Island and how she had hidden them. Ewing told Quaife about the felon's state of mind.

> Gabriel told me one day he grew up in the belief that his father and his sect had been persecuted and that his mother had been made to suffer by being shut out of society, and that her children had been compelled to fight their way against the prejudices of the public and at such a disadvantage that he always felt a grudge against society, and that this feeling had much to do with the life he had led. He was simply getting even in an underhanded way since he had no chance to be heard or be believed in open society. He always felt that he was condemned as soon as he was known to be a Strang and that accounted for his use of the alias George Sage.[31]

Gabriel Strang was released on probation in 1914, but within a few months had left the state, taking "French leave," as Milo Quaife called it. Wingfield Watson "[has] heard from Gabriel since he skipped parole, but gives me no information," Quaife recorded.[32] Watson had not only heard from him, the Strangite leader was the one who provided Gabriel with the money he needed to leave Michigan. Using another alias, Charles Harris, Gabriel wrote to Watson on December 30, 1914, from Houston Texas. "I managed to get down here by your assistance but don't know yet how I will get along," he wrote.[33]

Gabriel found work doing construction in Galveston. He owned property in Mexico and thought about trading it for land in Belize, his dream being to gather a colony of Strangites in that country. "There are so few of us in

---

30. A. E. Ewing to Milo Quaife, Apr. 9, 1919.

31. Ibid.

32. C. A. Engelbracht to Milo Quaife, Apr. 5, 1919; also Milo Quaife's notes.

33. Charles Harris [Gabriel Strang] to Wingfield Watson, Dec. 30, 1914, Clarke Historical Library.

the world," he wrote to Watson.[34] "I wish the few of us who are left who have the interest of the Work at heart were together at some place where we could receive those who are just and who will be dissatisfied with the Wars and hatreds of Nations. I think the time is near at hand when God will again call on those who desire to follow him to gather where his Law can be supreme."[35]

The dream of the Strang family scion was not to be. Before the end of the following year, Gabriel had badly bruised his foot and was being treated in a hospital in Terre Haute, Indiana. Still incognito as Charles Harris, he wrote to Watson on September 27, 1915: "This is the tenth day since my leg was amputated the third time and it is doing as well as could be expected. I feel that your visit was the turning point for the better."[36] He explained he had developed blood poisoning in his foot and that the doctors had given him no choice but amputation.[37]

Three months later he was staying with relatives—probably his sister Abigail and her husband, Ferd McNutt—who were nevertheless "very bitter here against everything connected with Beaver Island." Gabriel was looking for a job he could perform sitting down. "I could have got a job here at a news stand," he explained, if his family and acquaintances had not "objected and said they did not want me around this part of the country at all." According to Gabriel, his relatives harbored a "horror of everything connected with Beaver Island and Salt Lake; even Ferd and [Gabriel's sister] Abigail[,] who should remember you as a kind friend[,] [but] think you and 'Old Hickey' are the same horrid monsters and would as soon stop and listen to a snake rattle as to hear you preach.... I hope before they die they may see the folly of the whole business but the children know nothing of the real 'religion.'"[38]

Gabriel was the only descendant of James Strang who continued to ad-

---

34. Charles Harris [Gabriel Strang] to Wingfield Watson, Jan. 28, 1915, Clarke Historical Library.

35. Charles Harris [Gabriel Strang] to Wingfield Watson, Feb. 21, 1915, Clarke Historical Library.

36. Charles Harris [Gabriel Strang] to Wingfield Watson, Sept. 27, 1915, Clarke Historical Library. Gabriel was writing from St. Anthony's Hospital in Terre Haute.

37. Charles Harris [Gabriel Strang] to Wingfield Watson, Jan. 3, 1917, Clarke Historical Library. He explained that he had suffered from typhoid fever seven years previously and the medicines he took hardened the vein in his leg and reduced circulation. As a result, the slightest scratch would not heal.

38. Charles Harris [Gabriel Strang] to Wingfield Watson, Dec. 20, 1915, Clarke Historical Library.

here to his father's religious beliefs. He kept his faith in Strangism until his death in Houston, Texas, in 1937. "This I know," Clement wrote of his half-brother, "Gabriel had a very sad life. He finally ceased all practice of consecration" but remained "devoted to the church. He lost both wife and daughter, and when he was about 80 years old some time last summer, he died in Jefferson Davis Public Hospital." Clement said he had "received letters from both hospital and undertaker asking for cash to pay his burial expenses. But of course I had no money to send. I lost my wife last August."[39] On another occasion, Clement recorded that "as to Gabriel, I have letters from those who took care of him in his old age, in which are only words of praise for his good character. The church he belonged to was rejected by his neighbors, but he was faithful to it."[40]

Clement had some judgments about Elder Hickey and the concept of stealing for the Lord and shared his thoughts with Stanley Johnston, still a loyal Strangite:

> I understand that Apostle L D Hickey, really thought he was doing God's service when he had his sons and Gabriel Strang kneel down and receive divine blessings before they were sent forth to "consecrate" horses. And for this same reason he attributed the wisdom of the young men[,] by which they were able to escape capture[,] to the protective inspiration of God. The Old Testament is full of such interpretations of divine providence.[41]

Clement picked up the topic again later, writing to Johnson:

> I have my mother's testimony on the same subject. I have heard my uncles and aunts talking it over, and to a limited degree (in the earlier days, they changed later) justify the principle of consecration judiciously used, but tremendously against it as Hickey, Chidester, and the "Saint" in Grand Rapids practiced it.... They justified this because of the fact that their nice homes were taken from them, and they were driven away without means of resettling anywhere else.[42]

In a third letter to Johnson, Clement explained that he had heard people express a sense of disorientation, having wandered leaderless for so long, and

---

39. Clement Strang to Stanley Johnston, Apr. 23, 1937.
40. Clement Strang to Stanley Johnson, May 21, 1937, Clarke Historical Library.
41. Clement Strang to Stanley Johnson, Oct. 1, 1938.
42. Clement Strang to Stanley Johnston, Nov. 9, 1938, Clarke Historical Library.

a feeling of moral uncertainty about whether what they did on Beaver Island had been right. "These are the things that make clear to me why after the King was gone, they felt that God was against such things," he explained, "that either the prophet had been making false claims ... or else the future would bring a new revelation.... So they waited; and when no divine mani-festation came, ... they began to doubt themselves and their past. When they thought of the king's advice to take care of their families rather than jeopar-dize their safety for the sake of the church, "they did as he ordered, and they have been doing that since, as best they knew."[43]

---

43. Clement Strang to Stanley Johnston, July 17, 1938.

22

KEEPING THE FAITH

*"After the prophet was shot, & when
on board the Propeller for removal to Voree, while the boat lay at the pier;
he said ... [to] 'tell the brethren in a quiet way, that I think we will have
to draw off before our enemies.' His last directions were 'for every man to
take care of his family and do the best he could, till he found out what to do.'
... On a certain occasion, I being led by the spirit went to [James's] house
and told him I had been thinking of the work of Shiloh [the messiah],
what it would be. I then asked him if the Shiloh did not stand before me:
His reply was, 'I shall answer you as Christ answered Peter, Flesh and
blood hath not revealed it unto thee.'"* —Warren Post to Samuel Bennett.[1]

I n October 1856, some of Strang's apostles called a conference wherein they hoped to determine the future of the church. However, the
Saints were so scattered and deprived of funds that only a few were able to attend. Another attempt was made to meet in December, but poverty and severe
weather again prevented them. "The Strangites awaited word from the Lord
to tell them what to do. In anticipation of that word they set aside December
31, 1856 for fasting and prayer—yet the word did not come."[2] Five of
Strang's apostles, Lorenzo Dow Hickey, James Hutchins, Isaac Pierce, Lorenzo D. Tubbs, and Warren Post met in the woods six miles from Racine on
February 10, 1857, and "prayed and communed with each other all night."
They became convinced they could not lead the church without a prophet,
that only God possessed the power to appoint such a man. Elder Post wrote:

> We became satisfied, that the Twelve could not lead the Church without a
> Prophet; and concluded to take care of ourselves & families; and when occasion
> offered, minister to the necessities of the Saints, according to our abilities, until
> we have the word of the Lord to guide us on to other duties. This is truly a time

---

1. Warren Post to [Samuel] Bennett, May 16, 1858, Clarke Historical Library, Central Michigan University, Mount Pleasant, Michigan.

2. John Cumming, "Lorenzo Dow Hickey: The Last of the Twelve," *Michigan History*, Mar. 1966, 60-61.

for mourning, & fasting; for God has chastened us sorely for our sins, & we know not the extent of our sins, for God has not shown them unto us. The faithful among us are determined to wait upon the Lord, and trust in his mercies: for his mercy endureth forever.[3]

On Christmas Day 1863, seven years after the death of James J. Strang, more than a hundred Strangites met together in conference at the home of John Raymond in Hixton, Jackson County, Wisconsin. The purpose of this meeting was to "lay before the Saints the necessity of becoming united, in singleness of purpose, as one personage." Four apostles were present—Lorenzo Dow Hickey, James Hutchins, Warren Post, and Anson W. Prindle. At 10:00 a.m. the conference began with three men bearing their testimonies to the "truthfulness of Mormonism." In the afternoon, Hickey led a discussion on several matters, including how to best dispose of church records and what to do with the unbound copies of the Book of the Law of the Lord.[4] More importantly, the Strangites wanted to know what to do about Joseph Smith III, the son of the Mormon prophet Joseph Smith Jr.

A few years earlier, Mormons from northeastern Illinois and southern Wisconsin had met to discuss the leadership issue and resolved to await a direct descendent of Joseph Smith. Former Strangite adherents Jason Briggs, William Marks, Zenas Gurley, and others had left Strang when he began practicing polygamy. In 1856, Briggs and Gurley traveled to Nauvoo to persuade Joseph Smith III to assume leadership of the church. "Young Joseph" was not ready to talk about it at that time but four years later decided to accept the presidency of the church, named for legal purposes the Reorganized Church of Jesus Christ of Latter Day Saints. Members became known as "Josephites" to distinguish them from followers of Brigham Young, popularly known as "Brighamites."[5]

The Strangites at the Hixton conference, three years after the reorgani-

---

3. Warren Post, "The Record of the Apostles of James, Written During 1854-1863, Relating to the Events of 1844-1856, James J. Strang, the Mormons, and Beaver Island, Lake Michigan," unpublished manuscript, Clarke Historical Library,

4. Hixton Conference minutes, Dec. 25, 1863, Clarke Historical Library. It was decided that each Strangite family should purchase as many uncut sheets of the Book of the Law of the Lord as they could and that the proceeds would be used to put bindings on 100 copies.

5. The RLDS church was first headquartered in Amboy, Illinois, then relocated to Plano, Illinois. In 1881 the headquarters were transferred to Lamoni, Iowa. See articles in the quarterly *Restoration Trail Forum*.

zation was launched, wondered if they should join their Josephite colleagues or if they should continue to wait for a prophet of their own. Unlike the Brighamites, who believed the Twelve Apostles carried authority to appoint a new president, and unlike the Josephites, who believed in succession by bloodline, the Strangites held that only God or a living prophet could appoint a prophetic successor. Since James Strang had died without naming an heir, the choice was now up to God. Still, many wondered how long they should wait on God and what to do in the meantime.

Hickey argued a position at Hixton that he would continue to plead the rest of his life, a point that would split the Strangites into factions and render the church incapable of survival as a potent force in the Mormon religion.[6] The Saints had not been left leaderless, he maintained, because on November 6, 1846, about ten years before James Strang's death, James had quietly crept through a window at William Marks's home in Illinois and anointed the sleeping Joseph III to the First Presidency. The action was done quietly and secretly so that no harm would come to the thirteen-year-old boy from the enemies of the church.[7] According to Hickey, Strang's action meant Joseph III, the leader of the Reorganized Church, was also the leader of the Strangite Church, although not its prophet.

Hickey urged fellow Strangites to recognize young Smith on the basis of this revelation. The conference considered Hickey's plea and closed after adopting two resolutions. They stated that they were "deeply interested in the welfare and prosperity of Young Joseph and his family" and that they would "sustain" him "by our prayers and faith" in whatever office the Lord had called him.[8] It was only natural that the Strangites would be interested in the RLDS Church since the basic doctrines and beliefs of both churches were the same. In addition, many friends and family members had already joined the reorganization. More Strangites would become affiliated with the Josephites over the next few years, including members of Strang's own family. William Bickle exemplified the inclination in a letter to Wingfield Watson. "We have commenced a correspondence with what is called the new organization. If there is anything in Young Joseph's Claims we are going to know

---

6. Cumming, "Lorenzo Dow Hickey," 62.

7. Ibid., 63. At this time William Marks was living at Fulton City, Whiteside County, Illinois, about 140 miles upstream from Nauvoo.

8. Hixton Conference minutes.

it," he wrote.[9] Within a few years, the vast majority of the Strangites had gone over to the RLDS Church.

Young Joseph III welcomed the Strangites but would not acknowledge that Strang had ever been a legitimate successor to his father, Joseph Smith Jr. For the next thirty years, Hickey caused a considerable amount of dissension within the two churches as he tried to convince Strangites to accept Joseph III as a presiding priesthood officer and the RLDS Church that Strang had been God's prophet. For many years he ran a battle of words with Joseph Smith III over the supposed "ordination" by Strang, Hickey insisting it was true and Smith responding that it was not.[10] Hickey also called Wingfield Watson a pseudo and heretic for not accepting the story of Smith's secret ordination.[11]

By the 1890s Hickey was the last of James Strang's apostles, looked to by those who continued to watch for the emergence of a true successor to Strang. Realizing he would need to appoint someone to keep the tradition alive after he died, he attempted to interest Strang's sons, Charles, Clement, and Gabriel. None was interested. Hickey even traveled from Michigan to Utah at age seventy-seven to try to convince Sarah Wright's son, James Phineas, to accept leadership of the Strangite fold, but was again unsuccessful.

Gabriel Strang was with Hickey in Coldwater, Michigan, a few weeks before Hickey's death. He described the old man's insistence on finding someone to carry on the Strang legacy. Gabriel described how Hickey carried on part of the conversation with himself, as if Gabriel were not present.

> I was passing through the room where [Hickey] was sitting on April 6th, 1897. He called to me[,] and when I turned to look toward him[,] he motioned toward a chair at the end of the table and told me to sit down. When I did so he remarked that he was getting old and could not expect to be here much longer

---

9. William Bickle to Wingfield Watson, Apr. 19, 1862, Clarke Historical Library.

10. Joseph Smith III to Lorenzo Dow Hickey, Jan. 23 [1884], Joseph Smith III Letter Press Book, Library-Archives, Community of Christ, Independence, Missouri; also Cummings, "Lorenzo Dow Hickey," 67. Joseph III said it would have been impossible for Strang to creep through the window and ordain him because his father's old dog, Major, was always by his side.

11. Cumming, "Lorenzo Dow Hickey," 68-69. Hickey moved from Wisconsin to Coldwater, Michigan, in 1866 with two wives and twelve children. One wife, Sarah Linnell, lived with him while the other, Frances Miller, lived in a separate residence posing as an aunt. Hickey's deception was so successful, his obituary said he never practiced polygamy.

and felt it was his duty to ordain someone to the High Priesthood before he passed away.... He sat there a few minutes and then remarked that he had been studying a long time on who should be ordained. He said there is Gabriel Strang, but if I should ordain him, how long would it be before he would be in South America or on some Islands out in the ocean among strangers.[12]

Gabriel made no reply. Hickey suggested "Jim [James Oscar] McNutt" but then quickly discounted the idea. "He studied the matter for a while and then asked me if there was anyone else I could suggest," Gabriel recalled. "I told him there was Bro. Watson who had always had a desire to be a High Priest. He turned toward me with a look between a sneer and a laugh and said Watson? Don't you think he would try to start a little Kingdom of his own if he possessed the High Priesthood?" Hickey and Strang discussed the matter a little more and finally came to the conclusion that Wingfield Watson, even though he was at odds with Hickey, was the right man to lead the church. Hickey wrote a letter to Watson asking him to come to see him. Gabriel carried the letter to the train and mailed it so it could be delivered in Burlington the next morning.[13] Watson received it and traveled immediately to Coldwater, where the two men settled their differences and Hickey ordained him to be the Presiding High Priest of the Strangite Church.

Hickey died less than three weeks later on April 25, 1897. He had not doubted the prophet from the moment of his reinstatement, when Strang forgave him for disrupting the meeting in New York City, to his death. "I feel as Nebuchadnezzar did after he had been driven out from among men," the repentant disciple had written to Strang in 1849. "And all I have to say is I love you as I never loved before. I have confessed to God and man, and I ask your forgiveness and I ask your prayers that I may be just such a man as God shall own and bless in the future."[14] Twenty-two years after Strang's death, Hickey expressed his love for his deceased prophet in a letter he wrote to Charles and Clement Strang. Hickey related his emotions at seeing the two men and the memories the event rekindled.

It brought the days of other years to my mind, even the happiest days of my

---

12. Gabriel Strang to John Wake, Jan. 9, 1928, Clarke Historical Library.

13. Ibid.

14. Lorenzo Dow Hickey to James Strang, Dec. 6, 1849, Yale Collection of Western Americana, Beinecke Rare Book and Manuscript Library, Yale University, New Haven, Connecticut.

life when I met Charlie [Strang's son], as he came out of the work room to the business room, as he turned his back and as he walked, it brought such sensation ... just the form, just the turn, and it seemed as though I almost stood in the printing office of other years, where James J. Strang stood and met and parted with kind friends....

What added to my joy was that I found that gentle, quiet, yet firm and decided spirit for the right.... I hope you will not think I am flattering, for I am not.... [B]e assured that these are [also] my own traits of character.... [W]hen James was shot I soon came home from Wisconsin instead of sneaking off as did some.... No, gentlemen, I got a letter at Wisconsin from the captain of the propeller and got the medicine they sent for and hastened to the place where the good man lay. Even then the mob were on the alert and I stood my post when exposed to their shots. When the word came that he wanted E[dward]. Chidester and L[orenzo]. D. Hickey, I felt it an honor, as I do this day, to be one that was to stand by him through the storm. And all I ask of my father in Heaven is to have a home in His glory, even where the Father will place him.

But let the curtain fall until the sleeping dust shall arize and then, instead of being the object of scorn and ridicule, a crown of King and Martyr will be his to wear. And it will be his to be honored as one who like Moses tried to save the people from the ways of sin and death. Sirs, think not that I talk fiction, for it is all a reality and all I ask is to compare notes and time.[15]

Hickey could not have chosen a better leader for the church than Wingfield Watson. Considered a "gentleman in the finest sense," Watson was an earnest and kindly man who devoted his life to the preservation of the church. Among the Strangites he is regarded with admiration exceeded only by their reverence for Strang himself and remembered for his gentle character, steadfast devotion, and his vast knowledge of the scriptures.[16]

After leaving Beaver Island in 1856, Watson and his family stayed in Chicago while he earned enough money to go back to work in the lead mines in southwestern Wisconsin, where he had worked before and where his mother and siblings had settled. From there, the Watsons moved to Black River Falls, then to Boyne City, Michigan. In 1891, Watson returned to the Voree area of Burlington, Wisconsin, with the dream of purchasing back

---

15. Lorenzo Dow Hickey to Charles J. Strang and his brother [Clement], June 10, 1878, Clarke Historical Library. Like his father, Charles was a printer.

16. John Cumming, "Wingfield Watson: The Loyal Disciple of James J. Strang," *Michigan History,* Dec. 1963, 320.

Strangite land and gathering the people together again.[17] He was, in fact, able to purchase a large amount of land, but the dream of gathering the remnants of the scattered flock never occurred during his lifetime. He remained in Burlington until his death, preaching Mormon doctrine and publishing Strangite materials into his nineties. He and his children tithed themselves until they had enough money to reprint many of the church's publications from the Beaver Island era. Without his attention and care, most of the church's literature and records would have been lost. In 1919, at the age of ninety-one, he returned to Beaver Island with Milo Quaife—the only trip back to the island Watson ever made.[18]

On October 29, 1922, Watson died at the age of ninety-four, "convinced that the Lord would yet send a prophet into the world to lead the Saints and continue the work of Strang." So firm was his conviction, he left his property in trust for the day when a prophet would re-appear. The house and land are still administered by three Strangite trustees in accordance with Watson's wishes, maintained for the prophet to come.[19]

James Oscar McNutt was another Strangite who tried to keep the faith. The nephew of Betsy McNutt, James Oscar recorded a great deal of the history of the Mormon settlements of Beaver Island and of Knapp, Wisconsin. In 1924 he wrote to an adherent recalling some incidents in the church's history and bearing testimony of its rightness.

> Seeing that I lived on the Beaver Islands ... and was an eye witness to what happened in 1856, I will give you the facts in as few words as possible. The Mormons on Beaver Island were a law abiding people strictly living up to the law of the United States, and the state laws of the state of Michigan at that time, and God's laws.... They kept the eighth of July [commemorating Strang's coronation] and held a great feast and thanks offering to God for the blessings he bestowed on them the same as people now keep Thanksgiving Day. They did not drink any intoxicating liquor nor tea or coffee or smoke or chew tobacco.

---

17. Watson's own family was split by religious differences. His daughter Grace was a fervent Strangite whose husband was a passionate member of the RLDS Church. Daughter Janey married a man who was antagonistic to Strangism. Son Robert married a Strangite and moved to Colorado. Thomas's wife converted, and they remained in the Burlington area, similar to Elizabeth, whose husband Adelbert White converted and settled near Voree. See William Shepard, "Wingfield Watson and the Restoration," *Journal of the John Whitmer Historical Association* 16 (1996): 75.

18. Cumming, "Wingfield Watson," 317-21.

19. Ibid., 320.

They never used any profane language, and if they saw anything going astray took and returned it to its owner.[20]

They paid the tenth they raised or earned in tithing to keep the poor and anything to support the church work. They played cards and danced. They had large dances, old and young all attended both Christmas and New Years, also dances at other times. But they never gambled or bet on anything. The women all wore Bloomers made of dress goods, their dresses came half way down between their knees and feet. These people went on the island when there was very few whites [who] lived there and when there was nothing but fishermen. They settled up thru the Island and opened up farms....

There was a road running from Saint James down at the harbor up thru the island called the Kings Highway.... There was other roads that branched off from this highway these roads and farms were all built by the Mormons[,] and their houses and barns [were constructed out of] very large timbers, and all done in less than nine years. This ought to convince the world that those Mormons were not what their enemies paint them to be, I want to say right here there never was a child born there at that time but everyone knew who its father was, and never a young girl went astray. There was deeds done up around the Islands that was laid to the Mormons that they never done, and would not have [been] done by any of their people, but in those days every thing criminal was laid to the Mormons....

There are always some black sheep gets in the flock and it is the same with all churches, AND WHEN THOSE ARE CHASTISED PUNISHED OR CUT OFF, whichever it might be, then they turn against the church and do all they can to injure [those who have] been the cause of putting them out or whatever may be done to them. Look today at the ministers and some of the priests and the crimes they commit. If that was Mormons what [would] be said and done? But this does not make it the church's fault.... There was everything charged against them and they have been accused of every known crime, and brought before the bar of justice (and sometimes injustice), but NEVER CONVICTED. This ought to be evidence enough that they never done the crimes their accusers claimed they did.... James J. Strang served in the legislature of Michigan. His seat was contested but he was seated by a large majority and proved to be a highly respected man by his fellow members.... NOW WHAT GREAT CRIME DID THIS MAN JAMES JESSIE STRANG COMMIT that he should be assassinated?

McNutt recalled when he went to Voree in 1868 to see his father's grave:

---

20. J. O. McNutt to Lloyd Flanders, Dec. 12, 1924, Clarke Historical Library.

I went there ... later in the fall of 1868 and thought I would fix up the grave, but I could not locate the cemetery and while I was looking around a man came out of his house and asked me what I was looking for. I told him my father was buried there somewhere, and he said, "I made my hog yard right there over them Damned Mormons."

Now we had never injured him[,] then why should he have this kind of a feeling about the Mormons? It is only a religious belief when you get down to the bottom of it, and we all have a right to believe what we all have to do to be saved. The Mormons today are all divided[,] so are the Protestant Churches, but there is lots of good honest people in all of them, and because they do not believe as we do what right do we have to say they are robbers, thieves, murderers and criminals?[21]

In 1886, McNutt applied to the Millston township board to purchase land for a Mormon cemetery. It was granted under the condition that McNutt pay fifty cents each year to keep the cemetery in good repair. More than a hundred years later, a few stones still remain. Some of the surnames are still visible on the gravestones: Denio, Hostetter, Ketchum, McNutt, Pierce, and Tubbs. The apostle Warren Post is buried there, as is Betsy McNutt's older brother John.[22]

McNutt wrote how he was "the means" by which the cemetery came about.

I planned and laid out the lots and everything, and kept record of the Cemetery, until the Town of Knapp accepted the Cemetery as the Town Cemetery. Those I have given you, in this [plat] book, all died Strangites, except [two].... The following were on Beaver Island: Warren Post, John C. Hill, Harriet Hill, Sarah Alice Pierce, George C. Pierce, Mary McNutt, John McNutt, Elnora Jane Wallworth.... [In] 1884 ... [many] were moved from an old burying ground to the New Cemetery; which was bought, cleared, and fenced by donation, on purpose, so that the cemetery should never become like the one in Voree where my father, Tobias McNutt, is buried.[23]

Nearly all the Strangites who had lived on Beaver Island eventually

---

21. Ibid.

22. James O. McNutt, "Plat of the Mormon Cemetery at Knapp, Wisconsin," unpublished manuscript, Library-archives, Wisconsin Historical Society, Madison, Wisconsin. Burial information for the cemetery was recorded in 1971.

23. Ibid.

joined the Reorganized Church, but some held to old loyalties and remained in the Strangite strongholds in Wisconsin, at Black River Falls, Hixton, Manchester, and Warrens Mills. Eventually even those groups died out. By the 1930s there were only about twenty active members of the Strangite movement, including Edward Couch, Reuben T. Nichols, and Watson's daughter Jane and her children in the Boyne City, Michigan, area. The Strangite apostle L. D. Tubbs organized a branch in Muscatah, Kansas, at the start of the Civil War. Joseph Ketchum later replaced Tubbs, but the unofficial leader of the branch was a woman known as "Granny Flanders." Most of the members today—Samuel Martin, the Scott family, and John Wake—trace their church lineage back to the missionary efforts of this woman. Even so, the branch later split up over whether James Strang had appointed young Joseph Smith III to lead the church. A sizeable group immigrated to the San Luis Valley near Monte Vista in southern Colorado. When this branch broke up in about 1905, some of the members relocated to Pueblo, Colorado. However, the majority moved to Artesia in the southeastern part of New Mexico, where they started another branch. One segment of the Monte Vista group later traveled to Kansas City to establish a branch there.

Wingfield Watson remained in Burlington with his daughter Elizabeth White, her husband, and a few other Strangites. Stephen West and his family moved there from Pueblo in 1947 and revitalized the branch. Other members began arriving from Colorado, Missouri, and New Mexico until there was a large enough gathering to justify construction of a chapel. In 2003 there were about 100 active members of the Strangite Church in branches at Burlington and Artesia, New Mexico, as well as small clusters of Strangites in Colorado, Michigan, Minnesota, Missouri, and Texas. To date, the branch in Burlington is the only group that has a dedicated building to meet in.

Ordained by Lorenzo Dow Hickey, Wingfield Watson served as the presiding high priest, or leading member, of the Strangite Church until 1922, when shortly before his death he ordained Samuel H. Martin to be his successor. Shortly before his own death in the mid-1930s, Martin in turn ordained Moroni "Max" Flanders to be presiding high priest. After his death in 1947, Max was succeeded by Lloyd A. Flanders. Vernon Swift of Artesia, New Mexico, became the leader in 1955 and holds that office at this time.[24]

---

24. William Shepard and David Rhees to the author, Apr. 2, 2003. Shepard and Rhees are members of the Strangite Church in Burlington, Wisconsin.

Conclusion

GOD HAS MADE US A KINGDOM

> *"[Before 1847, Beaver Island] was the slough hole of eternal hell. The inhabitants were a conglomerate mass of French, Irish, Indian, with one McKinley ... as their leader and dealer, and his stock and trade was vile villainous whiskey. That Sir, was the condition of affairs when your father sought a home for himself and people upon those islands. Not a schoolhouse, habitation or Church, nor in its whole domain the leaf of a primer. What was its condition when your father left it? I have traveled somewhat upon that island with your father, and I saw churches, schoolhouses, farms, and in fact the whole island booming with the product of earth. I saw a mighty change as by magic, from a barbarous to an intelligent people.... Well Sir, I am a friend of humanity, and in favor of advancing, either by ecclesiastical power or otherwise. Therefore, I will always cherish the memory of your father. For he believed in bettering the condition of man.... If he had been left to follow out the chain of his thoughts, those islands would be fit for gods to dwell on."* —Dr. O. M. Aldrich to Clement Strang.[1]

As they left Beaver Island in July 1856, the Mormons must have realized they would never return. Once again they were an exiled people, rejected by God, driven from their homes, their property lost to a mob. When Strang died on July 9, 1856, the grief stricken Strangites had to

---

1. Dr. O. M. Aldrich to stranger [Clement J. Strang], March 15, 1898, Burton Historical Collection, Detroit Public Library. Aldrich's note was in response to an article he had seen in Salt Lake City's *Deseret Evening News*, February 19, 1898, and was enclosed with another letter from Stanley Johnston to Clement Strang, n.d., Clarke Historical Library.

decide what to do. Most obeyed Strang's last request by "falling back before their enemies" and carrying on the best they could. Four of these followers were Strang's plural wives, whose futures would be filled with sadness and hardship as they made the best decisions they could for themselves and their children.

Like their relatives and friends, these four Strangite women were ordinary people who had gone looking for religious freedom. Instead they found themselves embroiled in several matters of controversy, including the coronation of a king and the setting up of a kingdom that included polygamy and the doctrine of consecration. They found themselves in circumstances not entirely of their choosing and participants in events they may not have foreseen, but their faith and dedication ruled all. Everything they did was for the good of the kingdom.

Did the Strangites steal from the gentiles? Yes, they probably did. Strang himself stated his followers would return "blow for blow" anything that was done to them. "Consecration" was acknowledged by Elvira Field and her brother Albert, Samuel Graham, Stephen Post, Romeo Strang, the Chidester family, and others. The fact that consecration of gentile property was carried on after the Saints were driven from Beaver Island seems to support this premise.

On the other hand, it has to be assumed that the Strangites did not steal anything more than the gentiles stole from them. This was the frontier at its best and worst—best because men and women were required to draw on their own resources to succeed, worst because they were often in survival mode and willing to do anything to escape the cold and hunger. Success was often achieved at someone else's expense. Stealing for gain occurred over and over again during this period of time, from the harbor master who required additional funds after the Strangites had already paid their fare, ship captains who refused to unload their Mormon passengers on Beaver Island, and those who appropriated lost freight to the men who brazenly helped themselves to lumber stacked on docks and fishing boats tied up in harbors. Mormons and gentiles alike took over abandoned homes and properties in Nauvoo, Pine River, and St. James. Everyone who participated in this activity felt they had a reason and a justification. One of the differences between Mormons and gentiles was that the Mormons did their stealing as a group instead of individually. It was performed by a select few for the supposed good of all, with the overriding purpose being to drive away the gentiles so the Strangites could have a place of their own. Not all Strangites participated in this endeavor, but all can be considered complicit to the extent that they must have observed irregularities and ignored them even if unaware of the scale or official sanction of this activity.

The historical record is full of sensational stories about the Strangites as pirates and brigands who forced young girls to marry into polygamy, who stole horses, livestock, and even children, and spirited them away to a horrible life on Beaver Island. Skepticism is warranted. Strang was supposed to have seduced runaway women to be his plural wives, then repented of his actions on his death bed, asking his wife Mary to care for him as he lay dying. This is only one example of the many fanciful stories that made their rounds through Michigan and throughout the United States. In fact, there is no way James Strang and his followers could have possibly committed all the crimes they were accused of.

What is clear is that the Strangites made good copy for newspapers. A story about alleged "Mormon crimes" would circulate, and before members could refute the charges, navigation was closed for the season and for five months it was impossible for the Mormons to communicate with the outside world. In the meantime, the stories had time to ferment and become ever more sensationalized as they appeared time and again in newspapers across the country. A good example was an interview with Captain John V. Tuttle, who told the *Milwaukee Sentinel* about the Mormon "rascals" who flourished there. Even in setting up the context for Tuttle's story, the article exhibited unrestrained hyperbole.

> The Beavers are at the northern extremity of the lake, about forty miles from the mouth of Green Bay, and contain, I think, more thieves and rascals than any similar amount of ground on the continent.... Strong [*sic*] was a dissolute, licentious and unprincipled man. He stooped to almost any crime with a most graceful ease, and was totally indifferent to the lives, welfare, or property of what his sect termed the gentiles.... It was beyond question that the Mormons living thereon were rascals and thieves, but accusations were carried still further, and in many quarters they were regarded not only as non-respecters of property, but as non-respecters of human life.[2]

---

2. "Story of the Lake: A Captain's Reminiscence of the Beaver Islands," *Milwaukee Sentinel*, Dec. 20, 1885.

Tuttle claimed three vessels had sailed for Big Beaver Bay during the years 1850 and 1851 and were never heard from again. He cited the schooner *Willis*, which was seen to enter Beaver harbor loaded with provisions in 1851. "She was never heard of afterwards, none of her crew ever again appeared, and the general supposition among marine people is that she was taken by the Mormons, her crew murdered, the cargo stolen and the vessel scuttled," Tuttle said.

To bear out his assertion that the inhabitants of Beaver Island had the propensity to lug away everything they could carry, he related some experiences of his own. As his vessel was about to leave Beaver Harbor one day, the cable slipped and ninety fathom of chain attached to the anchor dropped into the water. Not having time to drag for it, Tuttle took bearings so he could retrieve it later and continued on his journey. On the return trip, he pulled into the bay for his lost chain and anchor. Having no lightweight boat aboard, he went ashore and hired a local fisherman to drag the bay with him for five dollars an hour.

After rowing back and forth for nearly two hours, the captain finally said, "Now, this is —— funny. I know my cable dropped right here."

"Don't doubt it," said his companion.

"Well, let's go over the ground again and maybe we'll make a catch," the captain replied.

"It's no use," the imperturbable fisherman noted, "for the chain isn't there. We raised it two hours after you left port, and the lighthouse-keeper has it now."

"Blankety, blank, blank, blank," exclaimed the captain, "why in blank didn't you tell me that before?"

"Because you didn't ask me," said the Beaver Island resident.

Tuttle recognized the force of the logic, paid the man ten dollars, and left to ask the keeper of the lighthouse about the missing property. The keeper claimed the chain and anchor were his by virtue of his having pulled it out of the water; he refused to relinquish it unless the captain paid him $500. Tuttle threatened force but was laughed at. He finally got his chain and anchor back by paying $250 for it.

To further illustrate his point, the captain related the experience of the ship *George Sherman* when it had gone ashore on Beaver Island the previous fall. "The crew left the vessel for a time fearing she would go to pieces," Tuttle insisted. "And when they returned the next morning they found they had been visited by the delectable residents of Big Beaver who had stripped her of every inch of rope and every yard of canvas she possessed."

The only problem with the stories spun by Captain Tuttle was that the Mormons had left Beaver Island nearly twenty years before the incidents he related, which took place in 1875.[3] Life was different on the Michigan frontier in the 1850s. There were different norms for what was considered virtuous and good than in an eastern urban setting. A good parallel is Brigham Young's forceful and pragmatic, rather than polite and highly ethical, approach to his rule in Utah. Even in church meetings, Young spoke of "justice being laid to the line and righteousness to the plummet, or of sending enemies to hell across lots."[4] Historian Klaus J. Hansen summarized Young's policies and philosophy of government to be "singularly un-American."[5] In both Michigan and Utah, it was a different time and place, and the context was important. Those engaged in a struggle for life and death, who chose to survive rather than submit to savage force, should not be judged too harshly —which is not to excuse them entirely, especially considering their often expressed pretension of living a higher law and of being more morally strict than gentile neighbors. To say they were worse is unfair. To say they were better is another question.

---

3. Ibid.

4. Phillip A. M. Taylor, "The Life of Brigham Young: A Biography Which Will Not Be Written," *Dialogue: A Journal of Mormon Thought* 1 (Fall 1966): 106-07. On one occasion Young "cursed every Gentile who should attempt to settle here with sickness, rottenness, and death," that their "flesh might consume away on their bones, and their blood be turned into maggots and their torments never cease" (Leonard J. Arrington, "Personal Reflections on Mormon History," *Sunstone*, July 1983, 44).

5. Klaus J. Hansen, "The Metamorphosis of the Kingdom of God: Toward a Reinterpretation of Mormon History," in *The New Mormon History: Revisionist Essays on the Past*, ed. D. Michael Quinn (Salt Lake City: Signature Books, 1992), 229-30.

M<small>APS</small>

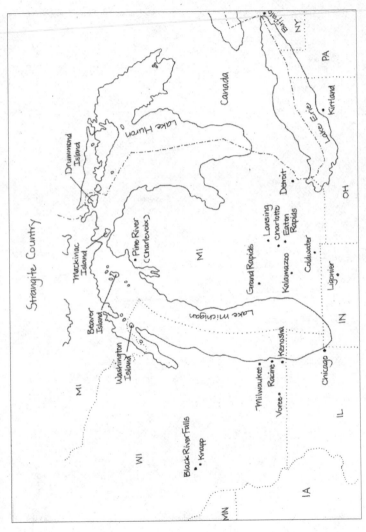

Followers of James J. Strang settled along the coast of Lake Michigan and on the islands of Lake Michigan and Lake Huron. When they were evicted in 1856, most gravitated to the Black River Falls area, where they lived incognito. *Maps by Keiko Jones*

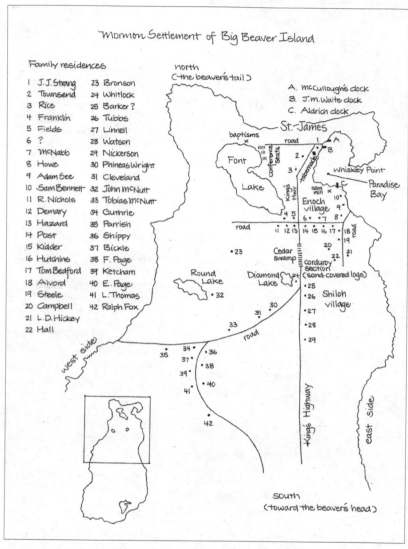

Rendering of a rough map by James Oscar McNutt, whose memory of where the most prominent Strangite families had settled was better than his sense of scale or orthography, both of which have been modestly corrected. Native Americans believed the island was in the shape of an upside-down beaver, tail to the north. *The McNutt holograph is preserved by the Beaver Island Historical Society.*

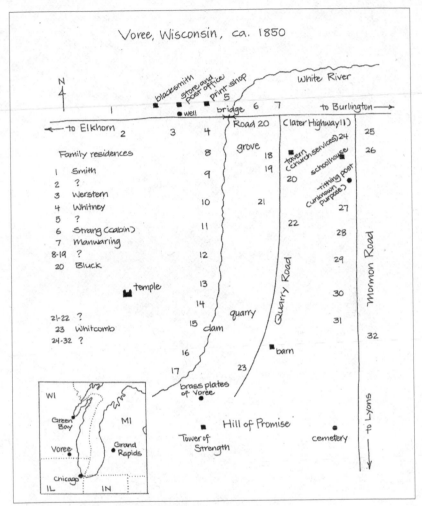

Voree, Wisconsin, ca. 1850

Based on several sources, including the early settlers' correspondence, recollections by Aaron Smith and Gabriel Strang, a memorial plaque from the Burlington Historical Society, and an archaeological survey conducted by the Wisconsin Department of Transportation in 1988, it is possible to reconstruct the original layout of Voree. The structure labeled "print shop" was a large stone house where James Strang's parents lived, but it was also where the printing press for the *Voree Herald* was quartered and where James Strang died. The log cabin, the first Strang domicile in Voree, would later become home to two of Strang's wives, Elvira and Betsy. It is thought that Mary Perce may have lived in the home labeled number 5. "Mormon Road" was presumably a later designation for the street heading to Lyons.

PHOTOGRAPHS

James Strang was a frontier attorney before converting to the Latter Day Saint movement and becoming prophet and king to the Mormons of Michigan and Wisconsin. *Courtesy Clarke Historical Library, Central Michigan University*

James Strang's parents, Clement and Abigail, were unconvinced by their son's religious claims but moved from New York to Wisconsin to be with their daughter-in-law and grandchildren. *Courtesy Clarke Historical Library*

"Charles Douglas," the sixteen-year-old nephew of James Strang, was really Elvira Field, Strang's first plural wife, in disguise. This photo was taken in 1849-50, probably in Buffalo, New York. *Courtesy Clarke Historical Library*

After the prophet's death, Elvira married John Baker, with whom she shared many interests, although she kept her religious beliefs private. *Courtesy Clarke Historical Library*

Six years after being banished from Beaver Island, Sarah Wright moved to Utah with her new husband, Joseph S. Wing. She became a well-known doctor in Springville, Utah. *Courtesy Springville Historical Society*

James Strang's fifth wife, Phoebe Wright, was considered hand-some and intelligent. She remained devoted to his memory all her life. *Courtesy Yale Collection of Western Americana, Beinecke Rare Book and Manuscript Library*

Although she was born on Beaver Island to Strangite parents and married a former Strangite, Evangeline Strang (right) later renounced her father's religion and joined the Reorganized Church of Jesus Christ of Latter Day Saints.

Born six months after the death of her father, Abigail Strang (below) married her first cousin, Ferdinand Juan McNutt, a union prohibited in the Strangite religion. She later joined the RLDS Church.

Raised without a father, Gabriel Strang (above) formed a close relationship with the Strangite apostle Lorenzo Dow Hickey, who taught him the principle of "consecration." In the 1880s and again in the early 1900s, Gabriel went to jail for stealing horses and buggies. *Photos on this page courtesy Clarke Historical Library*

Notorious in Mormon history, George J. Adams became one of James Strang's closest advisors. After defecting from Strangism, he led an unsuccessful effort to establish a colony in Palestine. *Courtesy Library-Archives, Community of Christ*

John C. Bennett was mayor of Nauvoo and a good friend of the Mormon prophet, Joseph Smith, before writing an exposé on Mormonism. Four years later, Bennett wrote to James Strang asking to be his general-in-chief. *Courtesy Library-Archives, Community of Christ*

Immensely talented but lacking in scruples, William Smith
became James Strang's first counselor. A proponent of polygamy, he was later excommunicated for adultery and apostasy.
Courtesy Library-Archives, Community of Christ

Benjamin G. Wright was one of James Strang's most trusted advisors. He became a successful businessman in Jackson County, Wisconsin. *Courtesy Church of Jesus Christ of Latter Day Saints (Strangite)*

Phineas and Amanda Finch Wright were ardent supporters of James Strang. Although Amanda died when their daughter Sarah was only ten, Phineas went on to become one of Strang's apostles and a member of his Privy Council. At age seventeen, Sarah became one of Strang's plural wives. Phineas, who previously had been a lumberman in Canada, found success in the business in the Black River Falls area of Wisconsin. *Courtesy Clarke Historical Library*

Thomas Bedford, one of the assassins of James Strang. Bedford never expressed regret for his act. *Courtesy Burton Historical Collections, Detroit Public Library*

Ruth Ann Bedford, wife of Thomas, refused to wear bloomers, the costume prescribed for women on Beaver Island. *Courtesy Burton Historical Collections, Detroit Public Library*

Apostle Warren Post became the unofficial leader of the Strangites who moved to Knapp, Wisconsin. *Courtesy Church of Jesus Christ of Latter Day Saints (Strangite)*

Much of what is known about the Mormon settlement of Beaver Island came from Wingfield Watson, shown in this portrait from the mid-1850s. Watson became leader of the church in 1897. *Courtesy Church of Jesus Christ of Latter Day Saints (Strangite)*

Of all the Strangites, none was more devoted to the prophet than Lorenzo Dow Hickey. At first opposed to polygamy, he eventually had four wives. The first child born to his first plural wife was named after Elvira Field. *Courtesy Church of Jesus Christ of Latter Day Saints (Strangite)*

Many former Strangite children were educated in the Wrightsville school near Black River Falls, Wisconsin. Once a prosperous town, Wrightsville no longer exists. The school has been moved from its original site nearly two miles east to its present location, shown here, near U.S. Highway 12. *Photo by author*

Appendixes

Nauvoo June 18th 1844

My dear son Your epistle of May 24th proposing the planting
a stake of zion in wisconsin and the gathering the saints there
was duly received & I with most of the breathren whom advise I called
in were of opinion that you was deceived by a spirit not of this world
great but not good brother Hyrum however thought otherwise and
favored the project not doubting it was of God I however determined
to return you an unfavourable answer for the present but oh the littleness
of man in his best earthly state not so the will of the Almighty, God hath
ruled it otherwise and a message from the throne of grace directed me
as it hath inspired you and the faith which thou hast in the shepherd the
stone of Israel hath been repaid to thee a thousand fold and thou shalt be
like unto him but the flock shall find rest with thee and God shall reveal
to thee his will concerning them I have long felt that my present work
was almost done and that I should soon be called to rule a mighty host
but something whispers me it will be in the land of spirits where
the wicked cease from troubling and the bands of the prisoner fall off
my heart yearns for my little ones but I know God will be a father to
them and I can claim face to face the fulfilment of promises from him
who is a covenant keeping God and who sweareth and performeth
and faileth not to the uttermost the wolves are upon the scent and
I am waiting to be offered up if such be the will of God knowing
that though my visage be more mared than that of any it will be un-
scared and fair when archangels shall place on my brow the double
crown of martyr and king in a heavenly world in the midst of
darkness and boding danger the spirit of Elijah came upon me and
I went away to inquire of God how the church should be saved I
was upon the hill of the temple the calm father of waters rolled
below changeless & eternal I beheld a light in the heavens above &
streams of bright light illuminated the firmament variedly beautiful
as the rainbow, gentle yet rapid as the fierce lightning. the Almighty
came from his throne of rest He clothed himself with light as with a garment.
He appeared & moon & stars went out, the earth dissolved in space. I trod
on air & was borne on wings of cherubims, the sweetest strains of heavenly
musick thrilled in my ear but the notes were few & sad as though they

A.

Letter of Appointment

Letter from Joseph Smith Jr. to James J. Strang, dated June 18, 1845, postmarked June 19, 1845, Nauvoo, Illinois. Two pages of the original letter are archived at the Beinecke Rare Book and Manuscript Library, Yale University, reproduced here by permission. The postscript was dropped when the letter was published in the Chronicles of Voree, *1-2, and the* Voree Herald, *Jan. 1846.*

My Dear Son: —Your epistle of May 24th proposing the planting a Stake of Zion in Wisconsin and the gathering of the Saints there, was duly received, and I with most of the brethren whose advise I called in were, of opinion that you was deceived by a spirit not of this world, great but not good. Brother Hyrum however thought otherwise and favored the project, not doubting it was of God. I however determined to return you an unfavorable answer for the present. —But oh the littleness of man in his best earthly state. Not so the will of the Almighty. God hath ruled it otherwise and a message from the throne of grace directed me as it hath inspired you, and the faith which thou hast in the Shepherd, the Stone of Israel hath been repaid to thee a thousand fold, and thou shalt be like him; but the flock shall find rest with thee, and God shall reveal to thee, his will concerning them.

I have long felt that my present work was almost done and that I should soon be called to rule a mighty host, but something whispers me it will be in the land of spirits where the wicked cease from troubling and the bands of the prisoner fall off. My heart yearns for my little ones, but I know God will be a father to them, and I can claim face to face the fulfillment of promises from him who is a covenant keeping God and who sweareth and performeth and faileth not to the uttermost.

The wolves are upon the scent, and I am waiting to be offered up if such be the will of God knowing that though my visage be more marred than that of any it will be unscarred and fair when archangels shall place on my brow the double crown of martyr and King in a heavenly world.

keep them under the shadow of my wing, the cities from whence
my people have been driven shall be purged with a high hand for I will do it,
my people shall be again restored to their possessions but dark clouds are
gathering for the church is not yet wholly purged. Now I command my
servants the apostles & priests & elders of the church of the saints that they
communicate & proclaim this my word to all the saints of God in all
the world that they may be gathered unto and round about the
city of Voree & be saved from their enemies for I will have a people to
serve me, I command my servant Moses Smith that he go unto the
saints with whom he is acquainted and unto many people & command
them in my name to go unto my city of Voree and gain inheritants
therein, he shall have an inheritants therein for he hath left all for
my sake, I will add to him many fold if he is faithful for he knows
the land and can testify to them that it is very good
            so spake the Almighty God of heaven
thy duty is made plain and if thou lackest wisdom ask of God in
whose hands I trust thee, he will give thee unsparingly for if
evil befall me thou shalt lead the flock to pleasant pastures
        God sustain thee
                                    Joseph Smith.

James j Strang
            PS Write me soon, keep me advised of your
progress from time to time

In the midst of darkness and boding danger the Spirit of Elijah came upon me and I went away to inquire of God how the Church should be saved.

I was upon the hill of the Temple. The calm father of waters rolled below changeless and eternal. I beheld a light in the heavens above and streams of bright light illuminated the firmament varied and beautiful as the rainbow, gentle yet rapid as the fierce lightening.

The Almighty came from his throne of rest. He clothed himself with light as with a garment. He appeared and moon and stars went out. The earth dissolved in space. I trod on air and was borne on wings of Cherubims. The sweetest strains of heavenly music thrilled in my ear but the notes were low and sad as though they sounded the requiem of martyred Prophets.

I bowed my head to the earth and asked only wisdom and strength for the church. The voice of God answered, My servant Joseph, thou hast been faithful over many things and thy reward is glorious, the crown and scepter are thine and they wait thee. But thou hast sinned in some things and thy punishment is very bitter. The whirlwind goeth before and its clouds are dark, but rest followeth and to its days there shall be no end. Study the words of the vision for it tarrieth not.

And now behold my servant James J. Strang hath come to thee from far for truth when he knew it not and hath not rejected it but had faith in thee, the Shepherd and Stone of Israel, and to him shall the gathering of the people be for he shall plant a stake of Zion in Wisconsin and I will establish it, and there shall my people have peace and rest, and shall not be mooved, for it shall be established on the Prairie on White River in the lands of Racine and Walworth, and behold my servants James and Aaron shall plant it for I have given them wisdom, and Daniel shall stand in his lot on the hill beside the river looking down on the prairie and shall instruct my people and shall plead with them face to face.

Behold my servant James shall lengthen the cords and strengthen the stakes of zion and my servant Aaron shall be his counsellor for he hath wisdom in the gospel and understandeth the doctrines and erreth not therein.

And I will have a house built unto me there of stone, and there will I show myself to my people by many mighty works, and the name of the city shall be called Voree, which is being interpreted, garden of peace, for there shall my people have peace and rest and wax fat and pleasant in the presence of their enemies.

But I will again stretch out my arm over the river of waters and on the banks thereof shall the house of my choice be. But now the city of Voree shall be a strong hold of safety to my people and they that are faithful and obey me[,] I will there give them great prosperity and such as they have not had before; and unto Voree shall be the gathering of my people, and there shall the oppressed flee for safety and none shall hurt or molest them.

And by this shall they know that I have spoken it; the people there and the owners of the land shall show kindness to them, for great calamities are coming on the church and such as have not been. & if they scatter[,] the ungodly of the world shall swallow them up, but if they gather to my city of Voree there will I keep them under the shadow of my wings and the cities from whence my people have been driven shall be purged with a high hand for I will do it, and my people shall be again restored to their possessions; but dark clouds are gathering[,] for the church is not yet wholly purged.

And now I command my servants the Apostles and Priests and Elders of the Church of the Saints, that they communicate and proclaim this my word to all the saints of God in all the world that they may be gathered unto and round about my city of Voree and be saved from their enemies, for I will have a people to serve me.

And I command my servant Moses Smith, that he go unto the saints with whom he is acquainted and unto many people, and command them in my name to go unto my city of Voree and gain inheritance therein, and he shall have an inheritance therein for he hath left all for my sake and I will add unto him many fold if he is faithful; for he knows the land and can testify unto them that it is very good.

So spake the Almighty God of heaven. Thy duty is made plain and if thou lackest wisdom ask of God in whose hands I trust thee and he shall give thee unsparingly[,] for if evil befal me thou shalt lead the flock to pleasant pastures.

God sustain thee, Joseph Smith

P.S. Write me soon and keep me advised of your progress from time to time.

B.

THE RAJAH MANCHOU OF VORITO

James Strang's translation of ancient texts was more modest in volume than Joseph Smith's Book of Mormon and Pearl of Great Price. What follows is the entire transcription of the Plates of Voree, "The Rajah Manchou of Vorito Plates, Translation of the Voree Record by the Prophet James, by Urim and Thummim, September 18, 1845," from Revelations of James J. Strang, *comp. Wingfield W. Watson (Spring Prairie, WI: Church of Jesus Christ of Latter Day Saints, Strangite: 1890s), 8.*

1. My people are no more. The mighty are fallen and the young slain in battle. Their bones bleached on the plain by the noonday shadow. The houses are leveled to the dust and in the moat are the walls. They shall be inhabited. "I have in the burial served them, and their bones in the death shade toward the sun's rising are covered. They sleep with the mighty dead, and they rest with their fathers. They have fallen in transgression and are not, but the elect and faithful there shall dwell.

2. The word hath revealed it. God hath sworn to give an inheritance to his people where transgressors perished. The word of God came to me while I mourned in the death shade, saying I will avenge me on the destroyer. He shall be driven out. Other strangers shall inhabit thy land. I an ensign there will set up. The escaped of my people there shall dwell when the flock disown the shepherd and build not on the rock.

3. The forerunner men shall kill, but a mighty prophet there shall dwell. I will be his strength and he shall bring forth thy record. Record my words and bury it in the hill of promise."

4. The record of Rajah Manchou of Vorito.

C.

DOCUMENTS PERTAINING TO THE
ORDER OF THE ILLUMINATI

*The following documents appear to have belonged together but may
have been purposely separated in the 1850s-60s when the Strangites
were persecuted in Wisconsin. Strang biographer Milo M. Quaife copied
the first item, the Covenant (also known as the Oath), in June 1921
from a book in possession of Heman Smith, historian of the RLDS
Church. Smith had borrowed the book from Henry Denio of Lamoni,
Iowa, a grandson of James Strang, and allowed Quaife to copy from it in
preparation for Quaife's book,* The Kingdom of Saint James: A Narrative of the Mormons, *published by Yale University Press in 1930.*

*The other documents included in this appendix were closely associ-
ated with the covenant, including the Colloquy with the Guard and
Colloquy with the Porter, containing secret passwords, phrases, and
signs; the Right Hand of Fellowship on Six Points, which described an
officiator embracing an initiate ("foot to foot, knee to knee, hand to back,
breast to breast, eyes all around, mouth to ear") in a symbolic way; and
the "Record of the Organization of the Kingdom," a list of people who
took the oath in July 1846. There were also various drawings of secret
tokens, symbols, and cipher codes considered important to the ritual.*

*The descriptions of the ceremonial colloquies and fraternal embrace
are preserved in the archives of the Beinecke Library at Yale University, which is also where the covenant and "Record of the Organization
of the Kingdom" now reside. The latter comes from Clement Strang,
whom the indefatigable Milo Quaife also contacted. Clement wrote the
following words of explanation on the first page of the document: "These
sheets were cut out of a record book about two inches thick. It was too
cumbersome to send complete. There was nothing else in the book." He
signed his name, then added: "P.S. The book was given me by a man
living near Black River Falls, Wisconsin, in the year 1890. The man's
name was Anson W. Prindle. His name is in the list." The names followed by an X on the list probably signify people who could not read and
put their mark next to their names.*

Covenant

I believe in God the Father Almighty Sovereign of Heaven and Earth: and in the Lord Jesus Christ, his son and right Lord of the earth: and in the Holy Spirit, which inspires men to rightiousness: and in the Holy Catholic and Apostolic Church of the Saints: and in James J Strang, the Prophet of God; Apostle of the Lord Jesus; and chief Pastor of the Flock: and in the revelations which God has given.

And for the purpose of drawing near unto God and entering into his oath and covenant, that my mind may be illuminated with intelligence knowledge and wisdom which is hid from the world and from the foolish: I do now, in the presence of God, Elect Angels and a Prince of the Illuminatti, solemnly promise, covenant and swear by the true, selfexistent and everliving God, that I will forever hail, ever conceal, and never reveal, any of the ceremonies, secrets and misteries of the order of the Illuminatti, which I may now or at any time hereafter be acquainted with, to any person in the world except it be an Illuminattus.

I do further, in like manner, promise covenant and swear that I will uphold sustain and obey the said James J. Strang and his lawful successors, if any he has, each in his time as the Imperial primate and actual Sovereign Lord and King on Earth and as my true and lawful Sovereign wheresoever and in whatsoever kingdom state or Dominion I may be; and in preference to the laws, commandments and persons of any other Kings, Potentates or States whatsoever, and will yield obedience to the revelations he shall give; the Laws made by the Grand Council of Nobles of God's Kingdom, with his concurrence: and the decrees he shall make, as the supreme Law, above and superseding all laws, obligations and mandates of any other person, authority or power whatsoever.

And I do further in like manner promise, covenant and swear, that I do now with my whole heart, without reserve and without regret, and according to the dispensation granted to me renounce all allegiance to any and every other Potentate State and Nation: and do yield myself wholly, heartily, and unreservedly to this Kingdom of God; and I will maintain its dominion integrity and inviolability in defiance of any and every power state and nation as long as life lasts.

I do further in like manner promise covenant and swear, that I will never intentionally, negligently, or indifferently injure an Illuminattus, his family or posterity, either in person reputation or property, nor suffer it to be done by others when it is in my power to prevent it, without violating parament [paramount] duties as a member of this order and a minister in the Kingdom of God.

And I do further in like manner promise, covenant and swear that I will maintain, in their purity, the principles of justice fraternity and equality; of devotion, courtesy and loyalty; and of hospitality, gallantry and courage among the Illuminatti.

And I do further in like manner, promise, covenant and swear that I will keep, maintain and uphold, order, subordination, and the rights of superiors, counsellors and nobles in this order of the Illuminatti, and will recognize as Superiors An Imperial Primate and two Vice Roys: As counsellors a General and Chief and eight other Privy Counsellors. And Nobles one hundred and thirty two noble men chosen from the various ranks of Nobility, as the Grand Council, of whom seventy shall form a quorum, for the transaction of business.

And I do further, in like manner promise covenant and swear, that I will yield implicit faith [and] confidence to all the oaths covenants and obligations herein contained, implied, and understood as long as I shall live: So help me God, the Lord Jesus Christ and the Illuminatti[,] and do good unto me, as they have covenanted.

But should I be so corrupt treacherous and abominable as to despise cast off and violate the covenant I this day make with God and with his chosen ones: May the just judgments of God, due to all like apostates traitors and perjured villains be executed on my head: May all men know me perjured: and may they look on me as loathsome and wretched: May God the Eternal father execute judgment and justice on me without mercy: And Jesus Christ the Redeemer turn from me and remember his loving kindness no more: Cast out from the society of the good on the earth: and cut off from hope in Heaven: may evil men and the worms destroy me always: May disease rot my bones within me: Parched and thirsty may I die without friends or succor: unloved of the good: cursed of evil doers: and the gates of Heaven closed against me: beholding bliss and feeling perdition evermore.[1]

---

1. At this point, the covenant included the paragraph preceding the names on the "Record of the Organization of the Kingdom," a duplication that has been eliminated here.

Colloquy with the Guard

Scene, North of the headquarters of <u>the Guards</u>, or at the North gate of the wall.[2]

1. W   Who comes there?
2. C   A true Companion.
3. W   Who accompanies you?
4. C   Not any one (or, True Companions all: or, otherwise according to the fact. If all is well, the W. proceeds).
5. W   What seek you?
6. C   Intelligence.
7. W   Where seek it?
8. C   In God's holy Sanctuary (or Tabernacle or island, Valley or Hill).
9. W   But have you a right there?
10. C   Truly I have.
11. W   How do you certainly prove it?
12. C   What right have you to ask?
13. W   I answer that to my superiors. To all others this is my answer (presenting arms).
14. C   Let me pass.
15. W   Stand you back.
16. C   Let me pass.
17. W   Prove your right.
18. C   I have smelled a sweet savor.
19. W   So has the Heathen.
20. C   I have tasted a sacrifice.
21. W   So has the Apostate.
22. C   And I have hands for feeling; Eyes for seeing; Ears for hearing.
23. W   Who has not?
24. C   Ears hear not; eyes see not; hands feel not.
25. W   Can you advance?
26. C   Who can hinder? (There stepping forward the C. gives the

---

2. The letter *W* stands for *warden* and *C* for *candidate*. In the subsequent Colloquy with the Porter, *G* stands for *guard* and *P* for *porter*. The initials "E.E." probably mean "enter exalted."

right hand of fellowship on <u>six points</u>; giving the common sign—three fingers of the right hand to the mouth—before the first; the common grip—three fingers within three—after the third; and the common <u>three words</u>—Obedience, Truth, Intelligence—after the sixth. If the situation be possibly exposed to observation; only two points of fellowship should be given, the first and the last; and if by possibility any one may be in hearing, only the first of the three words.)

27.   W   It is well God speed you; Be generous; be brave and (O) be fortunate.

Colloquy with the Porter

Scene, <u>At the door from the Ante room</u>.

(C. coming to the entrance to the Sanctuary at the station of the Master of Ceremonies, at the north, gives three and three and three distinct raps if a door; stamps if on land or whistles if on water; bowing as he catches the eye of the Porter; taking his cap in his right hand, which he raises a little; if the air is unpleasant, or takes off and presently transfers to the left if it is fair.)

1.   P   Who knocks there? (or stamps or whistles.)
2.   G   A true Companion.
3.   P   Who accompanies you?
4.   C   Nor any one (or True Companions all).
5.   P   What seek you?
6.   C   I seek Intelligence.
7.   P   Where seek it?
8.   C   In God's Holy Hill (or other lawful place of meeting).
9.   P   Have you a right there?
10.   C   Truly I have.
11.   P   Will you prove it to me?
12.   C   I have before been the way.
13.   P   Will you show it to me?
14.   C   The Eagle in the sky; the Lion on the rock and the Trout in the sea leave no track. So I. But they can go again.
15.   P   And can you?
16.   C   Strait is the way and narrow the gate that leads to life and few there be that find it.
17.   P   Who can stand on God's Holy Hill? (or other place of meeting.)

18. C   He that sweareth, and performeth, and though to his hurt draweth not back.

19. P   Have you sworn?

20. C   Truly I have.

21. P   How do you vouch your truth?

22. C   By this token (on the six points and with the common grip, gives the word "truth").

23. P   Have you performed?

24. C   Faithfully I have.

25. P   How do you assure me this?

26. C   By this token (as before and gives the word "integrity").

27. P   And have you not turned back?

28. C   To this moment I am faithful.

29. P   Can you satisfy me of this?

30. C   By this token (as before and gives the word "faithfulness." Note these three words are chang[e]able).

31. P   Who vouches you?

32. C   By command of the Most Majestic Imperial Primate the Most Excellent General in Chief, has vouchsafed me another token.

33. P   What is it?

34. C   The transient password.

35. P   You have it?

36. C   I have it.

37. P   Give it me.

38. C   How give it?

39. P   Speak it out.

40. C   I did not so receive it, and cannot so give it.

41. P   How did you?

42. C   In alternate parts.

43. P   How in parts?

44. C   Letters syllables or words.

45. P   Will you begin?

46. C   Which way divided?

47. P   Divide in syllables (letters or words).

48. C   Which way spoken?

49. P   As you choose.

50. C   At the beginning (middle or end. Example. "Truth is Eternal." C: <u>Truth</u>. P: <u>is</u>. C: <u>E</u>. P: <u>ter</u>. C: <u>nal</u>).
51. P   It is right, Companion. With joy we greet you.
E.E.

Note. The Porter now inquires his name and gives to the Master of Ceremonies, who introduces him to the presiding officers according to rank. 2. This colloquy does not include the writ[t]en tokens.

Right Hand of Fellowship on Six Points

Foot to foot; knee to knee; hand to back; breast to breast; eyes all round; mouth to ear.

Position.
The inside of the two right feet placed together; bring the inside of the knees together; place each left hand to the other's back, passing the arm over the shoulder; join hands with three and three; bring the breasts together; eyes in all directions within the semicircle to which each face is presented; and bring the mouth near to the other's right ear.

Instructions.
This teaches our relation to the order and to one another.

To the Order.
Foot to foot signifies that unitedly we will go the earth over to execute the Laws of God's Kingdoms.
Knee to knee signifies that all our united strength is consecrated to the establishment of God's Kingdom.
Hand to back signifies that we are joined in a living bond never to be broken, till the dominion of all the earth is given to the saints.

(Here the hands are joined.)
Breast to breast signifies that our hearts are joined in one, and all individuality is melted away in the unity of the order.
Eyes all round signifies that we should look everywhere for the enemies of the order and for their works.
Mouth to ear signifies that we report all enemies and evil doers to those who hold the keyes of judgement.

369

<u>To one another.</u>

Foot to foot signifies that we will go far for a Companion Illuminattus as for ourselves.

Knee to knee signifies that we will join our strength to his to uphold his cause.

Hand to back signifies that we are altogether joined to him in fraternal affection by a loving tie.

Breast to breast signifies that his secret is as safe in your breast as in his own.

Eyes all round signifies that you will watch for his enemies as for your own.

Mouth to ear signifies that you will whisper in his ear all approaching danger.

Record of the Organization of the Kingdom

We, whose names, are annexed, having witnessed for ourselves, the organization of the Kingdom of God, and the Crowning of the King of Zion, in fulfillment of the ancient Prophets: do now bear our testimony that this imposing ceremonial was consummated at the city of St. James, Beaver Island, Lake Michigan on the eight[h] day of July, in the year of our Lord, One Thousand, Eight Hundred and Fifty.

William Skimming
G. Brownson
Peltiah Barter
Zenas Gibbs
Nathan Foster
Franklin Bevier
Milo Weston [?]
Chauncey [blank]

George Adams
Andrew T. Hale
Hiram P. Brown
Charles Greenwood
Reuben Field
John Cole
Samuel E. Hull
Daniel Fillmore
Daniel F. Botsford
William H. Tripp

Stephen Post
Leonard Post
Christopher Dixon X
Alden Hale
Elisha C. Brown
William Chambers
Ansel Lake
Thomas P. Hoge

Joseph Hosmer
Azariah Parrish
John C. Hill
Susannah Campbell

Jonathan T. Pierce
Francis Fox
George L. Cole
Morrill E. Campbell

Deborah Tripp
William Bickle
Rhabeca Wright
Anson W. Prindle
Edward Chidester
Sally M. Aldrich
Sarah E. Chidester
Alanson G. Aldrich
James M. Greig
Ellen O. Greig
Samuel Baxter X
Ellen E. Greig
Delanah Baxter X
James M. Greig Jr.
Harriet Baxter X
Hyrum S. Hall X
Serena H. H.
Havens C. Hall

Sarah I. Bickle

Elizabeth Wright
Temperance Aldrich

Rachel Ann Aldrich

Hyrum Baxter X
William Baxter X

Cornelius Baxter X

Henrietta Baxter X

Royal Tucker
Catherine M. Tucker

Mary McNutt X
Sarah M. Tucker
John Guthrie
Nathan Wagener
Angeline Page
Liddy Wagener X
Elias Rice
Eliza Rice
Stratten Rogers
Catherine Rogers X
Serah E. Rogers
Ralph O. Fox
Polly Ann Fox
Elizabeth Pierce
Martha Purnell
Rachel Page X
Joseph J. Ketcham
Mary P. Ketcham

Huldah McNutt X
Sarah Jane McNutt X
Keziah H. Hopper

James Hickox
John Prince
Rachel Prince
Charles Tripp
Rebecca Tripp
Martha Ann Tripp X
Solomon Tripp X
Jonathan Tripp X
Hannah M. Tripp X
Alpheus Lawrence
Mary Jane Lawrence X
John A. Davis
George W. Hill X

371

Tobias McNutt

Gurdon Brown
Lucretia Brown X
Malvina Brotherton X
Huldah E. Brotherton X

David Heath
Moses Chase
Julius H. Hickox
Mary Jane Hickox X
Daniel Hickox
John C. Peirce
Eli Steel
Catherine Savage
Oren R. Hill
Susan Ann Hill
Cynthia Fox
Walter Ostrander
Alzina Ostrander
Stephen R. Sey X

Reuben T. Nichols
Eliza Ann Nichols
Joseph S. Ketcham X
Albert Ketcham X
Silas Campbell X
Sally Campbell X
Finley Page
Sally Page
Servilla Page
Nancy Page X
Ezra S. Ketcham X
Chauncey Loomis
Martha Loomis X
Seymour Page X
Daniel G. Wheelock

Benjamin Preston

James Renfel X
Ermina E. Humphrey
Samuel Chambers
Eri James Moore

Eliza Chidester
Benjamin Austin
Lois L. Austin
A. G. Hopper
John T. Grierson
Martha T. A. Grierson

Mary F. Steel

Betsy Hickox

Sarah Cole
Albert Field
Gilbert Watson
Cynthia Watson
J. M. Wait
Semour Wait X
Nephi Wait X

Eliza Field
John H. Brown
Albert Brown X

Albert M. Brown X
John S. Brown X

Simon Powers X

Melinda Powers X

Galon Cole

Lucinda Cole

Harriet Hill

Mary L. Hill

Violetta Rogers X

John L. Rogers X

Lorenza D. Wheelock X

Ruth C. Wheelock X

George C. Wheelock

Asa C. B. Field

Rhoda Field

Anna C. Field

James H. Field

Joel S. Field

Orria R. Brown

Harriet A. Brown

Sarah Brown X

Almira Parrish

David B. Whipple

Martha A. Whipple

H. D. McCulloch

James Smith

Catherine K. Hall

Augusta E. Hall X

William P. Clark X

Abigail Clark

William M. Clark X

Charles Clark X

Eliza D. Clark X

Annegenett Clark X

Margareth E. Tripp

Olive Adams

Oscar W. Hull

Albert Brown X

Joseph M. Brown X

Alexander Wentworth X

Franklin Johnson

Rispah Johnson

P. F. Johnson

G. F. Johnson

Marvin M. Aldrich Jr.

Saul Bennett

Selina Bennett

Elizabeth J. Bennett

Andrew J. Porter

Elizabeth A. Porter

Albert Newell Hosmer

Warren Post

Ebenezer Page

Mary Page

Francis Whitney X

Samuel P. Bacon

Elizabeth Bacon

James Blakeslee

Jehiel Savage X

George T. Preston

Caroline M. Preston

Cordelia A. Preston

Granger H. Preston

Frances Cooper

Catherine A. Cooper

Samuel Shaw

Mary Shaw

Samuel Graham

Leah Graham

Brigham Y. Graham

Wm. R. McLean

Aymes F. Hull   L. D. Hickey
Orson Campbell
Emily Campbell
Martha Ann Pierce
Estella Pierce

D.

WIVES AND CHILDREN OF JAMES J. STRANG

This information has been preserved by Myraette Strang in her history of the Perce family, various letters and documents, and the April 1980 Strang Family Newsletter, published from La Canada, California, and available at Central Michigan University's Clarke Historical Library.

James Jesse Strang
> b: Mar. 21, 1813, Scipio, New York
> d: July 9, 1856, Voree [Burlington], Wisconsin

Mary Abigail Content Perce
> b: Apr. 10, 1818, Madison County, New York
> m: Nov. 20, 1836, Silver Creek, New York
> d: Apr. 30, 1880
>> children by James Strang:
>> Mary Elizabeth, b. July 5, 1838, New York; d. Oct. 19, 1843, Spring Prairie [Burlington], Wisconsin
>> Myraette Mabel, b. May 23, 1840, New York; d. 1925, Colma, California
>> William J., b. Dec. 20, 1844, Voree, Wisconsin; d. Jan. 16, 1907
>> Harriet Anne, b. Oct. 17, 1848, Voree, Wisconsin; d. Aug. 16, 1868

Elvira Eliza Field
> b: July 8, 1830, Streetsborough, Ohio
> m: July 13, 1849, Beaver Island, Michigan
> d: June 13, 1910, Rockford, Michigan
>> children by James Strang:
>> Charles James,[1] b. Apr. 6, 1851, Beaver Island, Michigan; d. February 1916

---

1. Charles's indentureship was recorded three days after his thirteen birthday at the

Evaline,[2] b. Apr. 18, 1853, Beaver Island, Michigan; d. Sept. 1926

Clement J., b. Dec. 20, 1854, Beaver Island, Michigan; d. 1944

James Jesse Jr. (Charles J. Grier),[3] b. Jan. 22, 1857, Voree, Wisconsin; d. 1934

Elizabeth "Betsy" McNutt

b: Aug. 17, 1820, Preble County, Ohio

m: Jan. 19, 1852, Beaver Island, Michigan

d: Sept. 22, 1897, Lamoni, Iowa

children by James Strang:

Evangeline, b. 1853, Beaver Island, Michigan; d. Apr. 7, 1915, Lamoni, Iowa

David James, b. June 22, 1854, Beaver Island, Michigan; d. ca. July 2, 1854, Beaver Island, Michigan

Gabriel Strang, b. 1855, Beaver Island, Michigan; d. Sept. 1935, Texas

---

Eaton County Court House as "Charles Strang—90.106.21. Superintendent of Poor Order for Bond by Joseph Perkey for binding Charles Strang. Signed L. H. Ion (Supt. of Poor), E. Hayden (Deputy Co. Clerk). Dated 9 April 1864." See Joyce Liepins, "Easton County Indentures," *Eaton County Quest* 6 (1992): 70-72.

2. Evaline's indenture was recorded in ibid. as "Everline Strang—#90.106.9. Apprentice's indenture, Everline Strang, aged seven years, with the consent of her mother, Elvira E. Strang of the town of Eaton, has voluntarily bound herself to Samuel Waltersdorf of the town of Carmel, as a domestic servant, to serve until she is eighteen, or becomes married, whichever comes first. Indenture dated 29 December 1850. Signatures: Elvira E. Strang, Samuel Waltersdorf, L. H. Ion, E. A. Foote (Co. Clerk). A sworn statement, also dated 29 December 1860, from Elvira E. Strang follows, stating that her late husband, James J. Strang died 9 July 1856 in the state of Wisconsin. Signature: Elvira E. Strang and Henry Robinson (J.P. in Eaton Twp.)

3. The indenture of James J. Strang Jr. was recorded in ibid. as "James J. Strang—90.106.17. Apprentice's Indenture—Elvira E. Strang to David A. Greer/Grier. James J. Strang, of the town of Eaton, aged four years, by and with the consent of his mother, Elvira Strang, has voluntarily bound himself to David A. Greer of Carmel township, to learn the art, trade and mystery of Farming, until the age of twenty-one which he will be on the 22d day of January 1877. Signatures: L. H. Ion, Elvira E. Strang, David A. Grier, E. A. Foote (Co. Clerk). Indenture dated 29 December 1860. Statement given by Elvira before Henry Robinson, Justice of Peace in the township of Eaton, says James J. Strang, her late husband, died 9 July 1856 in the state of Wisconsin. Statement dated 29 December 1860, signed Elvira E. Strang and Henry Robinson."

Abigail Utopa, b. Jan. 1, 1857, Voree, Wisconsin; d. May 20,
1921, St. Joseph, Missouri

Sarah Adelia "Delia" Wright
b: Nov. 25, 1837, Leeds, Ontario, Canada
m: July 15, 1855, Holy Island, Michigan
d: Aug. 18,1923, Boise, Idaho.
children by James Strang:
James Phineas, b. Nov. 11, 1856 (or Aug. 18, 1856), Black River
Falls, Wisconsin; d. Nov. 1, 1937, Claresholm, Alberta

Phoebe Wright
b: July 25, 1836, Leeds, Ontario
m: Oct. 21, 1855, Beaver Island, Michigan
d: Nov. 9, 1914, Tacoma, Washington
children by James Strang:
Eugenia Jesse, b. Oct. 28, 1856, Black River Falls, Wisconsin; d.
ca. 1936, Tacoma, Washington

E.

WIVES OF STRANGITE POLYGAMISTS

This information is drawn from the "Beaver Island Record," notices in the Northern Islander, *and extant letters.*

George Brownson
    Mary Week, dead, sealed Sept. 14, 1851
    Sally Trevallee (widow of Bogordus Travallee), married March 10, 1851, sealed Sept. 14, 1851
    Sarah Griffis, married and sealed June 15, 1852

A.C.B. "Asa" Field
    Rhoda Stern, married before 1850
    Samantha Richmond, married and sealed on Oct. 21, 1851, in a double wedding with James Hickox and Elisa (Elsa) Kendal
    Mariah Arnald, married and sealed on Oct. 14, 1852

Lorenzo Dow Hickey
    Ann Davis, married Dec. 9, 1841; later separated or divorced
    Sara Ann Linnel, married July 13, 1852, on Beaver Island
    Frances Brownson (Miller?), sealed in Oct. 1853 on Beaver Island
    Unknown, died in childbirth on Beaver Island
    Adeline L. Scott, sealed July 26, 1855

Joseph Ketchum
    Two unknown wives, according to Lorenzo Dow Hickey in a letter to Wingfield Watson

George Miller
    Mary Catherine Fry, married before 1827
    Elizabeth Bouten-Miller (widow of Walter K. Miller), sealed to her and her child, Lewis, on March 3, 1851, on Beaver Island; died a few months later
    Martha Ann Bagley, sealed on Jan. 29, 1853

Joshua Miller, son of George Miller
    Elizabeth Ann Anderson, endowed in 1845 in Nauvoo
    Mary C. Miller, sealed Jan. 29, 1853
    Emily F. Miller, sealed posthumously on Jan. 29, 1853
Reuben Nichols
    Eliza Hickox
    Mary DeMary (widow of Harvey L. DeMary)

Ebeneezer Page
    Betsy, deceased prior to other marriages
    Hannah, endowed Jan. 2, 1846, in Nauvoo; they later separated but
        did not divorce
    Angeline

Finley Page
    Mary Lucinda Tharp, married in 1840 in Warsaw, Illinois
    Mary "Sally" Russell, married before 1850

Warren Post
    Elizabeth, married in 1830; divorced 1844
    Deborah, married in 1850 on Beaver Island
    Sarah Moriah, married in 1852, divorced in 1856 after they left Beaver
        Island

Benjamin Wright
    Margaret Finch, married Feb. 27, 1831, in Canada
    Rhonda Whitney (widow of Clarke Whitney), married July 9, 1853, on
        Beaver Island
    Adeline Whitney (widow of Clarke Whitney), married July 9, 1853, on
        Beaver Island
    Nancy Rickerson (widow of Clarke Whitney), married July 9, 1853 on
        Beaver Island
    Elizabeth Enoch, perhaps posthumously

Samuel Wright
    Rebecca Finch, married in Canada before coming to Voree, sealed on
        Oct. 12, 1851
    Edna Chidester, sealed on Oct. 12, 1851, on Beaver Island

INDEX

A

Adams, Caroline, 127, 127n

Adams, George J., 74, 76, 76n, 137, 142, 151, 154n; abandons sick wife, 127, 127n; appointed to first presidency, 50; character, 38-40, 38n, 39n, 41; at coronation, 119-22, 126; Council of Fifty, 20n; defection, 125-28; description, 38-39; and Elvira Field, 68, 76, 76n, 90; forgiveness of Lorenzo Dow Hickey, 85-87; Fourth of July conflict, 118, 126; "frigging spree," 69; missionary work, 156; ordains black man to priesthood, 81; polygamy, 40, 45, 90, 92, 126-27; praises Beaver Island and Voree, 69, 70-71; promotes free land, 70-71, 105-06; relationship with James Strang, 39

Adams, Louisa (Cogswell), 126-28, 127n, 128n

Albion, Michigan, 69, 75, 76

alcohol, 204, 206, 209, 211; Indian whiskey, 132. *See also* temperance laws

Aldrich, Marvin M., 85, 163, 231

Aldrich, O. M., 329, 329n

Alma, Wisconsin, 253, 287

Alvord family, 250

American Fur Company, 109

apostasy, at Voree, 48-50, 53, 55, 73

Archer, John W., 57n

Artesia, New Mexico, 328

Associated and United Order of Enoch, *see* Order of Enoch

Atkyn, Thomas, 211-213

Austin, Lois, 77-78, 77n

Austin, Sophia (wife of Eri J. Moore), 77n

Austin family, 198

Avery, Daniel, 307

B

Babcock, Amos, 49

Bacon, Samuel P., 95, 98, 121n, 148, 149, 150

Baker, Emma, 264

Baker, Helen (Paine), 267

Baker, John, 264, 264n, 265, 267

Baker, May, 264

Baker, Warren, 267

Barnes, Caleb P., 16, 17, 21, 96, 224, 242

Bates, David, 133, 134

Bates, George C., 138, 139, 161, 162

Baxter, Delana, 198

Baxter, F., 100

Baxter, Henrietta, 198

Beaver Island, books from library, 232, 276, 277n, 281; church services, 167; deaths on, 180, 180n; description of,

ABOUT THE AUTHOR

Vickie Cleverley Speek is a former newspaper and radio reporter, feature writer, and columnist in Illinois and Michigan, recipient of four first-place awards from the Illinois Press Association, the Red Ribbon Media Award from the State of Illinois, and professional praise from Associated Press. In 2001 she received the Award of Excellence from the Illinois Historical Society for her research and writing on the Civil War. She has also been a frequent speaker at professional and community gatherings, including two presentations about James Strang during Museum Week on Beaver Island, Michigan. She is a past director of the LDS Family History Center in Morris, Illinois. She and her family live in Minooka, Illinois.